DETERMINANTS OF FERTILITY IN ADVANCED SOCIETIES

RUDOLF ANDORKA

Determinants of fertility in advanced societies

THE FREE PRESS
A Division of Macmillan Publishing Co., Inc.
New York

The Free Press
A Division of Macmillan Publishing Co., Inc.
866 Third Avenue, New York, N.Y. 10022

First American Edition 1978

Library of Congress Catalog Card Number: 78-62993

Printed in the United States of America

printing number

1   2   3   4   5   6   7   8   9   10

Library of Congress Cataloging in Publication Data

Andorka, Rudolf.
    Determinants of fertility in advanced societies.

    Bibliography   p.
    Includes index.
    1. Fertility, Human.   I. Title.
HB901.A5 1978   301.32'1   78-62993
ISBN 0-02-900780-1

CONTENTS

Preface vii

Part one *Methodological introduction* 1
   1.1 Measures of fertility 3
   1.2 Natural fertility 8

Part two *Theories of fertility* 11
   2.1 Malthus's theory of population 13
   2.2 The theory of demographic transition 18
   2.3 Economic theories of fertility 27

Part three *Determinants of fertility in centuries preceding the
modern period* 39
   3.1 Literary sources on fertility and birth control 41
   3.2 Family reconstitution and genealogies 45
   3.3 Data on fertility of countries and regions from
official statistics, aggregation of the data in parish
registers, and stable population analysis 73
   3.4 The economic and social background of the
decline of fertility in some parts of Europe, and of
the relatively long maintenance of high fertility in
other parts 84

Part four *Sources of data on the social determinants of fertility* 107
   4.1 Time series of vital statistical data 109
   4.2 Census fertility data 140
   4.3 International and regional cross-sectional analyses
of fertility 163
   4.4 Fertility surveys 190

Part five *Social factors of fertility* 225
   5.1 Two intermediate demographic determinants:
marriage, and knowledge and practice of birth
control 227
   5.2 Income 234

5.3   Socioeconomic status 251
5.4   Education 259
5.5   Social mobility 266
5.6   Urban and rural residence 279
5.7   Migration 289
5.8   Employment of women and emancipation of women 292
5.9   Religious denomination and ethnicity 298
5.10 Psychological factors 333
5.11 Population policy 347

Part six Recent attempts to develop a theory of fertility 361
6.1   New developments in the economic theory of fertility 363
6.2   Outlines of a sociological theory of fertility 369
6.3   An attempt to combine the economic and sociological theories of fertility 371

Part seven Some tentative conclusions 377

Bibliography 385

Author index 420

Subject index 427

PREFACE

This book is intended to give an overall review of the research and theories on the social factors determining fertility in advanced countries. It is based on the conviction that the level of fertility and the factors influencing it will become an increasingly interesting problem in advanced countries. In the first two decades after the Second World War fertility did not seem to be causing any problems in these countries. Its level was almost everywhere sufficient to produce a moderate natural increase of the population, which was considered to be advantageous for economic development and prosperity. The low fertility levels which had caused some concern in prewar years seemed to be almost forgotten. On the contrary, the continuing baby boom aroused some fear that the fertility level of these populations might eventually prove to be too high, causing excessive population densities and ecological problems connected with pollution, etc. The present author, however, is convinced that Margaret Mead was right in stating that 'every human society is faced not with one population problem but with two: how to beget and rear enough children and how not to beget and rear too many' (Mead 1950, p. 210). This conviction is based on the special experiences of Hungarian demographers in the 1960s, who were faced with a fertility level lower than that necessary for the simple reproduction of population, and the persistent concern was how to raise fertility to that level. Considering that recently the birth rate in several advanced countries fell to even lower levels, it seems probable that demographers in these countries will face the same problem of the causes of low fertility. Therefore in this book the causes of low fertility in advanced countries are examined at least as carefully as the causes of high fertility in these societies.

The title and the subject of the book require some explanation. The book deals with *social* determinants of fertility. This concept is interpreted in an extended sense. Although naturally there are biological factors of fertility, these play a relatively minor role in advanced countries as compared to the social factors. It might be hypothesized that the possibility of birth control is well known by almost all adults in advanced societies, and also that methods of birth control are more or less freely available, so that the practice of birth control depends obviously on the motivation of individuals and couples, which in turn is determined by social factors (biological factors can also be seen to play a role in determining fertility, mostly in the case of sterility).

Social factors determining the number of children planned and desired by families, the spacing of births, and also age at marriage, as well as the proportion of celibacy, are interpreted here in an extended sense. Such factors as income, socioeconomic status and education are obviously social in nature. On the basis of recent sociological and socio-psychological research, however, individual personality also seems to be mostly the product of social influences; therefore, individual personality characteristics, as well as socio-psychological characteristics of collectivities, are included into the concept of social factors of fertility.

The concept of *advanced* countries is not unambiguous. Developed in the economic sense (i.e. from the point of view of *per capita* income or the share of industry and other non-agricultural branches in the production of national income) does not necessarily coincide with developed or advanced in the demographic sense (i.e. having completed the demographic transition of low mortality and approximately similar low level of fertility). Therefore a simple geographical criterion is used to define the countries considered. They are the countries of Europe (with the exception of Albania, for which we have very few demographic data), including the whole Soviet Union, with Siberia, as well as the United States and Canada, Australia and New Zealand. This delimitation is obviously objectionable. For instance, Japan is today clearly an advanced country from any point of view. It is, however, not included in this book, as it is often considered to be the prototype of the demographic development of societies which are at present at the beginning of demographic transition. Therefore it will be convenient to analyse Japanese fertility data in a parallel book dealing with developing countries. On the other hand, as the demographic history of the European and North American countries provides many interesting insights into the causes of fertility decline, not only present fertility, but also its historical changes are dealt with in Part 3 of this volume.

Three methods of systematization of research and theories on fertility are possible:

1 Describing the different types of *sources* of empirical data giving insights into the social causes of fertility.
2 Enumerating the different social *factors* of fertility.
3 Reviewing the *theories* of causes of fertility.

In the first method the reader gets acquainted with the different researches and surveys done, but the findings of different researches, which are often contradictory, are not summarized. In the second method he gets acquainted with our knowledge of the influence of particular factors, but does not see their joint and simultaneous effect. In the third method he is informed on the hypotheses concerning the interdependent and simultaneous influence of these factors, but can get only a very superficial idea of the empirical sources on which the often contradictory hypotheses are based. Therefore it has seemed advisable to combine all three methods of systematization (in Parts 4 to 6).

Theories of social processes, however, have a double function: in addition to summarizing and synthesizing the results of empirical research they also formulate new hypotheses and raise new questions, and by doing so they stimulate and orientate new empirical researches. The earlier population theories providing the framework of empirical investigations done in recent decades, therefore, are considered before the empirical sections of the volume in Part 2, while the theoretical constructions and controversies of the last few years, which are based mostly on the empirical findings described in the empirical parts of this volume, are discussed in Part 6.

Part 1 includes a short review of different measures of fertility, their merits and their shortcomings, as well as some empirical findings on fecundity, which are used as a baseline for the study of the impact of social factors.

The book is intended to be used by students at senior undergraduate and postgraduate level who are interested in the study of fertility. It is hoped that research workers, too, will utilize it as a textbook or guide. Studies on the factors of fertility in demographic literature are therefore reviewed as fully as possible. In consequence, the book contains only a very few of the author's original research findings. He hopes to be pardoned, however, for dealing rather extensively with Hungarian research works on fertility, which are probably mostly unknown, but might be interesting in English speaking societies.

No new comprehensive theory of the social factors determining fertility has been formulated here by the author. The aim of this book is, rather, to stimulate the reader to rethink the findings of different empirical researches and the different theoretical explanations. Therefore, many data from different studies are included in the text, to enable the student to review them critically and form his own opinion on them. In order to help clarify understanding of the results, a short description is given wherever necessary of the methods of research, the sample taken, and the questionnaire of the surveys under review.

The author wishes to acknowledge the scientific research of members of the Hungarian demographic school, from the works of whom he got many inspirations and ideas.

PART ONE

Methodological introduction

1.1 Measures of fertility

In order to analyse the social determinants of fertility, it is first necessary to review briefly the different measures of fertility, their advantages and deficiencies, what the different measures exhibit and what they do *not* show, because, on the one hand, due to lack of similar data, different measures of fertility are used in the particular studies of the factors of fertility, and, on the other hand, as there is no such perfect measure of fertility which might be adequate for all types of analysis, it is therefore necessary to use different measures when investigating different features of the causative mechanism of fertility.

The most frequently used measure of fertility is the crude *birth rate*, i.e. the number of births (or live births) per 1000 total population. Its advantage is simplicity, as well as the fact that, comparing it to the crude death rate, we get natural increase. It is therefore the fertility measure directly influencing the growth of population. Its deficiency is that the total number of population to which the number of births is compared includes males and children, as well as old people; therefore it is strongly influenced by the age and sex composition, which may be very different in particular populations and historical periods. Thus the birth rate gives only rather crude information on the real level and changes of fertility in a population.

The *general fertility rate*, i.e. the number of births per 1000 women of childbearing age (15–49 or 15–44 years old), is a somewhat refined measure as it eliminates the influence of sex composition, and to a certain extent also that of the age composition of a population. However, the age composition of women of childbearing age might be very variable.

The *age-specific fertility rates* eliminate, or in the case of five-year age groups, almost completely eliminate the influence of age composition on the fertility, as they display the number of births by a particular (15–19, 20–24, etc.) age group per 1000 women in that particular age group. They enable the differences and changes in the age pattern of fertility to be studied, which is very important as the changes of total fertility ensue from different changes in the particular age groups. They are, however, somewhat inconvenient because seven rates are necessary to characterize the fertility of a given female population.

Therefore the measure of *total fertility rate* is often used instead of the age-specific rates. This is the sum of the particular age-specific rates from

15 to 49 years; in other words, it expresses the number of children a cohort of 1000 women would bear if they all went through their reproductive ages with age-specific rates of fertility observed in the given year. It is thus the measure of fertility of a hypothetical cohort and should never be considered the measure of fertility of a real cohort, since it characterizes the situation of one particular year, while a real cohort is fertile during twenty-five years, and there is no justification to suppose that during these years they will bear with the frequencies observed in one given year. It should also be kept in mind that the age-specific rates and in consequence the total fertility rates neglect the number of children already borne by the women.

The *gross reproduction rate*, previously widely used in demographic analysis, is essentially a total fertility rate taking into consideration only the births of girls and expressed per single woman (not per 1000 women, as is the total fertility rate). It might be interpreted as the average number of daughters borne by one woman under the age-specific fertility rates of a given year. The *net reproduction rate* is the gross reproduction rate diminished by the influence of mortality. One deficiency of both these reproduction rates is their names, which suggest that they express the reproduction of a population, and they do not. They are measures of the fertility (and mortality) of a given year, as is the total fertility rate.

The general, age-specific and total fertility rates might be computed for married women only, in order to eliminate the influence of the composition by marital status. These are the *marital fertility rates*. They naturally disregard illegitimate births, which might be important in some cases.

It is often stated that in present-day advanced societies fertility is a function of marriage duration rather than of age, because women tend to concentrate births in the first years of marriage, irrespective of their age. Therefore *marriage-duration-specific fertility rates* might be better characteristics of fertility than age-specific rates. *Intervals* between marriage and first birth and between consecutive births might be used for the same purpose.

The number of children already born naturally has a strong influence on fertility in societies where family planning is widespread. Therefore *birth-order-specific rates* might be the correct measures of fertility. The probabilities of increase of the number of children, or *parity progression ratios* (Henry 1953, Pressat 1961), elaborated by French demographers take into consideration this aspect by displaying the probability that a married woman having no child (not having had a birth) bears a child in future (a_0), and that a married woman having one child bears a second child in future (a_1), and so on ($a_2, a_3, \dots$). The calculation of these ratios is relatively simple if the fertility date by order of parity and time since marriage, and since previous birth, are available. However, such detailed data are not often available. In that case estimates are necessary based on the data of births by parity order. These are the most sensitive measures of fertility when examining short-run changes.

Doubts have been expressed (e.g. by Pressat 1969a 1974a) whether fertility measures calculated from vital statistical data of a given year–i.e. the so-called period data–can be relied on when analysing changes of fertility, since they might be merely the effects of decisions on timing of births taken by couples under the influence of momentary circumstances, which do not influence substantially the number of children born to the given couples. Period fertility rates used to fluctuate much more than the average number of children borne by couples during their reproductive life span. It seems, however, that timing decisions are not unrelated to the decisions of couples on the number of children they want to have, in the sense that decisions to postpone births often result in a lower final number of children; similarly, decisions to advance births taken by couples under monetary influences might result in ultimately having a higher number of children. Thus the period fertility measures based on vital statistical data of a given year can be used for analysing the factors influencing fertility, bearing in mind, however, that they express the mixed effects of the number of births of women and the spacing of these births.

The most perfect measures of fertility would be parity progression rates for real cohorts, displaying the number of births of a given cohort (birth or marriage cohort) from 15 to 49, detailed by order of parity.'The total number of births of a cohort shows not only the true fertility, uninfluenced by short-run oscillations, but also the reproduction of the cohort. Unfortunately, *cohort fertility* measures are rarely available because of lack of data. Also these measures cannot be utilized immediately to evaluate the fertility of a given year, because the cohort measures can be calculated only at the end, or near to the end of the reproductive age of the cohort, while most births come from young women in the first fifteen years of their reproductive age. Therefore, cohort analysis is most useful in historical analysis (Whelpton 1954), but of less use when the actual demographic situation must be evaluated.

In addition to these measures of fertility based on vital statistics, there are fertility measures calculated from census and survey data. These are the *number of children ever born* or the number of living children of women at the time of the census. The problem with these data is that it is not at all certain that women always answer accurately when asked at the census about the number of births they have had. Single women particularly can be suspected of not always giving sincere answers. Therefore census measures of fertility are generally given only for married or ever-married (including widowed and divorced) women. The great advantage of census fertility measures, however, is that at the time of the census we get information on the total number of women in different categories, not only in age groups and marital status categories, which are generally known in other years too, but also in occupational categories, by residence, by religion, sometimes by migration, by income, etc. Therefore, differential fertility data are most adequately calculated from census or survey data.

Completed fertility of women (i.e. the number of children ever borne by them during their life) may be calculated from census returns and from vital statistics (number of children ever borne of women who died in a given year).

All these census fertility data display the fertility of longer periods, as opposed to the vital statistical fertility data, which display the fertility of given years.

If the number of children ever born was not included in the census questionnaire, another – very crude – measure of fertility, the *child/woman ratio*, can be calculated from census data. This is the number of children 0–4 or 0–9 years old per the number of women of childbearing age. This measure displays the fertility of the five or ten years before the census, minus the influence of infant and child mortality.

Coale and associates developed new measures to study the historical changes of fertility (Coale 1969, Demény 1968, Van de Walle and Knodel 1967). The basic idea was to separate the influence of proportion of unmarried women and of birth control in marriage on fertility decline in Europe. They defined four indices:

I_m = The index of proportion married of women in childbearing age, as seen from census data; this index has the value of 1, if all women aged 15 to 49 are married.

I_g = The index of marital fertility, i.e. the actual marital fertility as compared to the maximum biologically possible, which is considered equal to the marital fertility of the exceptionally healthy population of the Hutterite sect in North America, which prohibits every kind of birth control. The marital fertility of Hutterites is equal to 1.

I_h = The index of fertility of unmarried women, similarly compared to the fertility of married Hutterite women.

I_f = The index of overall fertility = $I_g \cdot I_m + (1 - I_m) \cdot I_h$.

In addition to the number of children ever born, fertility and family planning surveys use other measures of fertility attitudes, as:

(a) The *expected* number of children, i.e. the number of children actually expected at the end of reproductive age.

(b) The *desired* number of children, at marriage or at the time of the interview, or under different imaginary conditions (e.g. 'If you had plenty of money').

(c) The *planned* number of children, i.e. the number intended to be borne by those who plan the number of children.

(d) The *ideal* number of children, i.e. the number which is considered ideal in the given society or social stratum.

The questions in the surveys are not always formulated similarly, and there is no consensus as to the real meaning and content of the data obtained from the answers.

1.2 Natural fertility

In order to have a reference or baseline to evaluate the impact of social factors on fertility, some information on natural fertility is necessary. Following the definition of Henry (1961a), by natural fertility we mean the average fertility of a population where everybody is living in marriage during the reproductive life span and is not practising any deliberate control over childbearing, i.e. where the behaviour of couples is not modified according to the number of children ever born. Natural fertility is influenced by several kinds of biological factors – e.g. coital frequency, probability of conception in case of given coital frequency, the age of biological maturity and the age of the end of fecundity, the probability of final and temporary sterility in function of age, the length of infecund period after birth, the frequency of foetal deaths, the frequency of still-birth. All these may be very different in different populations and periods (and also not unrelated to social factors, such as coital frequency). Therefore there is no universal 'natural fertility' level valid everywhere and always. Bourgeois–Pichat (1965a) described 280 different types of biological fertility. It is even questionable whether a fertility level influenced only by biological factors and completely uninfluenced by social ones existed or exists in real life.

Nevertheless, fertility levels of populations living in conditions where the influence of social factors might be hypothesized to be minimal were investigated. The most famous example is that of the Hutterite sect whose members are very healthy and whose religious convictions forbid any kind of birth control (Eaton and Mayer 1953, Henry 1961a). The total number of births by a Hutterite woman married from 15 to 49 was shown to be more than twelve and almost eleven for those who marry at the age of 20 and remain married to 49 (obviously not all Hutterite women marry at 15, so that the fertility of the Hutterite population might not be called 'natural' in the strict sense). There is also a strong variation in fertility of individual women in the Hutterite population, caused by individual differences of fecundity (Bodmer and Jacquard 1968).

Henry calculated the fertility rates of thirteen populations most probably not practising birth control (Henry 1961b). Because these populations are not as exceptional as the Hutterite sect, the levels are somewhat lower, but also at these age-specific levels the total number of children borne by a woman married at 20 would be 8·4. Henry also calculated separately the rates for women who were not sterile, which are higher and very close to those observed in the Hutterite population (Table 1.1).

Table 1.1 Age-specific marital fertility rates of populations not practising birth control.

	Age group						
Population group	*15–19*	*20–24*	*25–29*	*30–34*	*35–39*	*40–44*	*45–49*
Hutterites	300	550	502	447	406	222	61
Thirteen populations observed by Henry, all couples	—	435	407	371	298	152	22
Thirteen populations observed by Henry (only fecund couples)	—	494	483	443	389	—	—

Source: Henry 1961a, Henry 1961b.

The proportion of women or couples becoming sterile or subfecund with age is a special problem of biological fertility. Henry (1961b) estimated that the proportion of infecund couples is 3 per cent at the age of 20, 6 per cent at 25, 10 per cent at 30, 16 per cent at 35 and 31 per cent at 40. Kiser and associates (1968) estimated higher proportions in the United States, distinguishing definitely sterile, probably and possibly sterile and possibly fecund couples (Table 1.2).

Table 1.2 Percentage distribution by fecundity, white couples with wife aged 18–39: United States, 1960.

	Age group of wife			
Fecundity	*18–24*	*25–29*	*30–34*	*35–39*
Total	100	100	100	100
Fecund	87	79	64	53
Subfecund	13	21	36	47
Definitely sterile:	3	6	13	19
Because of contraceptive operation	2	4	7	9
Because of remedial operation	1	1	4	9
Because of other cause	—	1	1	1
Probably sterile	1	2	3	7
Possibly sterile	4	5	9	13
Possibly fecund	5	8	11	8

Source: Kiser, Grabill and Campbell 1968.

Thus while it is not possible to determine exactly the level of fecundity for all developed societies (it might be between eight and thirteen children per woman), it is clear that actual fertility is much lower than the biologically possible level. The factors contributing to the difference are: most women marry later than the age of biological maturity, some women remain single, some marriages are terminated because of death or divorce before the woman reaches the end of the reproductive age, and, last but not least, birth control is practised in marriage in order to achieve planned family size. All these are determined by social factors, the investigation of which is the subject matter of this book.

PART TWO

Theories of fertility

Early theories of fertility, although often largely hypothetical or based only on common observation, played an important role when researchers began to formulate questions concerning the factors of fertility in advanced societies, for which answers were sought in empirical investigations and surveys; these surveys were intended to verify or disprove the statements of the early theories. It seems appropriate, therefore, to examine some of these theories before analysing the results of empirical researches.

2.1 Malthus's theory of population

The birth of the science of population has been attributed to the publication of John Graunt's *National and Political Observations* in 1662, since he was the first who systematically investigated demographic data in order to derive conclusions on the actual development of population. However, it was Thomas Robert Malthus who brought the demographic processes into the forefront of public – and partly also scientific – interest, by his much quoted and even much more disputed *Essay on the Principle of Population* (Malthus 1966 1970 n.d.). Although mortality and fertility share equal place in his theory, we are justified in beginning this review of the theories of fertility with his work, particularly since Graunt and the demographers of the eighteenth century were mainly interested in mortality, changes in which seemed to influence the development of population much more than fertility in that century and earlier, while demographers following Malthus became increasingly interested in fertility, and were influenced by Malthusian theory, even if they did challenge its statements.

As the statements of Malthus were so often misunderstood and misinterpreted, it seems advisable to deal with the circumstances of the birth and development of his ideas. These changed radically from the first publication of the *Essay* in 1798 to the sixth edition in 1826, which is more or less a completely new book (even the second edition published in 1803 'may be considered as a new work', as Malthus himself stated), and to the *Summary View of the Principle of Population*, written originally for the *Supplement* to *Encyclopedia Britannica* and issued separately with some modifications in 1830.

The first *Essay* was essentially a polemic against the optimistic views of Godwin and Condorcet on the progress of mankind towards a world of abundance, equality, justice and peace, in which overpopulation would not present a problem. The actual situation in England and other countries of Europe was exactly the opposite at that time: the greater part of the population, which had a high growth rate in England, lived in very poor conditions (for a more detailed description of the debate between Condorcet, Godwin and Malthus, see Flew 1970, and Eversley 1959).

The argument of Malthus in the first *Essay* can be summarized as follows: population, if unchecked, has a tendency or capacity to grow faster, in a geometrical ratio doubling perhaps every twenty-five years, than resources and food supply which at best increase in arithmetical ratio. Therefore necessarily checks come into operation, which maintain the balance between the growth rates of population and production. The checks mentioned in the first *Essay* are predominantly of a dismal nature, such as misery, disease, famine, war, all causing premature death. According to Malthus, the poor laws of England did not succeed in their intention, because by providing some livelihood for the poor and relieving their immediate misery, they stimulated population growth in the long run and thus effectively increased misery. Therefore the abolition of the poor laws would increase 'the mass of happiness' among common people. This extreme conclusion rightly scandalized all those who were trying to alleviate poverty in contemporary societies.

The scientific importance of Malthus, however, should not be judged on this extreme conclusion. If he had mentioned only the above checks on the growth of population, his theory would be purely a theory of mortality and thus not interesting for the investigation of the factors of fertility. However, in the first *Essay* Malthus mentioned another type of check, namely a preventive one, which influences the fertility of populations. This consists in restraint from or postponement of marriage, coupled with a strictly moral behaviour while unmarried. Malthus stated that the preventive check operated through all the ranks of society in England.

In the subsequent editions of the *Essay* he more fully elaborated the operation of this second kind of check. In this elaborated form of his theory the checks of population growth can be classified in two ways:

1 From the point of view of the way they influence the growth of population there are:
   (*a*) Positive checks which shorten life expectancy, i.e. increase mortality.
   (*b*) Preventive checks that diminish fertility, including on the one hand 'promiscuous intercourse, unnatural passions', as well as 'improper arts to conceal the consequences of irregular connections', by which Malthus probably meant abortion (Flew 1970) and contraception practised in sexual relations outside marriage. He never seems to have thought of married couples resorting to abortion.
2 From the moral point of view checks can be classified into:
   (*a*) Misery, i.e. famine, disease, war.
   (*b*) Vice, i.e. abortion, sexual deviance etc.
   (*c*) Moral restraint, the only method advocated by Malthus.

The main problem for scientific research is the investigation of the conditions under which the different types of checks operate. A great part in later editions of the *Essay* is devoted to a country by country investigation of this question, from Fuegians and Tasmanians to England, Norway and Sweden, with some historical examples, such as ancient Greece and Rome. Malthus in general found that in contemporary European societies preventive checks became more prevalent than in earlier historical periods and in non-European societies. Moral restraint should be encouraged further and by this the conditions of the poor could be improved. Thus the outcome of the arguments of Malthus is much more optimistic in the later editions of the *Essay*.

The real problem for social science, however, begins at that point, with the investigation of the factors contributing to the operation of the preventive checks, i.e. to a decrease of fertility. At this point the statements of Malthus are rather obscure and contradictory. On the one hand, he seems to hypothesize a positive correlation of fertility and standard of living – e.g. reviewing the English society of his time, he states (Malthus n.d., pp. 219–21):

A man of liberal education, with an income only just sufficient to enable him to associate in the rank of gentlemen, must feel absolutely certain that, if he marry and have a family, he shall be obliged to give up all his former connexions. The woman, whom a man of education would naturally make the object of his choice, is the one brought up in the same habits and sentiments with himself, and used to the familiar intercourse of a society totally different from that to which she must be reduced by marriage . . . . These considerations certainly prevent many in this rank of life from following the bent of their inclinations in an early attachment.

The sons of tradesmen and farmers are exhorted not to marry, and generally find it necessary to comply with this advice, till they are settled in some business or farm, which may enable them to support a family. These events may not perhaps occur till they are far advanced in life.

The labourer who earns eighteen pence or two shillings a day, and lives at his ease as a single man, will hesitate before he divides that pittance among four or five, which seems to be not more than sufficient for one. Harder fare and harder labour he would perhaps be willing to submit to for the sake of living with the woman he loves; but he must feel conscious, that, should he have a large family and any ill fortune whatever, no degree of frugality, no possible exertion of his manual strength, would preserve him from the heart-rending sensation of seeing his children starve, or being obliged to the parish for their support.

The servants who live in the families of the rich have restraints yet stronger to break through in venturing upon marriage. They possess the necessaries, and even the comforts of life, almost in as great plenty as their masters. Their work is easy and their food of the class of labourers; and their sense of dependence is weakened by the conscious power of changing their masters if they feel themselves offended. Thus comfortably situated at present, what are their prospects if they marry? Without knowledge or capital, either for business or farming, and unused and therefore unable to earn a subsistence by daily labour, their only refuge seems to be a miserable alehouse, which certainly offers no very enchanting prospect of a happy evening to their lives. The greater number of them, therefore, deterred by this uninviting view of their future situation, content themselves with remaining single where they are.

Analysing the trends of population growth in England, Malthus (n.d., p. 244) states that the increase in the demand of labour and the increased power of production strongly encourage a rapid increase of population, so that 'if the resources of a country will admit of a rapid increase, and if these resources are so advantageously distributed as to occasion a constantly increasing demand for labour, the population will not fail to keep pace with them'.

From these passages it seems that Malthus considered that it was the *fear of decrease in living standards that induced men and women to reduce their offspring* by postponing marriage, and in some cases by remaining single for life. Thus a general improvement of the living standards of a society would encourage higher fertility by earlier marriages, since the resulting burden would be – at least subjectively – less important.

There are, however, other passages in the works of Malthus that suggest that he hypothesized a negative correlation of fertility and socioeconomic development. For example, he states at the end of his book that 'there are some natural consequences of the progress of society and civilization, which necessarily repress' the full effects of the principle of population (p. 537). These consequences mostly act, in his opinion, by reducing fertility via encouraging the postponement of marriages. The motivation for this is provided by the 'desire of bettering our condition, and the fear of making it worse' (p. 539). Elsewhere he explains the causative mechanisms in the following way (p. 498):

In most countries, among the lower classes of people, there appears to be something like a standard of wretchedness, a point below which they will not continue to marry and propagate their species. This standard is different in different countries, and is formed by various concurring circumstances of soil, climate, government, degree of knowledge, and civilization, etc. The principal circumstances which contribute to raise it are liberty, security of property, the diffusion of knowledge, and a taste for the conveniences and the comforts of life.

He several times stresses the importance of education. As a historical example he mentions the improvement in the conditions of the labouring classes in France after the Revolution, accompanied by a decrease in the birth rate.

This latter *negative correlation of fertility and socioeconomic development* seems to fit better into the general spirit of the later editions of the *Essay*, in which Malthus formulated rather optimistic opinions on the future development of population and society and thus implicitly invalidated his principle of population. Nevertheless, it is clear that his work lends support to very different interpretations of the factors affecting fertility.

2.2 The theory of demographic transition

The demographic and socioeconomic development of the nineteenth century and the first half of the twentieth clearly supported the latter interpretation and seemed to show that the population principle, as formulated in the first *Essay* (and never clearly repudiated by Malthus), does not work in industrializing societies. On the one hand, production increased more or less at a constant rate, i.e. in a geometrical ratio, mostly under the influence of scientific progress, as predicted by Engels in his critique of Malthus in 1844 (Engels 1964). On the other hand, the rate of increase of population, being always lower than the rate of growth of production, showed a declining tendency in the first decades of the twentieth century in the advanced societies.

In view of this development, a new kind of demographic theorizing gained ground. Its different variants are commonly called the *theory of demographic transition* (Thompson 1929 1944, Landry 1934 1945, Notestein 1945 1953, Davis 1945, Blacker 1947, Coale and Hoover 1958, Cipolla 1962, Casetti 1968, Bogue 1969).

At first (Thompson 1929, Landry 1934 1945) the theory consisted only of a description of phases of demographic development. Landry distinguished three phases or systems ('régimes') of demographic transition: (1) the primitive phase, characterized by high mortality and fertility, when population growth is determined mostly by mortality, which in turn is determined by the availability of items necessary for subsistence; (2) the intermediate phase, when mortality and fertility are declining and population growth is controlled by the number of marriages in such a way that the standard of living will not decline; (3) the modern phase, when both mortality and fertility are low and population growth is no longer determined by economic factors (Landry 1934 1945).

Blacker (1947) distinguished five phases: (1) a high stationary phase in which mortality and fertility are high; (2) an early expanding phase when mortality begins to decline and fertility remains unchanged at a high level; (3) a late expanding phase, when the decline of fertility follows the decline of mortality; (4) a low stationary phase, when mortality and fertility are both at a similar level; (5) a diminishing phase, when fertility declines below the level of mortality, which ceases to decline, and so the population begins to diminish.

These, however, are not theories of the causes producing demographic transition; they are only generalizations of the demographic trends observed in the past history of many developed countries. From our point of view the interesting problem is: what causes the decline of fertility and what kind of factors determine the birth rate after transition has been accomplished?

As to the causes of fertility decline, there are several explanations. The simplest one states that the decline of fertility is caused by *the preceding decline of mortality*, because otherwise population would grow at a rate which would upset the balance of population and the economic environment. Obviously the next question is: what causes the decline of mortality? There are several hypothetical answers to this question, pointing variously to economic development and the higher levels of living connected with it, the improvement of public health conditions, and the development of medicine or ecological changes (e.g. the gradual extinction in Europe of the species of rat which might have been especially dangerous in transmitting the plague). However, it would require a separate volume to investigate which of these causes were the most important factors in the decline of mortality.

The decline of fertility obviously can only very roughly be explained by the decline of mortality, since a full explanation would require that the effective numbers of surviving children – i.e. fertility less infant and child mortality – were constant during the transition, and that they were similar in all societies. Actually there were very important variations both in time and between different societies. For example, Knodel (1974) estimated that in Germany 41 per cent of the decline in fertility from 1871 to 1939 could be explained by the decline in infant mortality in the same period, but the percentage varied from 15 to over 90 per cent in different regions within Germany.

Another type of explanation points to the *economic and social changes* connected with economic development. For example, Notestein (1953) wrote:

Peasant societies in Europe, and almost universally throughout the world, are organized in ways that bring strong pressures on their members to reproduce. The economic organization of relatively self-sufficient agrarian communities turns almost wholly about family, and the perpetuation of the family is the main guarantee of support and elemental security. When death rates are high the individual's life is relatively insecure and unimportant. The individual's status in life tends to be that to which he is born. There is, therefore, rather little striving for advancement. Education is brief, and children begin their economic contributions early in life. In such societies, moreover, there is scant opportunity for women to achieve either economic support or personal prestige outside the roles of wife and mother, and women's economic functions are organized in ways that are compatible with continuous childbearing.

These arrangements, which stood the test of experience throughout the centuries of high mortality, are strongly supported by popular beliefs, formalized in religious doctrine, and enforced by community sanctions. They are deeply woven into the social fabric and are slow to change. Mortality dropped rather promptly in response to external changes because mankind has always coveted health. The decline of fertility, however, awaited the gradual obsolescence of age-old social and economic institutions and the emergence of a new ideal in matters of family size.

The new ideal of the small family arose typically in the urban society. It is impossible to be precise about the various causal factors, but apparently many were important. Urban life stripped the family of many functions in production, consumption, recreation, and education. In factory employment the individual stood on his own accomplishments. The new mobility of young people and the anonymity of city life reduced the pressures toward traditional behaviour exerted by the family and community. In a period of rapidly developing technology new skills were needed, and new opportunities for individual advancement arose. Education and a rational point of view became increasingly important. As a consequence the the cost of child rearing grew and the possibilities for economic contributions by children declined. Falling death rates at once increased the size of the family to be supported and lowered the inducements to have many births. Women, moreover, found new independence from household obligations and new economic roles less compatible with childbearing.

Under these multiple pressures old ideals and beliefs began to weaken, and the new ideal of a small number of children gained strength. A trend towards birth restriction started in the urban upper classes and gradually moved down the social scale and out to the countryside. For the most part this restriction of childbearing was accomplished by the use of folk methods of contraception that had been widely known for centuries throughout the world. However, they were not intensively used until the incentive for birth restriction became strong. Later, presumably in response to the new demands, the modern and more efficient methods of contraception were developed and gained widespread acceptance.

Notestein and other authors dealing with the theory of demographic transition used to mention the following changes associated with the fall of fertility during the transition from the phase of traditional society to that of advanced society:

Traditional	Advanced
High mortality, particularly high infant and child mortality.	Low mortality, particularly low infant and child mortality.
Agrarian society.	Industrialized society.
Rural communities.	High level of urbanization.
Education brief, low level.	Education long, high level.
Low standard of living.	High standard of living.
Scant consumption possibilities.	Widening consumption possibilities.
Little opportunity for women to achieve anything outside the family.	New economic role, independence from household obligations, emancipation of women.
Cost of child-rearing low; economic contribution of children to the household of parents begins early in life.	Cost of child-rearing high; contribution to the household of parents begins late, if ever.
Work organized in families.	Work organized in factories and offices.
Role of family in providing economic assistance and security very important.	Assistance and security providing role of family declines, because of the development of social security.
Extended families and households.	Nuclear families.
Social immobility.	High degree of social mobility, striving for achievement.
Religious ideas favourable to large families.	Secularization, ideal of small family.
Folk methods of contraception.	Modern and more efficient methods of contraception (in the later phases).

Recently, however, doubts have been expressed concerning the relation of these changes to fertility (Coale 1965 1973). *No exact thresholds* at which the decline of fertility begins could be determined. For example, by investigating the demographic development of sixteen European countries, Van de Walle and Knodel (1967) found that at the time of the beginning of fertility decline the indicators of mortality, as well as levels of economic and social development, were at very different national levels.

The beginning of fertility decline was defined as the date when a 10 per cent decline occurred. That was before 1830 in France, in 1890 in Germany, in 1892 in England and Wales, and in 1929 in Ireland.

At this time infant mortality was rather high in some countries, e.g. in Germany (221 per 1000), and rather low in others, e.g. in Ireland (69 per 1000).

Similarly this 10 per cent decline occurred at very different levels of industrialization. This was measured by the percentage of male labour force in agriculture. This indicator was 13 per cent when the fertility decline occurred in Scotland (1894) and 66 per cent when it occurred in Spain (1918).

Urbanization, too, was very different when the fertility decline occurred. For example, the share of rural population was 26 per cent in the Netherlands (1897) and 85 per cent in Finland (1910).

Basic education does not seem to be strongly connected to the decline of fertility; at the onset of decline the percentage of illiterates in the population aged 10 or 15 and over was 21 per cent in Austria (1908) and 60 per cent in Bulgaria (1912).

One of the most conspicuous cases of different levels of economic and social development at the beginning of fertility decline is that between France and Germany. While both countries were roughly similarly industrialized and urbanized in 1880, and France was lagging behind Germany in literacy, the decline by 10 per cent was just beginning in Germany, but had begun at least half a century before in France (more probably nearer to a whole century before that date).

Thus, although the data presented were rightly considered to be too crude, Knodel and Van de Walle concluded that 'a simple statement of the threshold hypothesis and of the demographic transition is incapable of describing the actual experience of Europe'.

Coale (1969) came to a similar conclusion when he investigated the map of early fertility decline in Europe. In the analysis he utilized the I_f (total fertility), I_g (marital fertility) and I_m (proportion married) indices of different microregions (departments, counties, districts) in Europe. The maps for 1870 and 1900 displayed three large regions, or more exactly conglomerates of microregions, where marital fertility was low: (1) a Mediterranean region, including parts of Italy, France, Catalonia and southern Spain; (2) a Baltic region, including parts of Sweden, as well as the surroundings of St Petersburg, Latvia, Lithuania and Estonia; (3) an Atlantic region (with not so low, but rather moderate fertility), including Norway, northern Scotland, Ireland, Brittany and the Atlantic provinces of Iberia. A fourth region might be added (Demény 1968, Tekse 1969), including parts of the Habsburg empire (southern Transdanubia, the Banat region in the southern part of the Great Plain, and parts of southern Transylvania). It clearly cannot be said that these regions were more developed, more industrialized and urbanized, or more educated than other parts of Europe where no similar signs of fertility decline can be discerned.

The I_m index also showed clear geographical differences, confirming more or less the thesis of Hajnal that the European pattern of late marriage and widespread celibacy extended to a line from St Petersburg to Trieste; eastwards from that line the proportion of married adults was much higher, and it increased with the distance of the given microregion from the line.

Thus, according to Coale (1973), there are several demographic phenomena which cannot be explained by the demographic transition theory:

(1) Differences in the proportions married were rather different in the particular regions and countries before the onset of the decline of fertility. It might be said that in western Europe there were *two fundamental demographic transitions*: the first was the introduction of the 'European marriage pattern' described by Hajnal, which probably began in the sixteenth century, perhaps earlier, characterized by late marriage and a high proportion of celibacy until the upper end of the childbearing life span; the second transition was in the nineteenth century, when marital fertility began to decline. The first was called by Coale the Malthusian transition, since the method of reducing fertility was that advocated by Malthus, and the second the Neomalthusian transition, the method used being that propagated by the Neomalthusians. On the other hand, in eastern Europe only this second transition occurred, only a few decades later than in western Europe.

(2) There were large *differences in marital fertility in pre-transition populations*, some having fertility rates near to the level of natural fertility, others much lower fertility.

(3) The *decline of mortality did not everywhere precede* the decline in fertility; in some cases the two rates shared a parallel decline.

(4) *Fertility shows large variations in time in the post-transition societies*. Although the explanation of these variations would be most interesting from the point of view of this book, the theory of demographic transition cannot be used for that purpose.

(5) There were important *regional differences* in the decline of fertility which cannot be explained by socioeconomic characteristics.

(6) According to Coale, the extent of availability and knowledge of *contraceptive techniques* during the transition is not clear. Folk methods were known before the transition, and were probably used to a large extent in the period of transition, but new techniques must have become available in the nineteenth century.

Thus the only generalization from the demographic transition theory that remains valid is that there are traditional societies where fertility and mortality are high, characterized by more than 60 per cent of active population engaged in agriculture, less than 30 per cent of population living in urban places of more than 20 000 persons, and less than 50 per cent of the female population aged 6 to 13 enrolled into education, and there are modern societies with low fertility and mortality characterized by less than 30 per cent engaged in agriculture, more than 50 per cent living in urban settlements and more than 90 per cent of the female population aged 6 to 13 enrolled in education. What happens in between these two types of society is only very vaguely explained by the theory. The process of fertility decline 'was more complex, subtle and diverse than anticipated' by the theory (Coale 1969, p. 19).

Recently Coale (1973) hypothesized that three preconditions must be fulfilled – instead of one precise threshold being attained – for the sustained decline of marital fertility, namely:

1   Fertility must be within the calculus of conscious choice – i.e. beliefs and norms should not forbid family planning, or should not favour very large families.
2   Reduced fertility must be economically and otherwise advantageous for couples.
3   Effective techniques of fertility reduction must be available.

Under these circumstances, the actual process of demographic transition and the development of fertility within this process of transition might follow different paths, depending on economic and social conditions, beliefs and norms, as well as on the techniques of fertility reduction available.

Taking into consideration these shortcomings of the demographic transition theory, Caldwell (1976) proposed a restatement of the theory, which, however, amounts to a completely new theory of the secular decline in fertility. He dismisses two basic assumptions of the demographic transition theory: (1) that the poor underdeveloped populations are brutish and behave in an irrational way, and (2) that industrialization and urbanization are preconditions of the demographic transition. On the contrary, he states that: (1) in societies of every type and in all stages of development, fertility behaviour is rational, and (2) the decline of fertility is the consequence of emotional and economic nucleation of the family, which is only loosely connected to economic development.

In primitive societies (in which the largest organizational institution is the tribe, clan or village) and in traditional societies (in which the state and the church are able to provide some protection of the individuals and of nuclear families in times of disaster) the more children (and other relatives) the head of the family has, the more powerful and wealthy he is, as the direction of intergenerational wealth (i.e. income and labour services) flows from children to parents – i.e. children provide more income, labour and help to their parents than they receive from them. In modern societies, the direction of this flow is reversed as parents give more to their children than they receive from them. The 'great divide' when the direction of these flows changes, however, depends on the change in the type of family, from the extended type to the emotionally and economically nuclear type, which might occur long before industrialization (e.g. in Europe). In post-divide populations economic rationality of the couple would require a minimal number of children (essentially no child), but non-economic factors, which are of social and psychological nature, contribute to maintain fertility over the zero level, in the same way as non-economic reasons (e.g. spacing of births to contain infant and early childhood mortality, or the avoidance of very large families and the problems of control, noise and emotional deprivation connected with them) might induce couples to practice birth control in primitive and traditional societies.

Essentially the possibilities of many different ways or responses to given situations are taken into account by the *theory of multiphasic response*, elaborated by K. Davis (1963). The starting point of this theory is that no society has been geared to a sustained high rate of natural increase except by conquest. Therefore, when mortality begins to decline and natural increase grows in consequence, populations give some response to this change in the demographic situation. The basic motivation of this response is not the direct fear of poverty, but the fact that larger families are exposed to economic hardships and cannot take advantage of the opportunities provided by economic and social development. More children means that the resources and property of the parents must be divided, and more expenses are incurred by the parents because of the necessity of rearing and educating them, endowing their marriages, etc. Populations quickly become aware of this, when mortality declines, and try to accommodate themselves by different responses. These might be:

(*a*) Increased celibacy.
(*b*) Delayed marriages.
(*c*) Contraception by folk methods or modern methods.
(*d*) Induced abortion.
(*e*) Outmigration, which might take the form of migration within the given country to other areas, especially towns, or employment in other branches of the economy, as well as of emigration to other countries.

Populations faced with the problem of a rapid natural increase generally adopt several of these responses, but the relative importance of the different responses might be very varied. For example, it might happen that emigration is predominant and so marital fertility remains more or less unchanged; or it might happen that a population responds by delaying marriage and increasing celibacy without changing marital fertility; it is also possible that a population simply accommodates itself by a control of marital fertility, which again might be achieved by different methods of contraception, or alternatively by induced abortion.

K. Davis analysed several societies. The peasant societies of western Europe responded to the decline in mortality first of all by delaying marriage and by an increased celibacy. The Irish response was characterized by mass emigration, in addition to celibacy and late marriage, but with a very small decline in marital fertility. In the period of industrialization the response of peasant communities was chiefly outmigration to towns and the seeking of employment in industry. In Japan in the last decades the main form of response was firstly induced abortion and later contraception. However, in almost all cases several response possibilities were utilized. It might be added to the theory of K. Davis that all the different responses are not equally inconvenient, their psychological cost is different, and populations probably tend to choose the relatively less inconvenient responses.

2.3 Economic theories of fertility

Although the theories hypothesizing a negative correlation of economic and social development and fertility were more or less generally accepted by demographers until the 1960s, the idea of a positive correlation of income or economic conditions and fertility (i.e. the other interpretation that can be derived from the work of Malthus) also made regular appearances.

For example, Alfred Marshall in his *Principles of Economics* (1898) described several observations on the interrelations of economic and demographic processes, and stated that 'given the climate, the average age of marriage depends chiefly on the ease with which young people can establish themselves, and support a family according to the standard of comfort that prevails among their friends and acquaintances' (p. 258). Peasants in traditional agricultural areas where the value of land rises and land is becoming scarce 'incline to limit artificially the size of their families' (p. 260), sometimes also 'dissuading the younger sons from marriage' (p. 261), thus keeping their numbers almost stationary. 'On the other hand there seem to be no conditions more favourable to the rapid growth of numbers than those of the agricultural districts of the new countries' (p. 261), where land is abundant, railways and steamships carry away the agricultural products and bring in exchange other goods. The two contrasting examples he mentions are France and America. He also mentions the relations between short-term economic fluctuations and demographic phenomena, stating that the rise in the price of wheat early in the nineteenth century in England diminished the number of marriages in the working class (p. 267).

This line of reasoning was followed by the new formulations of the so-called *economic theory of fertility*. The two basic tenets of this theory are that

1 Couples behave in a rational way when they decide on the number of children they want to have.
2 Children are viewed by the couples more or less as consumption goods.

According to the Hicks–Allen consumption theory, the choices of goods or consumption decisions of individuals or families are determined by their relative preferences for the different goods available, the prices of these

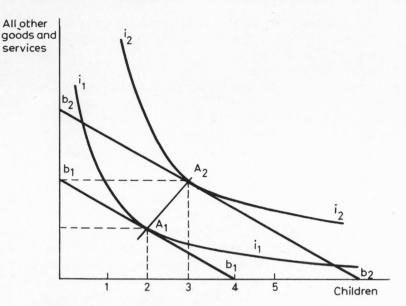

Figure 2.1   Indifference curves and budget lines.
    $i_1 - i_1$ Indifference curve representing a lower level of satisfaction.
    $i_2 - i_2$ Indifference curve representing a higher level of satisfaction.
    $b_1 - b_1$ Budget line representing a lower income level.
    $b_2 - b_2$ Budget line representing a higher income level.
      A_1 Combination of children and goods chosen at the lower income
          level. '
      A_2 Combination of children and goods chosen at the higher income
          level.

goods and their income. The logic of consumption decisions is illustrated in fig. 2.1 by indifferences curves and budget lines.

The indifference curves represent those combinations of two goods or groups of goods that provide equal utility or satisfaction to the given consumer. In the case of the economic theory of fertility the two goods are: (1) the children, (2) all other goods and services taken together. The slopes of the indifference curves express the rate at which the consumer would be willing to substitute the two goods for each other. It is assumed that the marginal utility provided by an additional unit of every good declines as its consumed quantity increases; therefore the consumer would be willing to sacrifice less and less of the other good in order to obtain an additional unit of the given good. It follows that the indifference curves are convex. The more the two goods considered are substitutes of each other – i.e. the less the marginal rate of substitution changes when the quantity of one of them increases – the nearer is the indifference curve to a straight line, and the less they can substitute each other the nearer is the indifference curve to two straight segments at right angles to each other (see fig. 2.2). In our case the indifference curve represents the combinations of the number of children the couple considers to provide equal satisfaction, and the slope of the curve expresses the willingness of the couple to trade off children for other goods. For example, if the indifference curves were of the orthogonally broken line type, it would mean that the couple is absolutely unwilling to change their family plans and plans to buy other goods depending on their relative prices.

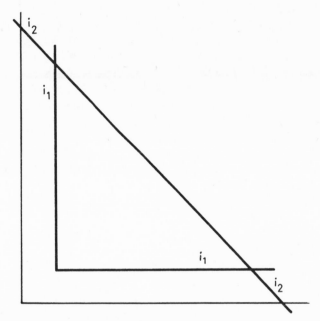

Figure 2.2   Two extreme shapes of indifference curves.
   $i_1 - i_1$ Indifference curve representing the case of no substitution.
   $i_2 - i_2$ Indifference curve representing the case of complete substitution.

The budget lines represent those combinations of the two goods that can be purchased by means of a given income. If prices are assumed to be fixed, budget lines are straight lines and the lines representing different levels of income are parallel, because with a higher income it is possible to purchase proportionately greater quantities of the goods.

The individual or family behaving in a rational way chooses that point of the budget line representing its income, i.e. the combination of goods that lies on the highest indifference curve, more exactly where the highest indifference curve is tangent to the given budget line. The line connecting the points where the budget lines representing different income levels are tangent to the respective highest indifferent curves represents the combinations of goods chosen by the couple at different income levels. In the case of the economic theory of fertility this line represents the number of children and quantity of all other goods and services the couple wants to have at different income levels. Depending on the shape of the indifference curves this line might be very different. In the usual form of the consumption theory, with the usual indifference curves and budget lines, however, a higher income level should be always associated with a more or less higher number of children per family.

This way of reasoning is obviously very elegant and has the advantage of integrating the theory of fertility into the broader deductive economic theory of consumer choices, or – as it has been called recently – the theory of household production and consumption. The problem, however, is how to reconcile it with the many known cases of societies or social strata where families with higher incomes have lower fertility than those having lower incomes. The authors of the new formulations of this economic theory of fertility have attempted various different solutions to this dilemma.

The simplest explanation is provided by Becker (1960). In his opinion the most important factor causing the apparent negative relation of fertility and income is the *level of information on methods of birth control*. Population groups having lower income can be assumed to be less well informed on contraceptive methods, and therefore have more children than they want. If, however, in future all population groups were equally well informed on birth control, the positive relation would prevail.

In the absence of differences of knowledge on birth control, all couples behave and calculate in the same way, as households do when they plan their purchases of consumer durables. They take into consideration the cost or price of the goods and of the children, as well as their disposable income. The higher the income, the more and the better goods they purchase and the more and the better quality children they want to have. Here Becker introduces an important new idea – that in addition to the number of their children, their quality also influences the satisfaction of the parents. *Quality of children* might be influenced by their education and in general by the amount of money spent on them. Parents having a higher income not only want more children, but also spend more money per child in order to enhance their quality. Obviously it is imaginable that the couples with higher income spend all their extra money on the improvement of the quality of a given number of children and do not want to have more children. Becker, however, seems to have assumed that this is not the case, the couples with higher income wanting more and at the same time better quality children, so that the income elasticity of both quality and quantity of children is positive.

Okun (1958) rejected the explanation of the number of children in terms of the simple consumption theory, because he considered that there is a fundamental distinction between children and commodities. In other words, while the price of commodities is identical for households at different income levels, that of children is a function of the family income and status. Unlike Becker, who believed that couples are free to decide how much money to spend on the education of their children in order to enhance their quality, Okun considered that the *minimum cost per child is lower for low income and low status families* than it is for high income and high status families, because children cannot be brought up at a much lower level of living than that of their parents – i.e. that of the average of the social and income group to which the couple belongs. In consequence, the budget lines at different levels of income are not parallel, but their slope (expressing the relative costs of children) is higher at the higher income levels (fig. 2.3). In that case it may well occur that the couples decide to have a smaller number of children at a higher income level. It is thus possible to explain why fertility declined over time parallel with the rise of income, as at the same time the costs of children increased, so that couples were induced to substitute commodities for children. It can

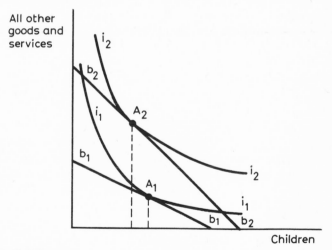

Figure 2.3 Indifference curves and budget lines in case of increasing cost of children.

$b_1 - b_2$ Budget line representing a lower level of income.

$b_2 - b_2$ Budget line representing a higher level of income and a higher cost per child.

A_1 Combination of children and goods chosen at the lower level of income.

A_2 Combination of children and goods chosen at the higher level of income.

similarly be explained why families with lower income have more children. It should be mentioned that Okun considered this scheme to be only an explanatory device, not a universally valid and verifiable theory of fertility.

Leibenstein (1957 1974), who was the first to formulate the new economic theory of fertility, described the development over time of different benefits and costs of children, in order to explain the relation between changes of fertility and economic development. He distinguished *three types of utility* for which a child is wanted: (1) consumption utility, i.e. the child as a source of personal pleasure, (2) work or income utility, i.e. the benefits derived from the fact that the child sooner or later enters the labour force and provides help either in the farm or the workshop of the family or earns an income to add to the common fund of the household, and (3) the security utility, derived from the fact that the child will be a potential source of security and help for the parents, particularly in old age. The *two types of costs or disutilities* considered by Leibenstein are: (1) the direct costs involved in feeding, housing, clothing and education, and (2) the indirect costs arising from the income-earning (or other) opportunities forgone by the parents because of the efforts needed to raise and educate the child.

These utilities and disutilities are variously influenced by socioeconomic development, and in particular by three aspects of this development: (1) the increase of *per capita* income, (2) the decline of mortality, and (3) changes in occupational structure.

Leibenstein considers that the analysis of fertility should not be concentrated on children of any birth order. He is not interested in explaining why the first two children are wanted, but in examining why families having two children shift to three, those having three shift to four, those having four shift to five.

While it might be assumed (though Leibenstein does not exclude a different assumption) that the consumption utility of the nth (third, fourth, fifth) child does not change when income rises, he considers that both work utility and security utility decrease, because at a higher level of *per capita* income children are educated for a longer period and therefore enter the labour force later, and because it is possible to assure other sources of security for the parents. Direct costs in money terms certainly increase with *per capita* income, but it is not certain whether the disutility of bearing these costs also increases in terms of the utility of the goods given up to bear these costs (out of a higher income). On the other hand, the indirect costs could be very important at higher income levels, because the parents might be obliged to give up important earning activities and very desirable consumption activities (e.g. recreation).

The decline of infant and child mortality tends to increase the utilities of children, since fewer of them die before the age of entering the labour

force to provide security for their parents. Changes in occupational structure certainly indicate that more and more families enter the occupational
strata where the direct costs of education are necessarily higher.

Also Leibenstein assumes that marginal utilities of the nth child are
lower than those of the $(n-1)$th child. When parents decide on wanting the
nth child, they compare the expected utilities and disutilities and decide to
have the nth if the utilities are higher than the disutilities. It is impossible
to deduce from this model – considered by Leibenstein to be an explanatory vehicle, rather than a device to predict the development of fertility –
whether the number of children of a representative family will increase or
decrease with the growth of income. That depends on the shape and slope
of the utility and disutility curves.

If the slope of the utility and disutility functions of the nth and $(n-1)$th
child are similar to those in the figure given by Leibenstein (1974), then
obviously at a lower level of *per capita* income the representative couple
will want to have more children (n) than at a higher income level $(n-1)$
(fig. 2.4). It might be conceived, however, that these curves could be of a
different shape and slope, e.g. that the disutilities of children decrease at

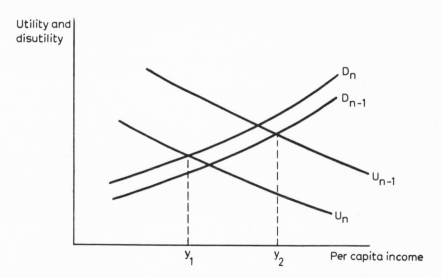

Figure 2.4 Utility and disutility of the nth and $(n-1)$th child for the repre-
sentative household, inverse relation of fertility to income ($y_1 < y_2$).
U_n, U_{n-1} Utility associated with the nth and $(n-1)$th child.
D_n, D_{n-1} Disutility associated with the nth and $(n-1)$th child.
$\quad\quad y_1$ Income beyond which the representative household would
$\quad\quad\quad$ decide not to have an nth child.
$\quad\quad y_2$ Income beyond which the representative household would
$\quad\quad\quad$ decide not to have an $(n-1)$th child.

higher income levels, because the utilities that must be forgone due to the larger number of children are less important at these higher income levels, and in that case the representative couple might want more children at a higher income level (fig. 2.5). Also the representative couple might consider that the utility provided by the nth child is not lower than that provided by the $(n-1)$th child or that the disutility per child is not increasing with each subsequent child, and in these cases the relation of fertility to income might be quite different.

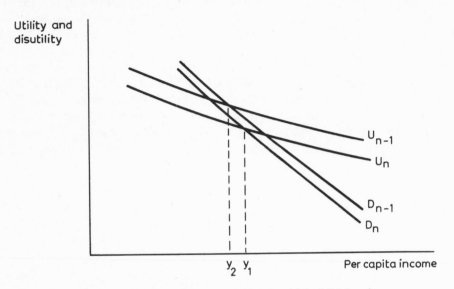

Figure 2.5 Utility and disutility of the nth and $(n-1)$th child for the representative household, direct relation of fertility to income ($y_1 > y_2$).

Mincer (1963) developed the line of reasoning further, accentuating the importance of indirect costs. He stressed that any consumption might entail *opportunity costs*, the most important of them being the *time spent* in connection with consumption. Among other examples he cites that of the children. Obviously the pleasure of having (i.e. consuming) children necessitates a great deal of time, most of all from the side of the mother, who for that reason might give up her gainful occupation. The *forgone income* of the wife who bears and cares for children might not have been a very important opportunity cost in a period when women had a low education and could attain only very low wages, but in an advanced society where both the education and wage inequalities of women and men are much smaller the wage of the wife might be a very important component of the income of the family.

Mincer specified the following equation for the demand of children:

$$X_0 = \beta_1(X_1 + X_2) + \alpha X_2 + \beta_3 X_3 + \mu$$

where X_0 is fertility, X_1 is the husband's earning, and X_2 is the wife's potential full-time earning, so that $X_1 + X_2$ is the potential income of the family, and X_3 the education of the husband, a proxy variable for the contraceptive knowledge. He stated that according to the economic theory of fertility the parameters should be $\beta_1 > 0$, $\alpha < 0$ and $\beta_3 < 0$. By means of different samples (e.g. 400 white urban families with a fully employed husband and a 35–45 year old wife employed for some time in the year), as well as average data for cities and areas in 1950 and in 1940, he found the predicted parameter values and concluded that the hypothesis on the importance of the opportunity cost associated with the forgone wages of the mother was valid and might be an important factor explaining the apparent inverse relation of fertility to income level. More exactly, however, the husband's earning is related positively and the wife's potential earning is related negatively to the number of children, so that the higher the female wage rate and the lower the husband's earning power, the lower is the fertility rate.

Simon (1969) also tried to incorporate the cases of the observed positive and negative relationships of fertility to income into a more general theory of fertility. His intention was to develop the theory of Becker by explaining the fact that desired fertility in many cases does not show the positive relation to income which was postulated by Becker. His model includes four economic and social factors of fertility: (1) income, (2) costs of child-raising, (3) investment value of children, i.e. their potential contribution to the support of the parents, and (4) a complex factor of *modernization*, including education, urban-rural residence, child mortality and contraceptive knowledge. Disregarding factors 2 and 3, he states that in cross-sectional studies in underdeveloped countries the unconditional effect of income on fertility (i.e. their simple correlation coefficient) is negative, even though its partial effect after abstracting from the other operative variables (i.e. the partial correlation coefficient) may well be positive, because the modernization factor is positively correlated with income and negatively correlated with fertility. Similarly, in long-term time series the modernization factor dominates the relationship of fertility to income, so it is negative. In short-term analysis, however, the positive effects of income changes are more apparent, because modernization does not ensue in two or three years. In developed countries the overall relation becomes more uncertain, as infant mortality approaches a level where it cannot be reduced further, knowledge of contraception becomes universal, and rural or farm residence approaches a level so low that even a large proportional change in the remaining farm population would be small relative to the rest of the society. Thus, according to Simon, the education component of the modernization variable may become crucial and may even be reversed at high education levels, so that the modernization variable might not overshadow the positive relation of fertility to income.

Independently from this American school of economic theory of fertility Smolinski (1965 1969) formulated a similar theory on the relation of fertility to income. He assumed that this relation is different in particular phases of economic development. In the first phase, when *per capita* income is below the minimum of existence, fertility is positively related to income; in the third phase, when *per capita* income is above the maximum of existence, the relation again becomes positive. In the second phase, however, when *per capita* income is between the minimum and maximum of existence and therefore many other goods are in competition with children, because the purchase of these goods is only possible if the number of children is restricted, the relation is decidedly negative, as the rise of income generates higher needs which cannot be satisfied by larger families. The meaning of *minimum of existence* is defined as the level of subsistence below which basic biological needs are not completely satisfied. The meaning of *maximum of existence* is more complicated. Smolinski considers that it is attained when all historically formed higher needs, such as consumer durables, dwelling, vacations at holiday resorts, etc., are easily satisfied. Obviously its level is changing and might be different in particular societies. Roeske-Slomka (1973), when utilizing the theory of Smolinski in an empirical study, stated that the maximum of existence might be set at approximately 2000 dollars *per capita* national income. The theory of Smolinski clearly reflects the recent demographic development of Poland and the problems connected with its interpretation – namely, why fertility was high and rose in the immediate postwar years when *per capita* income was very low, and why it declined beginning from the second half of the 1950s, when income rose rapidly, when at the same time the baby boom could be observed in countries with a higher *per capita* income level.

The economic theory of fertility has been strongly criticized by several demographers, perhaps most severely by Blake (1968). She considered that *children cannot be considered analogous to consumer durables* for several reasons. First, there are strong social pressures to marry and start a family, and people are even encouraged to do so in the face of financial difficulties; on the other hand, society considers that parents are obliged to provide a certain standard of care and education for their children, and they are condemned by public opinion if they have so many children that they are unable to provide them this standard. Therefore adults are *not as free to choose the number of their children*, as they are to decide to buy or not to buy consumer durables. Second, parents are *not able to choose the quality of their children*, since this depends on many other (e.g. genetic) factors in addition to care and education. Third, where parents are not satisfied with the number and quality of their children, they are not free to change them, as they may change consumer durables if they are not satisfied with them. Fourth, parents are not free to use (and abuse) their children, as they are free concerning the use of their consumer durables. Parents are socially and legally required to care adequately for their children. Fifth, the costs of children are misinterpreted by Becker, since on the one hand they include the indirect or opportunity costs of the time required for their care, and on the other hand the direct costs of children are also differentiated by social strata because of the different standards accepted by them. In consequence, according to Blake, a positive relation of fertility to income is most improbable. Her own analysis of data on the ideal number of children in the United States does not show any effective sign of a positive relation.

Instead of economic considerations families are influenced in their decisions on fertility by the norms and values of society. Societies channel motivation of adults in the direction of goals that imply the existence of children. To become a parent, to be a mother or a father, to be member of a family, are roles valued by society. All these roles imply children. Therefore it is unlikely that poorer families will abstain from having children. To become a parent, to be a mother or a father, to be a member of hand, there are institutions in developed societies which compete with the family, and which have a particular attraction for higher status people, who therefore might try to harmonize the pressures of society for having a family and the demands for participating in these other institutions by reducing the size of their families.

Thus the norm or ideal of two to four children developed in American society. On the one hand, it is universally considered that the only child is handicapped, because at least one sibling is necessary for socialization in childhood. On the other hand, too many children endanger the standard of upbringing, because of low *per capita* income in the larger families and because of high requirements and costs in the more well-to-do families.

Thus, according to Blake, 'fertility is determined by the characteristics of family and the general norms and values attributed to the concept of family in the given society, and the more fundamental changes of fertility are caused by the changes of the institution of family; therefore a theory of reproductive motivation is at the same time a theory of the family and society' (p. 24).

The problem with Blake's theory is that it does not explain the variation of fertility from two to four children per family, i.e. the differences of fertility found presently between different developed countries and between different population groups, as in almost all cases the average fertilities range from two to four children. These differences are actually

very important, because with an average of two children per family population would slowly diminish, while an average of four children per family
results in a very rapid growth rate.

Thus in the mid 1960s there were several theories of the determinants of
fertility in advanced countries – the theory of demographic transition and
that of multiphasic response, the economic theory of fertility, and the ideas
formulated by Blake as a criticism of the last-mentioned theory. The
predictions of these theories concerning the influence of different economic
and social factors were rather different, in some cases even contradictory.
In the next chapters we investigate how the empirical data from the
advanced countries fit these theories, and to what extent they confirm or
contradict them.

PART THREE

Determinants of fertility in centuries preceding the modern period

By the pre-modern period we mean here the period preceding the beginning of the regular publication of official national data or vital statistics. Official statistics began in different countries in widely different years, but generally the beginning of official statistics coincides with the attainment of a certain level of economic and social development, of industrialization. Thus, though it is not absolutely justified to identify the pre-official statistical period with the pre-modern period, it might be accepted as an approximation. Therefore in this chapter we deal with the period preceding the publication of official vital statistical data, which is at the same time the pre-modern period of the present developed countries.

We examine three kinds of sources concerning fertility during these centuries: (*a*) contemporary literary sources, (*b*) parish registers of births, marriages and deaths, evaluated either in a non-nominative way, or by the method of family reconstitution, as well as genealogical studies, (*c*) early census data for which the new method of stable population models provides new possibilities of evaluation.

The problems on which answers may be sought from historical demographic data might be summarized in the following four questions

1 What was the *level* of fertility in the pre-industrial period, and did it attain the level of natural fertility or was it lower?
2 If actual fertility was lower than the natural fertility level, what were the *immediate causes* (low marital fertility, late marriage, or high proportion of unmarried adults) of that difference?
3 *Where*, in which of the developed countries, in which regions of them, and in what periods, was fertility low or decreasing?
4 What were the economic and social *factors* and conditions associated with low fertility, and with the decrease of fertility?

3.1 Literary sources on fertility and birth control

There is a fairly widespread belief in demography that populations that have not yet reached modern economic and social development, or where modern industrialization does not have an important impact, do not know or at least do not practise methods of birth control to any great extent (see e.g. Beshers 1967, McKeown *et al.* 1972). Underlying this belief there is another general opinion, i.e. that the everyday philosophy, the mentality and the conception of the world of primitive or pre-industrial peoples is basically different from that of developed societies. Therefore, it is supposed, these people are ignorant of the biological mechanism of conception, and consequently of the possibility of birth control – or, if they do know about it, the idea of rational family planning and birth control is completely alien from their mentality. This belief, held by some demographers, is corroborated by the description given by the very distinguished ethnologist Malinowski of the sexual life of the population of the Trobriand Islands in northwestern Melanesia (Malinowski 1929). According to him, these people did not know the role of the father or of the sexual act in conception.

Recent cultural anthropological studies, however, discovered that even the most *primitive populations* know certain forms of birth control: infanticide in the most primitive case (Douglas 1966), different methods of induced abortion (Nag 1962, Devereux 1967, Murdock 1934), as well as most of the different methods of birth control, e.g. plugs, sheaths (De Laszlo and Henshaw 1954), douches (Himes 1963), vasectomy (Himes 1963) and, naturally, the most well-known method of coitus interruptus. There are also some customs and practices that result in the decrease of birth frequency, such as post-natal abstinence, periodical abstinence in connection with feasts, and prohibition of marriage of young people (Douglas 1966).

A demonstrative example of the use of such methods to limit the number of births is given by Firth (1936, 1939): the chieftain of the Polynesian population of Tikopia once a year addresses the population admonishing them to practise coitus interruptus, because otherwise too many children would be born, and in consequence theft and other social problems would spread. The real reason for birth control was the smallness of the island where they were living and the impossibility of extending the available food resources.

The knowledge and practice of birth control during the past history of the present developed countries is similarly not accepted by some scientists. For example, Aries (1953) states that in western Europe birth control was not generally practised, because its methods were not widely known. Riquet (1949) asserts that, although methods were known (which is proved by the fact that several prominent Christians, e.g. Augustine, wrote against them), birth control was not widely used because of general Church disapproval. Other authors, however, state that birth control was well known and widespread throughout the Roman Empire (Hopkins 1965–6) and in Byzantium (Patlagean 1969). According to Russell (1940) the Catholic Church in the Medieval Ages denounced the following methods of birth control, which implies that they might have been widespread: inducing infertility by drugs and incantation; aborting the foetus by violent exercise; killing the infant at birth; refusing to nurse one's child; accidentally sleeping on the child. Henry II of France made abortions a crime to be punished, in most cases by capital punishment (Chaunu 1966), which he would not have done if the practice of induced abortions had not been rather widespread. The fact that in the fifteenth century when illicit sexual relations were widespread in western Europe, the number of illegitimate children was low, was considered by Flandrin (1969) as a proof of the practice of birth control. He hypothesized that, beginning from the sixteenth century, two kinds of sexual behaviour developed: one in marriage, characterized by moderation and no birth control, and another in illicit relations, characterized by greater sexual indulgence and birth control.

There was a further practice widespread in Europe, that of prolonged breast feeding, which might have a certain contraceptive effect (although it is not a safe method) and which might have been practised with the deliberate intention of postponing conception (Eversley 1965a, Carlsson 1966). E. and F. Van de Walle (1972) examined medical and other literature of France in the period preceding demographic transition and found references to the connection between birth control and breast-feeding in the eighteenth century, but not before. However, in earlier periods they found instances of the opinion that during breast feeding the mother should not have sexual intercourse.

In the seventeenth century birth control methods were well known and widespread in France. Madame de Sévigné (1626–96) in a letter written in 1671 to her daughter quite openly suggests the use of certain 'restringents de Provence' in order to avoid a new pregnancy (Aries 1954). In the eighteenth century these methods were known by peasant families, as Moheau wrote: 'on trompe la nature jusque dans les villages' (nature is also cheated in the villages), and Mirabeau states in 1756 that 'la nature gémit des moyens que le luxe suggère pour éviter l'embarras d'une nombreuse famille' (nature groans because of the devices suggested by luxury to avoid the problems connected with a large family) (Pressat 1971, p. 67).

Not only in France, which was one of the most developed countries in Europe during the sixteenth to eighteenth centuries, but also in the relatively underdeveloped Hungary, occupied partly by the Turks and an area plagued by continuous wars in the sixteenth to seventeenth centuries, mentions of birth control methods were found in different contemporary literary sources.

In the records of evidence of witchcraft trials (Schram 1970) a frequent charge was that the alleged witch encouraged the witness to practise birth control or to induce an abortion, or offered abortives. For example, in 1582 a widowed woman was accused of having given a drink to a certain maidservant in order to induce abortion, and of knowing abortives that were effective in the fifth month of pregnancy. In 1739 an alleged witch – according to the witness – brought from her native region a certain medicament which prevented conception. In 1754 a women was alleged to have offered another who suffered frequent confinements something, probably some kind of operation, which would permanently prevent conception.

In the second half of the eighteenth century in the enlightened reign of Maria Theresa and Joseph II the first statistical data on population were gathered by the state, and to one of the reports an unknown state clerk joined some comments (Dányi 1960). Looking at the situation from a point of view characteristic of the mercantilist school, he stated that the population of Hungary did not grow at a sufficiently high rate. Actually, the growth rate at that time was one of the highest in Europe. In his opinion the causes of the unacceptably slow rate of growth were (1) high mortality, (2) dearth of marriages, (3) 'and finally the infertility of marriages. Hardly in four years is a child born in marriage . . . the cause being that the couples prevent conception, ignoring the divine laws, but feeling that they are unable to feed many children and foreseeing the future difficulties of their children.'

In the nineteenth century sources mentioning the widespread practice of birth control become more and more numerous. An agricultural journal, the *Magyar Gazda* (*Hungarian Farmer*), published a letter from a reader who relates that in a village in the county Nógrád the parish priest noticed the low number of baptisms; having spoken with the village midwives he learnt to his great consternation that the peasant women made use of methods handed on by old women to avoid confinement. He states that 'these means are the most horrible'. The editors of the journal add that similar facts are unfortunately known from other parts of the country.

In 1845 the chief medical officer of the county Baranya wrote a book on the county dealing in a detailed way with health and population problems. He stated that, according to his information and experiences, 'in most

Hungarian villages of the county the young wives consider it a shame to bear in the first four or even ten years of their marriage, and even the healthiest and strongest women bear not more than two children ... Many young wives hinder birth clandestinely and sinfully in order to maintain their beauty, while many others are induced by poverty to do this, because often three to four families have to live on a half plot of land. . . . They are taught methods of birth control by older people ... abortions are performed, . . . as is well known' (Hölbling 1845).

Both counties mentioned, Nógrád in the north and Baranya in the south, were regions that had relatively low fertility before being industrialized. Baranya in southern Transdanubia and its district Ormánság were particularly well known for their low marital fertility, popularly called the 'one child system'. At the end of the nineteenth century a 'One Child System Committee' was formed in the county to investigate its causes and possible remedies, and in the twentieth century several authors – scientists, journalists and novelists – have examined the problem. Traditional methods of birth control were investigated, and it was found that infanticide was first practised; abortion later became widespread, carried out by old women, and some kinds of contraceptives were used, e.g. a wooden plug inserted into the cervical orifice (Elek *et al.* 1936). Examples of methods of induced abortions were: a bath in hot water, drinking decoctions of poisonous plants, the insertion into the uterous for one or two days of spiked roots of poisonous plants, and the similar use of long needles (Kovács 1940). Later the plug was wound round with yarn powdered with quinine (Kovács n.d.). Naturally the traditional method of coitus interruptus was also used, as illustrated by the common saying, 'You should rather wash the sheeting than the baby's napkin' (Hidvégi n.d.).

Considering all this information from contemporary literary sources, it might safely be concluded that the methods and possibilities of birth control were not unknown in preindustrial European populations. However, we cannot ascertain from these sources the extent of the practice of these methods. For that purpose we must seek other sources.

3.2. Family reconstitution and genealogies

Family reconstitution is sometimes called the 'royal method' of historical demography. It is a method by means of which the most detailed and exact information can be obtained on the demographic characteristics of ancient populations, and is based on the nominative processing of the birth, marriage and death registrations in parish registers.

The first parish register in Europe begins in 1334 in Givry, Burgundy. In England registration became nationwide by a decree of Thomas Cromwell in 1538. In Germany the first register was that of Nürnberg in 1524. The Council of Trent (1545–63) prescribed registration for the Roman Catholic Church, although registration was not actually extended to all Catholic populations in different countries until later dates – e.g. in Hungary it became general in the second half of the eighteenth century (Dávid 1963). The introduction and generalization of registration more or less marks the attainment of a certain level of literacy, of organization of state administration, of economic and social development. Thus it is not unreasonable to treat the period of parish registers (until the introduction of official vital statistics regularly published by the state) as a definite period of economic and social, as well as demographic development of the given country. This is also necessitated by the fact that from the period before the beginning of parish registration we do not have at present any reliable data on fertility. Registration, naturally, was of very different quality and completeness in different periods and different countries, and thus the possibility of getting reliable data varies within the historical period of parish registration.

Genealogical studies use very similar sources, i.e. data on the date of birth, death and marriage of members of a given family. Family reconstitution, however, encompasses whole parishes, i.e. villages or districts of towns, while genealogical studies are restricted to one or several families, not necessarily living in the same settlement.

Parish registers, obviously, might be investigated by *non-nominative methods*, i.e. by counting the number of births, deaths and marriages in the given year and relating these absolute numbers to a population number obtained from some other source. Information may also be obtained from non-nominative processing – for example, distribution of deaths by age, distribution of marriages by age of bridegroom and of bride, etc. The method of *family reconstitution* (Fleury and Henry 1965, Wrigley 1966a), however, provides far better possibilities, since by processing the registrations nominatively we get sheets containing all the dates of one given family – i.e. the total history of the family from birth of the wife through marriage and births to the dissolution of marriage by the death of one of the spouses. From these family sheets all the most refined rates of demographic analysis can be calculated, such as age-specific fertility rates, birth intervals, completed family size, etc.

Family reconstitution, however, has some deficiencies which should be kept in mind when analysing the results of family reconstitution studies (see Hollingsworth 1968 1969).

The first problem is connected with the *completeness of registration*. Obviously, parish registers are not always complete. The opinion of scientists on the extent of omissions is very different. For example, Krause (1965) wrote of the registers in England that 'it seems that parochial registration was relatively accurate in the early eighteenth century, became somewhat less so in the 1780s, virtually collapsed between roughly 1795 and 1820, and then somewhat improved between 1821 and 1837' (p. 393). He estimated that around 1700 the omissions in birth registration amounted to 10 per cent. Recently, Razzel (1972) stated when trying to find the birth registration of people enumerated in the censuses of 1851 and 1861 that the rate of omissions might have amounted to one third, but did not change. Schofield (1971a), however, stated that in the family reconstitution study of Colyton the rate of omissions in birth registration – due to nonconformity – was not more than 4 per cent, although 9 per cent of the population was nonconformist, at the end of the eighteenth and in the first decades of the nineteenth century.

Omission of registration of births may be due to different causes. First, it may be the consequence of religious heterogeneity, as in the case of English parishes where nonconformists were living. This problem does not arise in countries where the population was homogeneous, or where all churches had registers. The second possible cause is that infants might not have been baptized immediately after birth. In the interval between birth and baptism some infants died and, since no baptism occurred, they might not have been registered. This apparently occurred mostly in Protestant populations, because Roman Catholics are said to have baptized the infants with a shorter delay. Razzel (1972), for example, found that in an English community from a total of 1292 cases only 112 infants were baptized in the first six days of their life and only 526 at the age of 7 to 27 days. Hollingsworth (1968) supposed that under-registration of births was the cause of the relatively low infant mortality found in Colyton (138 infants died, as compared to 1480 births) from 1600 to 1649. This delay, however, seems not to be characteristic for all Protestant populations; in the case of the family reconstitution of the Calvinist parish registers of

Vajszló and Besence in Hungary (Andorka 1972 1973) it was found that the interval between birth and baptism was never longer than six days, the general interval being one to two days in the nineteenth century, when in some periods the dates of both birth and of baptism were mentioned in the register. The main conclusion, after all, is that the researcher should always try to verify whether there was a delay between birth and baptism in the given parish, and whether those infants who died in this interval were registered.

A third cause of omission of registration of births might be migration. If spouses migrated during the reproductive years, the history of the family – i.e. the fertility of the couple – cannot be determined on the basis of one parish register. Migrant couples in general have no complete family sheet, so it is not used in the analysis of the results. A more serious problem arises, however, if the couple emigrated and later returned, because in this case the family sheet seems to be complete, although some births may be missing. In some settlements migration was frequent, in others it was more rare (Poussou 1973), so it depends on the parish register chosen for analysis to what extent it distorts the results.

The second problem encountered in family reconstitution is the fact that it is never possible to reconstitute all the families in the given parish because of lack of data – for example, because death registration is deficient or because marriage was not contracted in the village where the couple lived, one of the spouses having lived before marriage in another village. Hollingsworth (1969) put the proportion of families reconstituted at an average of 10 per cent. In the case of Vajszló and Besence the proportion was more favourable at 34 per cent, because the population consisted mainly of serfs holding land in villeinage and therefore not migrating. However, even a high proportion of reconstituted families always provides biased data, since the poorer families are likely to be left out, partly because in earlier centuries they tended to migrate more frequently, and partly because they might have omitted registration more frequently due to the costs associated with wedding and burial services, etc.

The third problem is that the results of family reconstitution for one parish cannot be considered representative for a whole country. Therefore it is necessary to perform family reconstitution for several parishes chosen in such a way that they constitute a representative sample of all parishes in the country. French historical demographers have followed this method (Fleury and Henry 1958, Biraben, Fleury and Henry 1960). The first results concerning Brittany and Anjou, as well as northwest and southwest France, have been published (Blayo and Henry 1967, Henry 1972, Henry and Houdaille 1973). The other possibility is to choose several parishes which differ from the point of view of population size, economic character (agricultural or fishing) and social composition (serfs having land and cotters working at large estates), etc., and try to evaluate the demographic situation of the country on the basis of these typical parishes (Schofield 1971a). The computerization of family reconstitution would provide great opportunities for increasing the number of reconstituted parishes, and by that the representativeness of the results (Blayo 1971, Henry 1971, Livi-Bacci 1971a, Beauchamp *et al.* 1973).

In spite of all these problems, however, family reconstitution seems to be the most important source of information on the two or three centuries preceding the regular publication of official vital statistics, as long as the results of family reconstitution studies are evaluated with precaution.

Table 3.1 shows the age-specific marital fertility rates derived from several different family reconstitution studies. It is at once clear that the rates are very different in each country, within given countries in the same historical periods, and also in given communities in different periods. Summing up the rates from 20 to 49 and thus calculating a hypothetical total marital fertility (the rates for the age group 15–19 are neglected, since in most communities only few women married before the age of 20), and considering that a similar summation (table 1.1) gives a total marital fertility rate of 10 940 for the Hutterite population and of 8425 for the thirteen populations investigated by L. Henry (not practising birth control), the following categories can be distinguished on the basis of the age-specific rates in table 3.1:

1 Populations definitely not practising birth control (total marital fertility rate higher than 9500):

French Canadians	1700–1730
Elversele in Flanders (Belgium)	1608–1796
Anhausen in Bavaria	1692–1899
The three villages in Brittany	18th century
The three villages in Ile-de-France	18th century
Sainghin-en-Mélantois	1690–1769 and 1800–1829

2 Populations most probably not practising birth control (rate 8500–9500):

Colyton	1560–1629
Sotteville les Rouen	1760–1790
Sainghin-en-Mélantois	1770–1799 and 1830–1839
Boulay and the three villages around it	from before 1780 to 1839
St Agnan	1730–1793
Bourgeois population of Geneva	1600–1649
St Joan de Palamos	1740–1779
Quaker population in America	before 1730

3 Populations where birth control might have occurred, but on a very limited scale (rate 7500–8500):

Colyton	1770–1837
Crulai	1677–1742
Ingouville	1730–1770
Tourouvre	1665–1765

4 Populations most probably practising birth control in marriage (rate 6500–7500):

Colyton	1630–1769
Thézels and St Sernin	18th century
Bourgeois population of Geneva	1650–1699
St Joan de Palamos	1780–1819
Alskog	1745–1794
Besence and Vajszló	1747–1790
Sárpilis	1760–1790
Velem	1753–1834

5 Widespread and intensive practice of birth control in marriage (rate below 6500):

Besence and Vajszló	1791–1895
Alsónyék	1760–1850
Sárpilis	1791–1850
Bakonya	1759–1830
St Joan de Palamos	1820–1859
Alskog	1795–1820
Quaker population in America	1756–1785

Age-specific marital fertility rates found in two regional studies of the historical trends of fertility in France (Henry 1972, Henry and Houdaille 1973) were published detailed by the age of the wife at marriage (table 3.2). Calculations performed on these data suggest that both regions belonged before 1770 to the category where birth control might have occurred, but to a very limited extent, the fertility of the southwest being markedly lower in this period. The decrease of marital fertility seems to have begun around 1770 in the southwest and around 1790 in the northwest, the drop, however, being more marked in the northwest.

Historical demographers have described other features of marital fertility which might be considered as further evidences of birth control in marriage. Four of these are described below.

(1) The evidence based on the shape of the curve of marital fertility rates. If the rates remain at a more or less steady level until the age of 35 or 40, birth control is supposed to be absent, as fecundity is supposed to decrease only slightly up to that age. If the rates drop sharply at a much earlier age, say around 30, birth control is supposed to be practised, since

Table 3.1 Age-specific marital fertility (children born per 1000 woman-years lived): results of family reconstitution in different communities and countries.

Community	Period of marriage	Age group							Source
		15–19	20–24	25–29	30–34	35–39	40–44	45–49	
England									
Colyton	1560–1629	412	467	403	369	302	174	18	Wrigley (1966b)
	1630–1646	500	378	382	298	234	128	0	
	1647–1719	500	346	395	272	182	104	20	
	1720–1769	462	362	342	292	227	160	0	
	1770–1837	500	441	361	347	270	152	22	
Flanders (Belgium)									
Elversele	1608–1649	—	571	406	310	343	232	23	Deprez (1965)
	1650–1699	444	430	432	407	386	202	37	
	1700–1749	666	542	492	396	348	166	18	
	1750–1796	666	661	572	452	272	171	0	
France									
Crulai, Normandy	1674–1742	320	419	429	355	292	142	10	Gautier and Henry (1958)
St Aubin, Brittany	18th cent.	—	582	520	489	358	—	—	Goubert (1968)
La Guerche, Brittany	18th cent.	—	507	487	458	270	—	—	Goubert (1968)
St Méen, Brittany	18th cent.	—	582	548	476	385	—	—	Goubert (1968)
Ingouville, north	1730–1749	—	450	412	400	279	103	7	Terrisse (1961)
	1750–1770	—	391	463	418	310	71		
Tourouvre, north	1665–1765	—	424	419	378	314	762	—	Charbonneau (1970)
Three villages in Ile-de-France	18th cent.	—	524	487	422	329	135	17	Ganiage (1963)
Sotteville-les-Rouen, north	1760–1790	—	491	440	429	297	125	10	Girard (1959)

Region	Period								Source
Saainghin-en-Mélantois, north	1690–1739	—	512	521	419	402	220	31	Deniel and Henry (1965)
	1740–1769	—	592	519	472	412	213	15	
	1770–1789	—	417	466	428	289	158	8	
	1790–1799	—	547	402	385	276	174	6	
	1800–1809	—	586	454	322	298	221	38	
	1810–1819	—	667	460	360	276	137	19	
	1820–1829	—	710	505	320	269	148	18	
	1830–1839	—	519	441	361	326	161	—	
Boulay, Moselle, east	before 1780	433	480	452	391	341	183	27	Houdaille (1967)
	1780–1809	—	532	399	385	296	165	20	
	1810–1839	—	504	403	353	266	—	—	
Seven villages around Boulay, east	before 1780	—	418	419	414	342	174	31	Houdaille (1971)
	1780–1809	—	460	412	395	325	158	16	
	1810–1839	—	479	404	351	269	127	8	
St Agnan, centre	1730–1793	245	403	429	378	242	246	63	Houdaille (1961)
Thézels and St Sernin, Bas-Quercy, southwest	18th cent.	208	393	326	297	242	67	1	Valmary (1965)
Germany									
Anhausen, Bavaria	1692–1799	—	472	496	450	355	173	37	Knodel (1970)
	1800–1899	—	482	525	525	362	148	12	
Switzerland									
Bourgeois population of Geneva	before 1600	264	389	362	327	275	123	19	Henry (1956)
	1600–1649	419	525	485	429	287	141	16	
	1650–1699	348	493	400	244	130	35	5	
Spain									
St Joan de Palamos, Catalonia	1700–1739	229	326	343	295	243	157	100	Nadal and Saez (1971)
	1740–1779	387	455	394	415	294	154	21	
	1780–1819	483	416	387	299	242	123	24	
	1820–1859	—	343	303	271	224	88	19	

Table 3.1—contd.

Community	Period of marriage	Age group							Source
		15–19	20–24	25–29	30–34	35–39	40–44	45–49	
United States Quaker population	before 1730	443	466	423	402	324	147	—	Wells (1971)
	1731–1755	446	408	410	326	228	171	—	
	1756–1785	347	351	346	275	215	101	—	
Canada French population	1700–1730	493	509	496	484	410	231	30	Henripin (1954)
	1630–1739	453	511	479	478	413	218	24	Charbonneau (1975)
Sweden Alskog	1745–1769	254	363	318	261	260	114	23	Gaunt (1973)
	1770–1794	307	372	374	279	204	94.5	14	
	1795–1820	439	345	337	265	174	91	12	
Estonia Rouge	1661–1696	462	350	375	325	—	—	—	Palli (1973)
Hungary Besence and Vajszló, south Transdanubia	1747–1790	306	350	311	266	189	141	45	Andorka (1972)
	1791–1820	251	291	244	198	152	66	16	
	1821–1850	211	248	219	172	112	29	6	
	1851–1895	232	245	160	119	32	13	0	
Alsónyék, south Transdanubia	1760–1790	173	288	248	214	156	60	1	Andorka (1976)
	1791–1820	139	227	182	148	75	45	0	
	1821–1850	137	227	211	145	84	30	11	

Sárpilis, south Transdanubia	1760–1790	369	393	331	276	282	182	4	Andorka (1976)
	1791–1820	234	315	310	231	181	83	19	
	1821–1850	288	273	239	151	82	36	9	
Bakonya, south Transdanubia	1759–1779	269	381	239	273	153	54	0	Moess (1973b)
	1780–1804	299	324	304	196	117	47	0	
	1805–1830	147	248	230	142	78	21	0	
Velem, west Transdanubia	1753–1793	303	390	369	359	256	82	32	Moess (1972)
	1794–1834	305	340	333	310	235	103	6	

when it is practised couples tend to concentrate parities to the younger ages. In table 3.1 the rates of the French Canadian population clearly display the first pattern, while the populations having the lowest fertility rates tend to display sharp decreases of fertility at relatively young ages.

However, the fact that the shape of the fertility curves of the populations in table 3.1 are not unambiguously convex – i.e. the greatest drop in the curve is not clearly at a relatively young age (as in the case of populations of present-day advanced countries) – suggests that this criterion of birth control might not be totally reliable. Obviously the sharp drop of the curve in young ages occurs only if the pattern of family planning follows that observed today in advanced societies, i.e. if parities are really concentrated to the younger ages and avoided later. This might not have been the case in all historical populations practising birth control, as suggested by the description of birth control in southern Transdanubia in Hungary by Hölbling (1845), who clearly stated that couples tried to postpone births in the first years of marriage.

(2) The evidence based on the fertility rates of women marrying at different ages. It is supposed that women marrying later have higher age-specific fertility rates in the same age groups than women marrying at younger ages, if both practise birth control, because couples tend to concentrate parities to the first years of marriage, and later, having attained the desired number of children, begin to avoid births by efficient methods of birth control. This is characteristic of populations of present-day advanced countries. However, this pattern is also dependent on modern methods of family planning, which might not have been similarly utilized by historical populations (see the above mentioned example in Hölbling 1845). Recently, Henry and Houdaille (1973) contested the relevance of this indication of birth control, since they found different age-specific fertility rates of women married at different ages in northwestern France (table 3.2) before 1770 when in their opinion birth control was not practised.

(3) Supposing that the pattern of family planning was to postpone parities at the beginning of marriage, long birth intervals might be the best evidence of birth control. Using this criterion it seems that, compared to the population of Crulai not practising birth control, the couples of Colyton from 1647 on and mostly from 1647 to 1719, those of Rouge in Estonia from 1661 to 1696, and the population of Vajszló and Besence in southern Transdanubia in the second half of the eighteenth century, and most of all in the nineteenth century, controlled their fertility (table 3.3).

(4) The simplest and most commonplace criterion of birth control is, naturally, the number of children borne by couples, i.e. the mean *completed*

Table 3.2 Age-specific marital fertility by age at marriage of women in two regions of France.

Region	Period of marriage	Age at marriage	Age group						
			15–19	20–24	25–29	30–34	35–39	40–44	45–49
Northwest France (Henry and Houdaille 1973)	1670–1769	–19	317	432	369	338	228	113	11
		20–24	—	459	414	359	273	134	11
		25–29	—	—	483	395	286	157	10
		30+	—	—	—	445	335	172	7
	1770–1789	–19	314	450	363	363	272	113	0
		20–24	—	480	404	342	249	103	6
		25–29	—	—	452	354	262	132	9
		30+	—	—	—	388	312	121	11
	1790–1819	–19	330	418	324	243	124	26	12
		20–24	—	470	338	229	149	62	13
		25–29	—	—	437	341	229	101	20
		30+	—	—	—	340	252	106	12
Southwest France (Henry 1972)	1720–1769	–19	275	353	311	288	215	129	14
		20–24	—	449	356	335	244	142	19
		25–29	—	—	433	373	282	157	27
		30+	—	—	—	401	331	166	34
	1770–1819	–20	289	352	324	262	204	93	5
		20–24	—	431	337	278	229	105	19
		25–29	—	—	391	325	242	130	12
		30+	—	—	—	398	296	129	14

Table 3.3   Mean birth intervals (in months), in Crulai, Colyton, Rouge, Vajszló and Besence.

| | Mean birth interval | | | | |
Community	Period	Marriage–first birth	First–second birth	Second–third birth	Third–fourth birth	Last birth
Crulai	18th century	16·6	22·4	25·3	27·2	33·0
Colyton	1560–1646	11·3	25·2	27·4	30·1	37·5
	1647–1719	10·3	29·1	32·6	32·1	50·7
	1720–1769	11·9	25·1	29·8	32·9	40·6
Rouge	1661–1696	18·9	33·3	35·7	27·9	36·3
Vajszló and Besence	1747–1790	23·9	34·3	36·5	36·7	—
	1791–1820	31·1	39·5	38·8	37·0	—
	1821–1850	34·8	48·3	49·9	44·8	—
	1851–1896	34·7	45·4	45·0	47·6	—

Source: Gautier and Henry (1958), Wrigley (1966), Palli (1973), Andorka (1973).

family size. When early Hungarian authors wrote about the 'one child system' they meant by that a completed family size (of living children) of approximately one child. The completed family size was actually decreasing sharply in Vajszló and Besence and reached very low levels in the second half of the nineteenth century, suggesting almost certainly a widespread use of birth control, although the average number of children borne by couples was always higher than two. Also the completed family size in Colyton changed in a way that seems to support evidence of the spread of birth control after 1647 and of a certain reduction of birth control after 1770 (table 3.4).

Table 3.4 Mean completed family size, in Colyton, England, and in Vajszló and Besence, Hungary

Community and period	Age at marriage			
	15–19	*20–24*	*25–29*	*30–39*
Colyton				
1560–1629		7.3	5.7	2.7
1646–1719		5.0	3.3	1.7
1720–1769		5.8	3.8	2.4
1770–1837		7.3	4.5	3.2
Vajszló and Besence				
1747–1790	6·8	6·0	4·5	—
1791–1820	4·3	4·9	4·3	—
1821–1850	3·6	3·5	3·0	3·3
1851–1895	2·8	2·8	2·3	1·0

Source: Wrigley (1966b), Andorka (1973).

The distribution of couples by the number of children born in Vajszló and Besence (table 3.5) also seems to demonstrate the pattern of the spread of birth control. Before 1790 the distribution is bimodal, one of the modes being at seven to eight parities, the other at four. It might be supposed that the first are the couples not controlling their fertility, and that the second ones are the birth controllers. In this period the birth controllers seem to be a minority, but an important one. Thus it seems again to be proven that even in populations not displaying unambiguous signs of birth control some families practised birth control. Four births were at that time more or less equivalent to the simple net reproduction of the parents, considering the infant and child mortality prevailing at that period. From 1790 the distribution becomes unimodal, the mode shifting gradually to three to four,

Table 3.5 Completed fertility (number of children born) in Crulai and in Vajszló and Besence

Community	Period	Age of wife at marriage	Number of children born												
			0	1	2	3	4	5	6	7	8	9	10	11	12
Crulai	18th century	–19												2	
		20–24	3	1		4	2	3	1	4	3	3	3		
		25–29	2	3		2	3	5	8	1	3	1	1		
		30–34	2	1	2	4	3	4		1	3				
		35–39			2	3				2					
		Total	7	5	4	13	8	12	9	8	9	4	4	2	
Vajszló and Besence	1747–1790	15–19	1	1	4	3	9	2	6	11	7	5	5	3	2
		20–24			2	2	4	4	2		4	3	1	1	
		25–34				1		1	1						
	1791–1820	15–19		5	9	15	14	10	5	5	3	2	2		
		20–24			6	4	7	3	5	5	1	2	1		
		25–34			2	1	2								
	1821–1850	15–19		6	16	15	15	6	2	1	3	1	1		
		20–24		5	4	7	3	4	2	1		1	1		
		25–34		1	2	2	1								
	1851–1895	15–19	2	12	15	10	12	4	1	1	1				
		20–24		4	10	9	5	1	1						
		25–34				1	2								
		Total	3	38	70	70	71	35	25	25	19	14	11	4	2

Source: Gautier and Henry (1958), Andorka (1973).

later two to three, and finally to two births. Couples having a mean completed fertility of two births were certainly near to the one child system, infant mortality still being relatively high at the end of the nineteenth century. However, even in that period some families seem to have had a rather high fertility, indicating that the one child system was not an absolutely universal norm in Vajszló and Besence. The number of children borne by couples in Crulai included in the table for comparison also demonstrates the fact that there were many families having relatively few births; this, however, might have been partly the consequence of late marriage.

Thus several kinds of evidence seem to prove that *in certain parts of present-day advanced countries birth control in marriage was practised on a more or less wide scale long before the industrial revolution.* The family reconstitution studies performed suggest that this was characteristic of at least part of the communities of the following regions of Europe: parts of England in the eighteenth century; southwestern France in the eighteenth century; most parts of France from the decades preceding the French Revolution or from the Revolution; Catalonia; Sweden; Estonia (see also Hyrenius 1958–9); southern Transdanubia in Hungary; and some early bourgeois populations, like that of Geneva from the middle of the seventeenth century, as well as the Quakers in America.

In order to arrive at conclusions concerning the social determinants of fertility in these communities in the above mentioned periods, it is necessary to investigate thoroughly the economic, social, sociopsychological, political, etc., conditions prevailing in the communities and regions where signs of early birth control were found, and compare them to those of the communities and regions where birth control does not seem to have been practised on a wide scale. Unfortunately this kind of interdisciplinary analysis of demographic phenomena and their economic, social, etc., factors is at present relatively scarce. The few investigations of this type will be examined while summarizing the results of historical demographic studies concerning the period preceding the industrial revolution.

Some hints concerning the influence of social factors on fertility in these periods can be found in data on differential fertility by denomination and occupation derived from family reconstitution studies. Such data are also relatively scarce, since most communities were inhabited by a population predominantly of one religion and occupations are generally not or very unprecisely mentioned in the registers.

In Remmesweiler, situated in Saarland, the age-specific marital fertility rates of Protestants were generally lower than those of the Roman Catholics (table 3.6). Protestants were mostly farmers owning land, but Catholics were mostly agricultural workers having no farm; thus the real cause of the

Table 3.6 Age-specific marital fertility (children born per 1000 woman-years lived) by religious groups: Remmesweiler en Sarre, France.

Period	Religion	Age group							
		15–19	20–24	25–29	30–34	35–39	40–44	45–49
Before 1780	Roman Catholics	286	439	416	372	323	189	15
	Protestants	571	500	344	370	257	115	0
1780–1809	Roman Catholics	320	430	410	350	320	131	0
	Protestants	349	335	380	300	225	110	14
1810–1839	Roman Catholics	333	338	287	244	105	48	8
	Protestants	295	346	244	243	117	58	0
1840–1869	Roman Catholics	483	393	365	231	147	101	20
	Protestants	383	376	286	239	166	54	11
1870–1899	Roman Catholics	625	440	382	338	202	89	7
	Protestants	267	494	280	242	90	74	6

Source: Houdaille (1970).

fertility difference might be the occupational or social differentiation, rather than the denominational one (Houdaille 1970).

A historical study of the population of Rotterdam (Van de Woude and Mentink 1966), not using family reconstitution techniques, found that in the years 1800–9 the birth rates of different denominations were:

Catholic	40·1
Lutheran	41·4
Reformed	33·1
Remonstrant	29·7
Other	31·8

These data certainly cast doubts on the hypothesis of a simple fertility difference between Catholics and Protestants, often voiced in earlier demographic literature, since here the fertility of Lutherans was somewhat higher than that of the Catholics, while that of the Reformed and Remonstrant denominations was lower. The two last-mentioned were, however, probably mostly wealthier bourgeois.

On the other hand, it certainly deserves attention that signficant parts of the communities where early birth control was verified by family reconstitution studies were Protestant ones – as, e.g., in Colyton and Geneva, among the Quakers in America, and in Vajszló and Besence in Hungary. However, although the communities in southwestern France and St Joan de Palamos in Catalonia were Roman Catholic ones, birth control also began at an early date. The results of the family reconstruction of two Catholic communities in Hungary, Bakonya and Velem (Moess ·1972 1973), are particularly interesting from this point of view, because Velem in western Hungary had a relatively high marital fertility, while Bakonya, which was situated near the Ormánság – i.e. near Vajszló and Besence in southern Hungary – displayed a similar declining fertility to that of the Calvinists of Vajszló and Besence, only there seems to be a certain time lag between the decline in the Calvinist and the Roman Catholic villages in the same region. It might be supposed, therefore, that the causes of the early fertility decline in these communities of Hungary should be sought in certain features of the economic and social conditions of Hungarian peasants in this region, rather than in denominational peculiarities.

Data on social and occupational differences of fertility from these periods are, too, relatively scarce. In Tourouvre, a community in northern France, Charbonneau (1970) was able to determine age-specific marital fertility rates of five occupational groups: peasants, merchants, artisans, producers of sabots (sabotiers), and unskilled dayworkers. Fertility rates of the three first-mentiooed groups, which were more wealthy and more educated, were consistently higher than those of the poorer and less educated sabotiers and unskilled day workers:

	Age group						
	15–19	20–24	25–29	30–34	35–39	40–44	45–49
1665–1714:							
Peasants, merchants, artisans	298	431	432	408	348	178	15
Sabotiers and dayworkers	122	386	416	324	309	136	0
1715–1765:							
Peasants, merchants, artisans	381	502	467	437	347	184	12
Sabotiers and dayworkers	216	400	375	337	258	136	8

Charbonneau, however, considers that these differences could not have been the consequences of birth control in the group having lower fertility. The fertility rates are indeed so high that no widespread birth control seems to be probable. Nevertheless, it cannot be excluded that conscious efforts to limit the number of children by the poorer couples might have played a certain role.

In Ingouville, a community near to Tourouvre, Terrisse (1961) compared the fertility rates of peasants and agricultural workers with those of artisans and workers and found the rates of the latter group to be lower in the period from 1730 to 1770:

	Age group					
	20–24	25–29	30–34	35–39	40–44	45–49
Peasants, agricultural workers	516	500	485	312	84	14
Artisans and workers	356	400	356	250	73	0

This, however, according to Terrisse, might be the consequence of the fact that artisans and workers tended to migrate more frequently, so that their family sheets might be less complete because of registrations in other communities. Again the alternative explanation of conscious limitation of births cannot be wholly excluded.

In Sainghin-en-Mélantois (Deniel and Henry 1965) the two social groups distinguished were the farmers and artisans on the one hand, and the dayworkers and weavers on the other, and the fertility of the first group (i.e. of the wealthier social groups) was found to be somewhat higher:

	Age of wife at marriage	Mean number of children born (completed fertility), marriages	
		Before 1790	1790–1829
Farmers and artisans	20–24	8·46	6·69
	25–29	6·79	5·70
Dayworkers and weavers	20–24	8·29	6·70
	25–29	5·60	5·44

The investigation of three communities in Lancashire (Loschky and Krier 1969) showed fertility differences by income categories, the fertility of higher income couples being lower, where also women married somewhat later.

A comparative study of Swedish parishes in the seventeenth and eighteenth centuries (Gaunt 1976) by methods similar to family reconstitution revealed important differences by the social and ecological types of village: the community inhabited by farmer–miners who owned their own farmsteads, and parallel with agricultural production engaged in mining iron ore, had the highest marital fertility, while a mixed (farming and transporting) community and three villages dominated by large estates had lower fertility rates. Celibacy was highest in the mixed farming community and lowest in the manor-dominated communities. Gaunt hypothesized that the demand for manpower in the farmer–miner community was an important factor of high fertility.

A census of serf households taken in 1828 in Hungary for taxation purposes provides an opportunity for investigating differential fertility in Vajszló and Besence, by combining the census data with the sheets of family reconstitution. Apart from some artisans and agricultural workers having no land held in villeinage and a very few serfs having relatively large farms, two categories of serfs can be distinguished, the first having farms about twice as large as those of the second category. The completed fertility and age-specific marital fertilities of these two groups were:

	Average completed fertility	Age-specific marital fertility in age group						
		15–19	20–24	25–29	30–34	35–39	40–44	45–49
Serfs with larger farms	5·4	259	337	258	240	188	85	19
Serfs with smaller farms	4·6	292	313	238	207	134	65	0

Thus the fertility of the more well-to-do peasants seems to have been higher in that period.

On the basis of these differential fertility rates no clear relation can be formulated. In some communities the negative correlation of fertility and socioeconomic status, well known in the period after the industrial revolution, seems to have prevailed. In others, the wealthier couples had somewhat higher fertilities, i.e. the correlation seems to have been positive, as has been found in recent decades in some studies of advanced societies. However, the fact that differences existed before the industrial revolution seems to prove that there was some conscious limitation of births in some parts of the populations and that it might have been influenced by economic and social conditions.

Historical demography produced two further studies which might be considered in investigations of social fertility differences: the study of the fertility of the French aristocracy by Henry and Lévy (1960) and that of the British aristocracy by Hollingsworth (1957–8 1964–5 1965). These studies were made by means of the genealogical method, which provides similar data to the family reconstitution studies. Their interest lies not only in the fact that the demographic history of the aristocracies is more or less in advance of that of other parts of the given society, but also in the difference of the development of the fertility of the French and British aristocracies.

The age-specific marital fertility rates of the French aristocratic couples married from 1700 to 1795 were already very low:

	Age group					
	20–24	25–29	30–34	35–39	40–44	45–49
French aristocracy	336	167	63	18	6	0

The total marital fertility rate from 20 to 49 computed from these age-specific rates is 2950. Henry and Lévy suppose that in the seventeenth century fertility was already low in the French aristocracy, and attribute this to widespread birth control.

The development of fertility of the British aristocracy was quite different. Not only was it higher around 1700, but also it increased in the eighteenth century and only began to fall in the second half of the nineteenth century. The total marital fertility rates from 15 to 49 were:

Birth cohort	Total marital fertility rate from 15 to 49, number of births per woman
1680–1729	6·97
1730–1779	9·13
1780–1829	10·54
1830–1879	7·98
1880–1939	4·81

Hollingsworth mentions that because of omissions the rate for 1680–1729 should be increased by 7·5 per cent and that of 1730–79 by 3·3 per cent to get the real rate. The cohort replacement rates calculated by Hollingsworth, i.e. the rates expressing the ratio of the number of children of both sexes attaining adult age and the number of the generation of parents, even more clearly display this remarkable development, since they show also the influence of mortality and of earlier or later marriage (table 3.7). In the

Table 3.7   Replacement rates, and computed family size of women living in marriage up to the end of the propagative period: British aristocracy.

Cohort born	Replacement rates*	Computed family size of woman living in marriage up to the end of the propagative period, number of children born per married woman	
		Wifes married before 25	Wifes married aged 25–34
1550–1574	1·517	6·88	2·70
1575–1599	1·714	7·29	4·46
1600–1624	1·242	6·51	3·48
1625–1649	1·021	6·15	3·60
1650–1674	0·999	6·40	3·02
1675–1699	0·957	5·90	3·55
1700–1724	0·819	5·17	3·26
1725–1749	1·023	5·86	3·44
1750–1774	1·311	6·20	3·56
1775–1799	1·360	6·45	4·20
1800–1824	1·389	5·91	3·96
1825–1849	1·275	5·00	3·28
1850–1874	0·880	3·31	2·44
1875–1899	0·891	3·25	2·33

* Combined replacement rate for males and females.
Source: Hollingsworth (1964–5 1965).

seventeenth century mortality increased slightly, the average age of marriage slowly increased and fertility slowly decreased. The cohorts born in the last decades of the seventeenth century did not achieve simple reproduction. However, in the first half of the eighteenth century these demographic trends changed; mortality decreased, the age at marriage did not increase further, celibacy declined and fertility increased. The fertility of the cohorts born in the last decades of the eighteenth century was the highest. In the subsequent cohorts fertility began to diminish slowly, and in the second half of the nineteenth century more rapidly. At the same time mortality decreased, but in the cohorts born in the second half of the nineteenth century the replacement rate again became lower than 1.0.

Family reconstitution studies provide information only on marital fertility, not on fertility in general. However, the fertility of a population is influenced by other factors besides marital fertility: by age at marriage and by the extent of celibacy, as well as by the fertility of unmarried women, i.e. illegitimacy. Family reconstitution studies, as well as other sources, offer possibilities for obtaining information on these other factors.

Hajnal (1965) formulated the famous thesis that in the seventeenth to nineteenth centuries there was a special pattern of marriage in western Europe – namely, that age at marriage was remarkably late and that a significant part of the population remained unmarried for life. It is not known exactly when this pattern first emerged; it might have been in the medieval period, but it certainly existed in the sixteenth century (e.g. in the English aristocracy – Hollingsworth 1957–8) and it disappeared only in the twentieth century. Hajnal stated that the eastern limit of the spread of this pattern was the line connecting Trieste and St Petersburg. Recently Sklar (1974) investigated age at marriage and celibacy at the end of the nineteenth century in areas near to this line and found the western European pattern to have been prevalent in Estland, Livland, Kurland and Lithuania, the western part of Poland, as well as Bohemia and Moravia, thus confirming the statement of Hajnal as to the limit of the area where the western European marriage pattern was prevalent.

When Hajnal wrote his article very few historical data were available, so he used mostly census data. Since that time the results of many family reconstitution studies have become available, which include data on the average age at marriage (table 3.8). These data confirm the statements of Hajnal, as the average age at marriage of men was between 27 and 32 years and that of women between 24 and 31 years in most parts and periods in western Europe from the seventeenth to the nineteenth century. The variations of the age at marriage in the communities are, however, rather large, so that the pattern does not seem to have been homogeneous throughout western Europe. It should be remarked that in Colyton age at marriage rose after 1660 and began to fall after 1720, i.e. the rise coincided with a decrease of marital fertility and the decline of the age at marriage more or less coincided with a new increase of marital fertility. A similar tendency seems to appear in Geneva. On the other hand, in Vajszló and Besence in southern Transdanubia the average age at marriage was 21–23 years for men and 18–20 years for women. This also seems to confirm Hajnal's thesis on the eastern limit of the west European marriage pattern, as these Hungarian villages lay eastward from the Trieste to St Petersburg line.

Table 3.8   Average age at first marriage.

Community, group of population	Period or cohort born	Men	Women	Source
England				
British aristocracy	1330–1479	22·4	17·1	Hollingsworth
	1480–1679	24·3	19·5	(1957)
	1680–1729	28·6	22·2	
	1730–1779	28·6	24·0	
	1780–1829	30·5	24·7	
	1830–1879	30·0	24·2	
Colyton	1560–1599	28·1	27·0	Wrigley (1966b)
	1600–1629	27·4	27·3	
	1630–1646	25·8	26·5	
	1647–1659	26·9	30·0	
	1660–1699	27·6	28·8	
	1700–1719	28·1	30·7	
	1720–1749	26·2	27·2	
	1750–1769	25·0	26·3	
	1770–1799	27·6	26·4	
	1800–1824	25·6	24·9	
	1825–1837	25·9	23·3	
France				
French aristocracy	1650–1699	25·5	20·0	Henry (1965)
	1700–1749	23·6	19·4	
	1750–1799	21·3	18·4	
Crulai	1674–1742	28·0	25·5	Henry (1965)
Ingouville	1730–1790	28·0	26·0	Henry (1965)
Sotteville-les-Rouen	1760–1790	27·4	26·2	Henry (1965)
Sainghin-en-Mélantois	1680–1699	32·3	29·2	Deniel and Henry (1965)
	1700–1719	31·2	28·4	
	1720–1739	31·9	29·4	
	1740–1759	30·8	28·0	
	1760–1779	29·7	26·6	
	1780–1799	28·4	27·3	
Tourouvre	1665–1699	28·2	24·1	Charbonneau
	1700–1734	27·6	24·9	(1970)
	1735–1770	27·5	26·2	

Table 3.8—contd.

Community, group of population	Period or cohort born	Men	Women	Source
Flanders (*Belgium*)				
Elversele	1608–1649	27·2	24·8	Deprez (1965)
	1650–1699	29·6	26·9	
	1700–1749	29·4	28·0	
	1750–1796	29·6	28·5	
Switzerland				
Bourgeois population				
of Geneva	1550–1599	27·2	21·4	Henry (1956)
	1600–1649	29·1	24·6	
	1650–1699	32·6	25·7	
	1700–1749	31·6	26·3	
	1750–1799	31·5	24·0	
	1800–1849	29·4	22·7	
	1850–1899	29·2	24·7	
Germany				
Anhausen	1692–1749	27·1	26·6	Knodel (1970)
	1750–1799	29·2	27·0	
	1800–1849	30·2	29·4	
	1850–1899	31·7	28·6	
Sweden				
Alskog	1745–1769	—	23·5	Gaunt (1973)
	1770–1794	—	24·0	
	1795–1820	—	24·3	
Hungary				
Vajszló and Besence	1747–1790	23·0	18·2	Andorka (1973)
	1791–1820	22·4	19·2	
	1821–1850	21·3	19·2	
	1851–1895	22·4	19·4	

The other part of Hajnal's thesis states that in western Europe celibacy was very widespread in the same centuries. Family reconstitution studies also provide some insight into the extent of celibacy, as the registrations of deaths generally contain some mention of the marital status of the deceased person – at least by naming a deceased woman either by her husband's name or by her own family name only. The latter might be presumed to be never-married. In the case of men marital status is much more uncertain. Therefore in table 3.9 only the percentage of single women at the age of 50 and over derived from family reconstitution studies is given. It seems that the rise of celibacy more or less coincided with the rise of average age at marriage in western Europe, although variations

Table 3.9   Percentage of single women at age 50 and of those who die aged over 50

Community, group of population	Period	Per cent single at 50
England		
British aristocracy	1330–1479	7
	1480–1679	6
	1680–1729	17
	1730–1779	14
	1780–1829	12
	1830–1879	22
France		
Crulai	1750–1800	2–11·6
Sotteville-les-Rouen	1760–1790	2·6–7·8
Tourouvre	1730–1793	max. 6·3
St Agnan	1710–1770	5·6
Seven villages around Boulay	before 1700	6·8
	1700–1719	9·5
	1720–1739	12·0
	1740–1759	16·5
	1760–1779	19·8
	1780–1799	19·6
Switzerland		
Bourgeois population of Geneva	1550–1599	2
	1600–1649	7
	1650–1699	25
	1700–1749	29
	1750–1799	31
	1800–1849	25
	1850–1899	17
Hungary		
Vajszló and Besence	1747–1847	5

between communities are very large – it remained low in Vajszló and Besence where age at marriage was low too. The highest proportion of celibacy was reported by Henry (1961c) in Iceland at the time of the census of 1703, when 24 per cent of the 50–59 year old men and 43 per cent of the women of the same age were single. Henry explained that fact by very strong efforts to control population growth because of the difficult natural conditions of the country. Actually population did not increase from 1703 to 1823.

It might be questioned, however, whether the high average age at marriage and the high proportion of never-marrying men and women was a result of conscious efforts to control general fertility in order to check population growth. Opinions of historical demographers on this problem differ, although one contemporary author, Cantillon, seems to give evidence of the fertility controlling motives of late marriage and celibacy. He wrote in 1755 in his *Essai sur la Nature du Commerce*:

In Europe the Children of Nobility are brought up in affluence; and as the largest sphere of Property is usually given to the Eldest sons, the Younger Sons are in no hurry to marry. They usually live as Batchelors in the Army or in the Cloisters, but will seldom be found unwilling to marry if they are offered Heiresses or Fortunes, or the means of supporting a Family on the footing which they have in view and without which they would consider themselves to make their Children wretched. In the lower classes of the State also there are Men who from pride and from reasons similar to those of the nobility, prefer to live in celibacy and so to spend on themselves the little that they have rather than settle down in family life. But most of them would gladly set up a family if they could count upon keeping it up as they would wish: they consider themselves to do an injustice to their Children if they brought them up to fall into a lower class than themselves. When Labourers and Mechaniks do not marry, it is because they wait till they have something to enable them to set up a household or to find some young woman who brings a little capital for that purpose, since they see every day others like them who lack of such precaution start housekeeping and fall into the most frightful poverty, being obliged to deprive themselves of their own food in order to nourish their children. (Cantillon 1931, pp. 77–9).

In addition Wrigley (1969) mentions that in some parts of western Europe legal prescriptions tended to postpone marriage and to produce frequent celibacy, such as where servants were prohibited from marrying until they could establish an autonomous household, and where in some regions the permission of the local landlord was necessary for marriage. It seems that the intention of these legal restrictions was to control the increase in the number of households, i.e. population, in order that the available production and marketing resources should not be stretched.

Laslett (1975) formulated the following 'ideal type' (in the Weberian sense) of marriage and household formation in western Europe. The rule of household formation requires that a new household shall come into existence only if an existing household goes out of existence, or if the means have been created to extend the whole society by adding a new constituent unit, i.e. if there is a new plot of land or a new workshop available for the new household. No marriage should be concluded without it constituting a new household (i.e. married couples – of parents and their children, or of brothers and sisters – should not live together in a common household). In that situation many sexually mature men and women will inevitably be in an unmarried state and waiting to get married and be heads of their own households. A proportion of them will never be able to marry. Although not all western Europe conformed strictly to this pattern, it was the prevalent type. On the other hand, eastern Europe seems to have been characterized in the same centuries by early and almost universal marriage and a higher proportion of married couples living together in the same household (Andorka 1975, Laslett 1972).

One might suppose that in the conditions prevailing in western Europe, where marriage was generally late and many adult men and women remained single, extramarital sexual relations would have been wide-spread, and that in consequence the number of illegitimate births would have been high. However, illegitimacy seems to have been comparatively rare in the communities investigated by the family reconstitution studies. For example, the proportion of illegitimate births was below 1 per cent in Crulai from 1604 to 1799, 0·8 per cent in Tourouvre from 1640 to 1769, and between 1 and 2 per cent in the villages surrounding Boulay until 1780, increasing after that date. One of the highest rates of illegitimacy was found in Ingouville (5·7 per cent) which was a suburb of Le Havre, an important port of France. It is possible that illegitimacy rates were much higher in towns that, in consequence of the size of their populations, were not investigated by the method of family reconstitution. For example, in Paris from 1770 to 1789, 31 per cent of all registered infants were found-lings, most of whom were probably borne out of wedlock by servant mothers (Henry 1965). On the other hand, Laslett (1965) found that in England the illegitimacy rate was not higher in towns than in villages. Anyway, urban population was relatively small at that time and its illegitimacy rate did not affect overall national illegitimacy rates too strongly.

Laslett and Oosterveen (1973) indeed found that in England in twenty-four parishes studied the illegitimacy rate moved more or less parallel with the number of legitimate births, and inversely with age at marriage. The percentage of illegitimate baptisms was 4·0 per cent from 1581 to 1630, 1·7 per cent from 1651 to 1720, and 5·1 per cent from 1741 to 1810, and – as shown by the family reconstitution of Colyton and other sources – the period from 1651 to 1720 was marked in England by later marriage and lower marital fertility than the preceding and subsequent periods.

Laslett and Oosterveen also stated that an important part of the ille-gitimate births came from a rather limited section of the population whose members were liable to have several illegitimate births and whose children and sisters also gave birth to children out of wedlock.

In this respect eastern Europe did not differ much from western Europe. The percentage of illegitimate births was below 2 per cent in the second half of the eighteenth and in the nineteenth century in the Hungarian villages Vajszló and Besence.

This obviously does not contradict the possibility that there were areas or whole societies in Europe where illegitimacy was frequent. For example, Sundbärg discovered long ago that in Sweden the illegitimacy ratio exceeded 10 between 1751 and 1775 and was above 17 between 1776 and 1800. Illegitimacy was similarly high in that period in Norway (Drake 1969).

Nevertheless, it seems that in most parts of Europe delayed marriage and high celibacy were not associated, as might be supposed, with higher illegitimacy. At present it is not possible to tell whether this was the consequence of birth control in extramarital sexual relations or of chastity until marriage, coupled with lifelong chastity for those remaining single. Laslett (1965) seems to adhere to the latter explanation. Shorter, Knodel and Van de Walle (1971) summarize the development of illegitimacy in western Europe in the following way: in the sixteenth and seventeenth centuries, as well as in the first half of the eighteenth century the proportion of illegitimate births might not have been higher than 1–4 per cent, according to all available information, and it began to rise only in the second half of the eighteenth century. Even this rise was not universal, since peasant and village communities generally were fairly intolerant of illegitimacy. Thus late marriage and a high proportion of celibacy did not coincide with high illegitimacy.

3.3 Data on fertility of countries and regions from official statistics, aggregation of the data in parish registers, and stable population analysis

The basic deficiency of family reconstitution studies, as mentioned, is that they only provide information on demographic conditions in small communities, and it is hazardous to draw conclusions on the basis of one or some communities on the fertility of whole countries or regions. Therefore, attempts have often been made to find birth and death rates, as well as the growth rate of countries or regions. There are three possible ways of doing this:

First, in some countries, aggregated statistical data on births and deaths are available from the period preceding the industrial revolution. These are, unfortunately, exceptional cases, and also the value of the data depends on the completeness of registration of vital events.

Second, it is possible to aggregate the number of marriages, births and deaths contained in individual parish registers.

Third, the method of stable population analysis enables us to estimate the historical development of fertility and mortality of larger populations. The method was elaborated originally (Bourgeois-Pichat n.d., United Nations 1955, Coale and Demény 1966) to determine the demographic characteristics of populations of present-day underdeveloped countries where some types of data, mostly vital statistical data are not available. If two of the following four types of data are known

1 Growth rate of population in a certain period (between two censuses)
2 Age structure of population at a given date (census)
3 Fertility by age
4 Mortality by age

then it is possible to estimate by this method the other two types of data, if the population can be considered stable (i.e. its age structure and consequently its fertility and mortality did not change in the period considered). At first it was considered that the stable population method could be applied only in cases of strictly stable populations. Recently, however, it has been elaborated for quasi-stable and destabilizing populations (Coale 1963, Demény 1965). If the hypothesis of a beginning decline of fertility and mortality in the eighteenth century in parts of present-day developed countries is correct, then these populations were mostly in the phase of destabilization.

In underdeveloped countries generally the growth rate and the age structure are known (on the basis of fairly reliable censuses), and the missing fertility and mortality data are estimated by the stable population method. In historical studies diverse kinds of data might be available – e.g. in addition to some census data there might be a contemporaneous mortality table, and the missing data could be the fertility rates and, say, age structure or the growth rate, etc. The method might be used to verify the consistency and compatibility of the not entirely reliable data originating from different sources, among others from family reconstitution (Van de Walle 1971). Thus stable population methods assist to an important degree in enlarging and improving our knowledge on demographic development in the period before official vital statistics, which was based formerly on rather questionable estimations.

One of the most interesting and controversial problems of historical demography is the development of fertility and mortality in *England and Wales before and during the industrial revolution*. Before 1837 the numbers of births, marriages and deaths contained in the registers were not aggregated officially. Around 1830 John Rickman collected this information from parish registers for every tenth year from 1700 to 1780 and for every year from 1780 to the beginning of the official aggregation of the data. The problem with these data, however, is that birth and death registrations were known to be rather incomplete. The extent of underregistration and its changes in time are not known. Krause (1965) has stated that parochial registration was relatively accurate in the early eighteenth century, deteriorated in the 1780s, virtually collapsed between 1795 and 1820, then improved somewhat again. The results of the censuses performed in ten year intervals regularly from 1801 also seem to be somewhat uncertain.

In order to arrive at the real number of births and deaths it is therefore necessary to use multipliers. Griffith used a ratio of $1 \cdot 15$ for births and $1 \cdot 10$ for deaths (see Glass 1965b) for the data before 1801, and then calculated back from 1801 the number of population by addition and subtraction (table 3.10). The birth and death rates so calculated were relatively low and thus supported the thesis of Marshall (1965) that the period of industrial revolution was characterized, contrary to the theory of Malthus, by a relatively low birth rate and an even lower death rate, the rapid increase of population being caused chiefly by the fall of the death rate. These multipliers, however, were considered by Glass to be too low.

Recently Razzel (1972) calculated much higher birth rates for England and Wales assuming a much higher rate of omissions in the registers (table 3.11). These data support the thesis that the high rate of growth of the

Table 3.10   Birth and death rates in England and Wales, estimated by Griffith.

1700	31·1	26·0
1710	27·5	26·7
1720	30·5	29·7
1730	32·0	33·4
1740	33·3	31·7
1750	34·1	28·2
1760	33·3	26·7
1770	34·0	27·9
1780	34·4	28·8
1785–1795	35·44	25·65
1796–1806	34·23	23·14
1806–1816	33·84	19·98
1816–1826	33·39	20·33
1826–1836	32·36	21·65
1836–1846	31·43	20·80

Source: Glass (1965a).

Table 3.11   Birth and death rates in England and Wales, estimated by Razzel.

Period	Birth rate	Death rate based on	
		Official population returns	Krause's population estimates
1801–1810	41·4	30·1	30·5
1811–1820	42·0	27·7	28·9
1821–1830	40·1	26·1	25·9
1831–1840	35·9	23·1	22·8

Source: Razzel (1972).

Table 3.12   Birth and death rates in England and Wales, estimated by Hollingsworth by means of stable population technique.

Year	Birth rate	Death rate
1781	44	35
1801	44	32
1820	44	30
1841	35	22

Source: Hollingsworth (1969).

population of England and Wales was caused by a rather high level of fertility. Krause (1958) also suggested that a rising birth rate might have been the major cause of the growth of population.

Hollingsworth (1969) utilized the stable population technique and arrived at even higher estimates (table 3.12). On the basis of these estimations and other caluclations, Hollingsworth summarized the historical development of English fertility and mortality in the following way:

1   The growth rate of population was high in the Middle Ages between 1143 and 1175, and after the Black Death between 1475 and 1556, with some recession between 1500 and 1510.
2   After 1560 population growth became slower as a consequence of the growing custom of later marriage.
3   In the seventeenth century the rate of growth was rather slow, but after 1688 a period of higher rate of growth followed, until 1719.
4   From 1720 to 1742 the population was maintained at an almost constant plateau, more or less corresponding to the full agricultural utilization of the disposable land; a slow growth then followed.
5   After 1759 the lack of great epidemics and the spread of higher standards of hygiene caused a continuous decline of mortality, while fertility remained approximately at the same level for the subsequent fifty years. Therefore the growth rate was high.
6   After 1820 fertility also began to decline, but when the decline of mortality was halted around 1840, fertility did not decline further, so that natural increase of population remained rather high. Fertility remained at a relatively high level till 1880.

Thus in England fertility did not immediately follow the decline of mortality, therefore in the period of industrialization the growth rate of population was high.

In France the development of fertility and mortality was quite different in the same period. Censuses were performed from 1801 and the numbers of births and death in France are known from 1806 onwards. At that time the birth rate was much lower than in England. Bourgeois-Pichat (1965b) made an evaluation of French birth and death rates from 1771 to the beginning of official vital statistics in 1806. Knowing the death rate from 1806 onwards he used for the 1770s the death rate calculated from the mortality table of Duvillard, published in 1806, but based on the data of the years preceding 1789. Knowing the number and age composition of population in 1775 and 1806 he could calculate the birth rates for the whole period, assuming that the death rate was regularly declining from the 1770s to 1806. The results of the estimate and the subsequent rates calculated from official vital statistics show that, in contrast with England and Wales where the natural increase was most probably higher than 1 per cent in this period, in France it reached 0·5 per cent only between 1816 and 1825 and between 1841 and 1845, otherwise it was lower. The net reproduction rate was around 1·1 (table 3.13).

Table 3.13   Birth rate, death rate, and gross and net reproduction rates in France, according to Bourgeois-Pichat's estimate.

Period	Birth rate	Death rate	Reproduction rate	
			Gross	Net
1771–1775	38·6	34·4	2·40	1·08
1776–1780	38·1	34·4	2·36	1·10
1781–1785	37·5	33·8	2·32	1·12
1786–1790	36·4	32·8	2·24	1·12
1791–1795	35·9	32·2	2·21	1·14
1796–1800	34·8	29·8	2·16	1·15
1801–1805	32·0	29·8	2·01	1·10
1806–1810	31·6	26·4	1·98	1·12
1811–1815	31·2	26·6	1·94	1·12
1816–1820	31·3	24·0	1·94	1·10
1821–1825	30·7	23·0	1·92	1·07
1826–1830	29·9	25·6	1·89	1·07
1831–1835	29·3	25·4	1·86	1·08
1836–1840	28·2	23·6	1·81	1·05
1841–1845	28·0	22·4	1·80	1·05
1846–1850	26·6	23·7	1·73	1·05

Source: Bourgeois-Pichat (1965b).

The utilization of the life table of Duvillard, the reliability of which was questioned by Henry (1965), is the weak point in Bourgeois-Pichat's estimate. Therefore the calculations of Van de Walle (1971) using the stable population techniques and based on the data of Blayo and Henry (1967) concerning Anjou and Brittany between 1740 and 1825 are of particular interest (table 3.14). Van de Walle used two alternative suppositions, the first being that of a closed population (neither emigration nor immigration) and the second that of 1 per cent emigration in five years. Although birth rates are lower in this estimate than in the Bourgeois-Pichat estimate, and the death rate is also lower (except for the 1770s and 1780s), Van de Walle's estimate supports the main conclusions of Bourgeois-Pichat – namely, that the decline of birth rate began much sooner after the decline of mortality than in England, so there was no period of high population growth in France comparable to that in England during the industrial revolution.

With a similar method Van de Walle (1974) reconstructed the number and age distribution, the overall marital and illegitimate fertility rates, and

Table 3.14 Birth and death rates in Brittany and Anjou, France, estimated by Van de Walle, supposing closed population and 1 per cent emigration per year.

Year	Closed population		1 per cent emigration	
	Birth rate	Death rate	Birth rate	Death rate
1740	36·5	42·3	33·5	38·8
1745	38·4	32·7	35·6	30·3
1750	39·0	30·8	36·6	28·8
1755	38·4	34·4	36·3	32·6
1760	39·7	31·8	35·1	30·4
1765	35·4	30·6	34·2	29·6
1770	32·3	35·8	31·5	35·0
1775	34·5	36·4	34·0	35·8
1780	35·8	35·3	35·6	35·1
1785	35·1	33·5	35·3	33·7
1790	33·8	27·3	34·3	27·7
1795	31·7	25·5	32·5	26·1
1800	27·6	26·9	28·6	27·9
1805	27·7	22·8	29·0	23·8
1810	27·7	20·3	29·3	21·4
1815	28·3	24·0	30·2	25·6
1820	26·3	21·1	28·3	22·7
1825	26·9	22·7	29·3	24·7

Source: Van de Walle (1971) calculated from data in Blayo and Henry (1967).

the proportion of married women (Coale's I_f, I_g, I_h and I_m indices), for eighty-two departments of France from 1801 to 1901 (some departments were omitted because of change of borders or because of very intensive migration). The calculations were based on existing but inaccurate census and vital statistical data. These fertility rates and proportions of married women make it possible to analyse the regional course of early fertility decline. He also calculated the birth rates for France, and his results were slightly lower than the rates estimated by Bourgeois-Pichat.

Considering the rather different demographic development of England and France displayed by the above estimates, it is interesting to investigate which pattern of demographic development prevailed in other European countries. Unfortunately, relatively few similar calculations concerning other countries are available. One of them is the estimate of fertility and mortality in Spain by Livi-Bacci (1968), which on the basis of data on population growth and age structure as well as a life table, calculated the development of fertility by means of stable population techniques. Although birth rate was relatively high in the second half of the eighteenth century (table 3.15), it was far from the maximum possible, as displayed by the value of I_g, and also lower than in the contemporary Netherlands, some parts of Scandinavia and Russia. Also there were rather pronounced regional differences, the decline being more significant and more rapid in the eastern regions of the country – namely, the Old Crown of Aragonia, Catalonia, Valencia and the Balearics. It should be noted that St Joan de Palamos, where family reconstitution studies found a rather low fertility at the end of the eighteenth and in the first half of the nineteenth century, is situated in Catalonia. The fertility of Madrid was also much lower than the national average of Spain at the end of the eighteenth century. It might safely be concluded, as Livi-Bacci did, that birth control was practised in parts of Spain in that period.

Table 3.15   Birth rate, marital fertility and the value of I_g in Spain, estimated by Livi-Bacci by means of stable population analysis.

Year	Birth rate	Births per 1000 married women aged 16–50	I_g
1768	43·84	280·4	0·767
1787	43·16	277·0	0·745
1797	42·27	274·6	0·735

Source: Livi-Bacci (1968b).

The four Scandinavian countries, Denmark, Norway, Sweden and Finland, introduced official collection of vital statistical data based on parish registers very early in the eighteenth century, so that their demographic development can be examined by means of these vital rates.

In Norway the birth rates were already relatively low by the eighteenth century (table 3.16). According to Drake (1969), this was mainly a

Table 3.16   Birth and death rates in Norway.

Period	Birth rate	Death rate
1736–1755	30·5	26·3
1756–1775	31·4	26·0
1776–1795	31·1	23·8
1796–1815	28·9	24·3
1816–1835	23·7	19·2
1836–1855	30·6	18·6
1856–1865	32·6	17·7

Source: Drake (1969).

consequence of late marriage, the mean age of brides (in marriages where both partners were married for the first time) being 26–27 years in the nineteenth century. The birth rate of Denmark was similarly low from 1735, but did not decline till 1800 (Matthiessen 1970).

From Närke, a region of central Sweden, birth and death rates are available from the end of the seventeenth century (table 3.17). Here too the birth rate was relatively low, a fact interpreted by Carlsson (1970) as a sign of birth control. The birth rates for the whole country, available from 1748, are similarly low, but the death rates were even lower in

Table 3.17 Birth and death rates in Närke, central Sweden.

Period	Birth rate	Death rate
1691–1695	34·2	26·3
1696–1700	32·6	41·7
1701–1705	33·5	21·9
1706–1710	28·6	30·4
1711–1715	35·4	17·1
1716–1720	32·9	29·0
1721–1725	38·1	24·0
1726–1730	34·3	22·7
1731–1735	31·5	23·4
1736–1740	30·0	31·1
1741–1745	30·7	28·6
1746–1750	33·7	26·6

Source: Utterström (1965).

Table 3.18 Birth and death rates in Sweden, based on official statistics.

Period	Birth rate	Death rate
1750–1754	34·4	25·1
1755–1759	31·8	26·9
1760–1764	32·2	27·7
1765–1769	31·6	25·3
1770–1774	29·2	31·6
1775–1779	32·5	24·0
1780–1784	30·0	26·6
1785–1789	30·2	25·7
1790–1794	31·7	24·0
1795–1799	30·8	24·5
1800–1804	29·3	23·3

Source: Van de Walle (1971).

consequence of the relatively favourable health conditions (except for the years 1706–10, 1736–40 and 1770–4), so that population increased at a relatively high rate (table 3.18).

In Finland the birth rate was higher than in Sweden and the death rate similar (except during the period of famine in 1742), so that the rate of growth of population was very high (table 3.19). The rise of the birth rate from 1722 to 1755 seems particularly interesting.

Table 3.19   Birth rates and death rates in Finland, based on official statistics, and estimates of Jutikkala.

Period	Birth rate	Death rate
1722–1728	34·2	19·9
1729–1736	38·9	22·2
1737–1743	36·2	37·5
1744–1749	40·3	25·3
1751–1755	45·3	28·6
1756–1760	44·5	29·6
1761–1765	43·7	32·3
1766–1770	41·7	28·4
1771–1775	38·8	23·7
1776–1780	41·3	26·0
1781–1785	40·4	27·7
1786–1790	37·5	31·9
1791–1795	41·1	29·3
1796–1800	39·2	23·8

Source: Jutikkala (1965), *Statistical Yearbook of Finland.*

Recently the data from the parish registers of Hungary in the period 1828–1900 were collected and aggregated by villages and counties. The results so far published (Klinger *et al.* 1972–5) show very high birth rates in 1836, no clear tendency of decline till 1870 and a rather sudden decline from 1870 to 1890 (table 3.20). It should be mentioned that capitalistic industrialization began in Hungary in the 1860s, so that the decline of fertility followed the onset of industrialization by ten or twenty years. This decline, however, might have been influenced by other factors, since the lowest level of fertility was experienced in 1890 by the two predominantly agricultural counties of Baranya and Somogy in southern Transdanubia. It will be remembered that the villages where early birth control was demonstrated by family reconstitution studies (see the first part of this chapter) are situated in the county of Baranya.

Cipolla published similar results concerning some regions of Italy preceding the unification of the country (Cipolla 1965). The regional

Table 3.20 Birth rates in some counties of Hungary, aggregated on the basis of parish registers.

Region and county	1836	1870	1890
Western Transdanubia			
Győr-Sopron	40·4	44·2	40·2
Vas	48·5	45·2	38·2
Zala	54·5	47·3	39·3
Veszprém	46·6	44·7	37·7
Southern Transdanubia			
Somogy	57·8	49·0	37·0
Tolna	53·3	47·7	42·1
Baranya and Pécs	49·3	45·8	35·0
Central region of Hungary, around Budapest			
Komárom	43·6	49·4	43·4
Fejér	47·1	48·2	39·0
Pest	48·2	49·9	44·8
Nógrád	46·6	49·3	43·3
Southern Great Plain			
Bács-Kiskun	53·5	48·3	41·1

Source: Klinger *et al.* (1972–5).

differences seem to be very significant. In Lombardy fertility seems to have remained high until the middle of the nineteenth century, while at the same time it was much lower in Tuscany, Liguria and Piedmont (table 3.21).

The available birth rates of countries and regions in the centuries and decades preceding the industrial revolution display marked differences: a

Table 3.21 Birth and death rates in different regions of Italy.

Period	Lombardy		Tuscany		Piedmont		Liguria	
	Birth rate	Death rate	Birth rate	Death rate	Birth rate	Death rate	Birth rate	Death rate
1770–1779	39	33	—	—	—	—	—	—
1780–1789	41	39	—	—	—	—	—	—
1790–1799	41	38	—	—	—	—	—	—
1800–1809	—	—	—	—	—	—	—	—
1810–1819	40	39	35	33	—	—	—	—
1820–1829	42	33	43	28	—	—	—	—
1830–1839	42	37	38	27	37	32	35	27
1840–1849	41	33	35	27	—	—	—	—
1850–1859	—	—	36	30	—	—	—	—

Source: Cipolla (1965), calculated from yearly data of source, some years missing.

relatively high and stable birth rate in England and Wales, a declining and relatively low rate in France, a low and relatively stable rate in Norway and Sweden, etc. It is an intriguing scientific problem to find out the factors contributing to the different levels and courses of development of these birth rates.

3.4 The economic and social background of the decline of fertility in some parts of Europe, and of the relatively long maintenance of high fertility in other parts

Family reconstitution studies and genealogical studies, as well as different estimates based on stable population models and other methods, and some official vital statistical data from the sixteenth to the nineteenth centuries, displayed rather important differentials of fertility in different parts, countries and regions, as well as in different social strata of Europe. It would be very rewarding to do a cross-sectional analysis by comparing the fertility rates and some quantitative measures of the economic and social conditions in different countries and regions in this period. However, we have almost no economic and social indicators (e.g. *per capita* national income or household income) that might be compared in an exact way, so this kind of cross-sectional analysis is not possible at present. But we do have some information on economic and social conditions in a few countries, regions and communities from which we have fertility data. Thus certain qualitative comparisons seem to be possible.

First it is necessary to verify the simple hypothesis that fertility differences and changes were not caused solely by different levels of mortality.

Some earlier variations of the theory of demographic transition (see Chapter 2) suggest that the decline of fertility in the process of demographic transition from the underdeveloped phase to the present-day developed phase was caused primarily by the decline of mortality. Naturally couples are planning the number of their living children, i.e. the number of children surviving to adulthood or to the death of the parents, and not the number of children born. Therefore lower mortality, and especially lower infant and child mortality, obviously parallels lower fertility.

The interrelation of fertility and mortality, however, does not seem to be very strong. Therefore the estimated yearly growth rates of different populations were rather different, e.g. (Wrigley 1969):

		Population growth rate (per cent)
England and Wales	1701–1801	0·45
	1751–1800	0·80
France	1700–1789	0·31
	1740–1789	0·45
Italy	1700–1800	0·45
Sweden	1749–1800	0·59
Wurtenberg	1740–1800	0·56
East Prussia	1700–1800	0·84
Pomerania	1740–1800	0·80
Silesia	1740–1804	0·94
Austria	1754–1789	0·94
Bohemia	1754–1789	1·18

Although recent estimates of the growth rate of the population of Hungary are lower than previous ones, and although it is at present impossible to discern the effect of natural increase and immigration, the rate of yearly natural increase of the population of Hungary might have been at least 1 per cent in the eighteenth century (Dávid 1957).

Also the comparison of fertility and mortality in family reconstitution studies does not seem to prove a strong relationship between fertility and mortality (tables 3.22 and 3.23). Fertility followed the main secular trend

Table 3.22   Infant mortality rates based on family reconstitution data.

Community	Period	Infant mortality	Source
England			
Colyton	1538–1599	120–140	Wrigley (1969)
	1600–1649	126–158	
	1650–1699	118–147	
	1700–1749	162–203	
	1750–1837	122–153	
British aristocracy	1550–1574	182	Wrigley (1969)
	1575–1599	189	based on
	1600–1624	189	Hollingsworth
	1625–1649	199	(1964–5)
	1650–1674	210	
	1675–1699	196	
	1700–1724	169	
	1725–1749	166	
	1750–1774	102	
	1775–1799	85	
	1800–1824	82	

Table 3.22—contd.

Community	Period	Infant mortality	Source
Flanders (*Belgium*)			
Elversele	1650–1699	151	Deprez (1965)
	1740–1749	152	
	1750–1796	215	
France			
Crulai, Normandy	1674–1742	172	Goubert (1968)
Thézels, southwest	1747–1782	191	
La Guerche, Brittany	1720–1792	285	
St Méen, Brittany	1720–1792	237	
St Aubin, Brittany	1749–1789	243	
Sotteville-les-Rouen, north	1760–1790	244	Girard (1959)
Ingouville, north	1720–1790	286	Terrisse (1961)
Tourouvre, north	1670–1679	273	Charbonneau (1970)
	1680–1689	274	
	1690–1699	305	
	1700–1709	298	
	1710–1719	278	
	1720–1729	266	
	1730–1739	236	
	1740–1749	273	
	1750–1759	187	
	1760–1769	174	
St Agnan, centre	1730–1793	240	Houdaille (1961)
Hungary			
Vajszló	1777–1790	200	Andorka (1973)
	1803–1810	220	
	1811–1820	200	
	1821–1830	310	
	1831–1840	260	
	1841–1850	250	
	1871–1880	200	
	1881–1887	230	
Besence	1801–1810	220	
	1811–1820	240	
	1821–1830	180	
	1831–1840	200	
	1841–1850	200	
	1851–1860	220	
	1861–1870	190	
	1871–1880	150	
	1881–1890	120	
	1891–1895	170	

of decline of mortality, with very different lags in different communities, and similar levels of mortality are accompanied by rather different levels of fertility. The problem with mortality data originating from family reconstitution studies is that death registration was most deficient, and therefore there are few data available on overall mortality. However, these sources of data have an important advantage – namely, that we can calculate infant and child mortality, which probably influenced fertility most strongly. In some cases the correlation of infant mortality and fertility seems to be positive. For example, the relatively low marital fertility in Thézels and St Sernin in southwest France was associated with a relatively low infant mortality, and both rates are high in Brittany, Ingouville, Tourouvre and Sotteville-les-Rouen. Also in Elversele in Flanders the rise of infant mortality and the rise of fertility seem to coincide in the second half of the eighteenth century. On the other hand, in Colyton the rates are not parallel, and also in Vajszló and Besence in Hungary infant mortality does not seem to have fallen to an important degree until the second half of the nineteenth century, although marital fertility had been declining since the end of the eighteenth century.

Data on expectation of life at birth are rather rare in family reconstitution studies. The few data available (table 3.23), however, suggest that the relation of fertility and mortality is not always positive, and surely not simple or very strong. For example, while in the case of the bourgeoisie of Geneva the improvement of expectation of life was accompanied by a decline of fertility, in Tourouvre the level of fertility hardly changed, while mortality declined, and in Colyton the period of highest mortality almost exactly coincided (although preceded by some years, in consequence of the plague) with the period of lowest fertility.

The second question to be answered is whether a pattern of late marriage and high proportion of celibacy (the marriage pattern called 'artificial' by Glass) might be interpreted as a form of control of growth of population, i.e. as an alternative to birth control in marriage. In addition to the statements of Cantillon quoted above, this interpretation seems to be supported by historical demographic data.

The family reconstitution study of a representative sample of communities in southwestern France (Henry 1972) most interestingly suggests that late marriage and control of marital fertility might have been alternatives. Two different patterns were found in the seven parishes investigated: in some of them (St Léger and surrounding communities) early marriage was a general custom (even today), and here marital fertility was lower, while in other parishes (Esbareich and surrounding communities) late marriage was customary and marital fertility was higher than in the first group (table 3.24). Although Henry does not exclude the possibility of

Table 3.23   Expectation of life at birth based on family reconstitution data.

Community	Period	Male	Female	Both sexes	Source
Britain					
British aristocracy	1550–1574	36·5	38·2	—	Hollingsworth
	1575–1599	35·3	38·1	—	(1965)
	1600–1624	32·9	35·3	—	
	1625–1649	31·2	33·2	—	
	1650–1674	29·6	32·7	—	
	1675–1699	32·9	34·2	—	
	1700–1724	34·4	36·3	—	
	1725–1749	38·6	36·7	—	
	1750–1774	44·5	45·7	—	
	1775–1799	46·8	49·0	—	
	1800–1824	49·2	51·7	—	
Colyton	1538–1624	—	—	43·2	Wrigley (1969)
	1625–1699	—	—	36·9	
	1700–1774	—	—	41·8	
France					
Crulai	1675–1775	—	—	30·0	Gautier and Henry (1958)
Tourouvre	1670–1719	—	—	25·0	Charbonneau (1970)
	1720–1769	—	—	33·1	
Switzerland					
Bourgeoisie of	1600–1649	30	35	—	Henry (1956)
Geneva	1650–1699	32	39	—	
	1700–1749	40	46	—	
	1750–1799	46	50	—	
	1800–1850	52	53	—	

The column headers: *Expectation of life at birth* spans *Male*, *Female*, *Both sexes*.

alternative interpretations, e.g. by biological factors, he also mentions that birth control might have been the cause of lower marital fertility in the first group.

In Vajszló and Besence in Hungary the pattern of early marriage and almost nonexistent celibacy associated with birth control in marriage appears very clearly. It should be remembered, too, that in these Hungarian villages birth control was not of the modern type, as parities were not concentrated to the first years of marriage. Demény (1968) suggested that the negative correlation of the I_m (percentage married) and I_g (marital fertility) indices in Hungary in 1880 proves that restriction of marriage and restriction of births within marriage might have been alternative means of achieving a lower overall fertility rate.

Table 3.24 Age-specific marital fertility in two microregions in southwest France, characterized respectively by early and late marriage.

Community	Period of marriage	Age at marriage	Age group						
			15–19	20–24	25–29	30–34	35–39	40–44	45–49
St Léger and surrounding communities	1720–1769	–19	270	345	321	286	213	113	9
		20–24		448	347	364	249	173	25
		25–29			382	411	281	182	33
		30+				382	296	147	43
	1770–1819	–19	233	356	329	270	214	101	0
		20–24		392	359	264	219	84	7
		25–29			415	297	221	140	22
		30+				391	308	150	12
Esbareich and surrounding communities	1720–1769	–19	310	381	389	388	307	205	30
		20–24		587	380	357	278	165	6
		25–29			507	410	328	164	28
		30+				563	394	215	8
	1770–1819	–19	393	405	323	348	255	140	25
		20–24		520	371	342	331	148	26
		25–29			410	364	278	145	15
		30+				358	304	152	13

Source: Henry (1972, p. 986).

The comparison of family and household structure in the smallholder (serf) families in Hungary with those found by Laslett (1972) and others in western Europe suggests an interesting hypothetical relation. In Hungary in the villages of southern Transdanubia showing early signs of birth control, the composition of households was more complicated; there were more extended households containing widowed parents and other relatives, and more multiple family households, containing several nuclear families, mostly married parents with married children, than in western Europe. At the same time the average size of households was not much larger than in western Europe. We might interpret this finding in the following way: parents allowed their children to marry and live with them in the same household, but strongly urged them to use birth control at the beginning of marriage. Many literary sources mentioned the strong influence, even dictatorial rule, of mothers-in-law on the fertility control of their daughters-in-law (Andorka 1976). On the other hand, in Russia (according to the census of 1897) high marital fertility and young age at marriage were existing in parallel with large and complicated household structures (Chojnacka 1976).

Matras (1965) summarized our knowledge on marriage and marital fertility patterns by stating that there are four possible strategies of family formation:

1 Early marriage and uncontrolled fertility
2 Early marriage and controlled fertility
3 Late marriage and uncontrolled fertility
4 Late marriage and controlled fertility.

Different populations follow different paths through these patterns. For example, western European populations might have gone from the first to the third and then to the second strategy. There is an alternative path from the first directly to the second strategy, which was perhaps customary in eastern Europe (Van de Walle 1968).

The populations investigated in this chapter might be tentatively classified into the above mentioned four strategies in the following way:

1 French population of Canada, British aristocracy in the Middle Ages
2 Vajszló and Besence in Hungary
3 Most French communities investigated
4 Colyton from 1647 to 1719, as well as Thézels and St Sernin in southwestern France.

Having reviewed the relation of fertility and marital fertility to demographic phenomena – mortality and marriage – we now proceed to investigate the economic and social background of differences and decline of fertility. The first obvious possibility is the comparison of the British and

French aristocracies, whose fertility developed in very different ways. In the seventeenth century the fertility of both was relatively low, associated with a moderately high age at marriage and similar mortality conditions. In the eighteenth century the fertility of the French aristocracy declined, while that of the British aristocracy increased, and did not begin to decline significantly until the second half of the nineteenth century. It is justifiable to suppose that these different tendencies were caused by different family planning and birth control attitudes.

What were the differences in the economic and social position of both aristocracies which might have contributed to the differences in attitudes concerning the size of planned families and birth control? A very important historical difference is at once obvious: while in France the political position of the aristocracy remained essentially unchanged until 1789, and then abruptly changed in the French Revolution, the British aristocracy had already lost its power base in the revolution of Cromwell (1645), but maintained much of its influence during the eighteenth and nineteenth centuries.

There are deeper economic and social causes. After Cromwell the British aristocracy had relatively few legal privileges, but intermingled to a large extent with the commercial and later industrial bourgeoisie, in whose hands lay economic and political power. This was caused partly by inter-marriage and also by the system of primogeniture, in consequence of which the second, third, etc., sons of British aristocrats did not inherit an estate and so were obliged to find an occupation, often in 'bourgeois' professions. On the other hand, the rich bourgeoisie often bought land estates in addition to their businesses. Thus in England the aristocracy became more or less assimilated with the bourgeoisie, the new privileged class.

On the other hand, in France such assimilation occurred rather rarely. Here all the noble sons inherited the noble status and the exemption from taxes. They lost these privileges, however, if they began some commercial or industrial enterprise (except long-distance commerce, glass manufacturing or coal mining). Therefore, most younger sons of aristocrats preferred to buy an office in the army, the church or the state bureaucracy. So the French aristocracy remained a separate privileged class, although with essentially diminishing economic basis (Habakkuk 1967). Thus it is understandable that the French aristocracy was much more interested in controlling the number of heirs, than was the British aristocracy for which the possibilities of economic expansion were open.

At the same time the French bourgeoisie seems to have been adversely affected by the social conditions prevailing in France before the Revolution (Blacker 1957). Infiltration into the class of nobility was possible, but difficult, since it required either the purchase of '*lettres du Roi*', which was used by the kings as a simple expedient for raising money, the purchase of an office which automatically carried the status of nobility, or the purchase of seigneurial estates. All these required great wealth, but the ambition to see their sons rise to social positions higher than their own, and to be exempt from taxation (as the nobles were), seems to have been a characteristic of the French bourgeoisie. The division of parental wealth between several heirs impeded this rise, as did also the custom of giving large dowries for daughters. Other routes of social upgrading for the bourgeois families seem to have been more scarce than in England, firstly because of the feudalistic social institutions in France, and secondly because of the time lag of the onset of the industrial revolution as compared with England.

Of all the family reconstitution studies the deepest and most detailed analysis of the interrelations of the development of fertility and economic conditions were made in the Colyton study by Wrigley (1966b). He found that the age at marriage suddenly rose and control of marital fertility became suddenly widespread in the middle of the seventeenth century – more precisely, after 1647. In the eighteenth century, most of all in its second half, marital fertility gradually increased again and age at marriage of women declined. It should be mentioned that similar tendencies can also be noticed in Nottingham (Chambers 1965) and Worcestershire (Eversley 1965b).

The reasons for these changes are connected, according to Wrigley, to the following events: from November 1645 to October 1646 about one fifth of the population of Colyton died as a result of the last great outbreak of bubonic plague. The population suddenly became aware of the fact that its number had outgrown its food base – using Wrigley's expression, 'it was overfishing'. Therefore the people of Colyton decided to control the growth of population by several different means: they married later, more people remained unmarried, birth control was practised in marriage, and the infants born were not so well cared for, so that infant mortality rose. In consequence, there was no population increase for several decades. Only when, in the middle of the eighteenth century, agricultural production began to develop, did the population allow its number to increase (Wrigley 1966b 1969).

Thus the population of Colyton controlled fertility by different means long before any impact of the industrial revolution appeared. More or less the same happened among the eighteenth century French peasantry, whose members had already become the *de facto* owners of their own land before the Revolution, so having more children meant the division of the land owned by the family. The *Code Napoléon* confirmed this tendency by proclaiming equal inheritance for all children (Blacker 1957).

Some insights may also be gained from available historical data on the economic and social background of the decline of marital fertility in

Vajszló and Besence, the two villages in southern Transdanubia. It should be kept in mind that here the decline of marital fertility was much more significant than in the western European communities studied by family reconstitution, but the custom of early and almost universal marriage did not change in the same period, from the middle of the eighteenth to the end of the nineteenth century. It is noteworthy too that infant mortality remained almost at the same level until the second half of the nineteenth century, a level which was rather low when compared with other infant mortality rates found in the eighteenth century, but relatively high in the middle of the nineteenth century. Also, adult mortality seems to have declined only slightly in this period. Thus, the decline in fertility was not caused or preceded by a decline in mortality.

In order to understand the background of the demographic development of the region of the Ormánság, in which Vajszló and Besence are situated, a short glance at the history of Hungary from the sixteenth to the nineteenth century seems necessary. During the sixteenth century an important part of Hungary, the Carpathian Basin, and a major part of its most agriculturally productive regions, came under Turkish rule. The Ormánság was also under Turkish rule. From 1526, the date of the battle of Mohács where the Hungarian army perished and the king died, to the peace of Karlóca in 1799 the country was (apart from some short relatively peaceful periods) a permanent battlefield of the Turkish, Hungarian and German armies. Then between 1703 and 1711 the liberated country was again devastated by a war between Hungarian freedom fighters and the armies of the Habsburgs. The armies regularly looted and burned the villages, killed the population or (in the case of the Turks) deported them into slavery, and even the most peaceful armies obliged the population to provide them with food. All this resulted in high mortality, as well as emigration of the native population from the Turkish-occupied territories. Although the decrease of population does not seem to have been as important as supposed earlier, it is probable that the population of the Carpathian Basin was approximately 4 million after the wars in 1720, i.e. more or less the same as two hundred years before, when the Turkish occupation began (Dávid 1957).

After the end of the wars in the first half of the eighteenth century the territory which was formerly under Turkish occupation was very sparsely populated, and a great part of the arable land was not cultivated. A real 'frontier' situation existed, similar to the western frontier of the United States (Gerhard 1959, Den Hollander 1960–1). The possibilities of expansion were limitless. Landlords were glad if somebody cultivated their land and encouraged immigration from western Europe, as well as from other parts of Hungary. At the same time landlords generally resided far away, in the parts which had not been occuped formerly by Turks, so their power over the serfs was not particularly strong. Also the state administration was not able to interfere in the life of the peasants.

The county of Baranya where the Ormánság is situated was also devastated and sparsely populated. Although after the wars there was a large amount of immigration, firstly of Germans, the native population which had managed to survive in the marshy parts of the county, e.g. in the Ormánság, faced great opportunities for economic expansion. Most probably, the larger households could profit best from these opportunities, since they were more able to organize their work. It seems that new land could be occupied by peasants legally or semilegally if they had the manpower necessary to cultivate it.

In the second half of the eighteenth century the situation gradually changed. Uncultivated land became scarce, and the landlords began manorial production which turned out to be profitable as methods of transport improved. In consequence, they tried to repossess the lands they had formerly given to serfs, or which were semilegally occupied by serfs. The use of woods and pasture lands by the serfs was curbed (Ruzsás 1964). State administration tried to defend the peasants, since they were the taxpayers (nobles did not pay taxes), and the empress Maria Theresa enacted the decree of 'urbarium' which ordered the rights, charges and lands of the serfs to be fixed on the basis of a detailed census. This effectively set a limit to the exploitation of serfs, but on the other hand it also set a limit to their own chances of economic expansion. As it became almost impossible to increase the land cultivated by a peasant family, from that time on having more children meant having to divide the farm between them. The other alternative was to send some of them to work as agricultural labourers in the large estates of the landlords. That, however, was considered by the relatively independent smallholder-serfs as intolerable social downgrading, not only because of the lower level of living of the labourers, but also because of the loss of independence and status. The ensuing situation might be characterized by the concept of Foster (1965) as one in which the 'image of limited good' prevails. Land and production were considered as given, and it was necessary to divide this given amount of production capacities and goods between the members of the family.

This image of the surrounding world is expressed in the following quotations from peasants in the Ormánság, interviewed much later in the twentieth century by writers and sociologists:

'One parcel, one child' (Buday 1909).
' "We do not make beggars" – said a young farmer today after having discussed for half an hour, as a conclusion. "The country is full of unemployed people," he continued, "There are more people than would

be necessary. What do you want from us? Give us land and the land will produce children" ' (Illyés n.d.).

Thus birth control and its most extreme form, the one child system (which, however, according to the results of the family reconstitution, was never dominant, only rather widespread), was considered by the sociologists investigating it (Kovács 1940 n.d., Erdei n.d.) to be a result of the conditions of agriculture, the large estates owned by the landlords and the bad possibilities of marketing the products of the peasants, which all resulted in the impossibility of economic expansion of the peasant population. They considered the one-child system to be a symptom of the general crisis or even bankruptcy of the peasant way of life.

Economic conditions, however, exerted their influence on fertility, not only directly, but also indirectly by the intervention of a special culture containing rather strict norms concerning the number of children considered desirable and permitted in a peasant family (Fälep 1929).

If a married woman remained sterile, she was sympathized with; if she had no living children, it was said 'it is her concern'; but if she had more than two children, she was ridiculed, despised, condemned – 'Can she not take care? or 'I would be ashamed if I littered as much' – and the mother or mother-in-law generally knew the proper time to recommend 'It is better to wash the sheeting than the baby's napkin' (Hidvégi n.d.).

In some cases this norm became so severely adhered to that some infants were killed.

A young peasant married. He wanted and desired children. A daughter was born and soon he was waiting gladly the second child. However, when the son was born, the old parents managed to change his feelings completely, and so dehumanize his parental instincts that he decided to kill the infant. They gave tablets of aspirin to the infant and when he began to perspire, they put him naked on the veranda. The result was pneumonia and quick death. The father said coldly and arrogantly: 'I do not buy the child shoes and dress. In my home the child will not howl. For me one child is enough!' (Kodolányi 1941).

These cultural norms prescribing a number of children which was lower than that necessary for simple reproduction, became later relatively independent from the economic base which had produced them, and even turned out to be sometimes dysfunctional for the population of the Ormánság, as the population slowly lost its lands and its economic position deteriorated.

Roheim (1950), who tried to synthesize the results of psychoanalysis and cultural anthropology, gave a different interpretation based on the results of the above mentioned writers and sociologists:

I think we must get used to a new kind of 'interpretation which combines the economic with the psychological.... These Hungarians disintegrate when the forests and swamps, owned really by the great lords but in which they could roam in freedom, are theirs no more. They have evidently suffered the trauma of separation from Mother Earth. In their unconscious, the whole estate was their own. Therefore they retaliate to the next generation, the child must be aborted, prematurely separated from the mother.... The immigrant has not been deprived of anything, he does not react in the same way.

All these explanations, however, do not answer the question why birth control was used just by the Calvinist smallholder-serf population of the Ormánság in southern Transdanubia, since it has not been proved that the conditions in this microregion were different from those in other parts of the country.

The first problem arising in this connection is whether the practice of birth control was not much more widespread in the peasant population of Hungary than generally supposed – i.e. whether the fertility conditions in the Ormánság were really as unique as often postulated. There are some data which indicate that a certain practice of birth control also took place in other population groups, e.g. in the similarily Calvinist smallholder population of the Sárköz (Pataki 1937, Kovács n.d.), where the villages of Alsónyék and Sárköz were situated, in Calvinist villages around Lake Balaton (Jankó 1902) and among the Calvinist population in general in southern Transdanubia. However, it was not strictly confined to Calvinist populations. Some decades later than in the Ormánság, in the first half of the nineteenth century signs of birth control were found by the family reconstitution method (Moess 1973b) among Roman Catholic groups in the county of Baranya, near to the Ormánság. Beginning from the 1820s in villages situated in the northern part of the Great Plain in Hungary the fertility of Catholics was much higher than that of Calvinists (Kápolnai 1962). On the other hand, in some parts of Hungary fertility was very high – e.g. in the town of Győr (Dányi 1973) in the second half of the eighteenth century. The growth rate of population between the tax census of 1720 and the population census of 1784–7 also suggests a rather high level of fertility, as the population of Hungary doubled in this period (including the population which immigrated in this period, the number of which cannot be estimated exactly at present). Also the non-nominative processing of registration data of Hungarian counties (Klinger *et al.* 1972–5) from 1836 to the end of the nineteenth century showed birth rates of 40–58 per 1000 (Table 3.20). Similarly, the family reconstitution of the western Transdanubian village of Velem (Moess 1972) gave rather high fertility rates in the nineteenth century. Thus it might be concluded that on the whole the fertility of the population in Hungary was fairly high until the last decades of the nineteenth century, but at the same time there were some social groups practising birth control relatively early in the nineteenth century, perhaps even in the last decades of the eighteenth century, one of these groups being the smallholder peasants in southern Transdanubia.

What kind of special features characterized the position of these population groups which might have contributed to the practice of birth control?

The first characteristic might have been the population density, or more precisely the proportion of free uncultivated land. According to Perjés (1973), between 1728 and 1784–7 the population of those settlements grew at a higher rate where (in 1728) the land was cultivated by two-stage rotation, i.e. half of it was left each year fallow, while the growth rate was lower in those settlements where at that time the three-stage rotation method was already being used, i.e. only a third of the land was fallow. It might be supposed, but at present it is not proved, that the smallholder-peasants of those areas began to practise birth control where the three-stage cultivation was introduced earlier, as here agricultural production could not be increased by changing over from the two-stage to the three-stage cultivation.

It is obvious that the serfs, i.e. the small-holders, had much more interest in limiting the size of their families than the agricultural labourers working at the large estates of the landlords, since the smallholders had something to lose by the division of their land among several heirs, while the labourers had practically nothing to lose.

It might be supposed also that the fact of being Protestant contributed to the acceptance of birth control, because the Habsburg kings tried to hold down the Protestants until Joseph II (1780–90) introduced the edict of tolerance, and also after that edict although with less harsh measures. The disadvantages of Protestants were especially strong in the western part of Hungary, where they were a small minority and where the power of central administration predominated more than in the eastern parts, which were further away from Vienna and where the majority of the non-Catholic population lived. The religious oppression also hampered the economic expansion of the peasants.

The difference between the position of Protestant and Catholic peasants was probably enhanced by the fact that most of the Calvinists were native to this region during Turkish occupation (they remained Protestant precisely because Turkish occupation made re-Catholicization impossible during the decades of the strongest counter-reformation drive of the Habsburgs), while the Catholics probably mostly immigrated. The native population tried to maintain the relative independence achieved under Turkish rule, which would have been lost by working as labourers in the large estates or by emigrating. Thus it seems that the social characteristics of these Protestants explain their lower fertility.

One question remains, however. Why did these smallholders not try to find some other solution, when the land became scarce and the possibilities of expansion narrowed down (e.g. why did they not emigrate or transfer over to other occupations in industry or commerce)? Emigration and seasonal emigration in summer for work was widespread in the northern and eastern parts of the country. The peasants of Transdanubia, however, had a higher living standard than those in other parts of the country and jealously tried to defend this standard, which would have been lost by emigration. In addition, for the Protestants emigration would most probably have meant the loss of contact with their church.

There are two other Protestant population groups among those whose fertility was found to be relatively low by family reconstitution studies (see table 3.1, p. 50): the bourgeoisie of Geneva, and the Quakers in America. However, it might be hypothesized that the principal factor of low fertility in these groups was not Protestantism, but the fact that both were 'embourgeoised' populations, i.e. having a rather high living standard and in consequence somewhat low mortality. Thus the motive of using birth control methods might have been similar to that found in the Ormánság in Hungary: fear of loss of status and of living standards, which might have ensued where there were many heirs.

The other regions where marital fertility was found to be relatively low were southwestern France and Catalonia. They are neighbouring regions on both sides of the Pyrenees, but another common feature seems to be more important: both underwent national subjection from the central power of France and of Spain. They approximate to the regions of 'langue d'oc' and the Catalan idiom. It would be intriguing to investigate the economic consequences of political centralization for these regions.

Going over to the comparison of the development of fertility in entire countries, and of their social and economic conditions, the most interesting problem seems to be the causes of the different demographic development of England and France. While in England fertility remained at a relatively high level from the second half of the eighteenth century to the last decades of the nineteenth century, resulting in a high rate of growth of population, fertility in France began to decline in the last decades of the eighteenth century almost parallel with the decline of mortality resulting in a much lower rate of growth.

What might have been the factors contributing to this difference?

The investigation of this problem would require a whole book, so only a few comparative elements of economic and social history can be mentioned here. One of the most important seems to be the different relation of population and food resources of the two countries. In France famines occurred often in the seventeenth century and in the first half of the eighteenth century (Meuvret 1965, Goubert 1965 1968). For example, in the region of Beauvais, north of Paris, famines took place in the following years: 1625, 1648–53, 1674, 1679, 1684, 1693–4, 1709–10, 1719, 1741–2 (Goubert 1960). In these crisis years the price of cereals increased and the number of deaths was from two to three times as high as in normal years – sometimes 10–20 per cent of population died, and the number of marriages and conceptions diminished. Peasants were eating grass from the fields and refuse from dung heaps.

In the middle of the eighteenth century a contemporary source stated:

> 'Le bécheur gagne six sols par jour qui ne peuvent suffire pour la nourriture de sa femme et de ses enfants dont il ne cherche qu'a réduire le nombre', 'the labourer earned only six sols daily, which was not sufficient to provide food for his wife and his children whose number he tries to reduce constantly' (Lautman 1972).

Summarizing these conditions, Sauvy (1963) concluded that France at the end of the eighteenth century was strongly overpopulated.

In neighbouring Belgium also, an investigation of the demographic and economic development of Liège (Ruwet 1954) showed a negative correlation between marital fertility and the changes in the price of rye from the middle of the seventeenth to the beginning of the eighteenth century. This period (1644–1715) was called by Ruwet the period of open famines. It was preceded by a period called the period of masked distress, and also after 1715 a similar period of masked distress followed, in which there were no famines and the negative correlation of fertility and prices of rye did not appear. Ruwet explains this fact by the beginning of the practice of birth control, which resulted in a better relation of population and the food base.

In the same period famines did not occur in England:

> Nearly all English registers which have been studied so far yield entirely negative conclusions; they contain no examples of harvest years where a conspicuous rise in burials was accompanied by a corresponding fall in conceptions and marriages. We may here be faced with a sociological discovery of the first historical importance, that our country in the seventeenth century was already immune from these periodical disasters, whereas France was not (Laslett 1965, p. 114).

The fundamental reason for the more favourable situation in England was probably the development of English agriculture, which was able to provide food for the population, even when it began to rise more rapidly in the second half of the eighteenth century. The factors contributing to the development of agrictulture in England were (McKeown, Brown and Record 1972);

1 The improvement of organization of work in agriculture in consequence of the enclosures which were well advanced by 1760 and almost complete by 1820.
2 Some extension of land under cultivation and the introduction of new technologies, e.g.
   (a) New crops (clover and other leguminous hays, and particularly root crops, among others the potato)
   (b) Crop rotation instead of the traditional grain–fallow rotation
   (c) Conservation of the fertility of soil by fertilizing, liming, mixed farming, new rotations, and a better balance between animal and plant husbandry
   (d) Seed production
   (e) Winter feeding of animals by clover and root crops, which made it possible to avoid slaughtering before winter
   (f) New farm implements, particularly the smaller, lighter, triangular plough with curved mouldboard, which could be pulled by fewer animals and worked by one man
3 Development of transport, mainly as a consequence of the development of canals.

This development of agriculture was followed by industrialization, beginning in the second half of the eighteenth century and becoming in the nineteenth century a source of more or less constantly increasing demand for manpower.

These economic processes might have caused the high rate of growth of population in England and Wales in the second half of the eighteenth century and its maintenance till the last decades of the nineteenth century.

It is not quite clear whether the rise of the rate of growth was caused solely by a decline of the death rate or was enhanced also by a rise of the birth rate. The different interpretations of the high rate of growth are based on different assumptions on the development of the birth and death rates, i.e. different assumptions on the extent and changes of underregistration.

It is not quite clear either what caused the decline in mortality: the growth of agricultural production and the better conditions of nourishment of the population, or a general improvement of living conditions, among them of dwelling and sanitary conditions, or an improvement of personal and public hygiene, or certain biological changes (the extinction of the black rat which was probably a major carrier of the flea causing the bubonic plague infection, or some other immunological changes).

As to the development of fertility, Krause (1958) hypothesizes that a rising birth rate was the major cause of the growth of English population around 1800. Chambers (1957) stated that in the region of the Vale of Trent in the second half of the eighteenth century both the crude marriage and birth rates and the ratios of the number of births to that of deaths were higher in the industrializing villages than in the traditional agricultural villages. Deane and Cole (1962) found that the birth rates in the industrializing northwestern parts of England were higher than in the agricultural region in southern England, from 1750 to 1830.

It is not quite clear through what kind of causative mechanism industrialization might have raised fertility. One reason might have been that by providing employment and an independent source of income for young men and women it freed the non-property-owning part of the population from the obligation to delay marriage or to remain celibate. There may have been some changes in customs, e.g. the period of breast-feeding might have been shorter in the case of women employed in industry, which might have tended to reduce the intervals between births (Wrigley 1969). Or, alternatively, the widespread employment of children in factories might have induced families to believe that it was economically advantageous to have many children, even if actually the income gained by the children was lower than the cost of their upkeep (Tranter 1973). Krause (1958) hypothesizes that the Speenhamland system of relief for poor families had a fertility-increasing effect, because the amount of relief was proportional to the size of the family and thus provided a guaranteed minimum level of living. Blaug (1963) doubts this kind of influence.

In spite of all these uncertainties, however, it is certain that the birth rate in England and Wales was higher around 1800 and began to decline much later than in France, where the decline was already well under way in the last decade or decades of the eighteenth century. Thus it seems to be most interesting to compare the economic and social conditions of England and France.

In France the development of agricultural technologies did not ensue, or at least was much slower in the eighteenth century (Dupaquier 1971). Moreover, the rate of development at the beginning of the nineteenth century became slower (Moulin 1972). The French population lived in danger of a demographic crisis, although the level of living slowly improved. Therefore it is understandable that the populations of villages – remembering the famines that had occurred some decades before – began to practise birth control when the decline of mortality would have resulted in a more rapid growth of population. As urbanization and industrialization was much slower than in England, and as emigration was almost impossible because of the loss of colonies, there were no alternative solutions for the surplus of population in the villages. This tendency might have been reinforced by the custom and later the provisions of the *Code Civile* (1804) which required Frenchmen to divide the bulk of their property equally between their children, as pointed out by Le Play, for example.

Sweden seems to have been in an intermediate position between England and France. The increase in agricultural productivity seems to have occurred later, in the first decades of the nineteenth century, and to have been smaller than in England (Utterström 1965, Heckscher 1949–50, McKeown, Brown and Record 1972). However, population density was low, so land was available, and mortality was lower than in England and France, so the relatively moderate fertility resulted in a population growth from 1740 to 1840 which was higher than in France, but lower than in England.

Around 1810 the rate of natural increase of the population increased, in consequence of lower mortality and higher marital fertility. This change was attributed to a more rapid economic growth, most of all in the peasant areas (as opposed to the manorial areas). Several factors might have contributed to that increase of fertility, like the introduction of potato cultivation by the independent peasants. The manorial economy, on the other hand, did not permit the development of the potential possibilities of the more intensified family cultivation of the potato (Fridlizius 1975).

In Finland, another Scandinavian country for which we possess vital statistical data beginning at a very early period (in consequence of the Swedish administration of the country in these centuries), the birth and death rates developed in a different way. The period for which we have data begins in the second decade of the eighteenth century. It was preceded by three decades of demographic catastrophes – namely, the famines in the 1690s and the Nordic War from 1698 to 1719. It was estimated that the famines caused the death of 30 per cent, the war that of 20 per cent of the population. The birth rate was moderate in the subsequent period, then in the middle of the eighteenth century a very bad harvest (1740) and a new war (1741) again caused high mortality and a natural decrease of population. From 1750, however, population began to increase at a high rate in consequence of high fertility and relatively low mortality. Famines and wars did not interrupt this development, land was abundant and agricultural production seems to have kept up with population growth, so that the period of high demographic growth rate was paralled by a relative prosperity of the population, as compared with the preceding decades (Jutikkala 1965).

The most well-known and odd case of historical demography, however, is Ireland. Here the first decades of the nineteenth century were characterized by a high growth rate of population, based on the expansion of Irish rural economy. Three factors contributed to this expansion. First, food scarcity in England increased the demand for Irish corn, in consequence of which land was transferred from pasture to tillage, i.e. to a more labour-intensive type of cultivation. In consequence, smaller farms became viable, so that holdings could be subdivided among the farmer's sons, providing the possibility of establishing new households. Second, the landlords also favoured the subdivision of holdings, because this facilitated the increase of rents. Third, the potato became an important part of the Irish diet, and as the yield of potato was much higher than that of corn, it was possible to produce the food necessary for a family in a much smaller plot. The possibility of obtaining a scrap of land and of establishing on it a new household resulted in the gradual breakdown of the earlier marriage customs, i.e. relatively late marriage and high celibacy, which had characterized Ireland in the same way as other parts of western Europe. In consequence, the rate of growth of population was very high from about 1780 to the 1840s (Connell 1965).

In the second half of the 1840s, however, the potato famine, caused by the appearance of the potato beetle, suddenly broke this economic and demographic expansion. The famine caused very high death rates and led to mass emigration. In consequence, the population of Ireland declined by almost 50 per cent between 1841 and 1911. In addition to emigration and to the deaths caused by famine, an important factor of the decline was the sudden change of marriage customs. Couples married very late and celibacy became frequent, so that the fertility of the population declined. Previously it was supposed that late marriage and celibacy were the main causes of the decline of fertility. Recently, however, it was suggested that conscious fertility limitation in marriage might also have contributed to it (McKenna 1974). By means of multiple regression analysis of data of the censuses of 1851, 1871, 1891 and 1911, it was found that holdings per 100 males in agriculture and median holding size had a positive effect on marriage frequency (percentage of females aged 15–44 married), but a negative effect on marital fertility in 1851 and 1871. It seems that in these years late marriage and lower marital fertility were alternative solutions of controlling family and population growth. In subsequent decades the influence of occupational structure (percentage in agriculture, education of women) seems to have become predominant in influencing fertility and marriage. The population history of Ireland thus provides clear examples of the adaptation of population by marriage patterns, marital fertility and emigration to the changing economic conditions.

Thus in the period preceding the introduction of official vital statistics, i.e. the period before the attainment of a certain level of industrialization (both periods coinciding in most countries, except Scandinavia, where official vital statistics were introduced earlier), the level of mortality had a certain influence on fertility. In other words, the decline of mortality tended to induce a decline of fertility. This relation, however, was neither strict nor strong, being influenced rather significantly by the available economic opportunities, in the sense that when economic opportunities were abundant and increasing the decline of fertility did not follow the decline of mortality. Economic conditions seem to have been important in determining the level and changes of fertility, unfavourable conditions promoting a decline of fertility and favourable conditions, abundant food supply, growing opportunities of employment and growing income tending to promote a higher level of fertility.

Thus fertility adjusted more or less exactly and with shorter or longer lags to a level which – combined with the given level of mortality – produced a population growth rate that in the long run did not exceed the growth of production, particularly of food production. There were several methods of adjustment of fertility to this level; birth control in marriage was only one of them, the others being late marriage and a higher pro-portion of celibacy. The population groups that had some property, and therefore had something to lose when there were several heirs, were more liable to practise birth control than those that had nothing to lose – i.e. the poorest strata of society.

It is obvious, however, that these economic factors do not influence fertility directly, but only indirectly by influencing on the one hand the individual decisions of couples and on the other hand the values and norms concerning the number of children prevalent in the culture of the given society, social stratum or group. This means that the favourable or disad-vantageous economic changes influenced fertility only if and when they became conscious in the given population. This would explain the lags of the responses of fertility to the changes in mortality or economic condi-tions, and also the fact that these values and norms sometimes seem to become independent of economic and social conditions, even dysfunctional in some circumstances, as e.g. in the last phase of the decline of fertility in the region of the Ormánság, when population actually diminished and its economic situation worsened.

All these findings support the thesis of Carlsson (1966) who stated that the spread of birth control is not an innovation, but an adjustment process. The innovation theory, which seems to be shared by many demographers, would mean that the introduction and spread of birth control was a recent innovation, something new in the culture of particular societies in the nineteenth century. This theory stresses the importance of knowledge of the methods of birth control and therefore of the information processes. It often assumes a 'trickle down' process in the spread of birth control, i.e. that the practice started in the most well-informed, most educated parts of population, in the metropolitan centres, reached the smaller towns with some delay and the villages still later; similarly, that it was first practised by the highest strata and gradually became accepted by the lower ones. The adjustment process accepted by Carlsson, on the other hand, means that birth control was practised by part of the population or by most of the population to a certain extent, with higher fertility goals, which were advantageous in the given economic and social conditions, and at the given level of mortality. When these conditions change, the decline of fertility ensues as an adjustment to new conditions. The demographic history of Colyton, as well as of Vajszló and Besence, provides examples of this adjustment process of fertility to the changes of economic and social situation.

The process of industrialization completely changed the various economic and social conditions of Europe, and in consequence also the demographic conditions, among them the level of mortality. It might be supposed that the causative mechanism of fertility changed in this period, as compared with the pre-industrial centuries. The social factors determining fertility in industrialized societies will be the subject of Part Four.

PART FOUR

Sources of data on the
social determinants of fertility

Four main types of data sources are examined in the following chapters:

1   Time series of vital statistical data from official statistical sources
2   Data on differential fertility from censuses
3   Cross-sectional data concerning fertility and other social variables of
    territorial units, i.e. countries, regions, communities
4   Data from surveys of fertility and family planning

The data from these different sources will be dealt with separately, since
each type provides somewhat different information, and (partly in
consequence) the conclusions they suggest on the nature and direction of
influence of particular social factors are often different, sometimes even
contradictory.

4.1 Time series of vital statistical data

During the nineteenth century the collection and publication of official vital statistical data was begun in all the present-day developed countries, providing annually detailed data on birth rates and more refined measures of fertility. These time series analysed in relation to the corresponding time series of economic and social indicators (though these are much scarcer and much less exact) facilitate the investigation of the effect of economic and social factors on fertility.

The period from the beginning of official vital statistics to the present day can be divided into three periods:

1. The period preceding the First World War, characterized by the decline of fertility
2. The period between the two World Wars, when fertility in the most developed countries reached a very low level, not to be equalled again until the 1970s
3. The period after the Second World War, characterized in most developed countries by the baby boom, while in other countries fertility continued to decline after a short upsurge immediately following the War.

Perhaps in a similar book written around the year 2000, a fourth period could be added, beginning around the middle of the 1960s and characterized by a new decline in fertility. At present, however, it is not yet possible to discern whether this new decline in fertility in some of the developed countries is the onset of a new trend, i.e. a new demographic period characterized by other relationships than those of the first twenty postwar years, or simply a short, temporary phenomenon.

The demographic development of the nineteenth century until the First World War can be interpreted apparently rather easily – at least so it was believed by contemporary demographers. Fertility declined in all developed countries parallel with their economic and social development (table 4.1). There are several different explanations for this decline to be found in demographic literature. Among others the following factors are mentioned as causing the decline of fertility, or contributing to it:

(a) The decline of mortality, which in turn was caused by a rise in the standard of living and/or by the development of medical knowledge, of personal hygiene, etc.

Table 4.1 Birth and death rates in selected countries, 1800–1920.

Period	Sweden Birth rate	Sweden Death rate	Finland Birth rate	Finland Death rate	United States Birth rate	United States Death rate	England Birth rate	England Death rate	Ireland Birth rate	Ireland Death rate	France Birth rate	France Death rate
1801–1805	31·3	24·4	38·4	24·7	55·0	—	—	—	—	—	—	—
1806–1810	30·4	32·0	34·3	39·0	54·3	—	—	—	—	—	—	—
1811–1815	32·9	27·0	37·0	28·0	—	—	—	—	—	—	—	—
1816–1820	33·7	24·6	37·7	24·9	52·8	—	—	—	—	—	—	—
1821–1825	35·8	22·1	38·7	25·7	—	—	—	—	—	—	—	—
1826–1830	33·5	25·1	37·8	24·2	51·4	—	—	—	—	—	—	—
1831–1835	32·4	23·1	34·2	31·5	—	—	—	—	—	—	—	—
1836–1840	30·6	22·5	32·6	25·0	48·3	—	—	—	—	—	—	—
1841–1845	31·3	20·2	35·5	22·3	—	—	35·2	21·4	—	—	28·0	22·4
1846–1850	30·9	21·0	35·4	24·6	43·3	—	34·8	23·3	—	—	26·6	23·7
1851–1855	31·8	21·7	36·3	28·2	—	—	35·5	22·6	—	—	26·1	24·3
1856–1860	33·7	21·7	35·6	29·2	41·4	—	35·5	21·8	—	—	26·4	23·9
1861–1865	33·2	19·8	37·0	25·8	—	—	35·8	22·6	—	—	26·6	23·0
1866–1870	29·7	20·5	31·8	38·6	38·3	—	35·7	22·4	—	—	25·3	23·3
1871–1875	30·7	18·3	37·0	21·7	—	—	35·7	22·0	26·2	18·1	25·0	23·9
1876–1880	30·3	18·3	36·9	22·7	35·2	—	35·4	20·8			25·1	22·6
1881–1885	29·4	17·5	35·5	22·0	—	—	33·5	19·4	22·8	17·4	24·6	21·8
1886–1890	28·8	16·4	34·5	20·0	31·5	—	31·4	18·9			23·0	21·9
1891–1895	27·4	16·6	32·0	20·6	—	—	30·5	18·7	22·1	17·6	22·2	20·9
1896–1900	26·9	16·1	33·1	19·3	30·1	—	29·3	17·6			22·0	21·6
1901–1905	26·1	15·5	32·4	19·2	—	16·0	28·2	15·6	22·4	16·8	21·6	19·6
1906–1910	25·4	14·3	32·5	18·2	29·7	15·0	26·3	14·7			20·2	19·1
1911–1915	23·1	14·0	29·2	17·1	29·1	13·6	23·6	14·3	21·1	16·0	—	—
1916–1920	21·2	14·5	24·9	20·8	27·6	14·4	20·1	14·4			—	—

Notes:
United States: Birth rates from 1800, 1810, 1820, 1830, 1840, 1850, 1860, 1870, 1880, 1890, 1900, 1905–1909, 1910–1914, 1915–1919.
England: Birth rates corrected by Glass (1951).
Germany: Birth rates and death rates 1845, 1860, 1875, 1880, 1885, 1890, 1895, 1900, 1905, 1910, 1920, always within boundaries of the German Reich at the given date.

(b) The rise in the standard of living
(c) Industrialization
(d) Urbanization
(e) The rise of education and the spread of rational thinking in all spheres of life
(f) The change or decline of the role of family
(g) Or simply the spread of birth control information and practice.

These explanations were almost universally accepted in earlier demographic literature. Recent development of fertility in advanced societies, however, has disproved the existence of such simple laws. Changes of fertility in the period before the First World War also cast doubts on

Germany		Belgium		Switzerland		Italy		Poland		Hungary		Russia	
Birth rate	Death rate	Birth rate	Death rate	Birth rate	Death rate	Birth rate	Death rate	Birth rate	Death rate	Birth rate	Death rate	Birth rate	Death rate
—	—	—	—	—	—	—	—	—	—	—	—	—	—
—	—	—	—	—	—	—	—	—	—	—	—	—	—
—	—	—	—	—	—	—	—	—	—	—	—	—	—
—	—	—	—	—	—	—	—	—	—	—	—	—	—
—	—	—	—	—	—	—	—	—	—	—	—	—	—
—	—	—	—	—	—	—	—	—	—	—	—	—	—
37·3	25·3	—	—	—	—	—	—	—	—	—	—	—	—
—	—	27·6	24·9	—	—	—	—	—	—	—	—	—	—
—	—	—	—	—	—	—	—	—	—	—	—	—	—
36·3	23·2	29·6	21·5	—	—	—	—	—	—	—	—	—	—
—	—	—	—	—	—	—	—	—	—	—	—	48·9	
—	—	32·7	31·3	—	—	—	—	—	—	—	—		
40·6	27·6	32·9	21·5	30·1	23·8	36·8	30·5	—	—	—	—	49·3	
37·6	26·0	30·9	22·0	31·2	23·1	36·9	29·4	—	—	45·6	36·5		
37·0	25·7	—	—	28·6	21·2	38·0	27·3	—	—	45·0	33·5	49·0	
35·7	24·4	29·0	20·6	27·5	20·4	37·5	27·2	—	—	43·7	32·4		
36·1	22·1	—	—	27·7	19·8	36·0	25·5	—	—	41·7	31·9	48·8	
35·6	22·1	28·9	18·9	28·5	18·2	34·0	22·9	43·6	25·6	39·9	26·8		
32·9	19·8	—	—	27·8	17·5	32·7	22·0	42·2	25·1	36·9	25·6	48·0	
29·8	16·2	23·7	14·9	26·0	16·0	32·7	21·2	39·8	22·8	35·8	24·0		
—	—	—	—	22·7	14·3	31·5	19·7	37·0	21·3	32·1	22·9	—	—
25·9	15·1	22·2	13·9	19·1	14·9	23·0	24·4	30·9	27·0	21·8	21·7	—	—

Ireland: Rates 1871–1881, 1881–1891, 1891–1901, 1901–1911, 1911–1926.
Italy: First rates 1872–1875.
Belgium: Rates 1846, 1856, 1866, 1876, 1880, 1890, 1900, 1910, 1920.
Poland: 1896–1900, 1901–1905, 1906–1910, 1911–1913, 1919–1920.
Hungary: Date of present territory of Hungary.
Russia: Zyromski (1975).

the universal prevalence of these simple relationships (Van de Walle 1969).

One of the facts which seem to contradict the alleged relationships is that fertility most probably rose at the beginning of industrialization, at least in some parts of Europe. Habbakuk (1963 1965a) hypothesizes that the higher rate of population growth was the precondition and driving force of industrialization in western Europe. Mortality declined and the postponement of marriage slackened, and therefore birth rates increased; the subsequent growth of population produced the cheap manpower and greater internal market necessary for industrialization and also rendered less costly in *per capita* terms the infrastructural investments necessary for the development of modern economy.

Other authors (Eversley 1961, Hofstee 1954 1966 1968, Petersen 1960, Deprez 1965, Wrigley 1969) found that fertility increased after the onset of industrialization in parts of England, Flanders (Belgium), Germany and the Netherlands.

Petersen (1960), for example, gives the following description and explanation of the rise of fertility in the first phase of industrialization in the Netherlands. Before industrialization it was a custom in the peasant class that only one of the male children married, the unmarried brothers and the unmarried sisters then living together in the household of the married brother. The function of this custom was that from generation to generation the family farmland remained undivided. Thus the family life and even the sexuality of an important part of the population was sacrificed to that goal. However, this situation caused many frustrations and was highly unstable. When economic conditions enabled new households to be set up, the number of marriages and the level of fertility rose suddenly. Examples of such economic changes in the Netherlands were the extension of land by reclamation in the area of the Zuider Zee, the introduction of fertilizers, and (most of all) rural and urban proletarianization connected with industrialization. It is characteristic that in the middle of the nineteenth century urban fertility was higher than rural fertility in the Netherlands. Rural and urban workers who found employment were released from prior institutional and normative restrictions and saw no effective bar to early marriage or procreation.

Similarly, Wrigley found that in Germany in parts of the Ruhr area the newly industrialized communities had very high fertility levels, higher than the agricultural areas and the older industrial communities. He supposed that the short-term effect of industrialization was everywhere to increase fertility.

Braun (1960) investigated changes in family life in some communities of Switzerland around Zürich in the last decades of the eighteenth century under the impact of the growth of industrial employment. He found a sudden decline in the age of marriage, and in consequence a higher overall fertility. While formerly the peasants had been reluctant to divide their farms between several sons, when the growth of industry offered greater opportunities for work, the traditional obstacles to early marriage, expressed in social norms, were abolished, and farm holdings were divided more readily, since a relatively small farm combined with industrial work provided a basis for livelihood for young couples.

On the other hand, it is indisputable that in the subsequent phases of industrialization fertility began to decline, and this tendency proved to be a secular one. Although the decline of fertility was more or less parallel to the decline of mortality, the correlation of the birth and death rates in the period preceding the First World War was not at all strong, the lags between the onset of the decline of mortality and fertility in different societies being very different. There were even some areas, e.g. in France, where the decline of the birth rate preceded the beginning of the decline of mortality (Van de Walle 1969). Thus the resulting natural increase of population in the period of early industrialization and the average size of families varied widely in the different countries of Europe. Two extreme examples in western Europe are again England and France, other countries (e.g. Sweden) being in intermediate positions. In England and Wales the rate of yearly natural increase from 1841 to the First World War was continually higher than 1 per cent, because the lag between the decline of mortality and fertility was long. On the other hand, in France the rate of natural increase was in the same period generally 0·2–0·3 per cent, since both rates declined almost in parallel, the death rate being somewhat higher and the birth rate much lower than in England. In Sweden the birth rate was lower than in England and higher than in France, the death rate being the lowest of the three countries. Natural increase, however, was higher in England than in Sweden.

The time series concerning this period were much shorter in eastern Europe, because industrialization processes and the keeping of official vital statistics lagged behind those of western Europe. By way of example, two countries will be compared here: Hungary and Russia. The last decades of the nineteenth century were characterized in Hungary by high birth and death rates, resulting in a high rate of natural increase (around 1 per cent). This period, however, seems to have been rather short, because probably in the preceding decades natural increase was lower (the population of 8·5 million in 1784–7 grew to 13·6 million in 1870, i.e. at a lower rate than from 1876 to the First World War) and this period of relatively rapid increase ended with the First World War.

On the other hand, the rate of natural increase in Russia was much higher, because of a higher and, till 1910, almost not declining fertility (Kvasha 1971):

	Birth rate (per 1000)	Death rate
1861–1865	50·7	36·5
1881–1885	50·5	36·4
1896–1900	49·5	32·1
1911–1913	43·9	27·1

Poland seems to have followed the Russian pattern of a very high rate of increase, but with lower birth and death rates.

The comparison of the economic growth rates of these countries suggests an explanation for the varied development of fertility. On the one hand, the rate of economic growth was much higher in England and Wales throughout the nineteenth century than in France (Blacker 1957; Marcz-ewski 1965). For example, in the two last decades of the nineteenth century the growth rates were as follows (Moulin 1972):

	Great Britain	France
Total product	2·9	1·1
Industrial product	3·5	1·7
Agricultural product	0·7	0·2

In consequence, Great Britain had a higher *per capita* income growth rate with a higher rate of population growth than France with its slowly growing population. The decline of the birth rate in England began only after the great depression of 1874 and the following years.

The comparative demographic development of England and Sweden was studied by Friedlander (1969) as a test of the theory of multiphasic response (Davis 1963).

He formulated two model cases. The first is characterized by rapid industrialization and urbanization. Here the main response in urban areas is a reduction of birth rates, and in rural areas it is migration to urban areas and employment in other fields than agriculture. The second model is characterized by a slow rate of industrialization and urbanization. In this case there is no important migration from rural to urban areas and the main response in both areas is a reduction of birth rate; this rate, however, is lower in rural areas than in the urban areas.

The relevant data of the two countries, characterizing their development, and used by Friedlander to test the theory, are as follows:

Year	Per cent (urban)	Birth rate			Per cent migration in following decade as compared to total rural population
		Total	Urban	Rural	
England and Wales					
1800	18·0	38·3	30·6	40·0	6·6
1850	50·0	35·6	29·2	42·0	22·0
1900	74·0	27·6	26·8	30·0	10·9
1920	77·5	18·1	17·8	19·0	3·2
Sweden					
1750	9·4	36·0	33·2	36·3	1·3
1800	9·5	30·8	28·0	31·1	1·5
1850	10·0	33·4	33·2	33·4	2·5
1900	21·5	27·0	27·2	27·0	4·1
1920	29·5	18·1	15·1	19·4	5·0

England fitted into the first model, its urbanization being very rapid in the nineteenth century and its rural birth rate being much higher in that period. On the other hand, Sweden was nearer to the second model, urbanization being slow and urban and rural birth rate being almost equal in the nineteenth century. In consequence of the higher rural birth rate the natural increase of England's population in the nineteenth century was much greater than that of Sweden.

These results coincide with those of the comparison of the development of England and Wales, as well as France – namely, that more rapid industrialization, which provided possibilities of finding employment outside agriculture for the underemployed peasants, was generally associated with higher fertility than that of the cases of slower industrialization.

The economic growth rates of eastern European countries are not so well known. For example, there are different estimates of the growth rate in Hungary from 1867 to 1913 (Berend and Ránki 1972, Berend and Szuhay 1973, Katus 1970). The estimate of 2·4 seems to be the most reasonable (Katus 1970). This is a relatively high rate of economic growth, although somewhat lower than that of Great Britain.

The decline of the birth rate in Hungary also began after economic depression – partly after the general depression in 1886, and partly after the agricultural crisis of the 1890s, which was the consequence of a decreasing market for Hungarian agricultural produce because of American and Russian competition, which resulted among other items in a 17 per cent drop in the price of wheat. The large estates tried to reduce their production costs by introducing agricultural machines. All this, however, impaired the position of the lowest class of Hungarian society, the landless agricultural labourers. In some parts of the country this class responded to the situation by beginning to emigrate to America, and at the same time fertility began to decline.

On the other hand, the 1890s were a period of rapid industrialization in Russia, followed by a crisis at the turn of the century. After 1905 the rate of industrialization again rose. In the years preceding the First World War there was a slight rise in the living standards of the peasantry and the working class in general (Gerschenkron 1966). The combination of very backward social conditions with rapid industrialization and an abundance of free land in the eastern parts, most of all in Siberia, might have contributed to the continued high level of fertility, while the death rate seems to have been comparatively low and steadily declining.

Thus the analysis of fertility trends before the First World War shows, on the one hand, the onset (or continuation) of the secular decline of fertility parallel with the general development and modernization of societies. On the other hand, however, in the short run a high rate of economic growth seems to have contributed to a postponement of the decline of fertility, while a slower rate of economic growth seems to have induced an earlier onset and a sharper decline of fertility. It also seems that periods of economic crises were strong precipitating factors in the initiation of the decline of fertility.

The positive correlation of the short-term economic fluctuations and changes of fertility (lagged by one or two years) was also demonstrated for the second half of the nineteenth century in England by Yule (1906) and for the period from 1870 to 1920 in the United States by Ogburn and Thomas (1922).

The period between the two World Wars in the most developed European countries saw fertility rates so low that they were never again equalled until the 1970s. With the notable exception of Germany and (to a lesser extent) Sweden and the United Kingdom, the birth rates continued to decline until the outbreak of the War (table 4.2). The level of fertility was so low in some countries (e.g. England and Wales, Sweden, Switzerland, Belgium, Austria, Germany, and even Hungary) that the net reproduction rate remained for several years below 1·0. The relatively high (that is higher than the present day) death rates also contributed to these low net reproduction rates, but the fact that even gross reproduction rates fell in some countries below 1·0 – e.g. in Sweden (table 4.3) – shows the extent of the decline of fertility. Although this decline might be interpreted as the consequence of the postponement of parities in the years of the Great Depression for economic reasons, never to be made up because of the ensuing War, the fact that not only yearly fertility rates, but also the cohort rates (table 4.4), were below the level necessary for reproduction seems to indicate that the decline was not simply a temporary phenomenon of timing of parities, but a symptom of deep changes of reproductive behaviour and attitutdes.

This was well known by the demographers and economists of the inter-war period. Spengler (1938) wrote a book with the suggestive title *France Faces Depopulation*. Keynes (1937) and Reddaway (1939) dealt with the consequences of a declining population for the economy. Hansen (1939) even considered that the stagnation of population growth was one of the causes of economic depression, which might lead to secular stagnation in the absence of a higher population growth rate. Population projections often predicted a diminishing population number in coming decades, as, for example, the projection made by Notestein and others (1944) on behalf of the League of Nations on the future population of Europe. The projection of Enid Charles for the population of England, using three alternative hypotheses of fertility – namely, the level of 1933 and the level of 1931 remaining constant and a declining level – predicted the beginning of decline of population number in 1939 and a population number equal to one tenth of the population of the 1930s after 100 years, in the case of the

Table 4.2   Birth rates in selected countries, 1920–1944.

Country	1920–1924	1925–1929	1930–1934	1935–1939	1940–1944
Austria	22·6	18·4	15·1	14·7	19·1
Belgium	21·1	18·9	17·6	15·5	13·8
Bulgaria	39·6	34·2	30·3	24·1	22·1
Czechoslovakia	26·8	22·9	19·7	17·1	20·8
Denmark	22·6	19·8	17·9	17·9	20·3
Finland	25·4	22·8	20·0	20·2	20·1
France	19·9	18·5	17·3	15·1	14·7
Germany	23·1	19·1	16·3	19·4	17·4
Greece	—	29·7	30·0	26·5	—
Hungary	30·2	26·6	23·2	20·1	19·3
Iceland	27·0	25·5	24·3	20·9	23·5
Ireland	20·5	20·3	19·5	19·4	20·9
Italy	30·1	27·2	24·5	23·2	20·7
Luxembourg	20·6	21·1	18·2	15·1	14·8
Netherlands	26·7	23·4	21·7	20·3	21·8
Norway	23·5	18·5	15·7	15·0	17·7
Poland[1]	34·3	32·9	28·9	25·4	—
Portugal	33·0	31·7	29·3	27·1	24·5
Romania	37·6	35·4	32·9	30·0	26·0
Spain	30·0	28·7	27·5	22·0	22·0
Sweden	20·3	16·3	14·4	14·5	17·7
Switzerland	20·0	17·8	16·7	15·4	17·9
UK	21·7	17·6	15·8	15·3	15·9
Yugoslavia	35·3	33·9	33·0	27·9	—
USSR	—	44·4	—	37·6	31·4[2]
USA	22·8	20·1	17·6	17·2	19·9
Canada	28·1	24·5	22·2	20·4	23·2
Australia[3]	24·4	21·6	17·6	17·2	19·5
New Zealand	23·0	20·2	18·1	18·8	22·8
South Africa[3]	27·6	26·1	24·5	24·7	25·6

[1] Prewar territory.
[2] 1940.
[3] White population.

third variant which was considered the most probable by Enid Charles (quoted by Petersen 1954–5).

There were two interpretations of this low level of fertility in the economically most developed countries. According to the first, it was caused by the secular negative correlation of fertility on the one hand, and industrialization, urbanization, higher educational and living standards and general modernization on the other. As Whelpton and Kiser wrote:

> As passing decades brought increasing urbanization, higher standard of living, and more education, birth rates declined much more rapidly than death rates and the previously wide margin of natural increase

Table 4.3 Generation total fertility rates, gross and net reproduction rates in Sweden.

Approximate year of birth	Total fertility rate	Gross reproduction	Net rate	Minimum total fertility necessary for net reproduction rate of 1·0
1850	4·171	2·030	1·326	3·145
1860	3·978	1·935	1·290	3·086
1870	3·722	1·809	1·206	3·086
1880	3·336	1·621	1·128	2·959
1885	3·055	1·484	1·064	2·874
1890	2·689	1·307	0·963	2·793
1895	2·338	1·135	0·859	2·755
1900	2·033	0·987	0·761	2·674
1905	1·821	0·884	0·712	2·558
1910	1·815	0·881	0·733	2·475
1915	1·915	0·929	0·791	2·421
1920	2·032	0·986	0·863	2·353

Note: Data for cohort born in 1920 based partly on projections.
Source: Glass (1968), based on computations of N. Keyfitz.

began to diminish. The stage of this process varies by area, but in most of the countries of northern and western Europe reproduction rates are now well below the requirements for continued population replacement and the existing increases are due only to a currently favourable age distribution. In our own country the present age-specific fertility levels barely meet permanent replacement requirements and the outlook is for cessation of population growth between 1970 and 2000 in the United States. (Whelpton and Kiser 1950, p. 139)

The second interpretation saw the cause of the very low level of fertility in the most developed countries in the extremely low and long depression in the 1930s. The First World War had resulted in a decrease of production in the participating countries (with the exception of the United States) and the prosperity of the postwar years broke down suddenly with the crisis of 1929, which was followed by a depression of a magnitude never before experienced in these capitalist countries. The War and the Great Depression shook the optimistic public opinion which had considered the depressions of the prewar years as temporary and superficial phenomena not endangering the continuous development of the societies based on free enterprise. Not only were the living standards of most parts of these societies lowered for a considerable period, but also the feeling of security disappeared, and an ultimate breakdown of the capitalist order and a

Table 4.4 Cohort total fertility rates for selected countries in Europe.

Period of birth	Denmark	England & Wales	Finland	France	Netherlands
1886–1895	—	—	3154	2065	—
1891–1900	—	—	2836	1980	—
1896–1905	—	—	2575	2145	—
1901–1910	2170	1810	2424	2220	—
1906–1915	2248	1836	2485	2335	2903
1911–1920	2324	1957	2592	2475	2984
1916–1925	2346	2120	2635	2535	2930
1921–1930	2366	2227	2637	2620	2843

Period of birth	Norway	Portugal	Sweden	Switzerland
1886–1895	—	—	2509	—
1891–1900	—	—	2160	—
1896–1905	—	—	1900	—
1901–1910	2058	—	1838	—
1906–1915	2093	3380	1904	—
1911–1920	2176	3098	2000	2162
1916–1925	2213	3034	2049	2229
1921–1930	2300	—	2089	2234

Note: Rates for the cohorts born in 1916–25 based on extrapolation beyond 40–44 years age group; rates for the cohorts born in 1921–30 based on extrapolation beyond 35–39 years age group.
Source: Glass (1968).

secular stagnation were considered as possible future outcomes. According to this interpretation, the social strata whose standard of living was endangered and even worsened in consequence of the depression, and whose feeling of security had disappeared, limited the number of their children in order to maintain as much as possible their standard of living.

Investigations analysing the correlation of fertility rates and business cycles in the United States and in Germany (Akerman 1937, Galbraith and Thomas 1941, Kirk and Nortman 1958, Kirk 1960) also confirm the above mentioned second interpretation, since fertility rates – and also marriage rates – were positively correlated with economic indexes, or more exactly with the deviation from the trend of these indexes.

England, however, does not fit into this pattern completely, since the upturn of the birth rate occurred in 1934 – i.e. in the crisis years. The ultimate number of children of married couples registered at the family census of 1946, and the ultimate family sizes of younger couples projected

Table 4.5 Total fertility rate for selected countries.

Year	England & Wales	France	West Germany	Belgium	Nether-lands	Italy	Portugal	Denmark	Norway	Sweden
1950	2190	2930	2100	2340	3090	2490	—	2580	2520	2310
1951	2140	2790	2060	2280	3050	2340	3170	2500	2470	2220
1952	2150	2760	2090	2330	3080	2290	3210	2540	2580	2240
1953	2210	2690	2080	2330	3030	2250	3060	2600	2640	2260
1954	2220	2700	2130	2370	3030	2320	2980	2540	2670	2180
1955	2220	2670	2130	2380	3030	2310	3160	2580	2760	2260
1956	2370	2660	2230	2400	3050	2300	3040	2590	2830	2280
1957	2460	2680	2330	2450	3080	2300	3170	2560	2830	2270
1958	2520	2680	2320	2500	3100	2280	3170	2530	2860	2240
1959	2550	2740	2400	2570	3170	2350	3160	2490	2880	2230
1960	2680	2370	2730	2560	3110	2370	3150	2540	2850	2170
1961	2760	2810	2460	2620	3200	2410	3190	2550	2890	2210
1962	2830	2780	2440	2590	3170	2430	3210	2540	2890	2250
1963	2870	2880	2520	2680	3190	2480	3080	2640	2910	2330
1964	2900	2900	2550	2710	3170	2620	3140	2600	2960	2470
1965	2830	2840	2510	2610	3040	2540	3030	2610	2930	2410
1966	2740	2790	2530	2520	2900	2490	2970	2620	2890	2370
1967	2630	2660	2490	2420	2790	2440	2890	2350	2800	2280
1968	2550	2580	2390	2310	2750	2400	23780	2120	2750	2080
1969	2450	2530	2210	2240	2750	2400	2700	2000	2700	1940
1970	2380	2470	1990	2230	2570	2310	2440	1950	2510	1940
1971	2360	2470	1910	2210	2380	2320	—	2043	2530	1980
1972	2190	2400	1720	—	2170	2339	—	2029	2390	1910
1973	2030	2290	1570	—	1890	—	—	1917	2240	1870
1974	—	2140	—	—	—	—	—	1897	—	—

Note: Data in Marchal and Rabut (1972) and Blayo and Festy (1975) were expressed per 1 woman; the total fertility rates given in this table are their data multiplied by 1000. Data of the USSR refer always to two years, i.e. 1957–8, 1958–9, etc.

on the basis of the data of the family census, however, demonstrate that the ultimate fertility of marriage cohorts, which declined strongly till the marriage cohort of 1925, continued to decline, but more slowly, until 1930 and then remained more or less stable at the level of 2·1–2·2 children until the years of the war. Thus, the fertility of marriages does not seem to have declined during the economic depression, but it remained at a low level (Glass and Grebenik 1954a).

After the Second World War the pessimistic population projections proved to be wrong. In the most developed western European countries, as well as in the United States and Canada, in Australia and New Zealand and in the white population of South Africa, the trend of fertility changed, with a rise of all fertility measures which was popularly called the 'baby boom'. In the less developed European capitalist countries, where the birth rates had been relatively high before the War (e.g. in Portugal, Spain and Greece), no baby boom occurred. Also the European socialist countries should be considered separately, as their demographic development was

Year	Finland	Hungary	Czecho-slovakia	Poland	East Germany	Romania	Yugo-slavia	USSR	USA	Canada
1950	—	—	3043	3660	—	—	3739	—	3030	3460
1951	3010	—	3286	—	—	—	3271	—	3210	3500
1952	3060	—	2968	—	—	—	3569	—	3310	3640
1953	2960	—	2871	3605	—	—	3396	—	3380	3720
1954	2930	—	2834	3580	2332	—	3371	—	3500	3830
1955	2930	—	2846	3605	2335	—	3172	—	3520	3830
1956	2910	—	2835	3505	2277	3028	3039	—	3630	3860
1957	2880	—	2752	3485	2114	2733	2772	—	3720	3920
1958	2680	—	2572	3355	2220	2589	2781	2822	3650	3880
1959	2750 } 2047		2387	3455	2360	2432	2757	2810	3670	3930
1960	2710 }		2394	2980	2367	2335	2814	2818	3650	3900
1961	2690	1939	2380	2830	2454	2174	2744	2799	3620	3840
1962	2640	1794	2344	2715	2451	2037	2678	2682	3480	3760
1963	2640	1818	2503	2695	2505	2006	2642	2596	3330	3670
1964	2530	1805	2512	2570	2542	1961	2614	2529	3200	3500
1965	2400	1807	2369	2520	2511	1906	2687	2456	2920	3150
1966	2320	1877	2221	2430	2449	1903	2633	2461	2730	2810
1967	2240	2008	2087	2325	2363	3657	2546	2431	2560	2590
1968	2070	2060	2008	2240	2322	3633	2468	2394	2460	2440
1969	1850	2042	2045	2200	2260	3194	2426	2369	—	2390
1970	1720	1962	2065	2200	2215	2886	2267	2389	—	2190
1971	1698	1912	2140	2225	2113	2660	2361	2442	—	2024
1972	1593	1930	2220	2240	1786	2550	2340	—	—	—
1973	—	1950	2380	2260	—	2440	2295	—	—	—
1974	—	2320	2510	—	—	2722	—	—	—	—

Source : Marchal and Rabut (1972), Blayo and Festy (1975), national statistical year books, Urlanis (1974).

rather different from that of the developed capitalist countries after the War.

The rise of fertility was first considered by demographers simply to be the well-known phenomenon of postwar replacement of part of the births which had failed to occur during the War. The high level of fertility, however, proved to be prolonged and demographers soon became aware that the secular trend of declining fertility had changed. This was demonstrated by the birth rates and total fertility rates (table 4.5) calculated from the yearly number of births and the cohort fertility rates (table 4.4) as well, although the latter, as usual, changed less than the period fertility rates. Careful analysis demonstrated also that the rise of fertility in some countries, particularly those that had been spared the devastations of the Second World War (e.g. Sweden, Switzerland and Iceland) but also to a certain extent in the United States, France and Great Britain (where the turning point had been reached in 1934), began to turn during the prewar and war years; thus the first signs of a change of the tendency to decline were appearing before the end of the Second World War. In some German occuped countries also fertility rose during the War. The development of German fertility was peculiar because although it had already begun to increase in the 1930s, it declined again during the War, due probably to the absence of young men in the army, and also to the hardships of the later war years.

The baby boom can be explained partly in terms of demographic factors – namely, the lowering of the average age at first marriage, the lower percentage of women remaining unmarried till the end of the reproductive life span, the concentration of parities to the younger ages and in consequence to the first years of marriage (Glass 1968). Nevertheless, the marriage-duration-specific fertility rates and the cohort fertility rates also increased in the marriages contracted after the War, so that in addition to the demographic factors, which themselves require an economic and social explanation, the social causes of the rise of fertility need to be investigated.

The simplest explanation in economic terms hypothesizes that, after having reached a certain level of socioeconomic development or of *per capita* personal income, the negative correlation of fertility and income turns into a positive one (e.g. Smolinski 1965). Although the basic positive relationship of fertility to the standard of living is hinted at by many research results in demography and by several demographers, it seems that a more elaborate interpretation of the baby boom seems necessary.

The baby boom can be interpreted, as can be the low fertility of the interwar period, in terms of economic cycles of prosperity and depression. The postwar years were much more prosperous than the interwar years and the higher level of fertility was considered a consequence of prosperity, and of the higher rate of economic growth.

The most developed theoretical explanation of the baby boom was given by Easterlin (1961 1966 1968). Analysing time series of the rates of change of production, national product, new construction, wage rates, hours of work per week, immigration, number of non-farm households, unemployment, fertility, etc., he formulated a general model of economic demographic interactions, i.e. not merely a theory of the economic and social factors influencing fertility.

The basic concept of his model is the so-called Kuznets cycle – that is, Easterlin states that between the several decades long Kondratieff cycle analysed by Schumpeter and the seven to ten years long business cycles there are intermediate cycles of fifteen to twenty years long. The existence of this type of cycle was observed by Isard (1942), Abramowitz (1961) and others, but it was Kuznets who investigated them most thoroughly (1930 1956 1958).

The Kuznets cycles are characterized by interactions of economic and demographic phenomena. A Kuznets cycle begins when for some reason the growth rate of non-agricultural output increases, followed (through the accelerator effect) by an increase of investments. The rise of investments (through the multiplier effect) results in an increase of aggregate demand, which again raises production, and also the wage level. At the same time unemployment diminishes. Soon a certain shortage of manpower appears in the places, i.e. mostly in the towns, where industrial and construction activity became intensified. The shortage of manpower, as well as the more favourable conditions on the labour market, elicit demographic responses. On the one hand, immigration is intensified, partly from agricultural areas and villages and partly from foreign countries. On the other hand, the participation of women, as well as of young and old people, in economic activity increases. At last the number of households increases, partly in consequence of immigration, but partly also in consequence of the rise of the number of marriages. Marriages which were postponed in the depressed years are now contracted, and people marry at younger ages, because the higher wages and employment rates allow the formation of new households. The newly formed households buy furniture, etc., and demand dwellings, which again gives rise to a higher aggregate demand for industrial products and building activity. The ensuing higher demand for municipal investment enhances and sustains the expansion. Thus the cumulative appearance of longer-term spending commitments constitutes the essence of the Kuznets cycle.

It is not quite clear whether there is an inherent automatic mechanism in the Kuznets cycles which causes a downturn after a period of Kuznets type prosperity. It might be supposed that the rise of wages and costs is the cause of this change from prosperity to Kuznets depression. On the other hand, a longer Kuznets depression might more or less automatically bring the beginning of a new upward swing, as marriages and the formation of new households are not postponed indefinitely, and a new wave of household formation initiates a new cycle. However, exogenous factors (e.g. the end of a war) may enhance the upswing, as after the war the postponed marriages are contracted, causing a great increase of their number.

According to Easterlin, the character of Kuznets cycles may change over time. The three main elements of the cycle – population, labour force, and number of households – are determined by the following factors:

Population
1   Mortality rate
2   Net immigration rate
3   Fertility rate

Labour force
1   Mortality and ageing
2   Net immigration rate

3   Labour force participation rates of women, as well as of old and young people

Households
1   Mortality and ageing
2   Net immigration rate
3   Household headship rates – i.e. the proportion of extended and multiple family households

The factors numbered 1 are largely exogenous in the given Kuznets cycle, but the factors numbered 2 and 3 are interdependent and to a certain extent are alternatives of each other. As a response to the increased demand for manpower the labour force might increase either as a consequence of immigration, or because of increased participation by women and by young and old people in the labour force. The number of households may increase either by immigration or by an increase of the household headship rate. And – what is most interesting from the point of view of this book – population might respond to the higher manpower demands and higher wages by immigration or by a higher fertility rate, i.e. a higher natural increase of the population residing in the area where the increased manpower demands arise. The mechanism of this last response is as follows: when immigration is restricted for some reason, either because of legal measures, or because the population of potential immigrants is small (e.g. in the case of a very low proportion of rural population), then wages increase to a higher level because of the shortage of manpower, young men and women easily get jobs, and in consequence they marry earlier and form many new households with consequently higher demands for houses, household equipment, etc., which in turn sustains prosperity for a longer period. The relatively better-off young couples are also inclined to plan larger families and consequently to have a higher fertility.

The economic and demographic development in the United States in the postwar years followed, according to Easterlin, the model described. Immigration from foreign countries was restricted for several reasons, and the manpower reservoir of rural population became almost exhausted. At the same time the population number of cohorts entering the labour market was relatively low because of the low fertility of the interwar years, and the quality of education and skills of these new entrants was high because of the rise of education level of these cohorts. Therefore with demand for manpower being high, and the supply being relatively low, they were in a very advantageous position on the labour market and achieved high wages and high participation rates. The relative wages of young people as compared to those of the older ones were never so high as in these postwar years. These factors contributed to earlier marriage, and with the addition of marriages that had been postponed during the War, there was a boom of marriage and new household formation, as well as a boom of fertility. Not only a higher number of births occurred because of the higher number of marriages, but also (because of the advantageous economic position of newly married couples) the number of children per family of these postwar marriage cohorts increased.

Other demographers (e.g. Livi-Bacci 1960 1961, Benjamin 1959) similarly stressed the important contribution of improved economic conditions and security to the baby boom. Several regression and correlation analyses of the factors of fertility performed on time series confirmed this interpretation. Kiser, Grabill and Campbell (1968) analysed data from 1917 to 1957 of the United States. Fertility was measured by birth probabilities differentiated by age and parity and three indicators to economic conditions were used: unemployment, personal disposable income in constant dollars, and industrial production. The variables were the deviations from five-year moving averages, i.e. the trends were eliminated. The calculations of correlation were performed separately for three periods: 1917–30, 1931–41 and 1947–57. The correlations found were mostly as expected – i.e. fertility rates were correlated negatively with unemployment and positively with industrial production, and most of all with income. It is notable that the correlations were stronger in the case of higher-order birth parities, which demonstrates that these births were not unplanned ones.

Gregory, Campbell and Cheng recently (1972b) investigated, by means of the model consisting of four simultaneous equations, the factors influencing the time series of birth rate in the United States from 1910 to 1968. The variables in the equations were: (1) birth rate, (2) labour force participation rate of women, (3) permanent income (taking into consideration in addition to current income also the future expectations of income), and (4) infant mortality. They found that income and birth rate were postively related, i.e. in the years when the income level of population was higher, *ceteris paribus* fertility was higher; however, the rise of education, the increase in female participation in the labour force, and the decline of infant mortality, all correlated to the rise of income, were negatively correlated to fertility. Thus the positive association of fertility and income seems to be confirmed, with the addition that the rise of income is accompanied by secular changes favouring a lower fertility.

Silver (1965–6) analysed the demographic and economic development of the United Kingdom and of Japan. As in the United States (Silver 1965), he found that the correlation of national income growth and the birth rate with one-year lag was positive and the responsiveness of the birth rate became stronger in the twentieth century than it was in the second half of the nineteenth century. Thus economic prosperity and depression periods were correlated to changes of fertility, and this relation seems to become stronger in England, as hypothesized by Easterlin for the United States.

Wilkinson (1967 1973) investigated by similar means the relations of economic and demographic development in Sweden based on data from 1870 to 1965. The dependent variable in his analyses was the birth rate, the independent variables were the real income of men and the potential income of husbands and wives separately, as well as the cost of children, infant mortality and emigration. Three periods were considered separately – 1870–1910, 1910–40 and 1940–65 – in order to ascertain the existence of structural changes in the factors influencing fertility. The earnings of husbands proved to be in positive correlation with fertility in all three periods, confirming the results found in other countries. The elasticity of fertility to the changes of husband's earnings increased from the first to the third period, suggesting the influence becoming stronger. The potential earnings of wives showed a significant correlation with fertility only in the second and third periods. Wilkinson distinguishes two effects of the earnings of wives: a substitution effect expressing the fact that with a larger number of children a wife can participate less easily in occupations outside the home, and an income effect – i.e. the higher the family income in consequence of the earning of the wife, the greater *ceteris paribus* is the size of the family. The income effect outweighed the substitution effect in the second period, so that the gross effect of the wife's earnings was positive. In the third period, however, the substitution effects became stronger, and so the gross effect was negative.

Cost of children showed a very small negative effect on fertility. Infant mortality exhibited the expected positive relationship to fertility, which was strongest in the first period. On the other hand, emigration showed a moderately negative influence only in the first period. The importance of emigration practically ceased in Sweden after the First World War, in consequence of restrictive legislation in the United States. It seems that while before the First World War the response of population to economic depression was a higher rate of emigration, after that it became a decline of fertility (Wilkisnon 1967). Long swings seem to be demonstrated also in Sweden, with important structural changes occurring in the causative mechanism of fertility. Thus all similar researches done in other countries seem to confirm the findings of Easterlin on the United States.

In some countries where birth rate fell to a particularly low level, measures of population policy were introduced intended to raise fertility. Some demographers in these countries tended to stress the influence of these measures on the increase of fertility during the baby boom period. Actually in two countries introducing such measures (although very different from each other) – namely, in Germany and Sweden – fertility had already begun to rise in the interwar years. In the case of Germany, however, it is difficult to distinguish the effect of the reduction of unemployment and of the population policy. Fertility declined again in the years of the War, obviously in consequence of the absence of young men in the army and due to the hardships of War for the civil population. On the other hand, in Sweden the rise of fertility to a level which was considered desirable (see Myrdal and Myrdal 1934) proved to be permanent.

The most interesting case, however, seems to be that of France. The *Code Familial* was enacted immediately before the War, introducing high family allowances and other monetary assistance for families with children. The rise of fertility began in 1942 and, since it was displayed by all measures of fertility, even by the refined parity progression ratios (table 4.6), it could not be an artefact. This rise of fertility is the more surprising, since it occured in a period when half of France was under German occupation, the standard of living was very low, there were all kinds of shortages, and the whole situation was characterized by insecurity and uncertainty. As the only factors favourable to higher fertility in these years seem to be the measures of population policy, it seems reasonable to attribute the increase of fertility, which brought a fundamental change to the secular tendency of low fertility in France, to these measures of population policy. After the War the fertility of the French population rose further and remained at a relatively high level until the 1960s, and even when the general decline of fertility occurred in western Europe in the second half of the 1960s, fertility in France decreased less than in other

Table 4.6   Parity progression ratios of married women in France.

| Year | Probability of having another birth of married women having already had the following parities | | | | | | |
	0	1	2	3	4	5	6
1929	703	685	572	581	604	625	630
1930	726	708	593	601	609	651	648
1931	718	687	590	594	611	646	641
1932	715	683	582	586	612	643	661
1933	687	652	558	544	573	612	628
1934	701	661	569	568	584	619	624
1935	695	641	552	545	563	592	607
1936	698	656	564	557	580	615	620
1937	706	652	572	565	584	618	629
1938	715	669	585	569	585	606	627
1939	731	677	598	581	605	621	630
1940	634	583	568	636	666	702	690
1941	665	593	552	561	606	628	639
1942	808	702	618	569	609	628	650
1943	812	768	652	606	628	626	671

Table 4.6—contd.

	Probability of having another birth of married women having already had the following parities						
Year	*0*	*1*	*2*	*3*	*4*	*5*	*6*
1944	806	806	688	645	637	645	681
1945	823	807	672	619	621	626	648
1946	836	1082	812	675	622	616	629
1947	794	902	745	640	620	619	630
1948 (I)	755	842	688	626	622	614	645
1948 (II)	810	768	675	613	607	604	638
1949	803	771	699	617	615	605	608
1950	799	755	699	630	618	611	618
1951	770	721	662	630	609	617	606
1952	778	733	652	620	629	625	621
1953	779	736	634	594	614	616	627
1954 (I)	792	753	643	595	616	640	640
1954 (II)	804	751	637	586	613	636	638
1955	810	748	632	580	607	633	647
1956	853	759	628	562	570	587	596
1957	869	785	646	576	577	581	604
1958	881	754	631	573	572	582	612
1959 (I)	904	765	629	576	578	599	626
1959 (II)	904	772	630	578	579	601	628
1960	904	741	613	559	558	582	612
1961	921	754	625	574	572	594	627
1962	913	735	609	556	556	572	591
1963	952	751	623	561	568	580	607
1964	934	756	625	559	564	581	607
1965	922	741	596	534	536	558	577
1966	919	742	583	521	533	543	572
1967	913	722	557	492	501	518	536
1968	916	720	544	475	476	494	521
1969	927	722	542	459	458	485	500
1970	932	714	525	444	453	471	495
1971	952	729	524	450	448	487	500
1972	946	709	487	415	423	450	479
1973	919	680	452	386	389	428	447

Notes: 1929–1948 (I): calculated on the basis of children ever born of women.
1948 (II)–1954 (I): calculated on the basis of children born in present marriage.
1954 (II)–1959 (I): calculated on the basis of children born in present marriage and living at present.
In 1959 change of method of calculation; in 1962 change of registration of data.
Source: 1929–1948: Pressat (1961).
1948–1963: Nizard and Pressat (1965).
1964–1970: Blayo (1972).
1971–1973: Biraben (1975a).

neighbouring countries – which again might be attributed to the existing measures of population policy.

Some doubts might arise, however, in connection with the effect of population policy in France. On the one hand, after the War fertility increased in all highly developed capitalist countries, whether they introduced a pro-natalist population or not, though the rise of fertility in France was somewhat more important and ensued after a long period of very low fertility. Also France was not exceptional for a rise in fertility during the War, since it also increased in some other German-occuped countries, e.g. in Denmark, Czechoslovakia and Austria. On the other hand, data on differential fertility show that the rise of fertility, experienced in all social strata, was not highest in those strata where the financial assistance provided by family allowances and other measures was most important – i.e. not in the middle class, but among the professionals (Febvay 1959).

Beginning in the mid-1960s a rapid decline in fertility began in all the advanced capitalist countries, in western Europe, North America, Australia and New Zealand (table 4.7) – i.e. in all the societies which had

Table 4.7 Recent changes of the birth rate in selected developed countries.

Country	1972	1973	1974	1975
United Kingdom	14·9	13·9	13·3	12·5
France	16·9	16·4	15·2	14·0
West Germany	11·3	10·2	10·1	9·7
Belgium	14·0	13·3	12·8	12·2
Netherlands	16·1	14·5	13·7	13·0
Italy	16·3	16·0	15·7	15·1
Portugal	20·3	20·1	20·0	20·3
Denmark	15·1	14·3	14·2	14·3
Norway	16·3	15·5	15·0	14·0
Sweden	13·8	13·5	13·4	12·6
Finland	12·7	12·2	13·3	14·2
Hungary	14·7	15·0	17·8	18·4
Czechoslovakia	17·3	18·8	19·8	19·6
Poland	17·4	17·9	18·4	19·0
East Germany	11·8	10·6	10·5	10·7
Romania	18·8	18·2	20·3	—
Yugoslavia	18·2	18·0	17·9	—
Bulgaria	15·3	16·3	17·2	—
USSR	17·8	17·6	18·0	—
USA	15·7	15·0	15·0	14·8
Canada	15·9	15·5	15·5	15·8
Australia	20·4	18·8	18·3	—
New Zealand	21·8	20·5	—	—

Source: Biraben (1975a 1975b 1976).

experienced the baby boom after the Second World War. This decline has not found an incontestable scientific explanation until now.

Some demographers consider that the decline might be a more or less temporary phenomenon (Blake 1974), while others believe that a basic change of tendency has occurred since the end of the baby boom (Bumpass 1975).

It was suggested that the decline might be simply the consequence of the diminishing number of unwanted births due to the spread of modern efficient birth control techniques, particularly the contraceptive pill (Westoff 1975).

Some authors (Campbell 1974) stressed the purely demographic factors contributing to the decline of the birth rates – namely, the continuing decline of the fertility of older age groups of women in consequence of the concentration of parities to younger ages, coupled to earlier marriage. The age at marriage, however, has stopped decreasing in the last few years, and because of that this source of the increase of the number of births, which was an important one in the baby boom, did not operate any more, while the opposite source of decline of the number of births – namely, the concentration of parities to younger ages – continued to operate. The Commission on Population Growth and the American Future considered that part of the decline might be caused by the gradually rising age at childbearing, which might be a temporary phenomenon or a permanent new tendency.

However, the same Commission considered that there is also a permanent factor of the decline of annual fertility rates – namely, that today's young people expect to have far fewer children than people a few years their senior in the United States. According to a survey in 1971, married women aged 18–24 expect to have an average of 2·4 children.

Easterlin (1968) suggested an explanation of the decline of fertility in terms of his explanation of the baby boom – i.e. in terms of a declining phase of the Kuznets cycle. In 1966 he predicted that the large cohorts born during the baby boom found a much less advantageous situation at the labour market than their parents after the War, simply in consequence of their greater number. Also the advantage of young over old cohorts in education has declined sharply. The relatively worse income and employment situation of the younger generation in the 1960s, essentially an echo effect of the baby boom, thus resulted in lower fertility. According to this interpretation, the United States and the most developed western European countries might be from the middle of the 1960s in the declining phase of a Kuznets cycle. It might also be conjectured that in general the development of these advanced capitalist countries became less self-evident, economic expectations became more uncertain, and in general the feeling of security declined in consequence of the higher rate of inflation;

thus it was this insecurity that tended to influence couples in the direction of greater caution when planning their fertility.

There are several problems concerning this kind of explanation. Most of all, the extent of decline of fertility does not seem to be clearly correlated to the changes of income level, or to the rates of inflation and of unemployment. For example, west Germany, where the economic hardships seemed to have been the least severe, experienced the lowest birth rate in the 1970s, and in consequence a natural decrease in population.

At the same time social atmosphere concerning the questions of fertility seemed to change. Anti-populationist opinions became louder and louder, voiced by very different groups in these societies, e.g. politicians (Draper 1969), some demographers (Freyka 1973), social and political comnittees (Commission on Population Growth and the American Future 1972), technocrats preoccupied with pollution (Meadows et al. 1972), the women's liberation movement, etc. Their propaganda might have influenced couples planning their fertility. It seems to be characteristic that the inconsistencies of the 'zero population growth for the year 2000' slogan were demonstrated and criticized most strongly just by demographers (Bourgeois-Pichat and Taleb 1970) in France where the decline of fertility was less pronounced than in other western European countries (although others, e.g. Ansley Coale, were also rather cautious in the evaluation of the desirability and feasibility of zero growth of population). It is, however, rather questionable whether these scientific, social and political movements had any important impact on the actual fertility behaviour of families.

Thus although the real meaning of the downturn of fertility since the mid-1960s in the advanced capitalist countries is not yet clear, it does raise new doubts on traditional simple explanations for the factors determining fertility.

The development of fertility in eastern European socialist countries after the War provides similarly interesting insights into the causative mechanism of fertility. First of all, fertility in these countries developed quite differently from that in the most developed capitalist countries of western Europe and America. Second, fertility followed very different paths in each of these geographically more or less adjacent countries, which had in addition similar social and economic institutions. After a short period of postwar rise of fertility which might be attributed to the effect of the postponement of births during the preceding War years, fertility began to decline in Hungary, Czechoslovakia, Bulgaria and Romania, and remained at a very low level, not even assuring simple reproduction of populations until the second half of the 1960s, when it rose again moderately. Romania is an exception here, with a very sharp increase and then a decline of fertility in recent years. On the other hand, in the Soviet

Union, in Poland and in the greater part of Yugoslavia fertility remained at very high levels for a long period after the War. At the beginning of the 1960s it seemed that these socialist countries were following quite different paths of development of fertility. However, in this decade the fertility of those countries with a high level of fertility declined sharply, while the fertility of those with low fertility increased, so that the fertility rates of the socialist countries became rather similar around 1970 (table 4.8). These countries will now be examined individually, in order to find the factors which might have contributed to this development.

Table 4.8   Gross reproduction rates in selected east European countries.

Year	Hungary	Czecho-slovakia	Poland	East Germany	Romania	Bulgaria	Yugo-slavia	USSR
1950	—	1·468	1·790	—	—		2·023	—
1951	—	1·463	1·806	—	—		2·049	—
1952	1·200	1·434	1·765	1·158	—	1·24	2·075	—
1953	1·330	1·390	1·751	1·143	—		1·633	—
1954	1·429	1·373	1·732	1·136	—		1·630	—
1955	1·354	1·379	1·742	1·132	1·49	1·17	1·531	—
1956	1·258	1·379	1·695	1·10	1·42	1·125	1·460	—
1957	1·102	1·329	1·687	1·02	1·34		1·340	1·38
1958	1·045	1·250	1·621	1·07	1·27	1·09	1·338	
1959	1·005	1·157	1·544	1·14	1·19	1·09	1·314	1·37
1960	0·975	1·159	1·438	1·16	1·15	1·123	1·36	1·37
1961	0·938	1·158	1·364	—	—	1·103	1·33	
1962	0·868	1·140	1·305	—	—	1·082	1·30	—
1963	0·880	1·217	1·302	1·197	0·978	1·072	1·293	1·227
1964	0·872	1·220	1·242	1·218		1·057	1·281	1·196
1965	0·875	1·151	1·217	1·198	0·924	1·004	1·315	1·195
1966	0·907	1·082	1·174	1·177	0·919	0·969	1·283	1·187
1967	0·970	1·017	1·127	1·135	1·780	0·975	1·256	1·171
1968	0·997	0·997	1·084	—	1·769	1·110	—	
1969	0·984	0·993	1·065	—	1·552	—	—	—
1970	0·953	1·011	1·064	—	1·402	—	—	—
1971	0·931	1·035	1·094	—	—	—	—	—
1972	0·931	1·078	1·082	—	—	—	—	—
1973	0·943	1·159	1·094	—	—	—	—	
1974	1·117	—	—	—	—	—	—	1·158

Source: Demographic Yearbook of the United Nations (1965 1969), national yearbooks, and Teitelbaum (1972).

In the Soviet Union the level of fertility was relatively high after the Second World War, continuing a trend that had prevailed before the War. However, fertility began to decline after 1960 and in the 1970s reached a level not much above the level necessary for simple reproduction. Fertility differentials between large towns, smaller towns and villages, as well as between different regions of the Soviet Union, are very important. According to Soviet demographers (Vostrikova 1962 1964, Urlanis 1963 1974, Katkova 1971, Arutyunyan 1975), the following factors contributed to the decline of fertility:

1   The rise of education, in consequence of which the level of information on methods of birth control rose, and also the demand for a higher standard of living was increased.
2   The rise of economic activity of women.
3   The housing situation of the population (those living in small dwellings and sharing a dwelling with another family having lower fertility).
4   Urbanization, the fertility of urban populations being lower.

Urlanis considered that growth of *per capita* income would have increased fertility, *ceteris paribus*; the other factors associated with economic development, however (as e.g. urbanization, the growing economic activity of women), overshadowed this positive effect and in consequence fertility declined parallel with economic development. Recently higher family allowances for families below a certain income level were introduced. Nevertheless, the relatively low level of fertility, most of all in the European parts of the Soviet Union, seems to be a serious preoccupation for Soviet demographers (Perevedentzev 1975a 1975b).

The history of fertility in Poland after the War raises fascinating questions. Its course was similar to that of the fertility of the Soviet Union, with firstly ten to fifteen years of relatively high fertility, then a sharp decline. The level reached after the War, however, was even higher than the level in these years in the Soviet Union, resulting in a very high rate of growth of population, partly replacing the losses caused by the War, which were proportionately the highest in Europe (6 million people died from a population of nearly 30 million). A slight decline in fertility began after 1951, although it remained at a very high level until 1959. Fertility during the 1950s in Poland was exceptional for Europe. From 1960, however, a rather sharp and continuous decline followed, so that in the second half of the 1960s the fertility of the Polish population was more or less similar to that of other western and eastern European countries. Since then the level of fertility has stabilized more or less at the level necessary for simple reproduction of the population.

Smolinski (1971) explained these two different periods of demographic development in terms of the economic situation and the socio-psychological expectations and needs of the population. During the War sheer survival was the central problem of the population, decimated by mass executions, deportation, extermination in concentration camps, and casualties of armed struggle and famine. The end of the War brought a fundamental change, as the satisfaction of basic necessities of life became assured. Basic needs, however, could not be satisfied at a higher level than that determined by the state authorities through the system of rationing, and very few goods of high quality (e.g. better dwellings, personal cars, other consumer durables – for some time even radio sets and wrist-watches) were available on the market. So that although on the one hand the population had assured incomes (unemployment disappeared) and basic needs were satisfied on a much higher level than in the preceding years, on the other hand no higher quality needs could develop, as their satisfaction was impossible. In that situation the cost of education of a larger number of children was not felt as a heavy burden, partly because the state provided family allowances and other social benefits to families with children.

However, around 1960 a new generation entered into the age groups which contribute mostly to fertility. This generation did not remember the War years and had also received a much higher education after the War, in consequence of the deliberate policy of the socialist government to enhance the level of education and culture. This generation had much higher expectations for material and non-material goods. Also, after 1956, the mass production of goods satisfying higher level needs began in Poland, so that the new needs could be satisfied, although by strenuous effort. In that new situation a higher number of children in the family was a real hindrance for attaining the new goals and aspirations, so that the young couples began to limit their offspring.

Yugoslavia is the third European country having a socialist economic and social system where fertility was very high after the War. This can be explained partly by the overall backwardness of the country, partly by the need for compensation following the War, which caused very high human losses. Unlike Poland, the fertility level in Yugoslavia began to decline very soon, and continued to decline until 1969, when it was more or less stabilized. Regional differences are very high: in the most developed parts of the country (Slovenia, Croatia, Serbia proper and Voivodina) fertility is rather low, the total fertility rate being around 2000; in the medium-developed parts (Bosnia and Hercegovina, Montenegro, Macedonia) this rate is between 2400 and 3000, while in the least developed Kosovo it still was higher than 5000 in 1970. Yugoslavian demographers (Breznik 1967 1969, Breznik et al. 1972 1974, Anicic 1971, Macura 1966, Rasevic 1971) consider that this decline of fertility can be explained by the theory of demographic transition, i.e. by rapid industrialization, urbanization, the growth of education, intensive migration and social mobility, the decline of infant and child mortality – in summary, by the general modernization of Yugoslavian society. The most developed parts of the country have already been through this transition and are supposed to enter a period of 'mature demographic development', while in the most backward Kosovo the transition has just begun. Differential fertility rates by education, etc., seem to support this view, as all indicators of modernization are negatively correlated with the fertility of families. The only phenomenon that apparently does not fit completely into this explanation is the constantly higher fertility of the most developed Slovenia as compared with the other somewhat less developed Croatia, Voivodina and Serbia proper.

Although situated geographically near to the regions of Yugoslavia having the highest fertility levels, Bulgaria already had a relatively low birth rate after the War, which declined till the mid 1960s, reaching a level of 14·9–15·0 (Kassabov 1974). At that time a population policy was introduced (family allowances and limited legal abortion), resulting in a somewhat higher birth rate, assuring more or less the simple reproduction of the population.

In Czechoslovakia (Srb *et al.* 1964) the development of fertility was similar, only the lowest point had already been reached in the first half of the 1960s, followed by the introduction of measures giving monetary help and other social benefits to families with children. Fertility rose slightly and oscillated around a gross reproduction coefficient of 1·0. Each successive population policy measure seems to have resulted in a slight increase of fertility, which after some years was to decrease again slightly. A special feature of Czechoslovakian fertility is the important difference between the fertility of Bohemia and Slovakia, that of the latter being higher (Vavra 1962 1964).

The demographic development of the East German Democratic Republic differed from that of the other socialist countries in one respect – the birth rate was already rather low in the postwar years, partly because of the disadvantageous age and sex composition of the population. The age-specific fertility rates, however, remained fairly stable and until 1970 the gross reproduction rate did not fall below 1·0. There seems to have been a decline since the early 1970s.

Among the socialist countries in eastern Europe which were characterized by low fertility in the first half of the 1960s the demographic history of Romania is somewhat different from that of the others (Ferenbac 1962 1971). After the War fertility declined rapidly. This was interpreted by Romanian demographers to be a consequence of rapid industrialization, urbanization and the collectivization of agriculture. The influence of collectivization seems to be proved by the fact that the decline was greater in the villages than in the towns, although a certain urban–rural difference exists also today. The lowest point of the birth rate was reached in 1966 at 14·3 per 1000. After 1 November 1966 population policy was completely changed; abortion which had been practically free was prohibited, except after having had four children, or after the age of 45, or in some other special cases. After nine months the birth rate rose until it reached 38·7 per 1000 in July 1968; it remained at that high level for three months and then began to decline. By 1972 it was under 20 per 1000 (David and Wright 1972, Teitelbaum 1972). The experiences of these recent years seem to prove that the prohibition of abortion only temporarily influences fertility, which is determined rather by economic and social processes, such as industrialization, urbanization, etc. Among the east European socialist countries, whose fertility was analysed and compared by Berent (1970), Hungary had the lowest birth rate in 1962, at 12·9 per 1000. Nevertheless, this country's demographic development bears a strong resemblance to that of Czechoslovakia and Bulgaria, so that its more detailed treatment here is justified only by the fact that the author of this book is obviously most familiar with the Hungarian facts. It might be considered, however, that the same conclusions could be drawn as from the development of fertility of these two other socialist countries. In Hungary fertility increased after the War. This might be interpreted as compensation for the lower fertility of the War years. This rise, however, was not as high as in other countries, and was relatively short lived. A decline had already appeared in 1951, followed by a more important decline in 1952. Then after the government introduced severe measures against illegal abortions, there was a rather slight and short rise in 1953 and 1954, the birth rate reaching a peak in this latter year at 23·0 per 1000. In 1955 and 1956 abortions were gradually legalized and at last became practically free, depending only on the wish of the woman concerned. Parallel with these measures the birth rate began to decline. However, it would be erroneous to attribute this decline to the liberalization of abortions, because the decline of fertility had already begun before the introduction of the new measures, most of all in Budapest, where the level of fertility declined in 1954 – i.e. in a period when clandestine abortions were severely punished. On the other hand, in the second half of the 1950s the economic and social conditions in Hungary underwent deep changes. Industrialization of the hitherto rather agricultural country proceeded quickly, agriculture was socialized (complete collectivization was achieved in 1962), and there was an intensive migration to the towns, especially to Budapest, causing housing shortages. Social mobility from the peasant stratum to that of the worker, and from the manual stratum to non-manual occupations was very intensive. The educational level of the population rose considerably after the introduction of compulsory eight-year elementary education. The level of personal incomes also rose at a high rate, although the needs of the population seem to have risen more rapidly. This might have been caused by the fact that the rise in the standard of living occurred to a great extent through the process of social mobility, in which people moved from lower strata to higher ones, having a higher income level, while the rise in living standard of each stratum was slower. Mobile families, however, soon adapted themselves to the needs and aspirations of their new stratum and tried to keep up with its standard of living. As in Poland, in the second half of the 1950s the possibilities of higher level consumption became available here too; it was possible to buy a car, to build a new home or a weekend house, and to travel in foreign countries. The acquisition of these desirable consumption items naturally depended on the income level of the family, which was in turn very much influenced by the number of children. The household income surveys carried out in Hungary show that the *per capita* income level of families is more strongly influenced by their number of children than by the wages of the economically active members of the family (Frigyes 1964).

The decline of the birth rate continued until 1962 and reached a low level (12·9 per 1000) in that year, never experienced before in Europe. The more refined measures of fertility show even more clearly the extent of the decline (tables 4.5 and 4.8), as the age structure of the population at that time was relatively favourable for fertility, and in addition the marriage rate had increased, the average age at first marriage becoming lower. Some demographers supposed that the decline was merely an 'echo' of the higher fertility in the years of severe prohibition on abortion, since during that period births planned for a later period might have been advanced, because of the impossibility of obtaining an abortion. Soon, however, it was found that the decline of fertility was a lasting phenomenon, firstly when surveys of family planning showed a continuously declining average number of planned family size and an increase in family planning and birth control (Acsádi, Klinger and Szabady 1970, Szabady 1968). The average of two children per family planned in 1966 seems to coincide with the total fertility rate of somewhat less than 2000 in the 1960s.

The low level of fertility caused concern, both in public opinion and among demographers. The government considered it necessary to introduce measures of population policy helping by monetary and non-monetary means families having two or more children. These measures had a double aim: on the one hand to induce a higher fertility, and on the other to lessen income inequalities caused by different numbers of earners and dependants in families. First in 1965 and in 1966, then subsequently in 1968, 1972 and 1974, family allowances were increased. A second important measure was the introduction of the so-called child care allowance – i.e. granting an employed woman a leave of absence for child bearing with an allowance equivalent to one third or a half of the average wage of employed women, until her child reaches its third birthday. Fertility increased parallel with the introduction of these measures, although it did not reach the level considered desirable, as the net reproduction coefficient remained somewhat below 1·0.

This rise of fertility might be attributed to several factors. The first might have been the introduction of the above mentioned measures – i.e. their direct effect on the cost of having children. The second seems to be a change in public opinion preceding and following the introduction of these measures. It is notable that the rise of fertility almost preceded the introduction of these measures – for example, the most important rise followed almost immediately after the introduction of the child care allowance, not eight or nine months later, as might have been expected. The reason was probably that the public already knew about the planned introduction of these measures from the media. As these media generally stressed the value to Hungarian society of children and the need for a higher fertility, a social atmosphere favourable for a higher fertility was created. This atmosphere was then strengthened by the introduction of the monetary measures, which very practically expressed the valuation of children by society. The change in atmosphere is well characterized by the fact that the popular political cabaret in Budapest had a programme running for several months with the title 'A Baby or a Car?', emphasizing the value of families with several children.

When investigating the causes of the increase in fertility, the fact should be stressed that never in the history of Hungary was economic development so rapid and constant. This surely contributed to a social feeling that a similar economic growth might also be expected in the future – i.e. the possibility of buying a car or the chance to travel were not temporary exceptional situations, but would be continuously available in future, so the birth of a child could not mean the loss of these possibilities for ever.

It can also be mentioned that in the second half of the 1960s cohorts entered the reproductive age groups, whose members had not experienced the shocks and uncertainties of the War and of the postwar years, but had grown up in a situation of stable and continuous development.

In 1974 the system of availability of abortion was somewhat restricted. Married women with less than two children were in principle not permitted to have abortions, except those with no separate dwelling, those living apart from their husbands, etc.; married women having two children were able to get permission for abortion if their social conditions justified it; married women with three children and unmarried women had the right to free abortion, as previously. The aim of these measures was not the increase of natality, but the reduction of the very high number of abortions. Therefore, at the same time as the new legislation on abortion, the supply of a wide variety of contraceptives was increased, and a strong propaganda and education campaign was initiated in order to bring into universal use family planning and contraceptive methods. In consequence, the number of abortions strongly declined and the birth rate increased (but to a much lesser extent) in 1974 and 1975. In 1976, however, the birth rate began to decline again, demonstrating that legal restriction on abortion has only temporary effects on the birth rate. It is hoped that the simultaneous rise and planned further increase of family allowances and of the child care allowance will contribute to the stabilization of the fertility of the Hungarian population at a level necessary for the simple reproduction of the population.

Analysis of the time series of fertility data seems to show different relations both in the short run and in the long run. While in the long run economic development seems to have been associated, at least until the Second World War, with a secular decline of fertility, in the short run a higher rate of economic growth (i.e. economic prosperity) seems to have a positive effect on fertility. Similarly, population policies providing monetary and other aid to families with children also have a positive influence on fertility. Depression periods, on the other hand, generally tend to have a negative effect on fertility.

However, the fertility rates calculated from yearly vital statistical data raise an important problem: it cannot be simply decided that the short-term fluctuations and changes in fertility rates are only responses to short-term situations considered either favourable or disadvantageous by the couples of reproductive age, and do not influence the number of children borne by women during their reproductive ages. Formulated another way, yearly changes in fertility rates might be only consequences of changes in the timing of parities, which in the end do not influence completed fertility. For example, the changes in fertility during a business cycle or the rise in fertility in consequence of some measure of population policy might merely be consequences of changes of timing, not of the completed fertility. Fertility data which are calculated from census results – e.g. the number of children ever borne by the age groups at the end of their reproductive period – do not suffer from this drawback.

4.2 Census fertility data

Census questionnaires often contain questions on the number of children ever born and on the number of those living at the time of the census of parents. As censuses provide data on age, occupation, education, residence, and often also on place of birth, income, etc., they are excellent sources of information on fertility and its relation to different social variables. As censuses generally use standardized methods which do not change very much from one census to the other, the changes of fertility of different population groups also can be studied.

Thus censuses provide data on differences of fertility by different social factors, i.e. on differential fertility. Vital statistics also give data on differential fertility, however these data are generally less detailed than census data, because it is impossible to ask for as many data on occupation, residence, income, etc., of parents of newborn children, as is usual in the case of censuses. Therefore, it seems to be more appropriate to investigate the information on the social factors of fertility that can be obtained from differential fertility data, on the basis of census differential fertility.

The rationale of using differential fertility data to analyse the effect of social factors on fertility is as follows: if we find a fertility difference between two population groups (e.g. between higher and lower income groups, or between urban and rural populations) then it might be surmised that increases of income or of urbanization have the same effect on fertility, as displayed by the differences found. This reasoning, however, is not completely correct, and it should therefore always be kept in mind that differences in fertility do not necessarily show correctly the influence of the given factors – i.e., if the position of a family or of a society changes in a given direction (e.g. its income increases, or it migrates to an urban area, or the percentage of urban population increases), these changes will not necessarily influence fertility in the same direction and extent as will the difference found at a given moment between the above-mentioned population groups.

Census fertility data have a further minor deficiency: as it is rather awkward to ask never married women about their fertility, the data are generally relevant only to ever married or currently married women. Therefore the influence of the proportion remaining unmarried and of illegitimacy is not taken into consideration.

There are plenty of good census fertility data in different countries, but all of them cannot be analysed in this volume. Therefore two countries have been selected, Hungary and the United States of America, both having good and detailed fertility data from several censuses. There is an added advantage in selecting these two countries in the fact that they represent different levels of economic and social development. The Hungarian data in 1920, 1930 and 1960 might be seen as presenting earlier stages of economic development, and those of the United States in 1940, 1950 and 1960 later stages of development. In Hungary the number of children ever born per married women from 1930 to 1960 declined in each age group, with the exception of the (rather few) 15–19 years old married women (table 4.9). The decline was greater in the older age groups, since the pattern of birth control which was increasingly practised by the Hungarian population was to concentrate births to the younger ages and increasingly limit fertility as age proceeded.

Table 4.9   Children ever born per 100 married women by age: Hungary.

| Year | Age of woman | | | | | |
	15–19	*20–24*	*25–29*	*30–39*	*40–49*	*50 and over*
1930	46	112	194	285	409	513
1949	45	93	159	238	298	370
1960	43	98	161	219	259	311
1970	45	88	140	192	220	251

Source: Termékenységi adatok (1966), p. 25.

Fertility differentials by education of women in 1960 showed the pattern well known to demographers of the nineteenth century and the first half of the twentieth century: the higher the education, the lower the fertility (table 4.10). Similarly, traditional differentials are found between three large social strata: peasants and manual workers in agriculture, manual workers in other branches than agriculture, and non-manual employees. Peasant women had the highest and non-manual working women the lowest fertility (table 4.11). Comparing similar differentials in 1920 and in 1960, no important changes are found (table 4.12), although fertility in each stratum declined. We also find the traditional difference of fertility between employed and dependent women, the latter having a higher fertility in each social stratum. From 1920 to 1960, however, there seems to be a tendency for this differential to decline.

If, however, we do not analyse merely these large social strata, but also make detailed analyses of smaller occupational groups, the overall

Table 4.10   Children ever born per 100 married women by age and education: Hungary, 1960.

| | Age of woman | | | | | | |
Education	15–19	20–24	25–29	30–34	35–39	40–49	50 and over
Did not attend school	107	209	315	442	498	506	500
1–3 years	80	160	229	309	350	369	392
4–5 years	61	129	189	258	289	296	334
6–7 years	50	109	171	211	232	247	300
8 years	37	89	147	172	181	177	159
12 years (secondary school certificate)	12	56	111	150	177	185	157
University diploma	—	42	94	133	160	174	138
Total	43	98	161	205	233	259	311

Source: Termékenységi adatok (1966), p. 31.

Table 4.11   Children ever born per 100 married women by age and social strata: Hungary, 1960.

| | Age of woman | | | | |
Social stratum	15–19	20–29	30–39	40–49	50 and over
Employed women					
Peasant	36	137	220	269	323
Manual	29	109	183	190	187
Non-manual	18	85	145	155	126
Total	29	108	186	218	250
Dependent women					
Peasant	54	166	276	342	388
Manual	51	152	238	274	305
Non-manual	42	140	208	217	205
Total	51	155	246	291	334

Source: Termékenységi adatok (1966), p. 29.

tendency of lower social groups having higher fertility does not appear so clearly.

Such detailed data are available from the census of 1930, which gives the number of ever born children by age and marriage duration. Some selected fertility rates (table 4.13) show that the fertility of agricultural labourers

Table 4.12 Children ever born per 100 married women: Hungary.

Social stratum	1920	1960	
		Actual	Standardized*
Employed women			
Peasant	282	245	227
Manual	244	162	164
Non-manual	176	121	126
Total	266	184	179
Dependent women			
Peasant	433	316	301
Manual	322	239	248
Non-manual	225	195	191
Total	378	263	261

* Standardized according to the age distribution of total population in 1960.
Source: Termékenységi adatok (1966), p. 28.

employed on one-year contracts, mainly in large estates, was the highest. This was the social stratum living in the most backward conditions, mostly residing not in villages but in small settlements around the manors on large estates, far away from schools, from cultural institutions, from mass media, almost outside society, and having almost no contact even with the village population. The income of these labourers was rather low, consisting to an important degree in natural benefits (wheat and other agricultural products, the possibility of rearing some animals, etc.). This income, however, was assured by yearly contracts, i.e. not so much exposed to fluctuations and uncertainties as the income of the lowest strata in the villages.

The other social stratum in a similarly low position in Hungary in the 1930s was that of day labourers in agriculture. Their income was even lower than that of labourers employed on one-year contracts, and was also much more uncertain than that of the contract labourers, because they were employed only for weeks, even for days at a time, to do the great seasonal work tasks on large estates and for smallholder peasants. The day labourers were unemployed for a great part of the year, mostly in winter. On the other hand, some of them had a small farm which, though not sufficient to provide work and income for the whole family, formed the potential basis for economic advancement. By efficient farming, by economizing, and with some luck, they had the opportunity of rising up to the social stratum of smallholders. Although this was rarely possible during the depression years of the 1930s, their opportunities for advancement

Table 4.13   Children ever born per 100 women in some selected age and marriage duration groups, by occupation:* Hungary, 1930.

	Age of woman				
	25–29	30–39	30–39	40–49	50–59
	Duration of marriage (years)				
Occupation	Less than 5	5–9	10–14	15–19	20 and over
Agricultural labourer employed on one-year contract in large estates	147	308	409	513	700
Agricultural day labourer	136	248	341	400	569
Farmer: less than 10 *hold***	118	240	299	378	519
Farmer: 10–50 *hold*	111	237	287	373	527
Farmer: 50–100 *hold*	105	207	293	385	593
Worker in mining	142	271	368	490	625
Worker in industry	98	180	264	306	486
Worker in transport	108	198	281	336	451
Worker in commerce	88	158	234	256	390
Self-employed in industry	103	195	269	301	466
Self-employed in commerce	86	166	227	251	407
Non-manual in industry	49	107	152	177	304
Non-manual in commerce	49	112	160	180	305
Non-manual in state administration	68	140	191	211	345
Self-employed professional	58	108	151	170	296

* In the case of employed women their own occupations, in the case of dependants their husbands' occupations were taken into consideration in the classification. Only the more important occupational groups are included in the table.
** *Hold* = 0·57 hectares.
Source: Thirring (1941), p. 169.

were not so hopeless as those of labourers employed on one-year contracts. Also, since they resided in the villages and were in daily contact with the smallholder peasants, they were not so much excluded from the culture of the other strata of society. The difference in the ways of thinking of one-year contract labourers on the large estates and of the agricultural day labourers can be illustrated by their different political opinions: at the elections the contract labourers always voted according to orders given by the employees of the landlords (i.e. they voted for the conservative government party), while the day labourers voted mostly for the opposition parties, as did the smallholder peasants. Also the number of ever born children of the day labourers was lower than that of the one-year contract labourers. This is noteworthy because – as has already been stressed – the overall income position of the day labourers was worse than that of the contract labourers. However, it might be hypothesized that the latter were less interested in limiting the number of their children, as they had no prospects of rising to another social stratum, while the day labourers were more interested in limiting the size of their families because a greater number of children depressed their already poor chances of rising into the smallholder stratum.

It is noteworthy, too, that there were no great or consistent fertility differences between the three strata of peasants – the smallholders having less than 10 *hold* of land often being obliged to seek work outside their farms in order to supplement their income, farmers having farms of 10–15 *hold* (i.e. medium-sized farms) employing workers for shorter or longer periods, and farmers having 50–100 *hold* already rising from the peasant class into the middle classes. Thus, it seems that there was no negative correlation between fertility and income or wealth in the class of farmers.

In addition to the labourers on one-year contracts on large estates, the other social stratum having the highest fertility in Hungary was that of the miners. This stratum was very heterogeneous, ranging from fairly well-paid skilled miners to part-time or seasonal miners, who were unskilled. It is certain that the income and social position of all of them was higher and better than those of the agricultural day labourers and the smallholder peasants. Yet their fertility was higher. However, this is not a specially Hungarian phenomenon for that period. Miners have been noted in other countries as well for a relatively high fertility.

Workers in other economic branches had lower fertility than that of the miners and those of the agricultural population. Here again, income differences between skilled and unskilled workers and between workers in different industrial branches were large, even though the available data differentiate only between workers in different branches, i.e. in transport, in industry and in commerce. Among these the fertility of transport workers was highest and that of workers in commerce was lowest. The explanation for these differences might lie not in the different incomes of these strata, but in the fact that the workers in commerce were nearest in their position, life conditions and goals, as well as in their beliefs and norms, to the middle classes. They were also most urbanized, while a large proportion of transport workers, many of them railway workers, originated from the peasant classes and were living in villages, with a small plot of land to cultivate.

It seems to be characteristic that the fertility of self-employed artisans was not much lower than that of industrial workers and that self-employed merchants and shopkeepers had a lower fertility than artisans. Fertility of self-employed shopkeepers was similar to that of the workers in commerce. The explanation might lie not in the different income levels of artisans and shopkeepers, but in the fact that the latter's way of life tried to imitate that of non-manual employees, and they made great efforts to help their children to rise into the non-manual strata, and even into the professional stratum.

The non-manual strata showed the lowest fertility, particularly the self-employed professionals. At that time this was a general tendency in European countries, although in Hungary an additional factor might have contributed to depressing the fertility of non-manual strata. There was fairly widespread unemployment among people with higher qualifications, even university degrees, in the 1920s and 1930s, partly as a result of the immigration of many Hungarian professionals from the territories which before the First World War had been parts of Hungary but after the peace treaty of Trianon were allotted to other countries.

Fertility differentials by employment status and social strata in 1960 do not show an unambiguous pattern of negative correlation of fertility and social status or income level (table 4.14). Fertility of employed women was consistently lower than that of dependent (i.e. non-working) women. The fertility of women belonging to the two strata in agriculture (i.e. agricultural workers and members of agricultural cooperatives on the one hand

Table 4.14   Children ever born per 100 married women by age and social stratum:* Hungary, 1960.

Social stratum	Age of woman				
	15–19	*20–29*	*30–39*	*40–49*	*50 and over*
Employed women					
Agricultural worker	38	145	242	292	324
Skilled in industry and construction	26	93	156	160	148
Skilled in transport	21	92	149	130	150
Skilled in commerce	22	92	153	157	140
Skilled in other branches	16	81	148	149	132
Total skilled	23	92	154	158	144
Semiskilled in industry and construction	29	104	179	185	175
Semiskilled in transport	33	118	191	203	190
Semiskilled in commerce	27	110	173	179	169
Semiskilled in other branches	27	122	203	211	201
Total semiskilled	29	106	180	187	179
Unskilled in industry and construction	33	123	203	208	200
Unskilled in transport	29	116	204	198	191
Unskilled in commerce	30	121	200	213	202
Unskilled in other branches	37	133	213	221	207
Total unskilled	33	125	206	213	203

Table 4.14—contd.

Social stratum	Age of woman				
	15–19	*20–29*	*30–39*	*40–49*	*50 and over*
Self-employed peasant	35	133	210	261	322
Self-employed artisan	31	128	166	152	136
Other self-employed (shopkeepers, etc.)	9	133	202	200	208
Non-manual clerical	19	86	141	144	117
High and medium level professional	17	84	155	170	154
Manager and executive	9	82	142	167	130
Dependent women					
Agricultural worker	56	168	274	336	383
Skilled in industry and construction	47	141	218	242	248
Skilled in transport	48	137	213	232	231
Skilled in commerce	54	145	199	201	193
Skilled in other branches	40	142	211	218	228
Total skilled	47	141	215	236	239
Semiskilled in industry and construction	49	156	258	315	322
Semiskilled in transport	50	153	248	283	300
Semiskilled in commerce	52	155	228	264	267
Semiskilled in other branches	46	165	273	304	325
Total semiskilled	49	156	253	302	313
Unskilled in industry and construction	58	162	274	339	331
Unskilled in transport	55	168	279	356	346
Unskilled in commerce	53	164	268	312	319
Unskilled in other branches	59	165	264	345	368
Total unskilled	54	164	272	342	342
Self-employed peasant	36	155	284	359	394
Self-employed artisan	55	163	213	230	267
Other self-employed (shopkeepers, etc.)	52	162	219	233	288
Non-manual clerical	42	139	199	203	196
High and medium level professional	47	147	213	228	234
Manager and executive	38	137	211	221	199

* In the case of employed women the social stratum is determined on the basis of the wife's occupation, in the case of dependants on the basis of the husband's occupation. Inactive earners, as well as dependants of inactive earners, are not included in the table.
Source : Termékenységi adatok (1966), pp. 177–87.

and self-employed peasants on the other – the latter were still in the majority in 1960 in Hungarian agriculture) was the highest. Then followed in decreasing order the fertility levels of unskilled, semiskilled and skilled strata, with some differences between the branches, workers in commerce showing a somewhat lower fertility than those in industry, building industry and commerce. Self-employed artisans and shopkeepers, however, do not seem to have a lower fertility than skilled workers, as earlier. This might be explained by the fact that these self-employed groups, whose number has diminished significantly, ceased to be the main source of recruitment for the professional and other non-manual strata, this role being taken over by the children of skilled workers, which group, or at least part of the families belonging to it, made great efforts in the past to raise its childrens' social position.

A new phenomenon appears in the fertility of the non-manual strata: the fertility of professional women and of wives of professional men was higher in some age groups than that of the simple non-manual administrative or clerical workers. This is the first sign of the appearance of the U-shaped curve of fertility in Hungarian census fertility data. The U-shaped curve means that there is no uniform negative association of socioeconomic status with fertility; the fertility of strata in more or less middle positions is the lowest, while the lower strata and the higher strata have higher fertility. The first sign of this curve is usually a higher fertility of the professional stratum than that of the medium-level non-manual stratum.

The higher fertility of professionals as compared to that of the simple clerical employees might be interpreted in the following way: the clerical employees in general try to follow the example of the living conditions and the way of life of the professionals, with whom they are in constant contact – i.e. the professionals constitute the reference group for the other non-manuals. However, the resources of the other non-manuals are generally much lower, because of lower wages and smaller possibilities of advancement in career, and therefore a greater number of children handicaps them in their efforts to achieve the standard of living of the professionals. The relative position of non-manuals also tends to deteriorate compared with other social strata – as e.g. when the average wages of skilled workers in Hungary slowly outgrew that of the simple non-manuals.

The most consistent and stable fertility differential seems to be that by type and size of settlements (table 4.15). Urban fertility is lower than rural fertility and the fertility of the population of Budapest, a metropolis of nearly 2 million people in 1960, is much lower than other towns having the administrative position of counties (four towns with populations of 100 000–200 000), and the fertility of these latter towns is lower than the fertility of smaller towns having the administrative position of districts.

There is another interesting fertility differential in Hungary: the difference in fertility between different regions (table 4.16). Census fertility data are published for the counties and the larger towns having the administrative position of counties. Differences are rather great. The most interesting fact, however, is that the neighbouring counties have similar levels of fertility, and that these 'fertility regions' do not coincide with the

Table 4.15 Children ever born per 100 married women per age and type of settlement: Hungary, 1960.

Type of settlement	Age of woman						
	15–19	*20–24*	*25–29*	*30–34*	*35–39*	*40–49*	*50 and over*
Budapest	33	72	122	150	166	166	179
Towns with the administrative position of counties	43	89	144	180	202	213	250
Towns with the administrative position of districts	44	95	157	200	229	250	293
Villages	44	105	175	226	260	301	361

Source: Termékenységi adatok (1966), pp. 33, 232–8.

Table 4.16 Children ever born per 100 married women by regions (counties): Hungary.

County or town	1920	1960	
		Actual	*Standardized**
Budapest	245	155	151
Baranya and Pécs	303	220	224
Bács-Kiskun	395	249	249
Békés	408	247	243
Borsod-Abaúj-Zemplén and Miskolc	365	254	265
Csongrád and Szeged	373	217	212
Fejér	387	250	258
Győr-Sopron	405	254	251
Hajdú-Bihar and Debrecen	389	295	278
Heves	391	234	239
Komárom	406	236	246
Nógrád	378	245	255
Pest	402	236	238
Somogy	325	223	222
Szabolcs-Szatmár	441	327	334
Szolnok	407	259	257
Tolna	327	238	238
Vas	399	259	250
Veszprém	385	253	254
Zala	365	247	244
Total	362	232	233

* Standardized according to the national age distribution of 1960.
Source: Termékenységi adatok (1966), p. 36.

regions which might be distinguished on the basis of economic development and industrialization. Thus the highest level of fertility is found in the eastern county of Szabolcs-Szatmár, which is well known for its economic backwardness. Two neighbouring counties, Hajdú-Bihar and Borsod-Abaúj-Zemplén have the next highest fertility levels, although only Hajdú-Bihar might be considered a relatively backward area, while parts of Borsod-Abaúj-Zemplén, and particularly the town of Miskolc situated in the county, are the centre of Hungarian metallurgy and heavy industry. Thus in the northeastern part of the country there is a region uniformly characterized by high fertility which is not homogeneous from the point of view of economic development.

The areas having the lowest fertility (apart from Budapest) are in the south – namely, the counties Csongrád (including the town of Szeged), Baranya (including the town of Pécs), Somogy, Tolna and Békés. Except for part of Baranya in the neighbourhood of Pécs and the town of Szeged these were rather underindustrialized areas in 1960, characterized by a predominance of agriculture.

Some of the highly industrialized parts of the country, on the other hand, such as the counties of Komárom, Fejér and Győr, had a higher level of fertility. Thus a cursory overview of regional fertility differences suggests that economic development and industrialization were not simply negatively correlated with fertility, and that other more complicated causative mechanisms seem to have played a role in determining these fertility differentials. In the next chapter we shall return to the interpretation of these regional fertility differentials in Hungary in connection with a multiple regression analysis of yearly vital statistical fertility rates.

One further fact about the regional differences, however, is worth mentioning here – namely, that some of these differentials appeared in the data of the census of 1920. The fertility of Szabolcs-Szatmár was outstanding at that time and the southern Transdanubian counties of Baranya, Somogy and Tolna already had a low fertility at that date. It is worth mentioning here that the communities where signs of early birth control were demonstrated by family reconstitution studies are situated in these counties. On the other hand, the counties of Csongrád and Békés in the southeastern part of the country which showed very low fertility in 1960 had a rather high fertility in 1920.

Fertility differentials evidenced by the census data of 1940, 1950 and 1960 in the United States differ in several respects from those found in Hungary (table 4.17). First of all, while in Hungary fertility declined from 1920 to 1960, as demonstrated by the census data, in the United States the number of children ever born in the cohorts of married women younger than 35 years increased from 1940 to 1960. Thus the baby boom is evidenced by census fertility data as well as by the yearly vital statistical

Table 4.17   Children ever born per 1000 white women of childbearing age, by age and type of settlement: United States.

Area (type of settlement) and year	Age of woman					
	15–19	*20–24*	*25–29*	*30–34*	*35–39*	*40–44*
Total United States						
1960	117	995	1959	2392	2475	2364
1950	92	701	1409	1847	2030	2132
1940	54	472	1088	1640	2112	2459
Urban						
1960	111	900	1835	2260	2314	2170
1950	75	582	1234	1625	1752	1825
1940	37	347	843	1325	1725	2047
Rural non-farm						
1960	148	1280	2246	2670	2815	2762
1950	135	962	1710	2193	2393	2492
1940	82	668	1396	1962	2413	2742
Rural farm						
1960	84	1171	2365	2933	3141	3147
1950	135	962	1710	2193	2393	2493
1940	82	668	1396	1962	2413	2742

Source: Kiser, Grabill and Campbell (1968), p. 76.

fertility data. The fertility of the age groups 35–39 and 40–44 declined from 1940 to 1950, then increased again, as the cohorts older than 35 years in 1950 experienced the baby boom after having finished the most fertile part of their reproductive ages, which more or less coincided with the years of lowest fertility, the 1930s, in the United States.

The fertility differentials by education of women showed in all the census years considered a negative correlation of fertility and education, as in Hungary, although the differences between the number of children ever born of women with low and higher education clearly diminished above the age of 30 years (table 4.18). Except for women aged 40 and more with very low education, fertility increased in all age and education groups; thus the baby boom affected all strata of population. Therefore the baby boom cannot be explained simply by a positive correlation between fertility and the standard of living appearing at a given higher standard of living, since in that case the population strata with lowest education (and consequently income) would have shown a continued fertility decline and only the fertility of the higher strata would have risen.

Table 4.18 Children ever born per 1000 white women, by age and education: United States.

Age of woman	Education		1960	1950	1940
15–19	College:	4 or more years	(*a*)	89	(*a*)
		1–3 years	43	19	9
	High school:	4 years	121	65	29
		1–3 years	103	81	40
	None or elementary		180	154	106
20–24	College:	4 or more years	296	191	65
		1–3 years	425	304	122
	High school:	4 years	912	573	280
		1–3 years	1539	989	650
	None or elementary		1510	1113	810
25–29	College:	4 or more years	1091	766	313
		1–3 years	1629	1056	613
	High school:	4 years	1894	1231	757
		1–3 years	2327	1663	1234
	None or elementary		2394	1913	1571
30–34	College:	4 or more years	1843	1285	704
		1–3 years	2223	1518	1050
	High school:	4 years	2294	1634	1164
		1–3 years	2577	1986	1692
	None or elementary		2796	2311	2233
35–39	College:	4 or more years	2028	1334	918
		1–3 years	2297	1639	1366
	High school:	4 years	2320	1687	1462
		1–3 years	2582	2066	2009
	None or elementary		2938	2582	2725
40–44	College:	4 or more years	1871	1249	1065
		1–3 years	2126	1628	1598
	High school:	4 years	2148	1657	1671
		1–3 years	2438	2153	2240
	None or elementary		2830	2724	2998
45–49	College:	4 or more years	1519	1079	1231
		1–3 years	1825	1513	1707
	High school:	4 years	1879	1643	1747
		1–3 years	2228	2852	2370
	None or elementary		2708	2852	3134

(*a*) Rate not shown, because the number of women in these categories is too low.
Source: Kiser, Grabill and Campbell (1968), p. 160.

A similar tendency is displayed by the fertility differences between different socio-occupational strata (table 4.19). The number of children ever borne by white married women increased in the baby boom period in all except the over 40 years old group of farmers. Thus the cause of the

Table 4.19 Children ever born per 1000 white women married and husband present, by age and social stratum:*
United States, selected age groups.

	Age of woman											
	20–24				30–34				40–44			
Social stratum	1960	1950	1940	1910	1960	1950	1940	1910	1960	1950	1940	1910
Professional, technical and kindred	1034	714	567	838	2377	1777	1321	1820	2311	1812	1926	2749
Manager and proprietor	1326	882	720	1035	2465	1867	1526	2206	2336	1942	2144	3259
Clerical, sales and kindred	1188	793	625	886	2387	1689	1365	1906	2230	1853	1978	2858
Craftsman, foreman and kindred	1498	1041	898	1218	2631	2075	1920	2605	2548	2399	2666	3854
Operative and kindred	1557	1112	968	1316	2738	2193	2084	2775	2690	2612	2931	4157
Service workers, including domestic	1407	1010	809	1121	2478	1880	1690	2325	2426	2164	2564	3596
Labourer, excluding farm and mine	1573	1195	1093	1491	2929	2457	2448	3248	2968	3162	3403	4633
Farmer and farm manager	1609	1294	1306	1629	3020	2713	2805	3706	3166	3344	3914	5292
Farm labourer and foreman	1741	1346	1233	1516	3617	2969	2800	3565	4017	3980	4281	4967

* Occupation of husband.

Source: Kiser, Grabill and Campbell (1968), p. 186.

baby boom must be sought in factors that influenced almost all the population of the United States. This influence, however, was stronger in the higher strata than in the lowest ones. In consequence, the shape of the curve of fertility differentials by strata changed. Earlier, as demonstrated by the data of the 1910 census, the same fertility differentials appeared as in Hungary from 1920 to 1960: the higher the socioeconomic status of the family, the lower the fertility. The only exception is the relatively high fertility of the manager and proprietor group, which, however, is so heterogeneous that it is rather difficult to interpret its relatively high fertility. The two groups employed in agriculture, the farmers and the farm labourers, had the highest fertility, as in Hungary, although with the slight difference that the fertility of farmers was somewhat higher than that of farm labourers. This might be interpreted as a manifestation of the fact that in the United States farm land was not so scarce as in Hungary before the Second World War. Skilled workers (craftsmen) had a lower fertility than operatives, and the latter had a lower fertility than unskilled labourers, as in Hungary. Service workers, being in an intermediate position between industrial workers and non-manuals as regards their life style, also had an intermediate fertility between these two social strata, in the same way as the workers in commerce in Hungary.

These fertility differentials also prevailed in 1940, i.e. before the baby boom. During the baby boom period, however, the fertility differences become blurred. U-shaped curves tend to appear, i.e. fertility is the lowest in the middle socioeconomic groups – namely, among the clerical, sales and kindred non-manual employees, the fertility of professionals tending to be rather higher than lower, although the differences are not consistent. The negative correlation of the level of skill and fertility in the non-agricultural manual groups remained unchanged, but the fertility of farmers became lower than that of farm labourers.

The U-shaped curve is demonstrated more clearly by the fertility differentials by income (table 4.20). By 1960 there was a clear tendency in the United States for the medium income groups to have the lowest levels of fertility, especially in the older age groups nearing the completion of family size. This phenomenon, which was evidenced by many other studies of fertility in the United States and in western Europe, might be considered the empirical basis of the new economic theories of fertility, which hypothesize that two tendencies might be manifested in the U-shaped curves of the relation between fertility and socioeconomic status – tendencies respectively of fertility and income. On the one hand, higher social status and the higher income connected with it tends to increase the aspirations and needs, which tend to depress fertility; on the other hand, a higher income makes it possible to achieve a greater number of children and maintain at the same time an average or a desired level of living.

Table 4.20 Children ever born per 1000 white wives with husband present, by age and income of husband in 1959: United States, 1960.

Income of husband ($)	Age of wife			
	20–24	*25–29*	*30–34*	*35–39*
15 000 and over	1366	2191	2651	2733
10 000–14 999	1448	2178	2579	2601
7000–9999	1532	2226	2571	2538
5000–6999	1498	2191	2531	2576
4000–4999	1401	2150	2554	2619
3000–3999	1359	2182	2643	2755
2000–2999	1299	2212	2773	2947
1000–1999 or less	1157	2247	2928	3097
None	1171	2090	2631	2905

Source: Kiser, Campbell and Grabill (1968), p. 209.

The nature of the relation between fertility and income is demonstrated more clearly if we analyse it in separate socioeconomic and educational categories. Some characteristic categories are included in table 4.21. In the case of couples where the husband's education was one or more years of college and his occupation was a professional, technical or kindred one, the correlation of income and fertility was positive in all the four age and marriage categories, with the exception of the lowest income group, which in two cases had a somewhat higher fertility than the next one. In the case of the clerical, sales and kindred group having high school education the correlation is positive in two cases and rather unclear in the two other categories. In the case of craftsmen, foremen and kindred workers having high school education there seems to be a positive correlation in two cases and a negative in one category. In the two lowest socioeconomic groups considered, the operatives and the labourers having no high school education, negative and U-type relations prevail. It might be conjectured that positive correlations of fertility and income seem to prevail in the higher social strata, while in the lower ones only the first signs of the overturn of the traditional negative correlation appeared in the census data considered if the influence of education level was kept constant.

Thus the fertility differences by social strata found in the United States in 1950 and in 1960 were different from those found in the pre-baby boom period, and also different from those in Hungary before 1960. Two fertility differentials, on the other hand, seem to be permanent features of both countries – namely, fertility differences between employed and dependent women and differences between urban and rural populations.

Employed women in the United States consistently had lower fertility than women not in the labour force, and those who worked thirty-five or

Table 4.21   Children ever born per 1000 white women, married once, husband present, by age, social stratum, education, and income of husband: selected age groups and marriage cohorts, United States, 1960.

Social stratum and education of husband	Income of husband ($)	Wives aged 35–44		Wives aged 45–54	
		Married at 14–21	Married at 22+	Married at 14–21	Married at 22+
Professional, technical	10 000 and more	2694	2551	2140	2018
and kindred, college 1	7000–9999	2645	2239	2064	1658
or more years	4000–6999	2469	2031	2125	1639
	2000–3999	2412	1925	2135	1594
	Under 2000	2571	1753	(a)	1668
Clerical, sales and	10 000 and more	2519	2298	2161	1662
kindred, high school	7000–9999	2540	2269	2045	1679
1–4 years	4000–6999	2504	2003	2253	1585
	2000–3999	2514	1660	2308	1397
	Under 2000	2553	1699	2114	1333
Craftsman, foreman	10 000 and more	2732	2311	2251	1817
and kindred, high school	7000–9999	2711	2324	2443	1820
1–4 years	4000–6999	2682	2108	2588	1747
	2000–3999	2764	1841	2850	1615
	Under 2000	2646	1673	2442	1471
Operative and kindred,	10 000 and more	2982	2284	2639	1616
no high school	7000–9999	2910	2273	2624	1929
	4000–6999	2990	2049	2843	1829
	2000–3999	3275	2058	3108	1812
	Under 2000	3627	2079	3313	1839
Labourer, except farm and	7000–9999	2860	2551	3201	2209
mine, no high school	4000–6999	3363	2117	3282	1932
	2000–3999	3631	2315	3731	2277
	Under 2000	4248	2499	4699	2447

(a) Rate not shown, base is less than 1000.
Source: Kiser, Grabill and Campbell (1968), pp. 213–15.

more hours a week had lower fertility than those who worked less than thirty-five hours; and among the dependent women those who had worked previously had lower fertilities than those who had never worked (table 4.22). These correlations appeared not only in the case of all women together, where it might have been the effect of unmarried women being more frequently employed, but also in the case of married (and widowed or divorced) women. The reason for this, however, might be of two different kinds. It might be supposed that employed women tend to control their fertility, because of the fact that they are employed, or it might be that women having more children tend to remain at home or seek employment for a shorter time, because of their larger families.

Table 4.22 Children ever born per 1000 white women, by age and employment status: United States, 1960.

| Employment status of woman | Age of woman | | | | | |
| | 25–29 | | 35–39 | | 45–49 | |
	Total	Ever married	Total	Ever married	Total	Ever married
In labour force	1160	1524	1880	2145	1817	2042
Employed	1132	1498	1863	2129	1802	2027
Worked 35 or more hours	960	1337	1678	1958	1692	1944
Worked less than 35 hours	1664	1907	2332	2454	2112	2245
Unemployed	1670	1938	2258	2448	2197	2364
Not in labour force	2360	2424	2839	2893	2532	2602
Last worked in 1959–60	1862	1920	2543	2592	2409	2471
Last worked in 1955–8	2102	2118	2401	2429	2103	2207
Last worked in 1954 or earlier	2783	2802	2878	2899	2316	2356
Never worked	2569	2806	3216	3391	3026	3168

Source: Kiser, Grabill and Campbell (1968), p. 221.

Table 4.23 Children ever born per 1000 women of childbearing age, by region: United States.

| Year | Region | Age of woman | | | | | |
		15–19	20–24	25–29	30–34	35–39	40–44
1960	United States	127	1030	2007	2452	2518	2407
	Northeast	83	799	1711	2157	2234	2119
	North central	112	1045	2091	2560	2589	2452
	South	164	1137	2114	2584	2694	2648
	West	144	1127	2103	2493	2531	2373
1950	United States	105	738	1436	1871	2061	2170
	Northeast	49	497	1152	1605	1787	1885
	North central	83	711	1433	1882	2026	2127
	South	154	912	1652	2101	2378	2540
	West	122	834	1509	1867	1956	2015
1940	United States	61	505	1129	1678	2156	2501
	Northeast	28	318	858	1401	1832	2201
	North central	49	461	1077	1614	2041	2405
	South	97	691	1413	2025	2644	3055
	West	65	554	1125	1595	1954	2201

Source: Kiser, Grabill and Campbell (1968), p. 75.

Also the urban–rural fertility differences, as well as the difference of the fertility of rural non-farm and rural farm areas in the United States, remained very constant, although the fertility level of all three types of settlement increased between 1940 and 1960 (see table 4.17).

As in Hungary, there are clear regional differences of fertility in the United States, and these differences seem to be fairly permanent (table 4.23). Fertility in the southern region was the highest from 1940 to 1960, then followed, in decreasing order, the western, the north central and the northeastern regions. There are also important and permanent differences within these large regions, as e.g. the high fertility of Utah which is inhabited partly by the Mormon sect who are characterized by high fertility. This latter case is a clear example of cultural features resulting in regional peculiarities of fertility.

Census data of the United States provide the possibility of analysing the effect of migration on fertility, by giving the region of residence at the time of the census and the region of the place of birth (table 4.24). The effect of migration seems to differ according to the region of origin and destination of migration. Those migrating from the south to the northeast adapt themselves to the lower fertility of the region of destination. Those migrating from the northeast to the south, on the other hand, retain the lower fertility of their region of origin. A similar tendency can be observed by migrants between the northeastern and the north central regions, where, whatever the direction of migration, migrants have a low fertility similar to the fertility of the northeast.

Migration from the south to the northeast means changing over to a more developed and more urbanized region, where living standards are generally higher, but where competition for jobs might also be higher, so it is especially difficult for migrants coming from more backward and traditional areas to keep up with the local population; therefore migrants try to control their fertility in order to be able to adapt to the new mileu. On the other hand, migrants from the northeastern region to the south might wish to maintain their relatively high level of living in a more backward area, offering relatively less opportunities, and therefore try to have small families.

On the basis of the census fertility data of the United States, it is possible to analyse a further problem – namely the influence of ethnic and cultural background on fertility. Fertility rates detailed by country of origin of immigrants, as well as by country of origin of the parents of second-generation Americans, provide most interesting information on the long lasting influence of cultural background, in spite of the fact that America is reputed to be a melting pot for immigrants of different nationalities. However, the fertility levels of population groups having different ethnic · backgrounds also differ between age groups, which might be explained by

Table 4.24 Children ever born per 1000 ever married native white women, by age, region of birth and region of residence: United States, 1960.

Region of residence	Region of birth			
	Northeast	*North central*	*South*	*West*
Age of woman: 15–19				
Northeast	736	697	754	(*a*)
North central	674	708	760	696
South	625	611	717	717
West	625	703	798	754
Age of woman: 20–24				
Northeast	1227	1177	1250	1282
North central	1212	1404	1516	1432
South	1134	1298	1403	1299
West	1196	1406	1588	1490
Age of woman: 25–29				
Northeast	2006	1912	2070	2012
North central	2070	2305	2285	2190
South	1940	2069	2195	2194
West	1897	2209	2356	2408
Age of woman: 30–34				
Northeast	2412	2460	2507	2530
North central	2565	2740	2681	2764
South	2383	2481	2576	2677
West	2334	2544	2603	2778
Age of woman: 35–39				
Northeast	2477	2593	2417	2576
North central	2614	2776	2729	2814
South	2479	2554	2702	2628
West	2301	2501	2612	2824
Age of woman: 40–44				
Northeast	2359	2358	2298	2353
North central	2374	2629	2760	2561
South	2215	2300	2695	2404
West	2167	2290	2461	2619
Age of woman: 45–49				
Northeast	2181	2081	2148	2161
North central	2141	2437	2577	2346
South	1857	2056	2646	2204
West	1838	2073	2323	2374

(*a*) Rate not shown, base is less than 1000.
Source: Kiser, Grabill and Campbell (1968), p. 109.

the fact that particular age groups consist of different kinds of immigrants (table 4.25). Also first-generation immigrants and second-generation immigrants do not always show the same patterns of fertility, the explanation again being possibly that they consist of different stocks.

Second-generation immigrants, i.e. those who have one or two parents born outside the United States, have generally higher fertility than first-generation immigrants born in foreign countries (exceptions are those originating from Ireland, Italy and Mexico, where the fertility of the first-generation immigrants is higher in some age groups). The most striking differences, however, are found in the case of immigrants from eastern and eastern central Europe. Those born in Austria, Czechoslovakia, Poland and the Soviet Union have relatively very low fertilities, although the last two had very high fertilities until the 1960s. The second-generation immigrants from these countries, i.e. those of foreign or mixed parentage, had higher fertility rates. The explanation might be that second-generation immigrants came mostly before the First World War and originated mainly from the peasantry or the working class, while first-generation immigrants might have been to an important degree intellectuals who fled partly from these countries before or after Nazi occupation. Those originating from Germany were characterized by a similar difference in fertility between first- and second-generation immigrants.

The fertility of women whose cultural background was Sweden and Norway is also relatively low. The much higher fertility of immigrants aged 35–44 than of those aged 45–54 seems to reflect the baby boom. A similar difference can be observed in the case of immigrants from all those countries where a pronounced baby boom occurred after the Second World War – i.e. in the United Kingdom, Germany and Canada, as well as in Sweden and Norway – while in the case of immigrants from the eastern European countries, where no similar lasting baby boom occurred, and also in the case of Italian immigrants, the difference between the fertility of

Table 4.25 Children ever born per 1000 ever married women, by age and national origin of the woman: United States, 1960.

Country of origin of woman	Age of woman		
	25–34	35–44	45–54
United Kingdom	2215	2402	1976
Foreign born	2023	2249	1850
Foreign or mixed parentage	2304	2467	2023
Ireland	2347	2725	2294
Foreign born	1997	2539	2539
Foreign or mixed parentage	2410	2749	2223

Table 4.25—contd.

Country of origin of woman	Age of woman		
	25–34	*35–44*	*45–54*
Norway	2398	2587	2275
Foreign born	1589	2167	1664
Foreign or mixed parentage	2489	2627	2330
Sweden	2277	2426	1912
Foreign born	1509	2094	1718
Foreign or mixed parentage	2328	2447	1942
Germany	2006	2320	2012
Foreign born	1613	1815	1565
Foreign or mixed parentage	2299	2490	2121
Poland	2105	2247	2081
Foreign born	1946	2015	1972
Foreign or mixed parentage	2123	2269	2107
Czechoslovakia	2136	2297	2175
Foreign born	1890	1953	2073
Foreign or mixed parentage	2173	2341	2194
Austria	2023	2133	1930
Foreign born	1623	1746	1781
Foreign or mixed parentage	2077	2166	1959
USSR	2059	2151	1878
Foreign born	2144	2011	1850
Foreign or mixed parentage	2055	2163	1886
Italy	2022	2233	2233
Foreign born	1893	2317	2554
Foreign or mixed parentage	2036	2225	2145
Canada	2385	2554	2215
Foreign born	2159	2415	2127
Foreign or mixed parentage	2477	2640	2271
Mexico	3267	4148	4580
Foreign born	3150	3982	4631
Foreign or mixed parentage	3311	4221	4508
Other countries	2059	2322	2123
Foreign born	1763	2157	2121
Foreign or mixed parentage	2199	2368	2124
Total foreign stock	2208	2392	2163
Foreign born	1949	2296	2226
Foreign or mixed parentage	2280	2412	2143

Source: Kiser, Grabill and Campbell (1968), p. 71.

the immigrants aged 35–44 and 45–54 is much smaller, or even non-existent.

Immigrants from Ireland, Italy and Canada had relatively high fertility levels, reflecting the high fertilities in their country of origin – i.e. these population groups maintained their high fertility in their new American surroundings. Similarly, Mexican immigrants retained their high fertility.

Thus traditional fertility levels of the immigrants were maintained to a certain degree in the United States, which seems to prove the strong and lasting influence of cultural patterns concerning fertility, even in quite different economic and social conditions. On the other hand, changes in these patterns can be observed in some cases, probably caused by the features and conditions of immigration and accommodation in America.

The study of Hungarian and American census fertility data on fertility differences thus suggests on the one hand that some traditional fertility differences (probably those by educational and social strata) are changing and may be diminishing. Some others, like the differences in fertility of urban and rural populations, seem to be fairly long lasting, or perhaps diminishing slightly in some societies. At the same time, there are some fertility differentials, like those by regions and by ethnic background, which seem to be maintained in spite of the tendency for equalization of regions and ethnic groups in other social aspects. The differences by income display the most conspicuous changes – namely, the traditional negative relation between fertility and income in the period of demographic transition seems to change into a U-shaped and even (in perspective) into a positive relation, at least for fairly homogeneous population groups. Because of these changes, however, it is rather difficult to come to any firm conclusions on the permanent relationships between these social factors and fertility.

4.3 International and regional cross-sectional analyses of fertility

As mentioned in section 4.1, the relation of fertility changes to economic and social factors was investigated by several authors by means of correlation and regression analysis based on time series of fertility and socioeconomic variables. However, it is well known in the social sciences that the use of time series data in correlation and regression analysis presents many pitfalls because of the frequency of multicollinearity and autoregression in these data and because there are usually important but unknown lags between the variables. For example, in the case of investigations of the social factors of fertility, these factors are often strongly correlated – i.e. *per capita* national income, industrialization, urbanization, the increase of education, and the increased employment of women, all develop in parallel, and it is therefore rather difficult to distinguish their separate effects, and even the sign of the correlation. Also it is obvious that fertility changes follow after a certain lag, at least of nine months, but generally some years. The exact length of this lag, and the distribution of the lags (as the lag might be different in the case of particular families or population groups), are more or less unknown. Correlation and regression analyses also used to suppose that the relationships of fertility to other variables are linear, whereas they might be (and probably are) curvilinear. A further technical drawback of time series regression analysis is the fact that the socioeconomic time series available are generally relatively short.

These drawbacks are partly avoided by cross-sectional analyses. The investigations of differential fertility data, described in the previous chapter, are essentially cross-sectional analyses. One type of cross-sectional data – the territorial cross-sections of fertility – is especially appropriate for multiple correlation and regression analysis of the factors influencing fertility, as generally rather good data on fertility, as well as on economic and social conditions of territorial units in given periods, are available, mostly on the basis of censuses.

The analyses based on territorial cross-section data, however, contain also a serious pitfall that has been called the ecological fallacy. The essence of this is that it is by no means certain that the correlations and regression coefficients displayed by the data on territorial units characterize individual families. For example, the fact that in areas where average income is higher there is a lower average fertility rate does not imply that families having a higher income achieve smaller family sizes, since it is quite possible that – while fertility is higher in the lower income areas in each income category than in the higher income areas – within a given area families with higher incomes have more children. Therefore, inferences from results of calculations based on territorial data on relationships prevailing at the level of individual families should be made with great caution.

International cross-sections

It seems obviously profitable to compare the fertility levels of different countries with data concerning their economic and social development and try to infer from this comparison the factors determining level of fertility. Several studies of this nature have been performed.

Weintraub (1962), using data of thirty developed and developing countries around the year 1950, found that the birth rate was positively correlated (as shown by the partial correlation coefficients) to the level of *per capita* national income, as well as to the percentage of agricultural population and to infant mortality. That is, *ceteris paribus*, the growth of income would increase fertility, the changes associated with economic development (e.g. industrialization and the decline of infant mortality) would cause a decline in fertility, and the effect of these latter associated changes overshadows the influence of the growth of income.

Adelman (1963) made a similar analysis based on the data of thirtyseven countries at different developmental levels between 1947 and 1957. She found that age-specific fertility rates are positively associated to *per capita* national income and negatively associated to the percentage of manpower employed outside agriculture, to an indicator of educational level (constructed from data of literacy and of *per capita* newspaper consumption) and to population density, the strongest correlation being that of fertility and education. These findings might be interpreted similarly to those of Weintraub. Later Adelman and Morris (1966) performed a factor analysis of different demographic, social and economic data of developing countries and found that the crude fertility rate was correlated with a factor of economic development and a factor of institutional modernization. They surmised that a fundamental underlying factor of modernization of thought and a spread of rationalism might be the cause of the decline in fertility.

Heer (1966), using data of forty-one countries at different levels of economic development, found a weak positive correlation between fertility and *per capita* national income, as well as a negative correlation of fertility to newspaper circulation and to population density, and a positive correlation to infant mortality and to *per capita* energy consumption. The last correlation seems to be the most interesting. Heer interpreted it by stating that the growth of energy consumption is an indicator of the rate of economic growth, and that a higher rate of growth tends to influence fertility positively in the short run while the long-term negative influence of economic development on fertility appears only with a certain lag, in connection with the general increase of the cultural level, expressed here by newspaper circulation, facilitating communication within the society.

Friedlander and Silver (1967), analysing separately developed industrial countries, the countries at an intermediate level of development, and underdeveloped countries, found that the strong correlations evidenced in the overall analysis of all the countries together became rather weak when analysed in the three separate groups, and some signs even changed. This fact suggests that only countries at a more or less similar level of development should be analysed together by the regression methods, as the separate effect of particular social factors on fertility might be different in countries at very different levels of development. For example, one of their findings was that fertility is correlated to *per capita* income positively in the developed countries, but negatively in the underdeveloped ones.

Gregory, Campbell and Cheng (1972a) went further in refining the techniques of analysing the relations of fertility and social factors, by using simultaneous equations. The basic idea was that not only was fertility influenced by different factors such as level of income and labour force participation rate of women, but also that these two variables were simultaneously influenced by fertility. The calculated coefficients of the model showed that fertility was positively influenced by the level of *per capita* income. The influence of the labour force participation rate of women on fertility was negative. The level of fertility was positively associated with two exogenous variables, illiteracy and infant mortality. On the other hand, a higher fertility had a negative effect on the partition rate of women and also on the level of *per capita* income.

Interregional cross-sections

Most international cross-sectional analyses tried to explain the factors contributing to the demographic transition from very high level fertility to the moderately low level of fertility characteristic for the average of the developed countries. In this book, however, we are interested in the factors differentiating the fertility of developed countries. For that purpose, the interregional cross-sectional analyses performed on the basis of data of different regions in particular developed countries might be of interest. The fundamental question in these analyses might be formulated in the following way: are the regional fertility differences within given countries caused by regional differences in social and economic development, or are there other factors connected with cultural, ethnic or denominational composition of the regional units which may have an important influence on the fertility differences?

In Poland important regional differences in fertility were observed after the Second World War. As there were relatively great changes in the pattern of these differences, and as the pattern of differences was rather unusual (the more developed western and northern regions having had higher fertility rates, and the urban rates in these regions being relatively high), the analysis of the Polish data provides interesting insights into the causes of development of fertility (table 4.26).

The correlation and regression analyses performed gave contradicting results according to the independent variables taken into account. The level of fertility around the year 1960 was negatively correlated to both *per capita* income and *per capita* consumption in the Polish regions (Roeske-Slomka 1973). When, however, in addition to *per capita* income, the percentages of agricultural population and infant mortality were also taken into consideration in a multivariate analysis, the partial correlation of fertility to income became positive, the partial correlation of fertility to agricultural population and to infant mortality also being positive (Vielrose 1965a). In another analysis the growth rate of *per capita* income was positively correlated to fertility changes – i.e. the decline of fertility, which was universal in Poland in that period (1956–61), was slower in the regions where the growth of *per capita* income was more rapid. These correlations can be explained partly by the fact that on the one hand the agricultural regions had much lower *per capita* income and higher fertility, and that on the other hand the more backward agricultural regions developed more rapidly in that period. Nevertheless, the appearance of the positive relation of fertility to both *per capita* income and the growth rate of it, when other manifestations of modernization (e.g. the percentage of non-agricultural population) are kept constant, is notable.

The history of mass migrations following the Second World War in Poland might help to explain some features of the regional fertility differences. The western and northern provinces (Bydgoszcz, Gdańsk, Koszalin, Olsztyn, Szczecin, Wrocław and Zielona Góra) and the town of Wrocław were populated after the War mostly by immigrants from the eastern part of prewar Poland, i.e. from the most backward regions of the country. In consequence of the migration, this population achieved far more favourable conditions than those in their area of origin, since these western and northern territories were relatively well developed, in spite of the devastations of the War. These favourable conditions combined with the high fertility norms and customs brought with them from their region of origin produced for several years higher fertility rates than those observed in the eastern parts of the country, which were less developed but where the population was largely of native origin and had in consequence cultural

Table 4.26 Regional differences of gross reproduction rates in Poland.

Region (city, province)	Total				Urban				Rural			
	1950–1951	1955–1956	1960–1961	1965–1966	1950–1951	1955–1956	1960–1961	1965–1966	1950–1951	1955–1956	1960–1961	1965–1966
Poland	1·799	1·719	1·410	1·203	1·563	1·514	1·116	0·918	1·978	1·927	1·744	1·577
City provinces												
Warsaw	1·210	1·258	0·778	0·594	1·210	1·258	0·778	0·594	—	—	—	—
Kraków	1·108	1·265	0·898	0·686	1·108	1·265	0·898	0·686	—	—	—	—
Łódź	1·220	1·137	0·836	0·669	1·220	1·137	0·836	0·669	—	—	—	—
Poznań	1·355	1·352	0·932	0·712	1·355	1·352	0·932	0·712	—	—	—	—
Wrocław	1·662	1·437	0·964	0·758	1·662	1·437	0·964	0·758	—	—	—	—
Provinces												
Białystok	1·794	1·818	1·647	1·415	1·756	1·666	1·285	1·053	1·814	1·874	1·847	1·681
Bydgoszcz	2·000	1·971	1·575	1·307	1·734	1·678	1·239	0·988	2·224	2·263	1·944	1·727
Gdańsk	2·106	1·918	1·473	1·236	1·886	1·662	1·186	0·980	2·485	2·487	2·137	1·922
Katowice	1·456	1·413	1·162	1·014	1·280	1·357	1·070	0·925	1·782	1·584	1·473	1·326
Kielce	1·939	1·799	1·548	1·294	1·732	1·676	1·215	0·976	1·963	1·840	1·700	1·468
Koszalin	2·396	2·330	1·806	1·478	2·181	2·060	1·408	1·077	2·529	2·512	2·198	1·985
Kraków	1·840	1·707	1·565	1·418	1·553	1·529	1·323	1·053	1·915	1·787	1·664	1·601
Lublin	1·635	1·633	1·439	1·282	1·534	1·601	1·113	0·932	1·659	1·633	1·572	1·478
Łódź	1·734	1·676	1·393	1·183	1·582	1·497	1·123	0·923	1·794	1·758	1·546	1·352
Olsztyn	2·309	2·263	1·594	1·589	2·021	1·855	1·321	1·067	2·444	3·507	2·190	2·012
Opole	1·630	1·572	1·485	1·309	1·565	1·480	1·290	1·024	1·662	1·628	1·628	1·548
Poznań	1·922	1·903	1·591	1·389	1·746	1·688	1·280	1·075	2·017	2·029	1·792	1·618
Rzeszów	1·804	1·678	1·541	1·408	1·553	1·534	1·191	1·017	1·862	1·729	1·664	1·577
Szczecin	2·355	2·125	1·483	1·258	2·108	1·822	1·181	1·007	2·724	2·632	2·089	1·886
Warszawa	1·782	1·768	1·449	1·294	1·563	1·447	1·063	0·956	1·840	1·898	1·734	1·505
Wrocław	2·147	1·946	1·480	1·227	1·884	1·723	1·287	1·034	2·340	2·178	1·748	1·519
Zielona Góra	2·309	2·152	1·616	1·326	2·055	1·915	1·369	1·113	2·480	2·364	1·920	1·637

Source: Smolinski (1971), p. 100.

traditions of a somewhat lower fertility. Also the relatively high level of urban fertility in these areas is explained by the fact that the urban populations had a rural background, while in the central and eastern part of postwar Poland the urban populations consisted at least partly of the original inhabitants of these towns.

The fertility differences of the first postwar years, however, changed rather rapidly, and already by 1965–6 another pattern of regional differences seemed to be appearing: the rural regions in northwestern, northern and eastern Poland showed the highest fertility rates and the most urbanized and industrialized regions the lowest rates. Rural–urban differences increased and became important in the western and northern territories too. These tendencies might be interpreted by the adaptation of the immigrant populations in the west and north and of the urban populations in general to the new economic and social conditions. The study of the development of these regional differences also explains some peculiarities of postwar Polish fertility development: the very high fertility until about 1960 and the sharp fall in the 1960s (Smolinski 1971).

Unlike in Poland, the regional differences of fertility in Yugoslavia seemed to remain rather permanent (table 4.27). The three regions which showed the highest fertility rates before the Second World War – namely, Kosovo, Macedonia, and Bosnia and Herzegovina – remained until 1970 the areas having the highest fertility, although their fertility declined. As the decline was very small in Kosovo, it was in the 1970s an outstandingly high fertility area in Yugoslavia. Croatia, Montenegro and Serbia proper (i.e. Serbia without Vojvodina and Kosovo) were territories having medium-level fertility in Yugoslavia. Vojvodina had the lowest fertility. Slovenia, on the other hand, which was before the War the second lowest fertility region in Yugoslavia, showed recently a somewhat higher birth rate than the regions with the lowest rates (Breznik 1967, Breznik et al. 1972). The change in the relative position of Slovenia suggests the possibility of a more highly developed region having higher fertility above a certain level of socioeconomic development.

Rasevic analysed fertility levels and other socioeconomic characteristics of seventy-nine regions in Yugoslavia by multiple correlation and regression methods (Rasevic 1965 1971). Fertility proved to be most strongly correlated to illiteracy and to the lowest educational level (1–3 years of schooling), as well as to infant mortality, indicating the traditional relation of high fertility in backward regions and low fertility in more advanced ones. The simple correlation of fertility to the income level of the region was negative, but the partial correlation coefficient became insignificant in the multivariate analysis. However, as the multiple correlation coefficient was rather low ($R = 0.72$), Rasevic concluded that some other factors had influenced the regional fertility levels.

Table 4.27 Regional differences of birth rates in Yugoslavia.

Period	Yugoslavia	Bosnia and Herzegovina	Montenegro	Croatia	Macedonia	Slovenia	Serbia			
							Total	Serbia proper	Vojvodina	Kosovo
1931–1935	31·9	39·0	31·3	29·0	35·0	24·6	30·6	32·3	24·3	36·9
1936–1939	27·4	36·9	28·9	25·4	34·2	22·4	24·4	24·6	20·0	34·1
1948–1949	29·1	37·6	30·6	24·3	41·1	22·8	27·5	26·8	25·0	40·0
1950–1954	28·8	38·2	32·1	23·2	38·4	22·8	27·4	26·1	23·3	43·5
1955–1959	24·8	35·3	30·1	20·3	34·0	19·4	22·0	19·6	18·4	42·3
1960–1964	22·1	31·7	26·9	17·2	29·4	17·9	19·7	16·6	16·3	41·7
1965	21·0	29·0	24·7	16·6	28·1	18·5	18·8	15·4	15·5	40·5
1966	20·4	27·6	24·2	16·5	27·0	18·6	18·1	14·9	14·8	38·5
1967	19·6	25·9	22·5	15·4	26·2	17·7	18·1	14·9	14·4	38·9
1968	19·1	24·6	21·4	15·0	25·4	16·9	18·0	14·8	14·1	38·5
1969	18·9	23·9	21·7	14·5	25·1	16·3	18·3	15·2	13·6	39·1
1970	17·8	20·9	19·8	13·9	23·3	16·4	17·4	15·0	12·6	36·0

Source: Breznik (1967), Statistical Yearbook of Yugoslavia.

An obvious interpretation would be the ethnic factor. The republics and territories of Yugoslavia are inhabited by populations of different ethnic compositions – for example, Serbia proper by Serbs, Vojvodina by Serbs and Hungarians, Kosovo by Albanians, Croatia by Croatians, etc. It might be argued that the different cultural traditions of the particular national groups cause differences of regional fertility. However, according to Breznik (1967), this explanation does not hold, since all ethnic groups have generally similar levels of fertility in the given regions – e.g. all have very high fertilities in Kosovo and all have low fertilities in Vojvodina, which incidentally has a very mixed population, so it provides a good experimental field in which to investigate national fertility differences.

Similar to Yugoslavia, regional fertility differences are rather large in the Soviet Union, where territorial differences more or less coincide with differences in the ethnic composition of these areas (table 4.28). Some Soviet demographers stressed the importance of the ethnic factors (Bondarskaya 1970, Bondarskaya and Kozlov 1971), while others mentioned the religious factor (Kozlov 1968). However, as there are also important differences in the socioeconomic development levels of the

Table 4.28 Regional differences of birth rates and total fertility rates: USSR.

Republic	Birth rate			Total fertility rate
	1960	1970	1973	1970
Russian SFSR	23·2	14·6	15·1	1970
Ukrainian SSR	20·5	15·2	14·9	2040
Belorussian SSR	24·5	16·2	15·7	2300
Moldavian SSR	29·2	19·4	20·4	2560
Estonian SSR	16·6	15·8	15·0	2140
Latvian SSR	16·7	14·5	13·9	1940
Lithuanian SSR	22·5	17·6	16·0	2350
Georgian SSR	24·7	19·2	18·2	2620
Armenian SSR	40·3	22·1	22·1	3200
Azerbaijan SSR	42·6	29·2	25·4	4630
Kazakh SSR	36·7	23·3	23·2	3310
Uzbek SSR	39.9	33.5	33.7	5640
Turkmen SSR	42·4	35·2	34·3	5930
Tadzhik SSR	33·5	34·7	35·6	5900
Kirgiz SSR	36·8	30·5	30·6	4850
Total USSR	23·2	17·4	17·6	2390

Sources: Pressat (1972b), Urlanis (1974), Arutyunyan (1975).

different territories considered, the fertility differences might be interpreted as related to socio-economic factors. Mazur (1967 1968), for example, found that fertility differences between ethnic groups can be explained fairly satisfactorily by differences in educational level and differences in age at marriage. In a subsequent study based on the data of 150 political-administrative units of the Soviet Union, Mazur divided the analysis into four groups by distinguishing urban and rural, as well as birth control practising and non-practising areas, the latter being the Armenian, Azerbaijan, Kazakh, Kirgiz, Tadzhik, Turkmen and Uzbek SSRs. Different social variables were found to have the strongest influence on fertility differentials in these four groups, namely:

(a) Education of women as the most important factor in urban birth control practising areas.
(b) The ratio of dependent women was the most important in rural birth control practising areas.
(c) The male–female literacy differential, considered to be an indicator of traditionalism, was the most important factor in urban and rural birth control non-practising areas.

The proportion of married women aged 16 and over was very strongly correlated with fertility in birth control non-practising areas and showed a rather weak correlation in the birth control practising areas. The results of this multiple correlation analysis might be interpreted in different ways. On the one hand, it might be suggested that all social variables are indicators of different aspects of socioeconomic development; thus the fertility levels of the different republics of the Soviet Union are determined by their level of modernization, and are not influenced to any important degree by cultural factors. On the other hand, the differences in fertility of the republics might be interpreted in terms of the different influences of their cultural (i.e. ethnic and denominational) backgrounds, which more or less determine the average age at marriage and also the extent to which birth control is accepted and practised.

Urlanis (1974) seems to accept the second interpretation, when he points out that within the Soviet socialist republics and the autonomous republics the populations of different ethnicity have very different birth rates. In addition to the purely scientific interest of this problem, it has very high practical importance for Soviet demographers, since, if the fertility differentials remain a long-lasting phenomenon (and, as Urlanis stresses, the differentials did not diminish but widened during the 1960s), they will influence strongly the composition of the population of the Soviet Union.

Yasuba (1961) analysed by means of simple rank correlation coefficients the socioeconomic factors influencing the refined birth rates he calculated for states and territories of the United States from 1800 to 1860. He found that in the early decades of the nineteenth century population density was rather strongly negatively correlated to the birth rates, reflecting the fact that in the traditionally settled areas the relative scarcity of land was a factor reducing the fertility of the population, while in the newly settled western regions the availability of free or relatively cheap land tended to stimulate a higher fertility. The influence of the density of population on the birth rates seems to have diminished in the later decades of the nineteenth century.

After the middle of the nineteenth century industrialization and urbanization assumed major roles in influencing the fertility differences of the states in America, the more industrialized and urbanized ones having lower fertilities.

The correlation between average income and the birth rate of states and territories seems to have been rather weak, but negative. The correlation disappeared when the degree of urbanization was held constant in the analysis. Yasuba suggests that average income might have been inversely associated with fertility in the more urbanized areas and positively associated with fertility in the rural areas.

Table 4.29 Regional differences of gross reproduction rates: Italy.

| | Period | | | |
Region	1881–1882	1910–1912	1930–1932	1935–1937
Piedmont	2·390	1·620	0·967	0·865
Liguria	2·234	1·608	0·906	0·780
Lombardy	2·459	2·226	1·261	1·131
Trentino–Alto Adige	—	—	1·394	1·290
Veneto	2·445	2·640	1·722	1·517
Venezia Giulia and Zara	—	—	1.235	1.106
Emilia–Romagna	2·450	2·432	1·365	1·143
Tuscany	2·486	2·042	1·140	1·027
Marches	2·415	2·464	1·692	1·456
Umbria	2·485	2·382	1·720	1·489
Latium	2·332	2·078	1·626	1·439
Abruzzi	2·568	2·280	2·038	1·880
Campania	2·449	2·351	2·169	1·948
Apulia	2·781	2·620	2·332	2·185
Basilicata	2·707	2·651	2·397	2·322
Calabria	2·436	2·474	2·240	2·134
Sicily	2·650	2·306	1·911	1·761
Sardinia	2·448	2·221	2·028	1·946

Source: Glass (1967), p. 266.

Potter (1965) was not convinced by the primary importance of the relative scarcity or abundance of accessible land at the beginning of the decline of fertility in the United States. Forster and Tucker (1972), however, confirmed Yasuba's conclusions by means of more refined regression techniques.

Easterlin also found that the decline in fertility of American farmers in the nineteenth century began in the old settlement areas, where available land had become less abundant, and therefore the prospective rates of return and the prospective growth of capital had declined. Under these conditions farmers were increasingly concerned about their ability to give their children a proper start in life – i.e. a farm of at least equal value to that of their own farm at the beginning of their career. Hence they began to limit the number of their children (Easterlin 1976).

At the present time, in western Europe fertility differences are especially high in Italy (tables 4.29–4.30). Differences which already existed in the

Table 4.30   Regional differences of cumulated fertility rates of women aged 39 for the cohorts born in 1906–1911 and 1926–1931 in Italy.

Region	Cumulated fertility rate of women aged 39 born in	
	1906–1911	*1926–1931*
Piedmont and Valle d'Aosta	1640	1513
Liguria	1490	1399
Lombardy	2134	1792
Trentino–Alto Adige	2364	2392
Veneto	2711	2167
Emilia–Romagna	2152	1698
Tuscany	1984	1671
Umbria	2594	1805
Marches	2582	1896
Latium	2588	2095
Abruzzi	3086	2153
Campania	3463	2752
Apulia	3777	2896
Basilicata	4015	2840
Calabria	3725	3061
Sicily	3232	2673
Sardinia	3605	3103

Source: Tabah (1971), p. 34.

first half of the nineteenth century (table 3.21, p. 82) became more and more accentuated as industrialization of the north proceeded at a high rate, while the south nearly stagnated in the second half of the nineteenth and in the first decades of the twentieth (Glass 1967). Federici (1967) calculated correlations and regressions of age-specific fertility rates and rates of employment of women in economic sectors (agriculture, industry and other branches). Fertility was found to be correlated negatively with employment in industry and other branches, but positively with employment in agriculture. As employment of women in agriculture generally means that they are family members helping in the work of the family farm, a higher economic activity of women in agriculture does not indicate a higher degree of emancipation of women or a higher degree of economic development, so the positive correlation is not surprising. On the other hand, employment of women in industry and tertiary branches is surely an indicator of social and economic development; thus it might be stated that fertility differences in Italy are correlated to the level of regional economic development.

The regional fertility differences in France do not show the clear tendencies and relations found in Italy (Chasteland and Henry 1956, Le Bras 1971, Noin 1973). The regional gross reproduction rates calculated for census years from 1921 to 1962 display a change in the pattern of regional differences. At the turn of the century and in the first decades of the twentieth century Brittany, Normandy, the Massif Central and Corsica showed the highest and the southwestern part of France the lowest fertility. It should be remembered that the southwest was found already to have a relatively low fertility by the historical demographic studies described in Part 2. The pattern of regional differences gradually became more crystallized, the north and the east having relatively high fertilities and the south relatively low fertilities. The area of low fertility extended from the region around the Loire through Languedoc to Provence. The area of high fertility formed a semicircular area beginning from the Vendée and ending in Savoie, while the area surrounding Paris had a relatively low fertility. The differences slowly became more accentuated, as in the baby boom period the fertility of the northern and eastern departments increased to a greater extent than that of the southern part of France.

No regression analysis of the regional data was performed. Different authors suggest different explanations of these regional fertility patterns. Le Bras considers that historical and geographical factors might have a more important influence on these regional differences than economic and social factors, although he does not specify these historical and geographical influences. Noin, on the other hand, sees a correlation between the higher level of education of the population and the lower fertility in the southern part of France. Another alternative explanation might be sought in terms of the different rates of economic development in past decades, as the northern and eastern parts of France experienced a higher rate of economic development than the south, and the relatively higher fertility and the more important growth of fertility in the postwar period might be influenced by this higher economic development rate.

The most detailed and sophisticated analyses of territorial differences of fertility were performed in the Netherlands (Derksen 1966 1970). First, Derksen investigated fertility differentials in 1931 of eleven provinces and six major cities in the Netherlands by multiple regression analysis. Later, Somermeyer repeated the same analysis with data concerning the periods 1955–7 and 1926–30 of seventy-eight socioeconomic regions of the country. Recently, a new analysis utilized the data of 1960 and 1967 concerning 129 regions. The repeated studies give an exceptional opportunity to analyse the changes of the factors determining the regional fertility differences. The following explanatory variables were taken into consideration:

(a) Proportion of Roman Catholic population (or, alternatively, the proportion of those voting for the Catholic Party).
(b) Proportion of Orthodox Reformed population (or, alternatively, the proportion of those voting for the Calvinist parties).
(c) Percentage of rural population.
(d) Percentage of population residing in cities above 100 000 inhabitants.
(e) Percentage of women 15–44 years old, who have received primary education only (six years of compulsory primary school) – or, alternatively, the percentage of all young men subjected to army intelligence tests in 1948–52 whose scores were in the two lowest classes.

Fertility was measured by average annual fertility per 1000 married women in the age group 15–49, adjusted for regional variations of the age structure.

Regression coefficients and their standard deviations for three periods investigated are given in table 4.31.

The strongest factor influencing positively the level of fertility was the percentage of Roman Catholic and Orthodox Reformed (Calvinist) population – i.e. where these denominational groups were less numerous and the members of the Dutch Reformed Church or of other denominations (as well as people without religious affiliation) were more numerous, fertility tended to be lower. However, the influence of the denominational factor, most of all that of the percentage of Roman Catholic population, declined; it was strongest in 1926–30 and constantly declined until the last analysis in 1967. This coincided with the findings of differential fertility analyses in the Netherlands, which showed that the fertility differential

Table 4.31 Regression coefficients and their standard deviations in cross-sectional analyses of interregional variations of marital fertility: Netherlands.

	Periods investigated		
Explanatory variables	*1955–1957*	*1960*	*1967*
	%	%	%
Religious affiliation:			
Roman Catholic	1·26	0·77	0·20
	(0·15)	(0·11)	(0·07)
Orthodox Reformed	0·86	0·69	0·51
	(0·45)	(0·39)	(0·24)
Degree of urbanization:			
In rural municipalities	0·31	0·15	0·17
	(0·13)	(0·09)	(0·06)
In towns with more than 100 000	−0·20	−0·25	−0·11
inhabitants	(0·09)	(0·08)	(0·05)
Education:			
Of women with primary education only	1·47	1·17	1·37
among all women 14–44 years	(0·86)	(0·53)	(0·32)
Coefficient of multiple correlation	0·81	0·71	0·68

Source: Derksen (1970).

between the Catholic population and the other population groups diminished in the 1960s.

The two variables indicating the degree of urbanization showed the expected signs – that in regions with a higher percentage of population living in rural municiplalities fertility was higher, while in the regions where the population living in large towns was great fertility was lower. The influence of these urbanization factors seemed to have diminished to a certain extent.

On the other hand, the influence of education of women did not seem to diminish – i.e. where education was lower, fertility tended to be higher.

The coefficient of multiple correlation decreased from 1955–7 to 1967. This was explained by Derksen partly as a consequence of the diminishing differences of marital fertility in the regions of the Netherlands.

No significant correlation of fertility to infant mortality or to *per capita* income was found, while the percentage of employed married women had a strong negative influence on fertility, although this percentage is relatively low in all the regions of the Netherlands. The fact that infant mortality showed no significant correlation might be interpreted as a consequence of the very low level of infant mortality attained in the Netherlands.

The influence of *per capita* income on fertility is further elucidated by a separate analysis of urban, mixed and rural regions in 1967. The influence of income, though hardly significant in each case, appears to be positive in the rural regions and negative in the mixed and urban regions. Derksen quotes an American investigation (Phillips *et al.* 1969) in which income of a rural farm population was found to be positively correlated to fertility, and considers that this is a proof of the positive influence of income on fertility in homogeneous occupational groups.

Thus the analysis of data on the regions of the Netherlands seems to prove the strong though diminishing influence of a cultural (denominational) factor on marital fertility. Two historical studies of fertility differences may contribute to the explanation of the development of these differences. Hofstee (1968) explained the regional differences by a diffusion theory, stating that birth control began to be practised in the northwestern part of the Netherlands (i.e. in the most developed, most urbanized region) and spread from there to other parts. The nearer a region is to the northwestern region, the lower its fertility, as it accepted the practice of birth control earlier. The least accessible and most distant parts of the country, North Brabant and Limburg in the south and Drenthe, Groningen and Friesland in the northeast, maintained the relatively highest fertility. The former two, however, are predominantly Catholic areas, while the latter three are inhabited by many Orthodox Calvinists.

Buissink (1971), on the other hand, explained the regional fertility differences by different attitudes to birth control, the resistance of the Roman Catholic and Orthodox Calvinist denominations to birth control being stronger than that of Dutch Reformed and other populations. According to Buissink, the fact that even those Roman Catholic regions that were situated relatively near the centre of diffusion of birth control retained their high fertility proves that cultural factors, not distance or accessibility, were determining the level of fertility. He gives a special explanation for the high fertility level of Drenthe. This formerly poor and backward region underwent a rapid development in the second half of the nineteenth century, as its cultivated area increased extensively due to peat cutting and land reclamation from the marshes and bogs. On the other hand, the relative geographical isolation of the region impeded the spread of new ideas. Thus the role of socioeconomic and cultural factors influencing fertility seems to be a mixed one in the regions of the Netherlands.

Livi-Bacci investigated differences in marital fertility in Portugal in the nineteenth and twentieth centuries. (Livi-Bacci 1971b.) The case of Portugal is of special interest, because it is a smaller and ethnically as well as denominationally more homogeneous country than any of the other countries analysed, and because regional fertility differences have increased in the last decades.

Utilizing the data of twenty-two districts of Portugal in 1911, 1930 and 1960, marital fertility (Coale's I_g value) was correlated to an index of illiteracy, the percentage of employment in agriculture, infant mortality and emigration, and in addition in 1960 to the percentage of births with no medical assistance (representing the level of medical organization), and to an index of religiousness.

It is interesting that marital fertility is never significantly correlated to illiteracy, which represents the level of education, one of the factors most strongly correlated to fertility in other countries. A significant positive association of marital fertility to infant mortality was found in 1960, to employment in agriculture in 1911 and 1930, to emigration in 1930 and 1960, and to the percentage of births with no medical assistance and the percentage of Catholics in 1960.

It seems, however, more interesting that the regional differences were not explained by these indices of economic and social development. An F test found that the regional means of marital fertility still differed significantly one from another after the effects of these variables had been removed from the means. The high fertility of the north and the low fertility of the south were specially outstanding. There is no evident difference between standards of living in the north and the south (the district of Lisbon being excluded from the comparison). The south has more illiteracy, more labour force employed in agriculture, is less industrialized and has lower participation of women in economic activities. On the other hand, the north is less urbanized, and has a much higher infant mortality rate, a higher death rate from infectious diseases, and a worse sanitary system. Thus neither region seems to be clearly more developed. The difference of fertility is explained, according to Livi-Bacci, by different attitudes which cannot be measured exactly by statistical indices. The north is more religious, more attached to tradition, has a stronger family life, and the population displays a patient and enduring character with an innate suspicion of innovation. On the other hand, the south is characterized by the lack of religious feeling, passivity, indolence and moral indifference of its population, and by the weakness of family ties. The social background of these differences is provided by the fact that in the north very small farm holdings prevail, while in the south the land is concentrated in a few *latifundia* and farm labourers constitute a large part of the agricultural population. Also the population of the north, which is much more densely populated, resorted to large-scale emigration, while emigration was much less important in the south.

Similar multiple regression analyses were carried out with the regional data of Hungary (Andorka 1967 1968 1969b 1969d 1970b 1971b). The data of the 1960 census combined with the vital statistical fertility data of the year 1960 provided very good opportunities for performing multivariate analyses based on territorial data. The variables taken into consideration were: X_1, total fertility rate; X_2, percentage of agricultural population; X_3, percentage of population aged 15 and over who had completed eight grades of primary school; X_4, percentage of active earners, i.e. of employed among women; X_5, percentage of population living in detached

Table 4.32 Regression and correlation coefficients and standard deviations in cross-section analyses of fertility: Hungary, 1960.

All Hungary $(n = 191)$

Correlation matrix:

	X_1	X_2	X_3	X_4	X_5
X_1	1·00000	0·53259	−0·62422	−0·50468	0·06155
X_2		1·00000	−0·88335	−0·37554	0·45232
X_3			1·00000	0·50606	−0·37023
X_4				1·00000	−0·09518
X_5					1·00000

Regressions and standard deviations:

$X_1 = 1815 + 9·38\,X_2$
        $(1·08)$

$X_1 = 2897 − 24·20\,X_3$
        $(2·20)$

$X_1 = 3106 − 27·34\,X_4$
        $(3·40)$

$X_1 = 2182 + 2·08\,X_5$
        $(2·46)$

$X_1 = 3044 − 1·51\,X_2 − 27·14\,X_3$
        $(2·14)$ $(4·71)$

$X_1 = 2534 + 7·03\,X_2 − 19·2\,X_4$
        $(1·08)$ $(3·32)$

$X_1 = 1842 + 11·17\,X_2 − 7·64\,X_5$
        $(1·18)$ $(2·27)$

$X_1 = 3206 − 19·22\,X_3 − 13·75\,X_4$
        $(2·46)$ $(3·46)$

$X_1 = 3067 − 27·02\,X_3 − 6·65\,X_5$
        $(2·31)$ $(2·02)$

$X_1 = 3097 − 27·27\,X_4 + 0·46\,X_5$
        $(3·43)$ $(2·14)$

$X_1 = 3211 − 0·05\,X_2 − 19·34\,X_3 − 13·73\,X_4$
        $(2·09)$ $(4·95)$ $(3·50)$

$X_1 = 3021 + 0·50\,X_2 − 26·10\,X_3 − 6·80\,X_5$
        $(2·18)$ $(4·61)$ $(2·11)$

$X_1 = 2532 + 8·69\,X_2 − 18·30\,X_4 − 6·56\,X_5$
        $(1·18)$ $(3·26)$ $(2·12)$

$X_1 = 3329 − 22·10\,X_3 − 12·60\,X_4 − 5·81\,X_5$
        $(2·60)$ $(3·39)$ $(1·97)$

$X_1 = 3182 + 1·73\,X_2 − 18·79\,X_3 − 13·02\,X_4 − 6·27\,X_5$
        $(2·13)$ $(4·85)$ $(3·43)$ $(2·04)$

Table 4.32—contd.

All Hungary ($n = 190$)

Partial correlation coefficients:

$r_{12\cdot3} = -0\cdot05$	$r_{13\cdot2} = -0\cdot39$	$r_{14\cdot2} = -0\cdot39$	$r_{15\cdot2} = -0\cdot24$
$r_{12\cdot4} = +0\cdot43$	$r_{13\cdot4} = -0\cdot50$	$r_{14\cdot3} = -0\cdot28$	$r_{15\cdot3} = -0\cdot23$
$r_{12\cdot5} = +0\cdot57$	$r_{13\cdot5} = -0\cdot65$	$r_{14\cdot5} = -0\cdot50$	$r_{15\cdot4} = +0\cdot01$
$r_{12\cdot34} = -0\cdot00$	$r_{13\cdot24} = -0\cdot27$	$r_{14\cdot23} = -0\cdot28$	$r_{15\cdot23} = -0\cdot23$
$r_{12\cdot35} = +0\cdot01$	$r_{13\cdot25} = -0\cdot38$	$r_{14\cdot25} = -0\cdot38$	$r_{15\cdot24} = -0\cdot22$
$r_{12\cdot45} = +0\cdot47$	$r_{13\cdot45} = -0\cdot53$	$r_{14\cdot35} = -0\cdot26$	$r_{15\cdot34} = -0\cdot21$
$r_{12\cdot345} = +0\cdot05$	$r_{13\cdot245} = -0\cdot27$	$r_{14\cdot235} = -0\cdot27$	$r_{15\cdot234} = -0\cdot22$

Multiple correlation coefficient: $R_{1\cdot2345} = 0\cdot68$.

1960 Four different regions of Hungary

Northeast ($n = 41$)
$X_1 = 3153 - 25\cdot53\,X_3$ $\qquad\qquad$ $r_{13} = -0\cdot60$
$\qquad\quad (5\cdot01)$

West ($n = 34$)
$X_1 = 3019 - 22\cdot41\,X_3$ $\qquad\qquad$ $r_{13} = -0\cdot73$
$\qquad\quad (3\cdot66)$

Centre ($n = 52$)
$X_1 = 2702 - 22\cdot01\,X_3$ $\qquad\qquad$ $r_{13} = -0\cdot77$
$\qquad\quad (2\cdot58)$

South ($n = 53$)
$X_1 = 2591 - 21\cdot41\,X_3$ $\qquad\qquad$ $r_{13} = -0\cdot68$
$\qquad\quad (3\cdot24)$

Note: For the definition of the variables see the text on p. 179–80.

farms, i.e. not in densely settled villages, but scattered in the countryside. Data from 191 towns and districts containing several villages were used in the analysis.

It was hypothesized that fertility is correlated negatively to indicators of economic and social development such as industrialization (a low percentage of agricultural population), education and employment of women, and positively associated to the percentage living in detached farms, since these people formed the population living in the most backward conditions (often without electricity, far away from schools, etc.).

The results (table 4.32), however, did not completely confirm these hypotheses. Namely:

1 The correlation of fertility to the percentage of the population living in detached farms was very weak, and even its partial correlation coefficient in the multiple regression analysis turned to negative, as if the population living in detached farms itself would have a negative influence on fertility. This negative coefficient can be explained by

looking at the geographical map of fertility and of the percentage of population living in those detached farms. The latter was especially high in the southern counties of the Great Plain in Hungary – i.e. in the southeastern part of the country, which was characterized by rather low fertility.

2 Both the percentage of agricultural population and the educational level showed fairly strong correlations to fertility. They were, however, very strongly negatively correlated to each other, so it seemed advisable to take into consideration only one of them in the final analysis of the results. As the educational level was more strongly correlated (negatively) to fertility, it was considered in the analysis as a main determinant of fertility. It represents, however, not only the level of schooling, but also the other factors of socioeconomic development associated with it, e.g. industrialization.

3 Employment of women showed the expected negative correlation to fertility. As it was not too strongly correlated to agricultural population and educational level, it was considered to be a relatively independent factor of fertility.

4 The multiple correlation coefficient was not very high, indicating that only half the variance of fertility can be explained by the variations of these four independent variables. It seems therefore that other factors must have had an important influence on fertility differences of regions in 1960.

Thus, other factors mentioned in demographic theories or held to be important by Hungarian public opinion were considered:

1 Infant mortality. This relation was not strong, because infant mortality is remarkably at the same level in urban and rural areas, while the latter have higher fertility than the urban ones.

2 Induced abortions. It would be obvious to hypothesize that where the rate of legal abortions is high, there fertility is low, although even in that case legal abortions could not be considered a fundamental cause of a low fertility level, only an intermediate one, mediating the influence of the fundamental factors. However, the rank correlation coefficient of fertility and the rate of legal abortions was rather low ($r = -0.26$, based on the data of countries and five great towns).

3 Income. Regional *per capita* income was not included in the regression analysis, because no income data concerning 1960 were available. However, as income and industrialization of different counties and towns were fairly strongly correlated in 1962 and 1967 (the years for which regional income data are available), it was considered that *per capita* income could not have an important independent effect on fertility in the regions.

4   Religion. It has often been stated in demographic literature that Roman Catholics have higher fertility rates than Protestants. As Hungary is a religiously mixed country (about two thirds Catholic and slightly less than one third Protestant in 1949), it might be supposed that denominational differences cause the fertility differences not explained by the variables taken into consideration. Data on denominational composition of territorial units were not available in 1960. However, a comparison of the geographical maps of fertility in 1960 and of denominational composition in 1949 gives cause for doubt about the validity of this hypothesis in Hungary in 1960, as the regions where the percentage of Protestant population was high in 1949 (the northeastern part of the country) showed a rather high level of fertility in 1960.

The examination of the scatter diagrams of correlations and regressions suggested another possible explanation for the fertility differences – that neighbouring districts and towns were situated in similar positions compared to the regression line. In other words, for example, the districts and towns in the northeastern part of the country were above the regression line, while the districts and towns in southern Hungary were generally below the regression line. That is, the deviations from the regression line (from the fertility values expected on the basis of the regression equation) seemed to show systematic patterns in different regions. In order to verify this hypothesis, the country was divided into four 'fertility regions', although these were not homogeneous regions in the economic and social sense. They were:

Northeast: characterized by high fertility; part of the region was rather underdeveloped, although another part was the centre of Hungarian heavy industry; this latter part also showed high fertility rates.

West: fertility rates slightly above the average, economically medium developed.

Central region around Budapest: lower than average fertility; an economically developed, industrialized region.

South: fertility rates below average, which is surprising because this is a rather underdeveloped agricultural area (the county of Baranya was not included in this region, although situated in the south, because its fertility was rather above the average).

The multiple regression computations were repeated separately for the four regions. All correlation coefficients became larger than they were in the computation concerning the whole country, and the error sum of squares declined to half of its previous value. Although the smaller number of observation units in the separate computations as compared to the national computation might have had an effect in improving the correlations, it seems to be proved that a strong regional factor was influencing the regional fertility differences. At the same time the regression equations and correlations of the particular regions were very similar: the regression coefficients had similar values, but the constants in the equations were different, as if the same relationships prevailed in all the regions, but at different levels. In table 4.32 the regression equations of fertility and education level are given for the four regions, to illustrate this finding. Other regression equations show similar features (Andorka 1969d).

The existence of this regional factor of fertility differences was confirmed by analysing the historical development of fertility of the four fertility regions. Birth rate data of the different counties and the greatest towns were available from 1920 and total fertility rates could be calculated in the 1960s. Data on birth rates, etc., are available also for the periods preceding 1920. Although they have a different regional breakdown, as country boundaries were changed, these data can be used for historical comparison. They prove that the regional differences were fairly stable, although the fertility level of the country and of the regional units underwent very important changes: a steady decline from 1920 to 1941, a rise after the Second World War, then another decline from 1954 to the first half of the 1960s, a slow rise in the second half of the 1960s, and recently a sudden rise in 1974. During all these changes the fertility levels of the particular regions changed almost in parallel, with some minor exceptions. It can thus be concluded that the regional factor found on the basis of the regression analysis of the data of 1960 is a traditional one. This also means that the regional differences are not the expression of some secular trend of fertility in the function of economic development.

Considering the birth rates and total fertility rates (table 4.33), as well as the analyses on previous periods (Kovács 1923, Tekse, 1969), the following patterns can be discerned.

The fertility of northeastern Hungary (the counties of Szabolcs-Szatmár, Hajdú-Bihar, and Borsod-Abaúj-Zemplén, as well as the eastern half of the county of Szolnok, and the two large towns situated in this region, Debrecen and Miskolc) was always much higher than the average and also higher than might be expected in view of the relative backwardness of the region. The counties of western Transdanubia (Győr-Sopron, Vas, Veszprém, and Zala) seem to have had mostly a fertility level above the average and certainly higher than might be expected in view of the relatively developed character of this region. Some southern counties – namely, those in Transdanubia (Somogy, Csongrád, and Tolna) – had a relatively low fertility for many decades; other southern counties situated on the Great Plain (Bács-Kiskun and Békés) entered the group of the low fertility regions at a later date. The low fertility of the two great towns situated in the south (Pécs and Szeged) reflects the same tendency. The relatively low

Table 4.33   Regional differences of fertility: Hungary.

Region, county and town	Birth rate				Total fertility rate		
	1925	*1935*	*1949*	*1954*	*1959– 60*	*1961*	*1962*
Central region							
Fejér county	29·9	19·2	22·9	26·0	2273	2169	1953
Heves county	31·8	23·1	19·6	21·7	1964	1883	1743
Komárom	32·1	20·9	21·6	25·5	2169	2042	1913
Nógrád county	33·0	25·4	21·2	23·2	2164	2050	1859
Pest county	31·2	21·7	21·5	23·2	1962	1915	1730
Budapest town	17·8	13·2	15·4	19·8	1235	1146	1081
Southern region							
Baranya county	27·4	18·2	20·9	23·9	2447	2413	2058
Bács-Kiskun county	29·5	18·2	20·7	22·5	2142	2019	1926
Békés county	30·5	23·1	20·4	22·0	2024	1964	1860
Csongrád county	26·5	24·4	15·5	20·0	1957	1869	1883
Somogy county	24·5	18·3	19·4	21·3	2139	2025	1791
Tolna county	24·7	18·8	21·0	22·9	2159	2043	1832
Pécs town	—	—	15·8	21·4	1779	1511	1368
Szeged town	—	—	26·5	18·6	1425	1372	1235
Western region							
Győr-Sopron county	29·1	23·7	21·8	23·0	2175	2060	1895
Vas county	27·6	19·9	20·6	22·1	2221	2144	2063
Veszprém county	28·7	21·7	21·0	24·6	2279	2190	2067
Zala county	27·7	21·3	20·1	21·7	2249	2187	1925
Győr town	—	—	—	—	—	—	—
Northeastern region							
Borsod-Abaúj-Zemplén county	32·4	24·4	24·8	25·8	2556	2464	2346
Hajdú-Bihar county	33·1	20·7	24·5	26·7	2662	2730	2495
Szabolcs- Szatmár county	40·3	31·7	28·7	29·1	2902	2802	2759
Szolnok county	31·5	24·0	20·8	23·3	2104	2113	1906
Debrecen town	—	—	20·6	25·9	1844	1671	1557
Miskolc town	—	—	20·1	25·9	1791	1609	1528
Hungary total	28·4	21·1	20·6	23·0	2039	1936	1795

Note: The births of the towns Pécs, Szeged, Debrecen and Miskolc are included in the data of Baranya. Csongrád, Hajdú-Bihar and Borsod-Abaúj-Zemplén in 1925 and 1935; the births of the town Győr are included in the data of Győr-Sopron until 1968.

fertility of this region does not fit into the theory of demographic transition, since it was and still is an area where the extent of agricultural production is above the average of the country. The central region surrounding Budapest has a somewhat lower than average fertility, which might be explained by its relatively more industrialized character.

1963	1964	1965	1966	1967	1968	1970	1971	1972	1973	1974
1945	1874	1921	2028	2141	2209	2112	2085	2134	2109	2501
1717	1683	1685	1785	1830	1911	1958	1984	1881	1869	2330
1872	1831	1853	1872	2022	2058	1993	1989	1958	1992	2446
1839	1837	1793	1976	2125	2017	2064	1974	1969	1956	2342
1789	1742	1766	1837	1967	2048	1991	2015	2021	1998	2429
1128	1163	1182	1249	1394	1429	1494	1365	1450	1455	1797
2120	2162	2128	2149	2234	2242	2074	2081	2046	2112	2501
1910	1897	1959	1999	2112	2185	2059	2018	2004	2073	2355
1886	1925	1983	2059	2110	2274	2040	1978	1999	2064	2558
1759	1835	1940	1911	2024	2117	1977	1964	1914	2024	2310
1861	1903	1870	1962	1996	2030	1912	2006	1953	1938	2250
1889	2001	2050	2064	2210	2236	2095	2039	1968	2023	2451
1404	1499	1380	1599	1633	1744	1674	1616	1584	1594	1906
1256	1308	1367	1346	1359	1489	1481	1321	1332	1456	1773
1920	1944	1964	2024	2184	2303	2304	2250	2174	2215	2554
2039	2023	2037	2138	2288	2294	2203	2172	2086	2103	2426
2032	2008	1972	2063	2173	2179	2149	2154	2209	2176	2517
2050	2098	2126	2124	2372	2468	2149	2100	2088	2154	2439
—	—	—	—	—	—	2042	1796	1921	1912	2198
2284	2325	2298	2355	2537	2571	2406	2300	2278	2301	2602
2529	2584	2553	2669	2852	2945	2566	2571	2642	2614	2821
2766	2787	2744	2892	3132	3139	2640	2651	2636	2689	2937
1983	2015	2006	2168	2279	2362	2166	2147	2066	2164	2538
1576	1612	1523	1607	1808	1853	1693	1588	1684	1728	2025
1532	1492	1565	1727	1915	1886	1903	1794	1830	1823	2161
1823	1811	1812	1882	2010	2060	1969	1919	1929	1969	2304

Source: Demographic yearbooks.

The most important exception to this more or less general stability of relative fertility levels is the county of Baranya. It should be remembered that the microregion of Ormánság where historical studies found early signs of birth control is in Baranya (see pp. 93–8). The fertility of Baranya was the second lowest among the counties in 1920 (the third lowest being neighbouring Somogy, and the lowest that of Csongrád, also in the south). Baranya was characterized by low fertility until the end of the Second World War. After the War the level of fertility in Baranya suddenly changed, becoming somewhat higher than the average for the whole country. This negative example might serve as a first illustration for explaining the stability of relative fertility levels, because a significant portion of the population of the county was changed after the war. This was caused partly by the gradual natural decrease of the native birth control practising population and partly by emigration of part of the German population of the county. The immigrants taking their place originated from very different parts of the country, e.g. from the county of Szabolcs-Szatmár, and also from territories outside the boundaries of Hungary, e.g. Hungarians from Transylvania, Moldavia, Croatia, and Slovakia. With the exception of the last group, almost all these immigrants came from areas characterized by high fertility. The extent of population change might be illustrated by the following data: at the census of 1949, 31 per cent of the population was found to be born outside the county, 20 per cent of them in other counties of Hungary and 11 per cent in foreign countries. Thus the relative fertility level of the county of Baranya changed because the population, and in consequence the cultural norms (including traditional norms and attitudes concerning fertility) changed after the War.

The low fertility rates of the other southern counties might be interpreted as reflecting long traditions, as – at least in southern Transdanubia – fertility levels were already low in the first decades of the 1800s, and perhaps even earlier (it should also be mentioned that the relative fertility level of Tolna changed to a certain extent, in connection with immigration from Moldavia at the end of the War).

The fundamental problem, however, is to determine how these traditions of low fertility and birth control in the south and of relatively high fertility in the northeast developed. Here we are compelled to have recourse to tentative hypotheses. It might be surmised that the southern parts of Hungary, which were under Turkish occupation in the sixteenth and seventeenth centuries, experienced a rapid economic development in the eighteenth century. In the southern parts of the Great Plain this development continued in the nineteenth century, while in the more densely populated southern Transdanubia the development might have slowed down earlier. In consequence of this development, the peasant populations of these areas, most of all the smallholders, attained a certain moderately high standard of living. When, however, the agricultural boom slowed down and later came to an end in the second half of the nineteenth century, this standard of living was difficult to maintain. In addition, industrialization began in the northern part of the country, where the mineral resources were situated. In consequence, the development of the southern countries lagged behind that of the northern ones. This situation lasted until the second half of the 1960s. It might have been the fundamental cause of the development of cultural traditions, norms and attitudes prescribing birth control and relatively small family sizes, resulting in lower fertility than in the north where opportunities for employment were generally more diversified. The very low level of fertility in small and fairly stagnant towns in southern Hungary in 1960 seems to prove this hypothesis. Thus the cultural traditions concerning the norms and attitudes of birth control and family size could be determined by long-run economic factors.

After having found – rather unexpectedly – a strong traditional regional factor influencing fertility and a stability of relative fertility differences between regions, it seemed interesting to replicate the multiple regression analysis of fertility at earlier dates. The data of the censuses of 1949 and 1930 provided a good basis for this kind of analysis. As, however, only fertility data for counties and some larger towns were available (counties are larger administrative units containing several districts and towns), the number of observation units was much smaller. The results of the computations were similar (table 4.34). The fertility level of each region was negatively correlated with the indicators of economic development, although the correlation was not very strong. The pattern was somewhat similar to that found when comparing the correlations and regressions in 1960 in the four regions: the constants in the regression equations are different, but the regression coefficients are similar, as if the same relationship prevailed in 1930, in 1949 and in 1960, only with its level shifted downwards. Also the position of the particular territorial units situated in the four regions above or below the regression lines showed considerable similarity, e.g. the county Szabolcs–Szatmár is in all cases far above the regression line.

In 1930 a further variable, X_6, the percentage of Protestant population, was added to the explanatory variables. The previous observations were confirmed, as the correlation of Protestant population to fertility proved to be positive both in the simple two-variable and in the multiple variable regressions. However, as differential fertility data of the 1930s showed more or less equal fertility levels for Catholic and Protestant populations, it would be erroneous to conclude, on the basis of the results of these regression equations, that Protestants had a higher fertility. Incidentally, this is a good example of the ecological fallacy occurring in cross-sectional territorial analyses. Protestants did in fact have a lower fertility in each region, but in predominantly Protestant regions each denominational group had higher fertility, and therefore the multiple regression equations based on territorial data displayed a positive correlation.

Table 4.34   Regression and correlation coefficients and standard deviations in cross-section analyses of fertility: Hungary, 1949, 1930.

1949 All Hungary $(n = 24)$

Correlation matrix:

	X_1	X_2	X_3	X_4	X_5
X_1	1·00000	0·40626	−0·56045	−0·28971	0·19699
X_2		1·00000	−0·92596	−0·40576	0·28653
X_3			1·00000	0·55252	−0·32330
X_4				1·00000	0·08167
X_5					1·00000

Regression and standard deviation:
$X_1 = 3141 - 26·26\ X_3$
$\qquad (8·28)$

1930 All Hungary $(n = 36)$

Correlation matrix:

	X_1	X_2	X_3	X_4	X_5	X_6
X_1	1·00000	0·69480	−0·70087	−0·68267	−0·00832	0·40603
X_2		1·00000	−0·96384	−0·71342	0·11919	0·22368
X_3			1·00000	0·82136	−0·07168	−0·17802
X_4				1·00000	0·12103	−0·13843
X_5					1·00000	0·15901
X_6						1·00000

Regression and standard deviation:
$X_1 = 3738 - 57·02\ X_3$
$\qquad (9·95)$

Similar results were obtained when simple correlations and regressions of fertility to the percentage of agricultural population were calculated on the basis of data between 1960 and 1964 (of counties and similar administrative units) in four neighbouring socialist countries:

East Germany	$X_1 = 2165 + 90·9\ X_2$	$r = +0·94$
Czechoslovakia	$X_1 = 1420 + 47·4\ X_2$	$r = +0·74$
Hungary	$X_1 = 1521 + 11·6\ X_2$	$r = +0·72$
Poland	$X_1 = 2048 + 21·9\ X_2$	$r = +0·79$
All four countries together	$X_1 = 2059 + 14·6\ X_2$	$r = +0·49$

More or less the same negative correlation of fertility to economic development seemed to prevail in each country, but at different levels – i.e. in areas at the same level of industrialization East Germany (the most developed of the four countries) and Poland (the least developed) showed relatively high fertilities, while Czechoslovakia and Hungary showed lower levels of fertility.

These results suggest two tentative conclusions. First, the regression equations computed on the basis of territorial cross-sections do not reflect long-term development tendencies of fertility – i.e. fertility does not necessarily decline according to the regression coefficients of variables indicating the level of economic and social development, when these variables progress slowly in the long term. Otherwise the particular regions would follow the regression line. However, regression lines tend to shift under the impact of economic and social changes.

Second, a regional factor not included in the general economic and social variables taken into consideration influences regional fertility differences, in some cases considerably. As this regional factor seems to be fairly stable over time, and changes only slowly, it might be surmised that it is connected with traditions and culture in general. Culture, i.e. norms and attitudes concerning fertility, naturally changes slowly and with certain lags compared to economic and social changes. The essence of this traditional regional factor is not clear: it might be simply a cultural characteristic, e.g. religion, or it might be developed under the impact of long-term economic and social conditions and trends. The problem might be formulated as follows: Is culture an ultimate factor of fertility that cannot be reduced to economic factors, or is culture developed under the long-term influence of economic and social conditions?

This conclusion seems to coincide with those of other studies based on data from territorial cross-sections. They all seem to display fairly stable regional influences which might be explained by cultural factors. It is an intriguing question to ask how stable these regional influences are. Knodel (1974) argued that in Germany the regional effects were stronger before demographic transition than they were during it. In Hungary the pre-transitional regional differences seem to be fairly persistent. The other important result seems to be that better economic opportunities, among others higher income, tend to be positively correlated to the level of fertility, if other indicators of socioeconomic development (industrialization, urbanization, etc.) remain constant. These latter indicators are, however, fairly strongly correlated with regional income level, so that it is somewhat difficult to separate the influences of different aspects of socioeconomic development by means of territorial cross-section analyses. On the other hand, because of the relation of the regional factor to these socioeconomic variables, it might interfere when the effects of the socioeconomic variables on fertility are studied by differential fertility analysis or fertility surveys.

4.4 Fertility surveys

Time series of birth rates and other fertility measures are beset by the problems of distinguishing temporary trends due to changes of nuptiality and timing of parities; census fertility data are difficult to use for analysing the factors of fertility, because they provide data on completed fertility only for the older cohorts of women; cross-sectional regression analyses of territorial data are always exposed to the risk of the ecological fallacy. In addition, all these statistical data provide only rather crude information on the social and economic situation of individuals and families, and on the possible motivations of larger and smaller families. Also it has been considered by demographers that data on the practice of fertility control would be necessary for understanding the causal mechanism of fertility. Therefore, at the end of the 1930s some American demographers accepted the idea of employing the survey techniques elaborated in sociology, i.e. interviews of samples by means of formalized questionnaires, to investigate the aspects of fertility not covered by the data obtainable from vital statistics. Subsequently this technique was adopted all over the world, leading to the more or less standardized surveys of fertility and family planning (the KAP – i.e. knowledge, attitudes and practice – concerning family planning and birth control) and the World Fertility Survey.

These surveys (though not all of them) used to include questions on:

1   History of fertility.
2   Plans, expectations, desires and ideals concerning size of family.
3   The practice of birth control, as well as knowledge and opinions on it.
4   The economic and social conditions of the family.
5   Motives and attitudes concerning size of the family, as well as other psychological characteristics of the parents.

Not only was the first fertility survey carried out in the United States, but this country also carries out the largest number of surveys, providing an opportunity for investigating trends in the results. These surveys will therefore be examined first in detail, as they give insights into the results and also the limitations of fertility surveys.

Two main series of fertility surveys may be distinguished in the United States: (1) the Indianapolis and Princeton surveys, which use special samples and focus on highly refined problems of causation of fertility, and

(2) the Growth of American Families (GAF) surveys and the National Fertility Studies, which use national samples of adult women and focus more on the description of trends in fertility and family planning, as well as birth control, and less on the verification of elaborate hypotheses on the influence of refined socioeconomic and psychological factors.

The first fertility study was conducted in Indianapolis in 1941 (Whelpton and Kiser 1950 1952 1954 1958). At this time American demographers were expressing great concern about the low level of fertility in the United States, especially in the cities (Kiser and Whelpton 1953). It was believed that a deeper knowledge of the social and psychological factors affecting fertility was necessary in order to introduce a population policy designed to encourage larger families. Also demographers were not satisfied with the census differential fertility data showing an inverse relation of fertility to socioeconomic status, because these census data did not give information on the practice of birth control of the couples, which in their opinion strongly influenced these fertility differences.

In order to be able to concentrate on the most important variables, it was decided to select a fairly homogeneous sample – namely, white, Protestant couples married in 1927–29, living in Indianapolis, both husband and wife having at least eighth grade education, neither of them previously married, husband under 40 and wife under 30 at marriage, and resident in a large city most of the time since marriage. This delimitation of the sample obviously precludes any possibility of drawing conclusions on the total population of the United States. On the other hand, the sample is very appropriate for testing hypotheses on fairly refined factors acting within the context of these families. There is an implicit underlying assumption in the study – that the type of couples selected into the sample, particularly all those practising birth control, represented the typical American couple of the future.

Altogether 1977 couples were interviewed. 1444 were found relatively fecund, i.e. having four or more children, or having less children but no good reason for supposing that conception was impossible during a period of at least twenty-four or thirty-six consecutive months since marriage (twenty-four months for never-pregnant and thirty-six for other couples). The other couples were considered relatively sterile and in most cases were not taken into consideration in the analysis of association between fertility and other factors. These relatively sterile couples were evenly distributed among the socioeconomic strata, so neglecting them did not alter the relations found.

The relatively fertile couples were divided into four groups according to 'fertility planning status': (1) couples having planned the number of births and the intervals between births (number and spacing planned), (2) couples having planned the number of their children, but not the intervals, i.e. the exact timing of births, (3) couples who did not plan the last pregnancy, but where husband and wife both wished that or another pregnancy (quasi-planned), (4) couples who had more children than planned (excess fertility). The relative percentages of these groups were: 28, 14, 31 and 27 per cent. Whelpton and Kiser suggested that – considering the high proportion of fertility planners – fertility planning would be universal in the near future, and therefore the relations of fertility to social and psychological factors found in the first two groups would be the most relevant for the future.

Twenty-eight hypotheses on the factors influencing the fertility planning status and the size of completed fertility of families were investigated (Kiser and Whelpton 1953). Only some of the most interesting of them can be described here.

Several indicators of social status were used (Kiser and Whelpton, in Whelpton and Kiser 1950, pp. 359–415): husband's annual earnings, husband's longest occupation, educational attainment of husband and wife, rating of household on Chapin's social status scale based on the material

Table 4.35   The relation of fertility planning status of relatively fecund couples to average annual earnings of the husband since marriage, and longest occupation of husband: Indianapolis survey.

Measure of socioeconomic status	Total	*Per cent distribution by planning status*			
		Number and spacing planned	*Number planned*	*Quasi-planned*	*Excess fertility*
Husband's annual earnings ($)					
3000+	100	45·5	16·5	23·1	14·9
2000–2999	100	33·0	14·7	35·1	17·2
1600–1999	100	30·1	14·0	35·3	20·6
1200–1599	100	25·6	15·2	29·8	29·4
Under 1200	100	16·2	11·1	30·3	42·4
Husband's longest occupation					
Professional	100	42·5	11·1	32·7	13·7
Proprietary	100	34·7	20·5	26·8	17·9
Clerical	100	31·1	13·7	30·5	24·6
Skilled	100	27·5	10·7	32·9	28·9
Semi-skilled	100	17·1	16·0	33·9	33·1
Unskilled	100	24·1	6·9	13·8	55·2

Source: Kiser and Whelpton, in Whelpton and Kiser (1950), p. 384.

equipment and cultural expression of the living room and condition of articles in the living room, rental status, etc. The distribution by fertility planning status, however, showed very marked correlation with social status, the proportion of successful planners being the higher, the higher the status of the couple (table 4.35). Two interpretations of this relation might be given: it might be supposed that the higher status groups are better informed on methods of fertility control or are more intelligent in using them, or alternatively it might be hypothesized that couples of higher status are more motivated to utilize birth control in order to have smaller families. On the basis of the data of the Indianapolis survey it is not possible to decide which of the two interpretations is correct – nor was the problem decided by any of the subsequent surveys of fertility, although it is a crucial one for the explanation of fertility differences between social strata and also for the construction of a theory of the factors of fertility.

The number of children ever born did not show any systematic association with social status in the group of relatively sterile couples, and in the case of the relatively fecund couples, when all were taken together, the relation proved to be negative, higher status couples having fewer children. When, however, the relationship of fertility to social status was analysed separately for each fertility planning status group, different correlations were found (table 4.36): (1) in the number and spacing planned group the

Table 4.36 Number of children ever born per 100 couples by fertility planning status, husband's average annual earnings since marriage, and longest occupation of husband since marriage: Indianapolis survey.

Measure of socioeconomic status	Number and spacing planned	Number planned	Quasi-planned	Excess fertility
Husband's annual earnings ($)				
3000	149	245	175	*
2000–2999	128	236	181	267
1600–1999	91	200	189	237
1200–1599	97	222	208	300
Under 1200	68	260	228	347
Husband's longest occupation				
Professional	126	*	176	219
Proprietary	127	231	184	279
Clerical	79	222	181	234
Skilled	126	250	210	330
Semi-skilled	92	225	213	306

* Rate not computed.
Source: Kiser and Whelpton, in Whelpton and Kiser (1950), pp. 395, 399.

relation was found to be clearly direct – i.e. the higher the status (measured by income), the higher the size of family; (2) in the number planned group the relation was U-shaped – i.e. the middle income groups have the lowest fertility; (3) in the quasi-planned group the relation is slightly inverse; (4) in the excess fertility group the relation is strongly inverse – i.e. the higher the status, the lower the size of family (table 4.36). These relations are also found, although not so clearly, in the case of other indicators of status, e.g. occupation of husband and education. Hypothesizing that planning of number and spacing of births will be fairly universal in future, it might be suggested that the direct relation of fertility to status will be prevalent in future. If however, on the contrary, it is supposed that the less widespread practice or less efficient practice of birth control is not caused by ignorance or lack of intelligence, but by lack of motivation, this prediction certainly does not hold.

These findings of the Indianapolis survey on the relationship of fertility planning and size of family to social status is one of the most often cited empirical results of demography, and theories of the social factors influencing fertility have been built on the observations of the survey.

The authors of the Indianapolis survey, however, intended to go much deeper into the analysis of the factors of fertility. In addition to the indicators of social status, they investigated many other economic, social and psychological factors which might have had an influence on the fertility planning status and on fertility. For example, they analysed the influence of the following factors:

(a) Economic security, measured among others things by the exposure to the possibility of unemployment since marriage.
(b) Economic tension, measured by the differences between actual income, home and car and those considered satisfactory by the couple.
(c) Intergenerational and intragenerational mobility.
(d) The number of siblings in the family of origin.
(e) Rural background.
(f) Denomination (different Protestant churches) and extent of participation and interest in religious activities.
(g) Traditionalism, measured by opinions on paid work of mothers, on divorce, on norms relating to the behaviour of women compared to the behaviour of men, etc.
(h) Tendency to plan, measured among other things by the frequency of running out of money between pay cheques.
(j) Marital adjustment.
(k) Psychological personality characteristics of the spouses and feelings and desires concerning children, such as feelings of personal inadequacy, fear of pregnancy, ego-centred interest in children, desire

to insure against childlessness, belief that an only child is handicapped, and general liking for children.

In some cases the hypothesized correlations were confirmed. For example: couples experiencing less economic insecurity had higher fertility; the number of siblings of the family of origin, most of all in that of the wife, proved to be correlated to fertility; rural migrants to Indianapolis had higher fertility and were less efficient planners of fertility than those living always in large towns; the more traditionally minded couples had more children and practised birth control less effectively; those who displayed a general tendency to plan their life were more efficient fertility planners; the couples whose marital adjustment was higher practised contraception more effectively, etc. In other cases, however, the expected relations were not confirmed by the data or proved to be very weak. The most conspicuous was the lack of strong correlations between fertility planning status and number of children and the personality characteristics.

Also Westoff and Kiser (in Whelpton and Kiser 1954, pp. 953–67), when they re-examined by correlation analysis the different hypotheses used in the Indianapolis survey, came to fairly negative conclusions concerning the results of the survey. The simple correlation coefficients of fertility planning status to particular social factors were:

Social factor	Wives	Husbands
Index of socioeconomic status	0·35	0·35
Husband's annual income	0·26	0·26
Husband's longest occupation	0·23	0·23
Education	0·24	0·23
Marital happiness	0·24	0·23
Index of general planning	0·20	0·19
Index of personal adequacy	0·17	0·20
Index of economic security	0·09	0·13

Thus the signs of the correlation coefficients are in accordance with the expectations, but their values are rather low (all indices used were constructed in such a way that they should be positively correlated with fertility planning status, e.g. a high index score of socioeconomic status means a high status in society). When examining the multiple correlation coefficients, it was found that other factors do not add much to the determining influence of social status, as the multiple correlation coefficients are not much higher than the simple correlation coefficient of fertility planning and social status:

Factor combinations correlated with fertility planning status	Wives	Husbands
Socioeconomic status and general planning	0·36	0·36
Socioeconomic status and personal adequacy	0·36	0·37
Socioeconomic status and marital happiness	0·38	0·38
Socioeconomic status, personal adequacy and general planning	0·36	0·37
Socioeconomic status, personal adequacy and marital happiness	0.38	0.38
Socioeconomic status, general planning and marital happiness	0·38	0·38
Socioeconomic status, marital happiness, personal adequacy and general planning	0·39	0·39

The correlation coefficients of the fertility of couples planning their fertility to the different social, economic and psychological factors were even lower:

Social factor	Wives	Husbands
Index of socioeconomic status	0·16	0·16
Marital happiness	0·11	−0·01
Index of economic security	0·32	0·31
Husband's annual income	0·24	0·24
Education	0·10	0·17
Husband's longest occupation	0·09	0·09

In this case, however, the strongest influence is that of economic security – i.e. couples who have experienced relatively secure economic conditions, little unemployment, and few fears of cuts in wages, tended to have higher planned fertility. Income is also relatively strongly correlated to fertility. Thus it seems that the higher planned fertility of higher status groups is correlated with their better economic conditions. The multiple correlation coefficients again are not much higher than the highest simple correlation coefficient, that of fertility to economic security:

Factor combinations correlated with size of completely planned families	Wives	Husbands
Economic security and socioeconomic status	0·32	0·31
Economic security and occupation	0·32	0·31
Economic security and education	0·32	0·32
Economic security and income	0·33	0·34
Economic security, income, education, and occupation	0·34	0·35

There seems to be important empirical evidence confirming the theories which hypothesize an underlying positive correlation of income and generally of better economic conditions to fertility. Westoff and Kiser, however, considered, that:

> such factors as socioeconomic status and feeling of economic security are, at best, only predisposing conditions in their effect on fertility behaviour. Feelings of economic security or insecurity, for instance, only facilitate or retard the operation of the other more complex attitudes surrounding the having or rearing of children. In other words, our current predictive instruments only indirectly approach the problem and are successful in predicting fertility planning and fertility only to the extent of their correlation with direct but more subtle factors involved (p. 867).

The second American survey, the Princeton survey, was planned explicitly to answer the questions that remained unanswered by the Indianapolis survey (Westoff, Potter, Sagi and Mishler 1961, Westoff, Potter and Sagi 1963). Like that of the Indianapolis survey, the sample of this survey was not nationally representative. However, the criteria of selection were different. As it was considered that the most interesting problem connected with fertility is that of the factors influencing the third parity, only couples having had a second birth in the four to seven months preceding the survey were interviewed. The sample was restricted to urban, native white couples whose marriage was uncomplicated by death, divorce, separation or extensive pregnancy wastage. Also while the Indianapolis survey tried to reconstitute the fertility histories of the couples and the factors having influenced fertility restrospectively, the Princeton survey used the method of longitudinal, i.e. repeated, interviewing of the couples in the sample. The first interview was made in 1957 after the birth of the second child, the second in 1960 and a third after six to ten years (Bumpass and Westoff 1969 1971). The results of the second interview (Westoff, Potter and Sagi 1963) of 905 couples will be discussed here.

A detailed hypothesis concerning the factors influencing the birth of the third child was elaborated (Kiser, Mishler, Westoff and Potter 1956–7). According to this hypothesis, there are four dependent variables influenced by several independent variables. These four dependent variables are: (1) personal desires regarding specific (third) pregnancies; (2) psychological availability of contraception, i.e. the attitudes toward contraception with reference to morality, aesthetics, convenience and effectiveness; (3) actual use and effectiveness of contraception; (4) actual fertility. The first two are the primary dependent variables influenced by the independent variables, the second two are determined by the primary dependent variables. Thus the framework of the hypothesis is very similar to that of the Indianapolis survey, as factors influencing desires regarding the number of children and those influencing the use of contraception are treated separately, actual fertility being considered an outcome of the desires and of the practice of contraception.

The independent variables are grouped in the following categories:

(1) Social settings (namely, occupation, education, religion, etc.), which determine, first, 'the relative benevolence of environment in the sense of resources of a psychological, social, or economic nature which are available to the couple as ways of defraying or absorbing the costs of child rearing'; second, 'the relative continuity or stability of the couple's relationships with their social settings with reference both to their transition to marriage and their future expectations'; and, third, 'the extent to which the couple has some sense of participation in or control over the effects of their social environment on their own life patterns'. The higher the benevolence of the environment, the more stable are the relationships, and the higher the sense of participation, the higher is the probability of the birth of the third child.

(2) Personal variables – namely, general attitudes and general psychological characteristics. The most important hypothesis here is that there are two distinct different life styles, a family based one and a work-mobility oriented one, the former being correlated with higher fertility than the latter.

(3) Family group variables – namely, marital adjustment, husband-wife dominance, family division of labour, family structure and interaction. For example, it was hypothesized that an unclear division of labour tends to be correlated with lower fertility.

The results of the survey, however, were more limited than the hypotheses that were intended to be verified. According to the authors, the main result was the demonstration of the influence of religion on fertility. 'Religious preference, that is preference for the Protestant, Catholic, or Jewish faith, is the strongest of all major social characteristics in its influence on fertility. Catholic couples want the most and Jewish couples the fewest children, with Protestants in an intermediate position' (Westoff, Potter and Sagi 1963, p. 238). Furthermore, while in the case of Protestants the difference in fertility between active and non-active Protestants is small, the fertility of the latter sometimes even being higher, in the case of the Catholics the fertility of the active ones is much higher than that of the non-active ones. The authors consider this to be a proof of the influence of religion, because the Catholic religion especially values a higher number of children. These fertility differences were caused mostly by the different number of children desired, the acceptance and efficiency of contraception having a much smaller role.

The influence of religion proved to be independent of social status, active Catholics showing a higher percentage of third pregnancies than other denominational groups in most social strata as determined by the occupation of the husband (table 4.37). Also the relation of fertility to social status seems to be negative in the case of Protestants, while it tends to be positive in the case of Catholics, although these relations are not unambiguous. In general, fertility differences by social stratum are not too large, certainly much smaller than the differences by denomination and religious interest.

Table 4.37 Per cent of women having an additional (third) pregnancy, by religion of the couple and social stratum of the husband: Princeton survey.

| Social stratum (occupation) of husband | Total | Religion | | | | |
| | | Protestants | | Catholics | | Jews |
		Active	Other	Active	Other	
Professional	54	43	56	77	80	32
Managerial, proprietary and official	46	26	53	90	64	25
Clerical	56	56	*	53	53	*
Sales	52	28	58	85	50	38
Skilled	55	43	52	67	63	30
Semi-skilled	57	60	67	59	54	*
Service	39	*	*	*	29	*
Unskilled	59	*	*	*	53	*
All couples	54	43	59	72	59	31

* Less than 10 cases.
Source: Westoff, Potter and Sagi (1963), p. 109.

One of the most ambitious new hypotheses formulated before the Princeton survey was that concerning the negative correlation of social mobility, especially upward mobility, to fertility (Westoff 1956). It was supposed that socioeconomic and psychological requirements for upward mobility are inconsistent with expenditures of time, energy and money for children. Actually, no important relations of fertility to social mobility were found, and even the slight relations observed were different in the case of the particular denominational groups. In the case of Protestants intergenerationally immobile blue collar couples showed the highest fertility, while immobile white collar, as well as mobile couples in both directions, had similar lower fertility (table 4.38). In the case of Catholics the immobile white collar couples showed highest fertility, the immobile blue collar families the lowest fertility, mobile couples having intermediate fertility.

Table 4.38 Per cent reporting at least one additional pregnancy since the second birth, by intergenerational social mobility: Princeton survey.

Longest occupational class of husband's father	Husband's occupational class and religion of couple					
	Protestants		Catholics		Jews	
	White collar	Blue collar	White collar	Blue collar	White collar	Blue collar
White collar	47	47	73	60	34	*
Blue collar	47	59	64	57	25	*

* Insufficient number.
Source: Westoff, Potter and Sagi (1963), p. 134.

The authors concluded that it is not surprising that the correlations of fertility to social mobility did not prove to be stronger, because the fertility differences by social strata were rather small and tended to diminish as compared to the earlier periods, so the change of social status naturally did not influence fertility very much. The findings, however, clearly prove that the hypothetical negative influence of social mobility on fertility does not prevail.

Similar to social mobility, the other economic and social factors considered (like migration, residence, change of income) from the first to the second interview seemed to have different, even opposite, influence on fertility in the particular denominational groups.

The importance of denomination and religious interest in determining fertility is a rather perplexing finding and it is not at all clear how the influence of religion is exerted. It is tempting to seek other background factors associated with religion, e.g. ethnic background. It is known from census fertility data (see pp. 158–62), and was also proved by the results of the Princeton survey, that different ethnic groups in the United States having the same denomination have rather different average levels of fertility. Also more recent researches seem to indicate that the denominational differences of fertility are strongly declining (Blake 1967a 1967b 1967c). Thus the main results of the Princeton survey do not seem to be applicable to the interpretation of the causes of fertility levels in later years in America.

Like the Indianapolis survey, the Princeton survey also failed to demonstrate correlations of fertility to different psychological characteristics. The psychological factors taken into consideration were: generalized manifest anxiety, nurturance needs, ability to delay gratification of impulses, self-awareness, compulsiveness, ambiguity tolerance, cooperativeness, need achievement.

Continuing the investigation of the influence of religion on fertility, especially the mechanism through which this influence is exerted, Westoff and Potvin reinvestigated one of the most interesting findings of the Princeton survey – that (contrary to all previous demographic theories) the correlation of fertility to education was positive in the case of Catholic women (Westoff and Potvin 1967). The positive correlation was found to be especially strong in the case of women having attended Catholic universities, although it was also observed in the case of Catholic women having attended non-Catholic universities. It was found in the Princeton survey that the higher fertility of Catholic women having university education was a consequence of their higher desired number of children (not of lesser acceptance of fertility control, although that factor had a certain role). It was not clear, however, whether the higher fertility of women having attended Catholic universities was a consequence of the influence of these universities, or whether it simply resulted from the fact that more religious Catholic women desiring more children generally go to Catholic universities. It was hypothesized (Westoff, Potter and Sagi 1963) that the higher fertility is the consequence of the educational experience in Catholic universities which strengthened religiosity and adherence to Catholic ideals, among them the Catholic ideas on fertility. In the Princeton survey, however, the degree of religiosity before going to the Catholic university could be determined only retrospectively, i.e. in a rather unreliable way.

In order to investigate the influence on fertility of attendance at a Catholic college, Westoff and Potvin selected a sample from women attending their first and fourth years at college. About 15 000 questionnaires were received (by mail). Owing to the peculiarity of the sample, instead of actual fertility only the desired number of children could be asked, because the women attending college were mostly unmarried. Desired number of children means the number of children the respondent would like to have. Obviously the desired number might not coincide with the actual number of children a woman will have at the end of her reproductive life span, so it cannot be interpreted as a measure of actual fertility. The reason for the difference between desired family size and actual completed fertility many decades later might arise from many sources: unwanted parities, unforeseen sterility, remaining unmarried, dissolution of marriage, change of desires, unforeseen major changes in economic and social conditions, or simply because the desired number of children given at the interview was not a statement based on mature consideration. The desired number of children thus reflects the cultural norms and values prevalent in the given social group rather than real fertility. Nevertheless, it is an indicator of these norms and values and personal opinions, so its differences might give insights into factors of real fertility.

On the basis of the results concerning the desired number of children of college women in the United States, the following main conclusions were formulated:

(1) The desired number of children of Catholic women is higher than that of Protestants, that of Protestants higher than that of Jews, and women having no religious feeling had the lowest number of desired children – i.e. the differences found by college women coincided with those found by other surveys in American population. The desired fertility of Mormons was also demonstrated by that survey and found to be near to that of the Catholics, indicating that high fertility values might be observed not only in Catholic groups. Here again, a special cultural milieu, the subculture of Mormons, seems to be playing an important role.

(2) College experience seems to have had no influence on fertility, as the desired numbers of children of women in their first and fourth college years showed very little difference. This finding disproves on the one hand the traditional thesis of demography that higher education tends to decrease fertility, but it also disproves the explanation given by Westoff, Potter and Sagi (1963) of the results of the Princeton survey – that Catholic college education tends to have an effect increasing fertility.

(3) While in the case of Protestant women the sectarian or non-sectarian type of college hardly influences fertility, in the case of Catholics women in Catholic colleges desire more children than Catholics going to other (non-sectarian) colleges. This difference appears in the first year of college, so it might be concluded that Catholic women desiring more children tend to go to Catholic colleges (table 4.39 and 4.40).

Table 4.39 Number of children desired by women attending first and fourth years of college, by denomination, and denominational or non-denominational type of college: American college women study.

Religion of woman	Type of college	Year of college attended	Mean number of children desired
None	Non-sectarian	1	3·2
		4	3·1
Protestant	Non-sectarian	1	3·5
		4	3·4
Jewish	Non-sectarian	1	3·4
		4	3·2
Protestant	Protestant	1	3·8
		4	3·4
Protestant	Catholic	1	3·7
		4	3·3
Mormon	Non-sectarian	1	4·6
		4	4·8

Source: Westoff and Potvin (1967), p. 36.

Table 4.40 Number of children desired by Catholic women attending first and fourth years of college by denominational or non-denominational type of elementary school, high school and college: American college women study.

Type of school			Year of college attended	Mean number of children desired
Elementary	*High*	*College*		
Nonsectarian	Nonsectarian	Nonsectarian	1	4·1
			4	4·0
Catholic	Nonsectarian	Nonsectarian	1	4·4
			4	4·3
Nonsectarian	Catholic	Nonsectarian	1	6·4
			4	3·3
Catholic	Catholic	Nonsectarian	1	5·0
			4	4·5
Nonsectarian	Nonsectarian	Catholic	1	4·8
			4	4·8
Catholic	Nonsectarian	Catholic	1	5·1
			4	5·3
Nonsectarian	Catholic	Catholic	1	5·5
			4	5·5
Catholic	Catholic	Catholic	1	5·7
			4	5·4

Source: Westoff and Potvin (1967), p. 40.

(4) In order to separate the effect of education on different levels, Catholic women were analysed separately by type of elementary and secondary school (high school) attended (table 4.40). It was found that Catholic elementary and secondary schooling is even more strongly correlated with higher desired fertility than attendance at a Catholic college. It is not clear whether the higher desired fertility was the consequence of Catholic elementary and secondary schooling, or whether the women attending these Catholic schools were already in childhood predisposed to desire more children. The influence of religiosity of parents on the selection of Catholic and non-Catholic schooling, as well as on the desired number of children, could not be demonstrated by the results of the survey.

A similar series of surveys using a sample not representing the total women population of the United States were repeatedly the Detroit area surveys, begun in 1954 and performed since that year. In the 1954 survey a representative cross-section of the adult population of Detroit, altogether 749 people, were interviewed. Here, in addition to actual fertility, another concept reflecting cultural norms and values concerning the size of family – namely, the ideal number of children – was studied by asking the following question: 'People have different ideas about children and families. As

Table 4.41 Ideal number of children by education, occupation, rural-urban background, income and religion: first Detroit area study.

Population group	Percent favouring two to four children	Mean ideal number of children
Education: years of school		
Less than 7	75	3·56
7–8	86	3·20
9–11	90	3·05
12	93	3·08
More than 12	93	3·04
Occupation of family head		
Operative, service worker, labourer	89	3·11
Craftsman, foreman and kindred	89	3·14
Clerical, sales and kindred	88	3·16
Professional, proprietor, manager, official	91	3·13
Rural-urban backgrounds		
Only urban background	91	3·10
Some rural background	85	3·25
Southern rural background	79	3·56
Northern rural background	89	3·08
Annual income of head of family ($)		
Less than 3000	87	3·21
3000–3999	89	3·17
4000–4999	91	3·00
5000–6999	92	3·01
7000 and over	94	3·19
Religion		
Catholic	84	3·38
Protestant	92	3·04
Total sample	89	3·15

Source: Freedman and Sharp (1954–5).

things are now, what do you think is the ideal number of children for the average American family?' (Freedman and Sharp 1954–5, Freedman, Goldberg and Sharp 1955). The ideal number of children was compared in the case of women aged 40 or more with actual fertility, and it was found that the ideal number of children is higher than actual completed fertility in all groups of the population, and also that the differences in the ideal number of children are smaller than those of actual completed fertility, but the sense of the differences is identical; it was therefore concluded that the answers given to the question relating to the *ideal* number of children might be used to conclude on the factors influencing the *actual* fertility differences. Thus in the case of women younger than 40 the ideal number of children was used for analysis (table 4.41).

The following main conclusions on fertility differences can be formulated on the basis of the results of the first (1954) survey:

(1) Differences in the ideal number of children by education are found only up to the eighth grade of elementary school, the average ideal number of children of those having this low kind of education being higher. Almost no difference is found from the ninth grade to over twelve years of schooling.

(2) Almost no difference by occupation of the family head was found.

(3) The relation of fertility to income of the head of family was U-shaped, although in the lowest income groups there are more families that consider large families (with more than four children) to be ideal.

(4) The ideal number of children is clearly higher in families having some rural background than in those having only urban background. However, only a Southern rural background is connected to higher ideal fertility, those with a Northern rural background having an ideal family size similar to those with only an urban background. Thus it is not rural background in itself, but rural background connected with a special cultural (Southern) milieu that tends to be related to higher fertility.

(5) Catholics showed a higher ideal number of children and a higher proportion of them considered families with more than four children to be ideal than Protestants. However, a particular group of Protestants (those with Southern rural background) showed as high ideal fertility as the Catholics. Thus it seems that it is not Protestantism itself, but Protestantism linked to a special cultural milieu that causes lower fertility.

The second great series of surveys of fertility in the United States consists of the two Growth of American Families (GAF) surveys in 1955 and 1960, as well as the two National Fertility Studies (NFS) in 1965 and 1970. These surveys were conceived as repeating each other (although with some modifications both in the sample and in the questionnaire), in order to provide a means of investigating tendencies of changes in the level of fertility, fertility differentials, and attitudes and opinions concerning fertility and family planning. These surveys were not intended to verify more refined hypotheses on the causative mechanisms of fertility – e.g. the influence of economic security, social mobility, marital adjustment or personal psychological characteristics.

All these surveys were based on national samples. The 1955 survey was confined to white married women aged 18–39, and the sample consisted of 2713 women. The sample of the 1960 survey, consisting of 3322 women, included in addition women aged 40–44, in order to provide possible comparisons between the interviewed persons aged 35–39 in 1955 and those aged 40–44 in 1960. The 1965 survey included non-white women (a small number of non-whites had been interviewed in the 1960 study), in order to compare the fertility of white and non-white women; the age coverage was also extended to 54 years, so that altogether 5617 women were interviewed. The sample of the 1970 survey consisted of nearly 7000 ever-married (not only currently married) women. It was considered that, although a longitudinal survey would have been ideal for investigating changes in fertility, it would have been very difficult and costly to reinterview the same women (as in the Princeton surveys), so it was decided to use, as a reasonable alternative, comparable repeated cross-sections.

New concepts of measuring fertility were elaborated for these surveys. In addition to the number of children borne by the interviewed women, and the number considered ideal by them for the average American family (i.e. not for themselves), the Growth of American Families survey introduced the concept of expected fertility, i.e. the number of children already borne by the interviewed women plus the number she most likely expects to have in future. By this concept, it was considered to be possible to compare the probable completed fertility of different cohorts – namely, those still at the beginning of their reproductive life span, those in the middle of it, and those who had already ended it. Obviously it is questionable whether these expectations are realized in subsequent years. The actual and expected fertilities of the same cohorts in the surveys at five-year intervals seem to indicate that the actually achieved average fertility levels were somewhat higher than the earlier expected average levels.

The National Fertility Studies distinguished the desired or wanted number of children, the intended number of children, and the expected number of children. The desired or wanted number of children was investigated by the questions 'If you could have exactly the number of children you want, what number would you want?' in the case of women having no children, and by the question 'What number of children would you really want?' in the case of women who already had children; the actual number of children is not identical with the number wanted. The total intended number of children was the sum of those already born and the additional number the respondent said she intended to have. The expected number of children was defined as the number actually expected, taking into consideration the eventual failure to achieve the intended number. The different measures showed somewhat differing averages, e.g. in the 1965 survey the average values were:

Expected fertility	3·36
Intended fertility	3·24
Desired fertility	3·29
Ideal fertility	3·29

In the particular subgroups of the sample there were far more different averages of these values. Thus, these measures reflect different aspects of fertility behaviour, attitudes and values. It does not seem, however, completely clear as to what are these different aspects. The authors of the book on the first National Fertility Study (Ryder and Westoff 1971) used mostly the expected fertility and in addition sometimes the desired and intended fertility.

By means of these different measures it was intended to distinguish two kinds of fertility differences. Firstly, some groups differ in their number of children because they differ in their ability to prevent unwanted pregnancies – i.e. in consequence of the different number of unwanted births – although they are similar with respect to the average number of children desired or wanted. Secondly, other groups differ in their fertility because they differ primarily with respect to the number of children desired or wanted.

The Growth of American Families surveys (Freedman, Whelpton and Campbell 1959, Whelpton, Campbell and Patterson 1966) showed that the most consistent and lasting fertility difference was that by religion, Catholics having and expecting more children than Protestants:

| | Current fertility | | Expected fertility | |
	1955	1960	1955	1960
Protestants	2·1	2·2	2·9	2·9
Catholics	2·1	2·5	3·4	3·7
Jewish			2·1	2·5
Total	2·1	2·3	3·0	3·1

The difference between the fertility of the two denominations increased from 1955 to 1960, so that its was stated that while many traditional group differences in fertility may almost disappear in America, religion seems to remain an important factor influencing fertility, its influence even seeming to increase.

The National Fertility Study of 1965 showed no further increase, but also no decrease in the denominational fertility differences (Ryder and Westoff 1971). Clearly this difference was caused by different ideals and desires concerning fertility:

	Current fertility	Expected fertility	Desired fertility
Protestants	2·3	3·0	3·0
Catholics	2·8	3·9	3·7
Jewish	2·1	2·9	3·0

From 1965 to 1970, however, this tendency changed. In spite of the publication of the Papal Encyclical, *Humanae Vitae*, which condemned the use of birth control methods (except the rhythm method), the acceptance of new birth control methods, among others of the contraceptive pill, by Catholics increased and the practice of Catholic couples approached that of the Protestant couples (Westoff and Ryder 1970). On the basis of the results of the 1970 survey it was predicted that by the end of the 1970s Catholics and non-Catholics will be virtually indistinguishable in their contraceptive practices. Since the current and expected fertility, as well as the desired number of children of Catholics, decreased more rapidly than that of Protestants from 1965 to 1970, the fertility difference by denominations diminished. The remaining difference of about 15 per cent was considered to be the consequence of a similar difference in the number of children desired. Thus it seems that the strongest and most lasting fertility difference found by the earlier surveys tends to disappear in present-day America.

Contrary to the difference in fertility by denominations the difference by whites and non-whites was caused by the different ability to prevent unwanted pregnancies (Ryder and Westoff 1971). The following figures emerged from the 1965 survey:

	Current fertility	Expected fertility	Desired fertility
White women	2·6	3·3	3·3
Black women	3·3	4·0	3·2

As the number of unwanted births strongly diminished recently as a result of the spread of efficient methods of birth control, it was predicted that in the 1970s the levels of black and white marital fertility will converge (Westoff 1975).

In other areas, the Growth of American Families and National Fertility Studies found the traditional fertility differences: more educated, urban and higher status (and income) groups having less children than less educated, rural, lower status (and income) groups. The differences were, however, rather small, and narrowed from 1955 to 1970, to a large extent because the number of unwanted births diminished strongly in consequence of the spread of the contraceptive pill.

In the opinion of Westoff (1975), analysing the results of the 1970 survey, the decline in marital fertility in the United States from the middle 1960s resulted simply from the reduction of unplanned fertility. The latter reduction was a consequence of the spread of knowledge on contraception, its acceptance and the use of the contraceptive pill. The National Fertility Studies amply evidenced these latter processes. In general a tendency can be observed in these surveys of putting more emphasis on methods and practices of family planning and less on the deeper social, economic and psychological determinants of fertility.

This tendency is understandable to a certain extent because of the failure of the Indianapolis and Princeton surveys to elucidate the causative mechanism of these deeper determinants. However, the facts of the increasing acceptance and practice of contraception do not add much to our knowledge of the social determinants of fertility, and the fertility differences by social groups shown by the Growth of American Families and National Fertility Studies do not present really new information compared with the census fertility data. In addition, the reliability of the answers of the interviewed persons concerning the ideal, desired, intended and expected number of children was queried by several demographers. For example, Hauser (1967) considered that the answers given to these questions reflect the number of children already born plus the desire of the interviewed person to win the approval of the interviewer. Others (Siegel and Akers 1969) stated that the expected number and the ideal number of children found in the fertility surveys are reliable bases for projections of fertility. Repeated interviews of families during a two year period in the Detroit area studies seem to indicate that the expected number of children of the families are fairly stable and the deviations in the answers cancel each other on the average (Freedman, Coombs and Bumpass 1965). Reinterviewing twenty years later of couples who had stated their family size preferences (Westoff, Mishler and Kelly 1957), however, gave rather ambiguous results. Many individual families attained a higher actual fertility, many others a lower actual fertility, than the preferred number of children stated twenty years earlier, so that the correlations of the preferred number (twenty years earlier) and the achieved number of children of the individual couples were rather low ($r = 0.26$ to 0.30), even in the case of couples practising birth control ($r = 0.45$). On the other hand, the averages of preferred and achieved fertility corresponded rather well.

Blake, who used to rely on the average ideal number of children for analysing tendencies of values concerning fertility (Blake 1967a 1967c), recently expressed doubts on the reliability of the data on birth expectations and ideal number of children in assessing the true character and causes of the recent decline of fertility in the United States (Blake 1974).

White Americans do not presently have a stable and consistent utility scale regarding family size. Although family-size ideals are well under three children, respondents are highly tolerant of large families and noticeably intolerant of the one-child family or childlessness .... These results suggest that some conservatism in interpreting recent data on birth expectations might be wise. Indeed, the suddenness of the shift in expectations to the two-child category should itself arouse suspicion (pp. 42–3).

She further suggests that the achieved completed fertility of the women today expressing preferences for two children might be much higher in future.

The most thoroughgoing critique of the GAF and NFS fertility surveys was written by one of the authors who participated in the analysis of the 1960 and 1965 surveys, Norman B. Ryder (1973a). The five main points of his criticism were:

(1) The population embraced by the samples of the surveys was not appropriate, because some population groups (Negroes in the first two surveys, populations of urban ghettoes, etc.) were left out, and because never-married women were never interviewed; these latter women should, in his opinion, be investigated, because fertility is strongly influenced by nuptiality – e.g. by the recent increase of the average age at first marriage in the United States.

(2) The expected number of parities is a mixture of hard (current fertility) and soft data (expected number of parities in future), with the proportion of each depending on the location of the respondent in the reproductive life span; as failures of contraception and changes of mind might happen, the soft part of this measure is not completely reliable.

(3) The retrospective data provided by the respondents on the history of contraception, family planning and fertility show not so much what has happened, as what they choose to say has happened;

(4) The answers of respondents on unwanted births do not reflect the real frequency of these unwanted births, but rather the extent to which the respondents rationalized or did not rationalize at the time of the interview the occurrence of unwanted pregnancies.

(5) No theory of the factors of fertility emerged from these surveys. Nor was any attempt made to formulate or verify theoretical hypotheses. Even the more sophisticated methods of multivariate analysis were seldom utilized; instead, cross-tabulations were used, adding variables until the number of cases in the cells begin to fall below 20, i.e. to a number on the basis of which it is hazardous to make inferences.

As in the United States, the main motive for the first surveys of fertility in the United Kingdom was the concern caused by the low level of fertility in the 1930s. A Royal Commission on Population was formed, in the framework of which several surveys were performed and published. The first of these was the survey of Lewis-Faning, which used a sample of women coming in contact with hospitals and other health institutions

(Lewis-Faning 1949). He found that fertility planning and birth control spread continuously. Parallel with this tendency, however, a clear change in the trend of planned fertility went on: after a declining phase the planned number of children began to increase. The turning point in the non-manual stratum occurred in the marriage cohorts married after 1930, in the stratum of skilled workers after 1935, while in the semi-skilled and unskilled strata it continued to decline until 1940 and began to rise in the cohort married after 1940.

The most important English survey was the family census of 1946, when more than 1·2 million married women were interviewed. The fertility rates by marriage cohorts (achieved ultimate family size for the earlier cohorts and projected ultimate family size for the more recent cohorts) demonstrated a continuous decline for marriages up to 1930, then a fluctuating low fertility level for the marriages contracted from 1931 to 1940, and an increase in fertility after that date. From the point of view of the study of social determinants of fertility, the most interesting results of the family census are those that display how the relation of fertility to socioeconomic status changed from an inverse relation to a U-shaped relation. In the marriage cohort of 1890–9, fertility was found to be lowest in the stratum

Table 4.42 Number of children ever born per 1 woman, by social strata and marriage cohorts: Family Census of Great Britain.

Social stratum	Date of marriage				
	1890–0	1900–9	1910–14	1915–19	1920–4
Professionals	2·80	2·33	2·07	1·85	1·75
Employers[1]	3·28	2·64	2·27	1·97	1·84
Own account[2]	3·70	2·96	2·42	2·11	1·95
Salaried employees[3]	3·04	2·37	2·03	1·80	1·65
Non-manual wage earners[4]	3·53	2·89	2·44	2·17	1·97
Manual wage earners	4·85	3·96	3·35	2·92	2·70
Farmers and farm managers	4·30	3·50	2·88	2·55	2·31
Agricultural workers	4·71	3·88	3·22	2·79	2·71
Labourers	5·11	4·45	4·01	3·56	3·35
Total	4·34	3·53	2·98	2·61	2·42

[1] Employers with ten or more employed persons.
[2] Self-employed with no or less than ten employed persons.
[3] Monthly or quarterly paid non-manual employees.
[4] Weekly or daily paid non-manuals, e.g. shop assistants, insurance agents, the lower ranks of the civil service, policemen, telephone operators.
Source: Glass and Grebenik (1954a), p. 111.

of professionals, while from the cohort of 1910–14 the lowest fertility occurs in the stratum of salaried employees (table 4.42). The fertility of the stratum of farmers is rather different from that found in other countries, because it was lower in England than that of all manual workers. This might be explained by the special position of farmers in England. The U-shaped curve is displayed even more clearly in the marriage cohort of 1925, when the cohort is differentiated by age of wife at marriage (table 4.43). While in the marriage cohort of 1910 professionals and employers had the lowest fertility, in that of 1925 this stratum shows a higher fertility in the case of women at marriage aged between 22·5 and 25 years than any other non-manual group. The change in shape of the relation of fertility to socioeconomic status from the 1910 to the 1925 marriage cohort occurred parallel with an overall decline of fertility. Thus the change in relative fertility differences had begun before the baby boom.

Table 4.43 Number of children ever born after twenty years marriage duration, of two marriage cohorts, by age of wife at marriage and social stratum: Family Census of Great Britain.

| | Marriage cohort of 1910 | | Marriage cohort of 1925 | |
| | Age at marriage | | | |
Social stratum	20–22·5	22·5–25	20–22·5	22·5–25
Professionals and employers	2·61	2·28	2·16	1·94
Own account	3·24	2·50	2·32	1·92
Salaried employees	2·79	2·35	1·82	1·63
Non-manual wage earners	2·94	2·65	2·34	1·86
Manual wage earners	4·09	3·34	3·06	2·41
Farmers and farm managers	3·63	3·20	3·04	2·32
Agricultural wage earners	4·19	3·55	3·13	3·07
Unskilled labourers	4·10	4·08	3·79	3·40

Source: Glass and Grebenik (1954a), p. 191.

In France a different approach was traditionally chosen: the so-called demographic opinion polls, which, in addition to the ideal number of children, asked questions concerning the level of information on the population number and demographic development of France, the demographic development considered desirable, the evaluation of the effects of population on economic prospects and unemployment, the influence of demographic development on the economic situation, and the desirability of population policy measures, etc. (Girard and Henry 1956, Girard and

Bastide 1960, Bastide and Girard 1966 1975, Girard and Zucker 1967 1968, Roussel 1969, Girard, Roussel and Bastide 1976).

The ideal number of children per family was requested from two points of view: (1) related to French families in general, and (2) related to the respondent's own circumstances.

As a series of similar public opinion surveys have been carried out since 1947, it is possible to follow the time series of the different opinions expressed. The ideal number of children clearly declined from 1965 to 1974 (from 2·82 to 2·54). It can therefore be concluded that the decrease of fertility in France was caused by a change of reproductive ideals.

The relation of fertility to socioeconomic status also changed in France (see table 4.44). In the surveys in the 1950s a very clear U-shaped relationship was demonstrated, this shape appearing more clearly in the case of the ideal number of children in the special circumstances of the respondents, since the medium-level socioeconomic strata tended to show the greatest difference between the ideal in general and the ideal in their own circumstances. According to earlier analyses of differential fertility in France (Febvay 1959), the inverse relation of fertility to socioeconomic status changed into a U-shaped one in the period of the baby boom in France. The U-shaped curve, however, does not seem to remain a permanent phenomenon, as signs of flattening of fertility differences by socioeconomic status can be observed, with the strongest decline in the

Table 4.44 Ideal number of children in general and in the special circumstances of the respondent, by social strata in France according to the demographic public opinion polls.

| Stratum | Ideal number of children | | | | | |
| | *In general* | | | *In the circumstances of the respondent* | | |
	1955	*1966*	*1974*	*1955*	*1966*	*1974*
Professional and executive	3·12	2·91	2·65	3·08	3·04	2·66
Medium-level technical and kindred	2·79	2·59	2·52	2·50	2·51	2·46
Other non-manual	2·79	2·61	2·49	2·55	2·42	2·22
Self-employed artisan and merchant	2·78	2·65	2·57	2·62	2·52	2·43
Manual worker	2·66	2·67	2·58	2·34	2·39	2·31
Agricultural worker	2·92	2·71	2·60	2·46	2·45	2·36
Farmer	3·02	2·83	2·72	2·91	2·80	2·64

Source: Bastide and Girard 1966 1975, Girard and Zucker 1967.

ideal number of children since 1955 being in the professional and executive stratum.

The relation of fertility to education and income was similarly U-shaped. Recently, however, the decline of the ideal was strongest in the groups having the highest education and the highest income.

The opinion polls also provide information concerning the general mood in France, and some inferences can be made on the influence of socio-psychological changes on fertility. For example, in 1956 only 34 per cent considered that in the next years an unemployment crisis would happen in France; in the mid 1960s this percentage suddenly began to increase and it had reached 83 per cent in 1974. Two-thirds of the respondents thought that it was difficult for young people to find employment, and the percentage of respondents believing that the total number of employment opportunities and workplaces in France would significantly rise in future clearly declined. Connected with these opinions, the percentage of people considering that a rise in the population is desirable has very strongly diminished since the Second World War (table 4.45).

Table 4.45 Opinions on the desirability of the further increase of the population of France: demographic public opinion polls.

Year		Percentage of respondents considering that it is desirable that the population of France should:			
	Increase	Remain more or less stationary	Decrease	No opinion	Total
1947	73	22	1	4	100
1949	54	33	3	10	100
1955	22	57	6	15	100
1959	27	59	8	6	100
1962	36	50	7	7	100
1965	29	59	7	5	100
1967	27	61	7	5	100
1974	23	63	10	4	100

Source: Bastide and Girard (1975), p. 737.

Several earlier surveys demonstrated that there are two clearly distinguishable currents of opinion in France concerning state intervention in the development of fertility by means of population policy measures: one in favour of an active natalist population policy, and the other opposed to it. This second opinion has slowly prevailed: in 1975, 46 per cent of those who had an opinion on this question (14 per cent of the respondents had no opinion at all) considered that the state should intervene with natalist measures to stop the decline of fertility, while 54 per cent of them were against this kind of intervention (Girard, Roussel and Bastide 1976). Thus it seems clear that the decline of fertility in France occurred against a background of change in public opinion about demographic matters.

Fertility surveys in West Germany, unlike the French surveys, followed the American pattern (Freedman, Baumert and Bolte 1959). A national representative sample of population in reproductive age was interviewed on expected, ideal and desired (financial and other conditions permitting) number of children. The average expected fertility was 2·1, the ideal 2·6 and the desired (in very good conditions) was 2·7.

Some important fertility differences were found. (1) Farmers had a much higher fertility than other socioeconomic groups, while other groups displayed a U-shaped relation of fertility to status. This U-shape was interpreted by the authors as, on the one hand, the consequence of an upward change in opinions on fertility in the professional stratum, and, on the other hand, by the fact that the stratum of unskilled workers shows a lag in accepting family limitation. (2) Fertility showed a U-shaped relation to education. (3) Discounting the farmers, almost no relation of fertility to income was found. (4) Smaller settlements consistently showed higher fertility rates. (5) The most clear relation was found between fertility and employment of women, working wives having lower fertility. This was interpreted by the authors as a consequence of the competition between extra-familial interests and the requirements of child care. (6) Catholics showed a somewhat higher fertility than Protestants. Within the Catholic group regular churchgoers had the highest, occasional attenders medium, and the seldom or never churchgoing group the lowest fertility. In the Protestant group differences in fertility by churchgoing were much smaller. Therefore, the higher fertility of Catholics in general is mainly produced by the higher fertility of churchgoing Catholics. In the larger cities and in the case of working wives, the Catholic–Protestant fertility differences almost disappear.

The developed socialist countries of Europe have also showed great interest in fertility surveys, because their results can be used in the elaboration of the population policy measures considered necessary in many of them in view of the decline of fertility. The first surveys were carried out in Hungary, where up to the present a series of surveys have been performed, so that the changes in characteristics of fertility and family planning can be observed. These surveys are:

1   The fertility and family planning survey of 1958, using a sample of women who had had contact with gynaecological services (birth, abortion, simple treatment) (Acsádi and Klinger 1959).

2   The fertility and family planning survey of 1966, using a probability sample of married women in Hungary (Acsádi, Klinger and Szabady 1969, Szabady 1967 1968b 1969a).
3   The fertility and family planning survey of 1974, using a probability sample of married women aged less than 35 in Hungary (Klinger 1975).
4   A longitudinal survey of a sample of the marriage cohorts of 1966 (reinterviews in 1969 and 1972) and of 1974 (Klinger 1975).

These surveys display some clear tendencies. (1) The percentage of women planning the size of their family at marriage strongly increased and is near to 100 per cent in 1974. (2) The percentage of couples practising some method of birth control increased. A switch to more efficient methods can also be observed, and the incidence of induced abortions has decreased in recent years. (3) The number of children desired, as well as the number of children planned at marriage of the couples who did plan their number of children, first decreased and recently slightly increased:

		Number of children	
Year of interview	Survey	Average planned	Average desired
1958	Fertility and family planning survey	2·25	2·33
1966	Fertility and family planning survey	2·05	2·10
1966	Marriage cohort of 1966	1·89	—
1972	Marriage cohort of 1966	—	1·97
1974	Marriage cohort of 1974	2·19	—
1974	Fertility and family planning survey	—	2·10

Thus a clear upturn can be observed, which might be interpreted either as a consequence of the improvement in living standards, or as a change in sociopsychological character influenced by the widely publicized population policy measures and a general discussion in the mass media of the problems of low fertility.

What seems remarkable is that the average number of children desired in 1972 by the marriage cohort of 1966 was higher than the number originally planned in 1966. Taking into consideration the fact that birth control is almost universal in this cohort and that until 1974 induced abortion was freely available to these couples, it does not seem justifiable to interpret this increase as a result of the failure to achieve smaller families in consequence of unwanted parities. Rather, it might be explained by a real change in plans and values.

From the point of view of the social factors of fertility, the most interesting results demonstrated by these surveys are the differences by social strata (tables 4.46, 4.47). While the number of children ever born by social stratum shows the traditional inverse relationship between fertility and social status, with minor signs of the fertility of professional women

Table 4.46 Children ever born per 100 married women, by social strata: Hungarian survey of 1966.

Social stratum	*Children ever born per 100 married women*	
	Working	*Not working*
Professional	135	178
Other non-manual	134	179
Skilled and semiskilled	152	194
Unskilled	188	252
Self-employed and member of industrial cooperative	166	225
Agricultural	233	230
Total	166	214

Source: Acsádi, Klinger and Szabady (1970), p. 93.

Table 4.47 Per cent distribution of married women by family planning status, number of children planned by family planning women at marriage, and desired number of children at present: Hungarian survey of 1966.

Social stratum	*Per cent distribution by family planning status at marriage*		*Planned number of children at marriage*	*Desired number of children*
	Planning	*Not planning*		
Professional	65	35	2·28	1·94
Other non-manual	64	36	2·13	1·78
Skilled and semiskilled	48	52	2·06	2·09
Unskilled	41	59	2·10	2·45
Self-employed and member of industrial cooperative	51	49	2·32	2·22
Agricultural	35	65	2·21	2·57
Total	47	53	2·14	2·22

Source: Acsádi, Klinger and Szabady (1970), pp. 107, 132.

becoming higher than that of the simple non-manual women, the planned fertility of those couples who did plan their fertility clearly displayed the U-shaped relationship observed in some western European countries. The percentage of family planners, however, was still much higher in the professional and others non-manual strata than among the manual strata. However, as family planners are rapidly becoming predominant in all social strata in Hungary, the same U-shaped pattern may soon characterize the total population in Hungary. The fact that the desired size of family at the time of the interview began to show the U-shaped curve seems to point in the same direction.

The longitudinal survey of the marriage cohort of 1966 demonstrated further changes in the planned and intended levels of fertility. The planned number of children at the time of marriage was highest in the stratum of non-manuals and lowest among the peasants, and the number of children already borne plus the number intended to be borne in future was almost equal in the three strata (table 4.48). On the other hand, achieved fertility after three years of marriage was highest among the peasants and lowest among the non-manuals. The different pattern of planned and achieved fertility might be explained by the fact that the percentage of planners, although very high in each stratum, was highest among the nonmanuals and lowest among the peasants, and it might be surmised that the non-planners had a higher fertility than the planners. On the other hand,

Table 4.48   Average planned and intended number of children and achieved fertility of the marriage cohort of 1966: Hungary.

	1966		1969	1972		
Social category	Planned number of children	Percent-age of planners	Number of living children	Intended number to be borne in future	Percentage of those who tell intentions	Number of living children
Social stratum						
Non-manual	1·85	87·5	0·87	0·97	92·8	—
Manual	1·71	83·9	0·99	0·83	93·3	—
Peasant	1·72	78·0	1·04	0·86	94·1	—
Residence						
Budapest	1·70	89·5	0·77	0·92	93·6	1·10
Other towns	1·80	88·5	0·91	0·92	94·0	1·26
Villages	1·78	80·4	1·04	0·85	92·5	1·46
Total	1·77	84·6	0·95	0·89	93·2	1·34

Source: Klinger *et al.* (1974).

however, the non-manuals showed most frequently a downward revision in their planned number of children after three years of marriage:

	The intended total number of children after three years of marriage, compared to the originally planned number				
	Lower	Higher	Unchanged	Unknown	Total
Non-manual	14·2	2·8	78·2	4·8	100·0
Manual	10·1	5·3	79·8	4·8	100·0
Peasant	6·1	5·4	84·3	4·2	100·0
All planners	11·5	4·2	79·5	4·8	100·0

These results prove that differences in planned fertility by social stratum cannot be interpreted as exact predictions of the differences in completed fertility by social stratum.

On the other hand, differences in planned, intended and achieved fertility by residence showed the traditional pattern: the villages show the highest fertility and the capital (Budapest) the lowest, the smaller towns being in intermediate position.

The fertility survey carried out in Poland in 1972 (Smolinski 1973a 1973b 1974), compared with the Hungarian survey, is interesting because the decline in fertility began in Poland several years later than in Hungary, and the postwar level of fertility was much higher. This is reflected by the expected (ever borne plus expected in future) number of children of women in different age groups:

Age group of married women	Average expected number of children
20–24	2·22
25–29	2·31
30–34	2·53
35–39	2·72
40–44	2·85
45–49	2·91

Clearly, the fertility level of the youngest Polish cohorts was very similar to that of Hungarian cohorts of the same age. Thus Poland attained a similar phase to that of Hungary in the development of fertility. The older age groups, on the other hand, show much higher fertility levels than in Hungary.

Taking together all married women of reproductive age, the Polish data show rather traditional fertility differences, namely: (1) fertility is much higher in villages than in towns, (2) there is a strong negative correlation of fertility to education, (3) the agricultural population shows much higher fertility than other populations, (4) non-manuals show much lower fertility than manual workers, and (5) dependent women have much higher fertility than employed women (table 4.49).

Table 4.49 Ideal number of children, planned number of children of family planners, number of children ever born and expected total fertility: Poland, 1972.

Social category	Number of children per married woman			
	Ideal	*Planned*	*Achieved*	*Expected*
Residence				
Town	2·64	2·30	2·07	2·37
Village	3·20	2·69	2·97	3·32
Place of birth				
Town	2·56	2·18	1·98	2·31
Village	3·03	2·54	2·68	3·01
Education				
Less than elementary	3·30	2·81	3·56	3·69
Elementary (7 years)	2·88	2·40	2·37	2·74
Secondary	2·50	2·12	1·67	2·07
University	2·32	2·06	1·39	1·73
Branch				
Agriculture	3·30	2·80	3·22	3·51
Other than agriculture	2·72	2·27	2·16	2·50
Occupation				
Employed total	2·87	2·40	2·39	2·73
Manual worker	2·81	2·31	2·38	2·70
Non-manual	2·52	2·14	1·71	2·07
Self-employed	3·33	2·83	3·25	3·53
Dependent total	2·90	2·46	2·59	2·91
Manual worker	2·96	2·49	2·67	3·01
Non-manual	2·70	2·32	2·25	2·47
Self-employed	3·06	2·65	2·91	3·25
Total	2·89	2·43	2·45	2·85

Source: Smolinski (1974).

Similarly, a more or less traditional pattern in fertility differences was found in the survey of birth control and family planning in Czechoslovakia (Srb, Kucera and Vysusilova 1964), the number of children desired by families in 1958 being as follows:

Professional	2·22
Medical employee	2·06
Commercial employee	2·26
Transport employee	2·27
Industrial worker	2·33
Agricultural worker	2·62
Member of agricultural cooperative	2·58
Self-employed peasant	2·73
Other	2·46
Total population	2·30

Several surveys of family planning have been carried out in the Soviet Union, showing on the one hand the widespread practice of birth control, among other methods the practice of induced abortion (Katkova 1971, Belova and Darski 1968), and on the other hand the differences between ideal and desired number of children by social stratum and residence (town and village population), as well as by region of the USSR and ethnic group (tables 4.50, 4.51). The results clearly demonstrate that in large parts of the country, particularly in the western regions (Estonian and Latvian SSRs, Kalinin and Novgorod districts, central and northwestern Russia, Ukrainian SSR), in the towns (Moscow, towns of Latvia), and in the non-manual strata, the desired number of children is well below the level necessary for simple reproduction of the population, while in the eastern regions of the country and among rural populations this number is much higher. Thus the family planning surveys demonstrate the clearly different desires and values which influence fertility differentials by socioeconomic stratum and by region in the Soviet Union.

Some recent surveys of fertility in ten European countries (Belgium, Czechoslovakia, Denmark, England and Wales, Finland, France, Hungary, Netherlands, Poland, Yugoslavia), as well as Turkey and the United States, have been analysed comparatively (United Nations 1976). As the surveys were carried out around 1970, the results provide information on changes in fertility differentials (current fertility, expected fertility and ideal number of children) during the process of the recent decline of fertility in the United States and most west European countries.

In some western countries, particularly in England, certain fertility differentials have tended to diminish. This, however, could be interpreted as a temporary phenomenon connected with the recent decline in fertility in these countries. In other countries, particularly in east Europe, fertility differentials seem to be fairly persistent.

Table 4.50 Average ideal and expected number of children, from a national family planning survey in the Soviet Union in the 1960s.

Republic and region	Average number of children	
	Ideal	Expected
Russian SFSR	2·52	2·21
Central	2·52	1·94
Northwest	2·50	1·99
Black soil area	2·79	2·22
Volga-Vyatka	2·63	2·25
Volga	2·79	2·29
Ural	2·69	2·31
Northern Caucasus	2·82	2·32
Far East	2·83	2·37
Western Siberia	2·84	2·41
Eastern Siberia	2·88	2·46
Ukrainian SSR	2·63	2·07
Don-Dnieper	2·60	2·04
South	2·65	2·11
Southwest	2·67	2·11
Latvian SSR	2·60	2·11
Lithuanian SSR	2·75	2·20
Moldavian SSR	2·74	2·25
Estonian SSR	2·74	2·29
Belorussian SSR	2·93	2·41
Georgian SSR	3·95	2·88
Kazakh SSR	3·38	3·19
Armenian SSR	4·10	3·42
Kirgiz SSR	3·94	3·72
Turkmen SSR	4·10	3·79
Tadzhik SSR	4·18	4·08
Azerbaijan SSR	4·52	4·25
Uzbek SSR	4·55	4·31

Source: Belova (1971), Heer (1973).

Rural/urban differentials seem to be the most persistent ones in most societies, although more so in economically less developed ones. This might be a consequence of the diminishing differences in urban and rural living conditions and ways of life in the more developed societies.

Differentials by employment status of wives also seem to be fairly persistent, although as employment of women (at least in some periods of their adult life) is tending to increase, the importance of this differential seems to be diminishing for the fertility of the population as a whole.

Differences in fertility by socioeconomic status of the husband are tending to diminish and to turn from an inverse relationship to a U-shaped one

Table 4.51   Average desired number of children of
married women in the Soviet Union in the 1960s, from
several family planning surveys.

Soviet Union	2·42
Moscow, industrial workers	1·8
Moscow, Onde district	1·6
Estonian SSR	1·8
Latvian SSR	1·78
Urban population	1·68
Rural population	2·07
Kalinin district, rural population	2·4
Novgorod district, rural population	2·6
Udmurt Autonomous Region	
Manual workers	2·4
Non-manuals	2·0
Chuvash Autonomous Region	3·0
Southern Kirgiz SSR, Kirgiz population	3·1
Celinograd district, Kazakh SSR	
Urban population	
Russian	2·7
Kazakh	3·7
Rural population	
Russian	3·0
Kazakh	4·3

Source: Urlanis (1974), p. 138.

in at least half of the countries considered, the number of children of
high-status non-manuals being higher than that of other (lower status)
non-manuals.

Similarly, in many of the countries education of the husband and/or of
the wife seems to show a U-shaped relation to the number of children,
spouses with post-secondary (university and similar) education having
slightly more children than those with full secondary education.

It might be conjectured that the appearance of these U-shaped relations
reflects a corresponding relation between fertility and family income,
which has again appeared in several countries (in Belgium the relation was
positive).

As the relation of total expected fertility to these social variables
changed within the particular countries from the older cohorts to the
younger ones, it seems that fertility differentials are in a process of transition, although a clear pattern of these differentials will only be ascertain-
able after several years, when the fertility changes initiated since the mid
1960s settle down.

Thus surveys of fertility have provided many interesting insights into the
determinants of fertility and into the attitudes, values and norms concern-

ing fertility, although the following significant facts must be kept in mind:

1 It seems to be clearly demonstrated that ideal, desired, intended and planned number of children should by no means be considered indicators of real achieved fertility.
2 Analysis of fertility factors which are more fundamental than those indicated by the fertility differentials displayed by census fertility data has been unsuccessful.

It seems clear from the results of the surveys that fertility differences by social strata, educational and residential groups, and religious and ethnic communities, are not simply caused by the differential knowledge and practice of birth control, but also by different ideals and values. Actual achieved fertility seems to fluctuate to a certain extent around these values and norms under the influence of different factors (economic conditions, etc.). In addition to the investigation of the causes of these fluctuations, it would be most interesting to discover the causative mechanisms shaping the attitudes, values and norms of fertility. At present, however, the surveys of fertility do not provide information on these, partly as attempts to elucidate these mechanisms have failed to bring the expected results, and partly because more recent fertility surveys have tended to give up the search for these deeper causative mechanisms.

PART FIVE

Social factors of fertility

Having reviewed the different sources of data and the possibilities of investigating the influences of social factors on fertility and having illustrated some results gained from different sources and by different methods, let us turn to the separate analysis of each of the different social factors.

First we deal with two demographic factors – marriage and the knowledge and practice of birth control – which are considered here to be intermediate determinants of fertility levels, not their ultimate causes. Then the factors taken into consideration in demographic researches on the determinants of fertility are treated in turn. We begin with fairly objective factors, like income, socioeconomic status, education, residence and employment of women, as well as their changes, like social mobility and migration. Following them we deal with cultural factors, like religion and ethnicity, then with the psychological ones that might have an influence on fertility. As it turns out, however, this distinction of 'objective' and 'subjective' determinants is not as clear as is sometimes supposed. We finish this chapter with a review of the influence of population policies. which, as it will be seen, influence fertility both directly, through changing the objective situation of families, and indirectly, through influencing their subjective beliefs, attitudes and values.

One major factor influencing fertility, the level of mortality, is not dealt with in a separate chapter. Obviously couples want and plan for their children to survive to adulthood, at least to the age when the parents will probably die. Therefore, the fact that in one population group the probability of newborn children surviving to adulthood may be about 50 per cent (as was probably not exceptional in earlier centuries in Europe), while in another population group less than 5 per cent of the newborn children die before adulthood, strongly influences the fertility differences of these two population groups, the couples of the first group probably wanting and planning, if all other circumstances were identical, almost twice as many parities, simply in order to have as many grown-up children as the couples of the second population group. In advanced societies, however, the levels of mortality are more or less equal at present, and also no important improvements in mortality seem to be realizable in future. So that the difference in some percentages of probability of survival of newborn children might not significantly influence the number of parities wanted by the couples. Nevertheless, it should be kept in mind that in the historical development of fertility in present-day advanced societies, the decline of infant and child mortality was certainly an important factor in the development of fertility.

In each of the following chapters dealing with particular social factors of fertility, the results of the investigations described in Parts 3 and 4 are summarized, then some special researches are analysed which have concentrated on the factor under examination. Some theoretical interpretations of the given factor are also given. However, these theories concentrate on the given factor, and they do not try to deal with the causative mechanism of fertility as a whole.

5.1 Two intermediate demographic determinants: marriage, and knowledge and practice of birth control

In advanced societies most children are born inside marriage, so that the age at marriage, the divorce rate and the remarriage rate of divorced and widowed men and women, as well as the percentage of them remaining unmarried until the end of their reproductive ages, obviously strongly influence fertility.

Non-marital fertility, however, should not be neglected, because in some societies and at some periods it could be an important component of total fertility. Available data seem to suggest that, in the sixteenth and seventeenth centuries and in the first part of the eighteenth, illegitimacy was rather low, only 1–5 per cent of all births being illegitimate. Around the middle of the eighteenth century a secular increase in illegitimacy seems to have begun in many parts of Europe. The period of the French Revolution and of Napoleon witnessed a swift acceleration in this increase, which continued until around the middle of the nineteenth century. Since 1880, however, a secular decline in the percentage of illegitimate births was apparent in almost all European countries (Shorter *et al.* 1971). The causes of these changes in illegitimate fertility and in the rate of illegitimate births among all births are not clear. The connection with changes in marital fertility in the last hundred years, however, seems to be rather general, although not universally valid (e.g. in France marital fertility began to decline earlier than illegitimate fertility).

Investigating the long-term trends in illegitimate fertility in England, Laslett and Oosterveen (1973) found that the percentage of illegitimate births rose at the end of the sixteenth century from about 2 per cent to nearly 5 per cent, then declined in the seventeenth century to 1–2 per cent, began to rise in the first decades of the eighteenth century, reaching more than 6 per cent in the first half of the nineteenth century, and declined from that period until the most recent decades. Their most important conclusion concerning changes in illegitimate fertility is that, in direct contradiction to the natural expectation that when marriage is late and many grown-up people are unmarried, illegitimacy is high, these changes do not seem to be positively correlated to the percentages of unmarried women at fecund ages. In fact, illegitimate fertility was lowest in England during the period when men and women married the latest and when the highest percentage of them remained married, i.e. in the second half of the seventeenth century. Also the illegitimacy ratio rose when couples tended to marry slightly earlier, marital fertility rose, and in consequence the population growth rate was higher – i.e. in the second half of the eighteenth century.

It seems that in past centuries in England illegitimate births might have occurred for very different reasons, ranging from the existence of sub-societies where illegitimacy or casual unions of couples might have been frequent (Laslett and Oosterven 1973), to laws restricting legal marriage (Knodel 1970), and the custom of contracting marriage only after the birth of the first child (i.e. after the woman has proved her ability to produce an heir to the family farm).

Table 5.1 Illegitimate live births as percentage of total live births in selected countries.

Country	1960	1967	1968
Austria	13·0	11·5	12·0
Belgium	2·1	2·5	—
Bulgaria	8·0	9·7	9·6
Czechoslovakia	4·8	5·4	—
Denmark	7·8	10·2	—
England and Wales	5·4	8·4	8·5
Finland	4·0	5·1	—
France	6·1	6·1	—
East Germany	11·4	10·7	—
West Germany	6·1	4·5	4·8
Hungary	5·5	5·0	5·0
Ireland	1·6	2·5	2·6
Italy	2·4	2·0	—
Netherlands	1·3	2·1	2·0
Poland	4·5	4·9	4·9
Spain	2·3	1·5	1·4
Sweden	11·3	11·5	—
Yugoslavia	8·7	8·3	—
United States	—	9·7	9·0

Source: Glass (1968), p. 143, UN Demographic Yearbook 1969.

Similarly, today (table 5.1), when the percentage of illegitimate births in European countries ranges from 1 per cent to more than 10 per cent, and when the trends are rather different (e.g. slightly rising in Sweden, England and Wales, Bulgaria, declining in East and West Germany), there are most probably very different reasons for illegitimacy. On the one hand, it might occur in marginal low-status population groups having a traditional subculture which does not conform to the norms of society requiring a legal marriage for cohabitation and birth of children, but on the other hand it most probably occurs also in the case of high-status couples and single women who consciously adopt an anti-traditional attitude concerning the necessity of being married in order to bear a child. In both cases, however, it seems that illegitimate children are mostly not unwanted children, and it might be conjectured that the factors influencing illegitimate fertility are not very different from those influencing marital fertility.

As for marriage, both the average age at first marriage and the percentage of population remaining unmarried until the end of the reproductive period varied strongly during the historical development of the advanced countries. There were also fairly significant differences between the different countries and within given countries between different population groups. Historical development was examined in Part 3, its most important feature being the late marriage and high proportion of celibacy in the western part of Europe, to the west of a line connecting Trieste and St Petersburg, until the first decades of the twentieth century, while early marriage and a very low rate of unmarried adults characterized the part of Europe to the east of this line (Hajnal 1965). It was conjectured that late marriage and a high rate of celibacy might have been strategies more or less consciously adopted by population groups to control the growth of their number (Wrigley 1966b).

In the twentieth century, most of all during the baby boom period, the age at marriage declined and the percentage of married population in the reproductive ages increased all over the advanced countries, most of all in those western European societies where late marriage and high celibacy had been fairly widespread (table 5.2). Some demographers (e.g. Glass 1968, Campbell 1974) considered that the change in patterns of marriage was a major cause of the baby boom. Clearly, a process of lowering age at marriage does tend to produce a rise in period fertility rates, as the high fertilities in the first years of marriage of several subsequent birth cohorts are superposed on each other.

It seems that recently, in most cases probably since the mid 1960s, the trend of lowering the age of first marriage was stopped or maybe reversed in some of the advanced societies (Prioux-Marchal 1974, Commission on Population Growth and the American Future 1972). It does not seem possible at present to judge whether this is only a temporary phenomenon, caused by the economic recession and inflation characteristic of these years, or whether it is the beginning of a new trend in marriage patterns. Similarly, it is difficult to state whether the decline of the period fertility rates in America and western Europe has been caused only by this change in the trend of earlier marriage or by a change in the family plans of the young couples. The most probable explanation seems to be that both the

Table 5.2 Percentages of single men and women in selected age groups in census years around 1930 and 1960: selected countries.

| | | Percent single in the age group | | | |
| | | Males | | Females | |
Country	Year	25–29	45–49	20–24	45–49
England and Wales	1931	47	11	74	17
	1961	29	10	42	11
Ireland	1936	82	35	86	26
	1961	67	31	78	22
Sweden	1935	66	17	78	23
	1960	41	15	57	11
West Germany	1933*	54	6	74	12
	1961	36	5	55	9
Italy	1931	49	10	67	13
	1961	55	9	61	14
Poland	1931	41	4	61	7
	1960	29	4	41	9
Hungary	1930	39	5	52	6
	1960	23	5	31	7

* In 1933 the whole of Germany in the 1933 frontiers.
Source: Glass (1968), p. 104.

stopping of the tendency of the lowering of age at marriage and its eventual rise, and the decline in fertility, were codetermined by similar economic and social factors.

Similar to marriage, the divorce rate might also influence fertility, particularly if divorce meant a definite rejection of marriage. Although we do not have exact data on remarriage, it seems that a large proportion of divorced men and women tend to remarry. For example, in France it was estimated (Roussel 1975) that in the 1960s 62 per cent of divorced men and 55 per cent of divorced women sooner or later undertook a new marriage. In these conditions it is very difficult to tell (without appropriate data) whether the growth of the divorce rate, which can be observed in many advanced societies (table 5.3), has a negative or positive effect on fertility, since it might be conceived that remarried men and women might have children in the new marriage which would not have been born in the previous marriage.

Thus it is not very clear how marriage patterns and divorce rates influence fertility, or what are the factors influencing marriage and divorce patterns. Clearly, it would be necessary to know the determinants of marriage and divorce, as well as of illegitimacy, in order to explain the changes and differences in fertility, as these phenomena are only inter-

Table 5.3   Number of divorces per 10 000 married women in
selected countries around 1937 and around 1968.

Country	Number of divorces per 10 000 married women	
	Around 1937	*Around 1968*
England and Wales	37	38
Sweden	27	59
West Germany	32*	44
France	27	33
Hungary		79
United States	85	131

* Whole of Germany within prewar frontiers.
Source: Roussel (1975), p. 126.

mediate variables, mediating the influence of the more basic economic and
social forces that affect both marriage and fertility. It might be conceived
that·at least partly the same forces influence the marriage patterns and
marital fertility, since marriages are concluded, at least partly, with the aim
of producing children, so that the same factor might tend to increase or
decrease both the frequency of marriage and marital fertility. In addition,
however, there might be factors that influence only one of these. In the
following chapters the determinants of marriage and of marital fertility are
in general not distinguished, since most demographic studies do not make
this distinction. It should be kept in mind, however, that conceptually these
two kinds of factor ought to be distinguished.

Another demographic factor of fertility considered by the author of this
book to be an intermediate one is the knowledge and practice of different
methods of birth control. Several demographers used to consider this to be
a basic explanatory factor for fertility changes and differences.

According to these latter conceptions:

1   The basic cause of the secular decline in fertility during the demographic transition was the increasing knowledge of and practice of birth
control.
2   Fertility differences of social strata and other types of population
groups are caused by differential knowledge and practice of birth
control (Becker 1960).
3   The recent decline in fertility in some developed countries, especially in
the USA since the mid 1960s, was mainly caused by the decline in the
number of unwanted births due to an increased practice of birth control
(Westoff 1975).

Although it is undeniable that the decline in fertility (both the secular process and short-term changes) is primarily caused by the increased use of birth control, it is very doubtful whether differences in knowledge of birth control methods had really strong influence on changes and differences of fertility. On the one hand, it seems to be proven that all advanced societies, and even most societies in a pre-modern phase of development, had knowledge of the possibility and of at least some methods of birth control. Thus the practice or lack of practice, as well as the extent of practice of birth control in a given society during a given historical period might not have been influenced to any significant degree by the knowledge of birth control.

On the other hand, taking into consideration the almost universal knowledge of birth control possibilities, the concept of 'unwanted children' does not seem to be an appropriate one. If there is any decision or will of the couples concerning fertility, it is rather of a negative type – i.e. they decide to prevent a parity or want to avoid a parity, and for that purpose use adequate methods of birth control (Bourdieu, Darbel and Febvay 1964). Although sometimes efforts are made by couples to have children (in the case of subfecund couples), in most cases the efforts are necessary to avoid a parity. Thus the birth of a child in a family might result either from the decision to have a child, or from the lack of decision to avoid a parity or the lack of sufficiently strong motivation for that purpose. Thus what is usually called an 'unwanted birth' should be named more correctly 'a birth resulting from the lack of sufficiently strong motivation to avoid it'.

In some cases, strong motivation is in fact needed to avoid a parity – i.e. when no efficient or low cost (both in the monetary and psychological sense) birth control method is available. Traditional methods of contraception are not very efficient, producing many contraceptive failures, and in addition causing certain psychological risks. Modern contraceptive methods, such as the pill and the intrauterine device, are efficient, but might be difficult to obtain in some circumstances. Induced abortion is an almost 100 per cent certain method, but one that entails grave psychological strains, and eventually health risks; also in some circumstances it might have a high monetary cost. Thus couples may probably consider all these strains, risks and monetary costs when deciding to use some method of birth control and by that method to avoid a birth. With sufficiently strong motivation, however, they are almost certainly able to avoid a birth. This seems to be proved by the fact that, although European populations have in recent years used very varied birth control methods (e.g. coitus interruptus was still prevalent in some societies, while in others more than half the population used the contraceptive pill or the intrauterine device), all these societies have achieved similarly low fertility levels (United Nations 1976).

This means that the basic research problem is that of the motivations to have and to avoid a further child, and the actual practice of birth control ought to be considered as an intermediate factor, having – through its costs – a certain influence independent of the above mentioned motivations.

5.2 Income

The different types of data sources described in Part 4 showed rather contradictory relations of fertility to income.

Historical demographic investigations seem to suggest that in the period preceding industrial revolution a higher standard of living was correlated to higher fertility, and that a rising standard of living tended to favour a higher fertility level than stagnating economic conditions. A lower level of mortality, particularly infant and child mortality, however, which was often connected to a higher standard of living, tended to depress fertility.

Analysis of long-term trends in fertility has shown that from the beginning of industrial revolution to the Second World War the secular rise in income level was associated with a secular decline in fertility. However, also in this period, short-term changes of income level connected with business cycles tended to be positively correlated to fertility. After the Second World War the long-term tendency for the decline in fertility to be associated with the rise in income level seemed to have changed in the economically most developed societies, as fertility first rose, then remained more or less stable parallel with the continuous rise in the level of *per capita* income. The decline in fertility in the second half of the 1960s, however, seems to reverse again the long-term tendency. This recent decline can be interpreted either as a return to the normal association of socioeconomic development with a declining fertility, or as a consequence of economic insecurity (unemployment, inflation) and a slower rise of income level in the economically most developed countries.

Recent census fertility data also show a blurring of the traditional fertility differentials that occur where, in the earlier phases of socioeconomic development, strata having higher income show lower fertility levels. Although there are some indications that this correlation did not prevail universally in these earlier phases, recently several clearly contradictory tendencies seem to be appearing. On the one hand there is a tendency for decline in the differentials, and on the other hand there are signs of the development of a new U-shaped or even positive relationship between income level and fertility of social strata.

Multiple regression analyses of the factors of fertility based on territorial cross-sectional data tended to show a positive relation of fertility to income. This latter, however, was rather strongly associated with other

factors (industrialization, urbanization, etc.), which were strongly negatively associated with fertility.

Fertility surveys, like census fertility data, seem to indicate that the
simple negative correlation between income and fertility does not prevail,
at least in the most advanced societies, and possibly also at relatively lower
levels of national development. Income level seems to be positively associated with the percentage of family planners and with the practice of birth
control. These differences, however, rapidly diminish with the almost universal acceptance of family planning and birth control. On the other hand,
within fairly homogeneous population groups, income seems to be positively related to fertility. Other elements of economic conditions, like
economic insecurity, also seem to have an important influence on fertility.

Thus the basic question is: whether the traditional thesis of negative
correlation of fertility to income, formulated in the various versions of the
demographic transition theory, is still correct in advanced societies; or,
alternatively, whether the signs of U-shaped and positive association found
recently in some investigations reflect the true relationship of fertility to
income, as formulated by the economic theories of fertility, with the
relationship being masked by other factors (e.g. urbanization or urban
residence, higher education) correlated with both fertility and income
level.

One of the earliest descriptions of a clearly positive relation of fertility to
income is given by Stys (1957 1959) who analysed the fertility of Polish
married women born in the 1870s in twenty villages. Daughters of more

Table 5.4 Number of children ever born per married woman, and other
demographic characteristics of peasant women, by size of farm in twenty Polish
villages about 1872–1914.

Demographic characteristics of women	Size of farm (hectares)				
	Landless	0–1	1–4	4–7	7 and over
Number of births per women	3·9	5·4	6·4	7·7	9·1
Number of surviving children per women*	2·9	4·1	5·0	5·9	8·0
Age at marriage	31	25	24	22	20
Number of births per year of marriage to age 45 of women	0·28	0·26	0·30	0·35	0·37
Number of births per year of marriage to the last birth of women	0·43	0·35	0·36	0·39	0·41

* Surviving to their marriage.
Source: Stys (1957).

Table 5.5 Average number of children ever borne by married women, by birth cohorts in twenty Polish villages.

Year of birth	Size of farm (hectares)										
	Total	Landless	Up to 0·5	0·5–1	1–2	2–3	3–4	4–5	5–7	7–10	10–15
1855–1880	6·48	3·89	5·46	5·30	6·10	6·57	6·40	7·54	7·83	9·08	9·00
1881–1885	6·16	3·50	3·50	4·94	5·38	5·84	7·23	7·30	8·09	8·17	6·00
1886–1890	5·50	6·00	3·55	3·75	5·15	5·39	6·26	6·00	6·67	7·00	9·80
1891–1894	4·84	4·33	4·31	5·16	4·43	4·83	4·81	6·12	5·56	5·40	7·00
1895–1897	4·59	2·00	4·28	3·74	4·54	4·77	5·29	4·53	5·00	3·75	5·50
1898–1900	3·97	4·50	3·71	3·20	3·49	4·07	4·57	4·84	3·88	7·17	6·50
1901–1902	3·98	—	4·40	2·85	3·80	4·02	4·27	4·60	5·14	4·75	7·50
1903–1904	3·48	4·00	3·64	2·94	3·42	3·72	3·72	2·64	2·67	4·40	—

Source: Stys (1957).

opulent peasants clearly married earlier, began to bear at an earlier age and had births till a higher age, as well as being confined more frequently during marriage. These differences remained unchanged in subsequent generations, although there was a general decline in fertility, presumably as a result of a spread of birth control (tables 5.4, 5.5). Thus the differences might not have been caused by differences in the knowledge of birth control. The obvious interpretation, therefore, is that wealthier peasants could afford to have more children, or that the peasants having larger farms could find employment for more children on their farms.

Data from Germany in 1925 based on income tax statistics (Burgdörfer 1932) reveal interesting tendencies: while in the whole of Germany the relation of fertility to income proved to be negative, with some signs of a U-shaped curve beginning at the highest income levels, in the largest cities the relation was strongly positive, and positive also in the medium-sized towns. The negative relation found in other settlements, however, dominated the relation at the national level. This finding might indicate that after the transition to the modern fertility pattern, which was completed in the larger towns at that time, a positive association prevails (table 5.6).

Table 5.6 Average number of children per 100 families by income groups, based on income tax statistics: Germany, 1925.

| Income group (Reichsmarks) | Number of children per 100 families | | | | | |
	Germany	Large cities	Berlin	Munich	Medium-sized cities	Other settlements
Up to 1500	160	96	75	98	129	176
1501–3000	174	110	87	110	147	199
3001–5000	164	116	91	107	145	189
5001–8000	152	119	94	107	150	176
8000–12 000	144	125	109	108	148	166
12 001–16 000	142	124	106	115	145	162
16 001–25 000	141	129	110	120	150	160
25 000–50 000	142	131	120	114	154	160
50 000+	148	140	130	121	157	164
Total	162	109	88	105	140	181

Source: Burgdörfer (1932), p. 59.

Data relating to the population of Stockholm in the 1920s (Edin and Hutchinson 1935) similarly demonstrated a positive relation of fertility to income. The authors were able to use data from several sources: they combined individual data from the 1920 census and from the vital statistics of 1919–20 with data on the income of husbands and their occupation. Unstandardized number of births per 1000 married-women-years showed a U-shaped relation. When the data were standardized for marriage duration and age of parents, the relation became more clearly positive (table 5.7).

Table 5.7 Live births per 1000 years of married life by income class: Stockholm 1919–22.

	Income class of husband in 1920 (Swedish kronor)			
Standardization	Under 4000	4000– 6000	6000– 10 000	10 000 and over
Unstandardized	118	112	119	142
Standardized for marriage duration only	110	112	124	153
Standardized for age of parents only	112	110	125	157
Standardized for both age of parents and marriage duration	110	112	125	159

Source: Edin and Hutchinson (1935), p. 53.

When the population was differentiated by social strata, the standardized fertility rates showed a negative relation in the stratum of industrial workers, while in all other strata the relation was positive (table 5.8). These results could be interpreted by surmising that the modern pattern of relationship appeared in the non-manual strata, while in the manual group the traditional pattern prevailed (although the relation was very weak in this case).

Another data source used the combination of the 1920 and 1930 censuses with maternity hospital records. As income of husband was available from both 1920 and 1930, it was possible to investigate the influence of changes in income. A fairly clear tendency was found – namely that among families having similar education and income in 1920, and having married at similar age, fertility was higher in those who experienced a favourable change of income. Also there was a clear positive relation of fertility to income level in 1920 in all strata differentiated by education level (table 5.9).

These investigations were repeated by Moberg (1950–1) on the basis of the data of the census of 1935. The investigation embraced not only the population of Stockholm, but all urban families with marriage duration of 0

Table 5.8   Live births per 1000 years of married life, standardized for age of wife and marriage duration by income and social strata: Stockholm, 1919–22.

| | Income class of husband in 1920 (Swedish kronor) | | | | | |
Social stratum	Under 4000	4000– 6000	6000– 10 000	10 000 and over	Total	Unstan- dardized
Industrial workers	111	109	105	—	110	107
Technicians, overseers, office staff in industry	104	120	125	152	124	122
Employees in stores, banks and transportation and others in trade and commerce	110	115	131	154	124	128
Professionals, state and municipal employees	110	112	127	154	123	125
Total	110	112	125	154		

Source: Edin and Hutchinson (1935).

Table 5.9   Average number of live births per family in the first ten years of marriage by income and education of husband: Stockholm, 1917–30.

| Education of husband in 1930 | Income class of husband in 1920 (Swedish kronor) | | | |
	Under 4000	4000– 6000	6000– 10 000	10 000 and over
8 years or less	1·15	1·18	1·18	1·56
More than 8 years but without matriculation	1·18	1·34	1·35	1·62
Matriculation, or university degree	1·46	1·45	1·46	1·85
Total	1·16	1·21	1·31	1·74

Source: Edin and Hutchinson (1935), p. 78.

to 20 years. A negative correlation of fertility to income was again found in the stratum of industrial workers, and in the group of employers and non-manuals with low education. The relation was U-shaped in the group of these latter having medium education and it was clearly positive in the case of employers and non-manuals having at least attained matriculation (table 5.10). When this last group was analysed in more detail, it was surprisingly found that the same positive relation was observed in the group who matriculated in 1920 as in the group who matriculated in 1910, but that in 1920 fertility rates were higher. This proves that, in the period

Table 5.10 Average number of children ever live born, by income, occupational group and education of husband: Swedish urban marriages, 1935–6.

Occupation and education of husband	Income class of family (Swedish kronor)				
	Under 3000	3000– 5000	5000– 10 000	10 000 and over	Total
Industrial workers	1·64	1·37	0·93	—	1·49
Employers and officials whose education was:					
(a) Not more than elementary	1·44	1·30	0·91	0·97	1·33
(b) Beyond elementary, but without matriculation	1·24	1·26	1·19	1·36	1·25
(c) At least matriculation	1·18	1·22	1·38	1·61	1·46

Source: Moberg (1950–1).

when fertility was at its lowest level in Sweden, important changes in the fertility differentials were already occurring, the fertility of the highest educational groups beginning to increase and showing a clearly positive relation to income.

These and other signs of a positive relation of fertility to family income have led some demographers to formulate new hypotheses concerning the impact of income. In addition to simply hypothesizing a positive relation, it has been supposed that, although the overall relation prevailing in the whole society is fairly negative, at least temporarily, within homogeneous social or occupational groups a positive relation exists, because the income of the family relative to the income of other families in the same social group (i.e. relative to the average income of the group) tends to be correlated positively to fertility. This is the so-called relative income hypothesis. Another hypothesis is that it is not or not only the level of income, but rather the change in family income over time, or the expected change of income in future, that is correlated positively to fertility.

It was again in Sweden, where the population registration provides excellent sources for investigating the factors of fertility, that these new hypotheses were confronted in a most detailed way with data on individual families (Bernhardt 1972). A national sample of 3·3 per cent was taken from the marriage cohorts of 1954–8, where the women were under 25 at marriage, and their fertility history was followed until 1967. Fertility was analysed by distinguishing parities by birth order.

Husband's average income from 1964 to 1966 displayed a U-shaped relationship with total fertility – i.e. the couples in the middle income groups had the lowest total fertility. However, the same type of relation was not found in the case of all birth orders. First and second parities showed a positive relation to income, in the case of the third child the relation was U-shaped and in the case of fourth and higher order parities the highest income group had a higher fertility than the two subsequent groups, but much lower than the lowest income group (tables 5.11, 5.12).

Table 5.11   Parity progression ratios by husband's income 1964–6 for marriage cohorts 1954–8, wife's age at marriage under 25: Sweden.

Husband's income (Swedish kronor)	Parity progression ratios		
	a_0	a_1	a_2
Under 10 000	918	876	584
10 000–15 000	942	798	493
15 000–20 000	952	813	414
20 000–40 000	955	856	384
Over 40 000	950	948	543

Source: Bernhardt (1972), p. 179.

Table 5.12   Fertility after 9–13 years of married life of marriage cohorts 1954–8, wife's age at marriage under 25, by husband's income: Sweden.

Husband's income (Swedish kronor)	Number of births of specified order per 1000 marriages				
	1	2	3	4+	All
Under 10 000	918	804	470	322	2514
10 000–15 000	942	752	371	222	2287
15 000–20 000	952	774	320	115	2161
20 000–40 000	955	818	314	72	2159
Over 40 000	950	901	489	142	2482

Source: Bernhardt (1972), p. 177.

The relative income hypothesis was investigated by dividing the sample into four social strata: non-manuals with advanced education, non-manuals without advanced education, manuals, farmers and farm labourers. The families in these strata were then differentiated according to their income relative to the average of the stratum. Total fertility again showed in all social strata a U-shaped relation to relative income. However, when fertility was investigated by birth order, the first and second order parities showed a positive correlation with relative income, while the fourth and higher order parities showed a negative correlation.

Bernhardt interpreted these results by two factors. On the one hand, there is a positive correlation of fertility to income, and to relative income, until the ideal number of two to three children is attained. It is characteristic that in the case of the third child the positive correlation is confined to the highest income group. On the other hand, the differences in the higher order parities are influenced by the fact that differences still exist with regard to the efficiency with which family limitation is practised, some families in the lowest income groups being somewhat inefficient family planners. This, however, is not caused by deficient knowledge of birth control methods, but by a weaker motivation for controlling the number of children, because the costs of child-rearing are lower in these strata.

American surveys of fertility have also dealt with the relation of fertility to income. The original results of the Indianapolis survey showed a negative relation of fertility to income with a slight rise in the fertility of the highest income group as compared to the second highest (both in the case of all couples interviewed and of the relatively fecund couples – table 5.13). Goldberg (1960) and Duncan (1965), however, in reanalysing the results found that, if couples with farm background are neglected, a clear positive correlation of fertility to income appears. This seems to be a proof of the relative income hypothesis, since the couples interviewed in the Indianapolis survey constituted a fairly homogeneous population.

Table 5.13 Number of children ever born per 100 couples by fecundity status, husband's average annual earnings: Indianapolis survey.

Measure of socioeconomic status			
Husband's annual earnings	*Total*	*Relatively fecund*	*Relatively sterile*
$3000+	159	180	94
2000–2999	149	176	87
1600–1999	163	194	76
1200–1599	189	229	70
Under 1200	227	266	121

Source: Kiser and Whelpton, in Whelpton and Kiser (1950), p. 376.

The Indianapolis survey also tested the hypothesis that economic insecurity might influence negatively the level of fertility. Economic insecurity was measured among other things by the answers given by wives and husbands to the following questions: 'How much time since marriage have you (or your husband) been faced with the possibility that you (or your husband) might have a large pay cut or be out of work for several months?' The answers clearly verify the hypothesis:

Frequency of facing probability of husband's pay cut or unemployment as expressed by wife	Number of children ever born per 100 couples		Per cent childless
	All couples	Fertile couples	
Very seldom	126	159	20·6
Seldom	118	162	27·4
Sometimes	88	146	39·8
Much or nearly all of time	71	140	49·0

This measure of economic insecurity proved to have the strongest influence on number of children among all the factors investigated (see p. 196).

The other economic factor investigated in the Indianapolis survey, called economic tension, did not show the expected influence on fertility. It was measured by the difference between actual income, home and car and those considered satisfactory by the couple. It was hypothesized that the greater the difference between the actual standard of living and the standard of living desired, the higher the proportion of couples practising contraception effectively and the smaller the planned families (Riemer and Kiser, in Whelpton and Kiser (1954). The hypothesis, however, was not confirmed, because couples experiencing more economic tension practised less birth control and had larger families.

In the Princeton survey the influence of income on fertility seemed unclear, because different relations were found in the case of denominational groups, as well as between completely successful planners and others. It seems that the relation of fertility to income was fairly positive in the case of Catholic couples, particularly among completely successful Catholic family planners. In the case of Protestants and Jews the relation is less clear, so that in the case of all couples together the pattern seems to be blurred.

The peculiar character of the sample of the Princeton survey (only couples with two children) and the longitudinal character of the survey made it less suitable for investigating fertility differentials in cross-section, but more adequate for studying the influence of changes in the economic conditions of families on their fertility. The influence of changes in income during the three-year interval between two interviews was investigated (table 5.14). This influence, however, seemed to be different in particular denominational and religious activity groups. In the case of active Protestants the correlation of income change to fertility was negative, while in

Table 5.14   Relationship between the directions of annual income changes during the three-year interval and number of pregnancies (per cent having additional pregnancy): Princeton survey.

Direction of income change	Religion				
	Active Protestants	Other Protestants	Active Catholics	Other Catholics	Jews
Downward	58	54	69	59	23
Stable	47	53	64	54	
Slightly up	38	62	62	59	40
Upward	43	63	83	67	26
Correlation of the index of income change with number of pregnancies	−0·06	0·11	0·15	0·09	0·03

Source: Westoff, Potter and Sagi (1963), p. 139.

the groups of other Protestants, and active and other Catholics the correlation was positive, couples whose income increased showing slightly more third pregnancies. The correlations, however, were fairly weak. It is puzzling what might have caused different relations in the group of active Protestants to the other groups. The positive correlation might be explained by an economic theory of fertility – namely, by the higher propensity of families with growing income to have more children, since they can afford to have more at the same level of cost per child. The negative correlation might be caused by a background factor connected to values and aspirations – namely, that families who strongly strive for improvement of their income situation are liable to limit the number of their children, since more children require more time and effort and consequently permit less time and effort for the occupational career. These, however, are conjectures.

The Growth of American Families surveys and the National Fertility Studies, on the other hand, were designed in such a way that fertility differentials by national cross-sections could be thoroughly investigated. The results concerning fertility differentials by income, however, were again not consistent in the interviewed populations and subpopulations. On the one hand, the negative relation of fertility to income, which had almost disappeared in 1960 (almost no differences in the expected number of children of different income categories), was fairly marked in 1965 (tables 5.15, 5.16, 5.17). On the other hand, Catholics in both years showed a U-shaped relation, while the relation in the case of Protestants was almost zero in 1960 and negative in 1965. Also the differentials by family income in the black population were much higher than in the case of

Table 5.15 Number of children born by 1960, and expected number of children, by husband's income: Growth of American Families survey, 1960.

	Average number of births	
Husband's income	By 1960	Most likely expected
Total ($)	2·3	3·1
10 000 and more	2·5	3·1
7000–9999	2·3	3·0
6000–6999	2·4	3·1
5000–5999	2·3	3·1
4000–4999	2·3	3·2
3000–3999	2·2	3·3
Under 3000	2·1	3·2

Source: Whelpton, Campbell and Patterson (1966), p. 104.

Table 5.16 Expected number of children, by husband's income and by religion: Growth of American Families survey, 1960.

Husband's income ($)	Total	Protestant	Catholic
Total	3·1	2·9	3·7
7000 or more	3·0	2·9	3·8
5000–6999	3·1	2·9	3·5
Under 5000	3·2	3·0	3·9

Source: Whelpton, Campbell and Patterson (1966), p. 105.

whites. The larger differences in the case of Negroes were explained by Ryder and Westoff partly by the fact that poor black couples were less efficient family planners, i.e. they had more unwanted births. This is demonstrated by the large differences between expected and desired number of children of black couples in all except the three highest income categories.

D. S. Freedman (1963) reanalysed the data of the Growth of American Families survey by taking into consideration the following economic variables: husband's absolute income, his relative income (as compared to the average income level he ought to have on the basis of socioeconomic status, age, education and residence, calculated by means of multiple regression equation), wife's income, years the wife worked since marriage, wife's labour force status, wife's future work expectations. Couples married for five to nine years and married for ten and more years were analysed separately. In the former group neither absolute nor relative income

Table 5.17 Expected and desired number of children, by family income: first National Fertility Study, 1965.

Family income ($)	Expected number of children				Desired number of children	
	White	Black	Protestant	Catholic	White	Black
15 000 and over	3·0	2·1	2·6	4·2	3·4	2·7
10 000–14 999	3·0	2·6	2·7	3·8	3·2	2·8
8000–9999	3·3	3·2	3·0	3·8	3·3	3·0
7000–7999	3·3	3·5	3·1	4·0	3·3	2·8
6000–6999	3·3	3·6	3·1	3·9	3·3	3·0
5000–5999	3·4	3·9	3·1	3·7	3·3	3·1
4000–4999	3·4	4·3	3·3	4·2	3·4	3·3
3000–3999	3·5	4·7	3·2	} 4·3	3·4	3·6
0–3000	3·9	5·3	3·7		3·7	3·9
Total	3·3	4·0	3·0	3·9	3·3	3·2

Source: Ryder and Westoff (1971), pp. 60, 78.

of the husband showed any significant correlation to fertility. However, in the latter group – i.e. those married for ten or more years – absolute income level showed a weak negative correlation, while relative income level of husband was rather strongly positively correlated to fertility. Years the wife worked since marriage were negatively correlated to fertility in both groups. The correlations did not change when eight demographic and social variables (duration of marriage, age of wife, education of wife, occupational status score of husband, education of husband, farm background of couple, religion of wife and attitude of wife towards family limitation) were introduced. Thus it seems to be proved that, at least in the United States, at present relative income is positively correlated to fertility.

The repeated Detroit Area Studies gave excellent opportunities for reanalysing new hypotheses on the factors of fertility (Freedman and Coombs 1966a, 1966b). For example, the relative income hypothesis was analysed by asking wives about the level of family income, (1) relative to couples where the husband has similar education and occupation, and (2) relative to the income of the families of three women friends. It was found – as in the reanalysis of the Growth of American Families data – that in the first years of family building there is no consistent correlation of fertility to relative income, but after the fourth parity a clear strong positive correlation of fertility to relative income is displayed.

The income change hypothesis was also investigated and found to be valid in the Detroit Area Studies. Both the expected number of children and the number of live births between the first and third interview was higher in the group of couples whose income increased in the meantime, than in the group where there was no change or a downward change of income (table 5.18). The relation becomes even stronger when the influence of absolute income level and religion is controlled by an adequate adjustment. The impact of income changes is especially strong in the group of couples with lower income. In the latter group a major part said that they would want more children if money were no obstacle than in the group of couples with higher income.

Table 5.18 Expected number of children and number of live births per 1000 from first to third interview, by income change from first to third interview: Detroit Area Studies.

Income change	Expected number of children at third interview		Number of live births per 1000 from first to third interview	
	Mean	Adjusted*	Mean	Adjusted*
Changed up	5·04	0·23	439	54
Mixed change**	4·84	0·06	411	6
Down or no change	4·63	−0·23	330	−76
Grand mean	4·85		398	

* Adjusted for religion and income.
** Income up at one follow-up interview and down at the other.
Source: Freedman and Coombs (1966a).

It was also supposed that not only actual income changes, but also expected changes during the whole life cycle influence fertility. Questions on expected income and living standard changes were asked separately. There was a general trend for couples who were expecting favourable changes in the following ten years to predict a higher number of children: valid in the Detroit Area Studies. Both the expected number of children and

Expected income change	Expected living standard change	Expected fertility
No change	No change	4·53
Slightly higher	No difference	4·76
Slightly higher	Big difference	4·71
Much higher	No difference	4·41
Much higher	Big difference	5·25

Although fertility seems to be positively correlated to increases in income, it was surmised that, parallel with the rise in family income, aspirations also tend to rise; the standard of living to which parents aspire for themselves and for their children tends to be higher, and new alternatives for spending may compete with a larger family, so that in consequence fertility may be reduced. An aspirations for children index was constructed based on parents' aspirations for separate bedroom, private lessons, membership in clubs or scouts, summer camp experience, etc. The higher the aspirations were, the lower fertility tended to be. Also college plans for children tended to be negatively correlated to the number of children. As to the aspirations of the parents for themselves, second car ownership by the family was investigated and found to be negatively correlated to fertility.

The Detroit Area Studies (Freedman and Coombs 1966b) also demonstrated a reverse relation between income and fertility. Not only did family income influence fertility, but also the number of children and the spacing of births influenced the level of income of the family. Couples interviewed several times were divided into three groups: (a) long spacers, where intervals between subsequent births were relatively long, (b) short spacers, where the intervals were relatively short, and (c) premaritally pregnant couples, where the first birth occurred after less than nine months following marriage. This last group was also characterized by lower education, lower age at marriage, shorter subsequent birth intervals and in general more unwanted pregnancies. In the first years of marriage long spacers showed the most favourable economic conditions; the short spacers, however, caught up with them in the subsequent years of marriage. The premaritally pregnant group, on the other hand, remained in a relatively disadvantaged position after a longer marriage duration. The fact that higher fertility seems to have a depressing effect on family income even more underlines the finding of the above mentioned studies that, *ceteris paribus*, a higher relative income or expected income is positively associated with fertility, because otherwise the negative reverse effects of higher fertility on income would completely mask the positive correlation.

Simon (1975a 1975b) investigated the influence of fertility on the basis of the one per 1000 sample of the 1960 census in the United States. His basic idea was that the influence of income on fertility is different at the particular birth orders, higher income reducing the tendency to stop at zero children or one child, but also reducing the tendency to add children after the third and fourth child. In other words, the relationship between income and the probability of another birth is assumed to be positive at low birth orders, but negative at high birth orders. If this relationship, were seen to apply to long-term historical development, in the same way it applies to this one cross-sectional example, it might explain the reduction of the variance in the number of children per family parallel with economic development.

The sample taken from the census was subclassified by race, degree of urbanization, husband's occupation, wife's and husband's education, and wife's age. The units of observation were women aged 35–54 with husband present. The dependent variables, measuring fertility, were parity progression ratios calculated from the census data, as well as birth order transition coefficients. It was found that husband's income is positively related to fertility at the first and second birth, almost neutral at the third birth, negative at the fourth and fifth birth, but surprisingly again positive at the sixth birth.

By further analysing the same data, Simon (1975b) found that education influences the impact of income on fertility. For example, income was seen to have a more positive effect on fertility for more highly educated women than for less educated women. This finding suggests that income interacts with other variables in determining fertility.

Recently the relation of fertility to total family income was investigated in Poland by means of a sample taken from married couples in Poznan and other towns in the region of Poznan, together with another sample of couples where one member of each couple had studied at the University of Economics in Poznan in the 1950s and the early 1960s. Correlation and regression of fertility and family income were calculated separately for different age groups and for persons employed in industry and transport on one hand, and in non-material branches on the other hand. It was found that below the level of 3000 *zloty* monthly income and above the level of 8000 *zloty* the correlations were positive, while between 3000 and 8000 *zloty* they were negative. The author stated that the results confirm the theoretical hypothesis of Smolinski (see p. 36), according to which at very low levels of income fertility and income are positively correlated, at medium levels the correlation is negative, and at a high level of income the relation again turns over and becomes positive (Roeske-Slomka 1974).

Thus investigations carried out in different societies and different historical periods seem to suggest unanimously that level of income, positive changes in income level and the more optimistic evaluations of future income tend to have a positive impact on marital fertility, when all other factors influencing fertility are kept constant. This is a very important conclusion, which has an impact not only on discussions of the theory of fertility (verifying the basic statement of the economic theories of fertility), but also on population policies (implying that by improving the economic conditions of families with children fertility can be raised). However, the condition that all other factors influencing fertility are kept constant can prevail only in the very short run and in homogeneous population groups, because these factors (e.g. socioeconomic status, residence, education, etc.)

tend to be correlated rather strongly with income level of populations, groups and individual families, and clearly have an influence on the costs of children on the one hand and on the aspirations of couples concerning their living standard on the other hand.

5.3 Socioeconomic status

The investigation of the influence of socioeconomic status on fertility is one of the traditional fields of demographic research. However, no consistent pattern of differences was found, as described in Part 4. In many cases, particularly in societies in the period of transition from high to low fertility, a more or less negative correlation of fertility to income was found, the higher socioeconomic status groups having lower fertility. Recently, however, the so-called U-shaped relation of fertility to socioeconomic status was demonstrated in several developed countries, the status groups at the medium level of social hierarchy having the lowest fertility. It was also hinted that the true relation, which prevailed before demographic transition and might prevail in the future, is a positive one, the higher status groups having higher fertility (Clark 1967). Forecasts of fertility differences by status and education are also different, even contradictory. Some authors maintain that there is a tendency for fertility differences by status to disappear, others suppose that a positive relation will be prevalent, and a third group supposes that agricultural populations – farmers and farm workers – will probably always have the highest fertility because of the special living conditions of these occupational groups.

Table 5.19   Number of children ever born in current marriage, per 100 married women: England and Wales, 1911.

Social stratum	Unstandardized rate	Rate standardized for age at marriage of women and duration of marriage
Upper and middle class	249	277
Intermediate (including farmer)	311	321
Skilled worker	350	353
Semi-skilled worker	356	359
Unskilled worker	399	392
Textile worker	308	319
Miner	423	433
Agricultural worker	433	399

Source: Glass (1967), p. 69.

The available data on differences of fertility by social status, originating from censuses, fertility surveys, and sometimes from vital statistics (these latter data are calculated in such a way that the yearly numbers of births are divided by the number of population in the different socioeconomic groups taken from a census or a microcensus), do not provide unambiguous answers to these questions.

The fertility differences in the United States, described in Chapters 4.2 and 4.4, seem to display both a gradual decline and a gradual reversal from the traditional negative relationship to a U-shaped pattern. However, even the National Fertility Study of 1965 demonstrated the existence of differences (Ryder and Westoff 1971):

Socioeconomic status	Average number of children			
	Expected		Desired	
	White	Black	White	Black
Upper white collar	3·1	2·8	3·3	2·8
Lower white collar	3·0	3·4	3·3	2·8
Upper blue collar	3·3	3·5	3·3	3·0
Lower blue collar	3·5	4·2	3·4	3·3
Farm	3·6	6·0	3·7	4·5
Total	3·3	4·0	3·3	3·2

The development of fertility differences by socioeconomic strata can be studied very accurately on the basis of British fertility data. Data from the census of 1911 (Glass 1967) seem to show a negative relation of fertility to status, although there are some interesting exceptions. The fertility of textile workers, for example, is surprisingly low, and this might not be due to the fact that the textile workers' status is higher than that of any other working class group. On the other hand, miners showed a very high fertility – when standardized, their fertility rate was the highest – and again it cannot be said that miners were at the bottom of the social hierarchy. Rather it might be conjectured that textile workers on the one hand, and miners on the other, each had a special subculture which tended to depress or to increase fertility (table 5.19). Data from 1939 (Hopkin and Hajnal 1947–8) already show the first signs of the appearance of the U-shaped relationship, as professionals and employers had a higher fertility than clerks, whose position in the social hierarchy was lower than that of the professionals. The relatively low fertility of textile workers and the high fertility of miners is even more outstanding than in 1911 (table 5.20). In 1961 (Glass 1968) the differences by strata are smaller, but the U-shaped

Table 5.20 Total fertility rates of men by social strata: England and Wales, 1939.

	Number of births per 1000 men	
Social stratum	All men	Married men
Professional and administrative	1485	1562
Employer	1760	1837
Clerk	1349	1497
Shop assistant and personal service	1725	1923
Police, armed services	1706	1777
Skilled manual worker	2103	2291
Semi-skilled manual	2425	2703
Unskilled labourer	2733	3309
Textile worker	1596	1767
Miner	2765	3211
Farmer	1938	2233
Agricultural labourer	2316	2932
All social strata	2136	2379

Source: Hopkin and Hajnal (1947–8).

Table 5.21 Number of children ever born, by duration of marriage of women married once only and enumerated with their husband, with age at marriage under 45 years, by social strata: England and Wales, 1961.

	Duration of marriage (years)		
Social stratum	10–14	15–19	20–24
Employer and manager: large establishments	1·81	1·85	1·79
Employer and manager: small establishments	1·78	1·83	1·80
Professional: self-employed	2·17	2·18	2·04
Professional: employed	1·86	1·90	1·84
Intermediate non-manual	1·76	1·80	1·76
Junior non-manual	1·68	1·76	1·72
Self-employed (not professional)	1·88	1·92	1·81
Personal service	1·90	2·00	1·86
Manual foreman and supervisor	1·90	1·99	1·92
Skilled manual worker	2·00	2·11	2·06
Semi-skilled manual worker	2·02	2·15	2·11
Unskilled manual worker	2·30	2·34	2·30
Farmer: employer and manager	2·22	2·25	2·30
Farmer: self-employed	1·99	2·05	2·01
Agricultural worker	2·10	2·24	2·29

Source: Glass (1968), p. 123.

curve is displayed more clearly, as the fertility of self-employed professionals, most probably the group on the highest level in hierarchy, is
higher than that of all other non-manual groups, including foremen and
supervisors, and is as high as that of the skilled workers (table 5.21).

Similar tendencies of changes in fertility differences were observed in
other western European countries (Johnson 1960). In France a slightly
U-shaped relation was found before the Second World War, professionals
having a higher completed fertility than medium-level executives, other
simple non-manuals and small self-employed merchants. On the other
hand, unskilled workers, miners and semi-skilled workers had much higher
fertility levels. After the Second World War fertility of all socioeconomic
strata increased. This rise was more pronounced in the case of the professional group than in the others (Febvay 1959, Bourdieu, Darbel and
Febvay 1964, Bourdieu and Darbel 1966). Recent data (table 5.22) show
the persistence of this U-shaped relation. However, the fertility of the two
strata working in agriculture – self-employed peasants and agricultural
workers – remains much higher than that of any other group.

Table 5.22 Number of children ever born per 100 married women, husband
present, by marriage duration and social stratum: France, 1962.

	Marriage duration (years)				
Social stratum	*5*	*10*	*15*	*20*	*30*
Professional, high executive	106	163	193	193	195
Medium-level executive*	93	139	164	173	180
Other non-manual, employed	103	152	184	201	213
Self-employed in industry and					
commerce	104	155	186	201	211
Worker	117	178	219	241	251
Self-employed in agriculture	146	222	266	288	295
Agricultural worker	142	219	275	310	328
Total	118	178	216	236	246

* *'Cadre moyen'*
Source: Tabah (1971), p. 40.

The U-shaped curve is found even more clearly in the Netherlands in
1960, with all manual workers having almost the same fertility levels as
professionals and high-level executives, and self-employed peasants having
the highest fertility; the actual number of children ever borne by women
living in first marriage was (Tabah 1971, p. 45):

Professional	2·6
High-level executive	2·6
Other non-manual	2·3
Self-employed outside agriculture	2·9
Manual worker	2·7
Self-employed peasant	3·7
Agricultural worker	3·2
No occupation (including helping family members)	3·9
Total	2·8

Table 5.23   Number of children ever born, expected and desired, by marriage duration and social strata: Belgium, 1960s.

	Number of children						
	Ever born			*Expected*			*Desired*
	Marriage duration			*Marriage duration*			
Social stratum	*5–9*	*15 and more*	*Total*	*5–9*	*15 and more*	*Total*	
Professional, high executive	2·0	3·1	2·2	2·4	2·9	2·8	3·0
Medium-level executive*	1·8	2·5	1·8	2·3	2·4	2·5	2·7
Other non-manual, employed	1·7	2·2	1·9	2·2	2·2	2·3	2·5
Self-employed artisan, shop-keeper	1·7	2·1	1·8	2·3	2·0	2·2	2·6
Skilled worker	1·8	2·6	1·9	2·4	2·5	2·3	2·3
Unskilled worker	1·9	3·0	2·2	2·3	2·9	2·4	2·4
Farmer and farm labourer	2·6	4·0	2·6	3·0	4·1	3·1	3·2
Total	1·9	2·7	2·0	2·3	2·7	2·4	2·5

* *'Cadre moyen'*
Source: Tabah (1971), p. 36.

Similar differences were recently found in Belgium (table 5.23), as well as in Sweden, where the number of children ever borne by women married at an age of less than 30 years was in 1967 (Tabah 1971, p. 50):

	Marriage cohort		
	1945–9	1950–4	1955–9
Non-manual with university level education	2·28	2·25	2·16
Non-manual without university level education	2·03	2·07	1·93
Manual worker	2·18	2·21	2·08
Peasant	2·79	2·63	2·39
Total	2·22	2·23	2·08

In Hungary, where social structure is from several points of view very different from the structure of western European societies, the first signs of similar changes in fertility differences can be observed in recent years (see Chapters 4.2 and 4.4). In one respect, however, the recent Hungarian data differ fundamentally from those of western European countries and the United States. The age-specific fertility rates calculated from yearly vital statistical data show that these rates were more or less at the same level for peasants and manuals working in other branches in 1968, and even somewhat lower for peasants than the manuals in other branches in 1960 (table 5.24). This is rather exceptional, because in all other national studies

Table 5.24   Age-specific fertility rates by social strata: Hungary, 1960 and 1968.

Social stratum	Number of live births per 1000 women aged				
	15–19	20–24	25–29	30–39	40–49
1960					
Peasant	43	163	108	41	4
Manual in other branches	71	179	109	42	4
Non-manual	24	122	92	30	2
Total	52	159	106	39	4
1968					
Peasant	56	195	113	37	3
Manual in other branches	65	182	120	39	3
Non-manual	22	131	113	32	2
Total	52	164	116	37	2

Source: Klinger (1969), p. 1174.

peasants had higher fertility rates than other social strata. It is not quite clear whether this peculiarity of the Hungarian socioeconomic fertility differentials is a temporary phenomenon or not, since the average birth order of peasants (2.22) continues to be higher than that of other manual workers (1.94). Recent fertility surveys performed in Hungary do not give clear answers to this question, since the planned number of children seems to be equal or higher in the non-manual and manual strata than in the peasant stratum, but the achieved fertility is slightly higher in the peasant stratum (see Chapter 4.4, p. 218). It is clear, however, that the fertility of peasant couples is at least not much higher than, and is perhaps at the same level as that of manual workers in other branches than agriculture. Different reasons for this special feature of Hungarian fertility differences might be suggested. One might be that, because of socialization of agriculture (almost no independent peasants remained in Hungary), the living conditions of peasants (i.e. of manuals in agriculture) became very similar to those of manuals in other branches; therefore, it is obvious that their fertility will also be similar. Another reason might be that social benefits (family allowances etc.) of members of agricultural cooperatives are somewhat lower in Hungary than those of workers in other branches and in agricultural state farms, and, as they constitute the largest part of the agricultural population, the somewhat lower benefits of the members of cooperatives might depress the fertility of the total agricultural population. It might also be supposed that after the intended equalization of social benefits for employees and members of agricultural cooperatives, and because of the rise in income of the peasant population to equal that of industrial workers, fertility of the peasant population would increase at least to the level of non-agricultural workers living in villages, the social group having the highest fertility in Hungary in the 1960s.

Thus fertility differences by socioeconomic strata are constantly changing and are somewhat different in different societies, characterized by different social structural features. In view of these findings, it does not seem to be possible to formulate some universal relationship, according to which socioeconomic status influences fertility.

In addition, it is not at all clear through what kind of causative mechanism socioeconomic status exerts its influence on fertility. Is this influence mediated by income differences and modified by the efficiency of birth control in the particular strata, as hypothesized by the economic theory of fertility of Becker (1960)? Or are the very different child-rearing costs in particular social strata, and also in different societies, having an important influence? Or is there a special factor connected with social status influencing fertility independently of income, costs of child-rearing and efficiency of birth control? This special factor might be conceptualized as a special subculture: special norms and values concerning the number of children, accepted by the given social strata, functioning as reference group norms and values for the members of the strata.

If these values and norms have a decisive influence on the relative fertility levels of socioeconomic strata, it is not inevitable that future fertility differences will be levelled, or even that a positive relation between fertility and socioeconomic status will prevail – for example, because of the universal acceptance and efficient practice of birth control.in all strata, or because of the supposed positive relation between income and fertility – since it is quite conceivable that in some socioeconomic strata (e.g. among peasants and workers living in villages) a subculture will be maintained which is favourably inclined to larger families. These subcultural norms and values are not necessarily similar for identical strata in different societies. Thus no universally valid generalization on the influence of socioeconomic status on fertility seems to emerge from the studies on this subject. The real causes determining the level of fertility probably lie at a deeper level, socioeconomic status only mediating the impact of these deeper causes.

5.4 Education

Education was often conceived as a factor influencing directly (i.e. without mediating factors) the size of the family. This might have two causes: first, more educated couples, particularly wives with higher education, might prefer smaller families than women having a lower level of education, because people with higher education might have more interests unconnected with family life, and might be engaged in more roles outside the family, such as professional careers; second, it might be supposed that more educated couples simply have access to more information on birth control and might be more efficient family planners.

Essentially the greater fertility decline in advanced countries in the nineteenth century and the first half of the twentieth was accompanied by a rise in the level of education. In addition, multivariate regression analyses based on cross-sectional data used to demonstrate a negative correlation between fertility and education, which was sometimes stronger and more consistent than the correlation between fertility and other indicators of socioeconomic development (e.g. industrialization or a rise in income level). Earlier census results seemed to confirm this negative relation. On the other hand, the results of fertility surveys cast some doubt on the general prevalence of this negative relationship.

The appearance of the U-shaped relation between fertility and socioeconomic status raises the question as to whether a similar relation between fertility and education is emerging. In that case, the nature of the influence of education on fertility would be similar to that of socioeconomic status – i.e. mediated by other factors, so that the direct negative influence of higher education on the size of family would be disproved.

The relation of education to income also raises problems. As higher education is mostly in strong correlation with higher income, the existence of a positive correlation between relative income and fertility might cause a similar positive correlation of education to fertility.

Unfortunately, since data on fertility classified by both education and socioeconomic status and by both education and income are rather scarce, it does not seem possible to find conclusive evidence for deciding these questions. We are compelled to have recourse to fertility data by level of education.

The earliest data of this kind are those published by Edin and Hutchinson on couples married in Stockholm and observed longitudinally in the years 1917–30 (Edin and Hutchinson 1935). They found a clearly positive correlation. Two remarks should be added, however: on the one hand, education is measured by the education of the husband, so that the data really do not reflect the influence of the wife's education; on the other hand, only urban couples were included in the investigation. Therefore, the results cannot be considered valid for Swedish society as a whole. The authors nevertheless considered that this positive association between fertility and education was not a temporary phenomenon, was not merely a result of a generally more favourable economic position in the more educated class, and was not attributable to differences in age distribution or frequency of employment of wives (table 5.25).

Table 5.25 Number of live births per family in the first three years and in the succeeding seven years of marriage, by education of husband: Stockholm, 1917–30.

Education of husband in 1930	*Age of wife at marriage*			
	Under 25	*25–29*	*30–34*	*Total*
First 3 years of marriage				
8 years or less	0·83	0·67	0·53	0·71
More than 8 years but without matriculation	0·96	0·76	0·53	0·79
Matriculation	0·87	0·88	0·72	0·84
University degree	1·16	0·80	0·72	0·94
Total	0·89	0·71	0·55	0·75
Succeeding 7 years of marriage				
8 years or less	0·54	0·45	0·36	0·47
More than 8 years but without matriculation	0·66	0·55	0·42	0·57
Matriculation	0·80	0·73	0·40	0·69
University degree	0·93	0·75	0·55	0·79
Total	0·60	0·50	0·39	0·52

Source: Edin and Hutchinson (1935), p. 76.

In the United States the Indianapolis survey demonstrated a slight positive relation between fertility and education in couples planning their fertility. All couples were urban dwellers.

The National Fertility Study survey, on the other hand, which was based on a national sample of married women, showed a more or less negative relation of education to the number of children already born, as well as to desired and expected fertility. Only the women having the highest education, i.e. four years of college or more, displayed a slightly higher desired and expected number of children than the women immediately below them (table 5.26).

Table 5.26 Number of children ever born, desired and expected of married women, husband present, by education of women: USA, first National Fertility Study, 1965.

Education of women	Current parity		Total desired number of children		Total expected number of children	
	White	Black	White	Black	White	Black
Grade school	3·5	4·8	3·8	4·0	4·1	5·2
High school 1–3 years	2·9	3·5	3·3	3·2	3·4	4·1
High school 4 years	2·4	2·6	3·2	2·9	3·1	3·4
College 1–3 years	2·1	1·4	3·2	2·7	2·9	3·1
College 4 and more years	2·1	1·4	3·3	2·8	3·0	2·3
Total	2·6	3·3	3·3	3·2	3·3	4·0

Source: Ryder and Westoff (1971), p. 54.

Recent data from western Europe suggest that the U-shaped relation of fertility and education is much more developed there. In France (table 5.27) a survey of the INSEE showed that the number of children ever born was lowest in the group of women with secondary education without baccalaureate, and that the fertility of those having a higher than baccalaureate education (i.e. university or similar education) showed a number of children almost as high as the group having the lowest education, at least in the first fifteen years of marriage (i.e. in the younger cohorts interviewed in 1962).

Table 5.27 Number of children ever born per 100 married women, husband present, by marriage duration and education of the women: France 1962.

Education of woman	Marriage duration				
	5 years	10 years	15 years	20 years	30 years
Less than full primary	122	185	226	249	260
Primary with certificate	110	164	196	208	210
Secondary	102	153	182	189	202
Baccalaureate	113	168	193	196	225
Higher than baccalaureate	121	189	223	229	187*
Total	118	178	216	236	246

* Rate calculated from a very small number of cases.
Source: Tabah (1971), p. 40.

Similar tendencies, though less marked, were demonstrated by the fertility survey performed in the second half of the 1960s in Belgium (Morsa 1967 1970). Here, women with secondary education at a higher level (more or less corresponding to the baccalaureate level in France) show the lowest fertility, and those with university or similar education have a somewhat higher fertility. When the expected number of children is investigated, the U-shaped curve is displayed more clearly (table 5.28).

In the Netherlands, on the other hand, the fertility survey embracing the 1958, 1963 and 1968 marriage cohorts did not show any relationship between the wife's education and the expected number of children, while for the husbands the relation seems to be very slightly positive (Moors 1974):

| | Expected number of children of the marriage cohort of | | |
Education	1958	1963	1968
Wife			
Primary school	2·7	2·7	2·8
Secondary school	2·7	2·8	2·8
Grammar school	2·6	2·7	2·8
College and university	2·8	2·6	2·7
Husband			
Primary school	2·7	2·7	2·7
Secondary school	2·7	2·7	2·7
Grammar school	2·6	2·7	2·8
College and university	2·8	2·7	2·9

These results clearly contradict the hypothesis of an eventual direct negative impact of the wife's education on her number of children, while the positive correlation of husband's education and fertility might reflect the positive effect of income, those having higher education attaining a higher income level. Moors, however, conjectures that the real completed fertility of these marriage cohorts – estimated by him on the basis of fertility data of earlier cohorts and family planning patterns of the investigated cohorts – will probably be different from the expected fertilities. His estimated completed fertilities, however, do not display any consistent relationship between fertility and the wife's education.

In Hungary the first signs of the appearance of a U-shaped relation can be observed. Yearly vital statistical data suggest that the fertility of women with university degrees (thirteen and more years of education) is slightly higher than that of women with secondary education (nine to twelve years). As these fertility rates might be distorted by the different age distribution of women in the particular education level categories (the women with

Table 5.28 Number of children ever born and expected per married woman, by marriage duration and education of the women: Belgium, 1966.

	Marriage duration				
Education of woman	*Up to 5 years*	*5–9 years*	*10–14 years*	*15 years and over*	*Total*
Average number of children ever born					
Primary	1·1	1·9	2·3	2·8	2·2
Lower level secondary	0·8	1·7	2·1	2·5	1·8
Lower level technical	1·0	1·9	2·2	2·6	1·9
Higher level secondary	1·0	1·7	2·1	2·4	1·7
University and similar	1·0	2·0	2·8	2·9	1·9
Total	1·0	1·9	2·3	2·7	2·0
Average number of expected children					
Primary	2·2	2·4	2·4	2·7	2·5
Lower level secondary	2·2	2·2	2·3	2·4	2·2
Lower level technical	2·4	2·3	2·4	2·5	2·4
Higher level secondary	2·6	2·3	2·1	2·4	2·4
University and similar	2·9	2·3	2·9	2·8	2·7
Total	2·3	2·3	2·4	2·7	2·4

Source: Tabah (1971), p. 39.

university education being on the average younger than any other group), the average birth order is also given, since this is an indicator which probably contains a bias in the opposite direction (younger women having lower average birth orders). However, this measure of fertility indicates a somewhat higher fertility for the women with university degrees than for the women with secondary education (Klinger 1969):

	Number of live births per 1000 women aged 15–49		Average birth order	
Years of education of women aged 15–49	1960	1968	1960	1968
0	122	164	4·25	4·98
1–3	60	52	3·40	3·63
4–5			2·79	3·03
6–7	57	57	2·41	2·59
8 (finished primary)			1·62	1·67
9–12 (secondary)	55	56	1·50	1·40
13 and over (university)	69	65	1·63	1·43
Total	59	59	2·18	1·93

As in other countries, the planned number of children of couples using family planning methods displays a different tendency from the traditional fertility differences by education, when compared with the number of children ever born. In the case of the marriage cohort of 1966 the current fertility in 1972 showed an inverse relation, while the planned number of children showed a U-shaped relation to the education of the wife (Klinger *et al.* 1974):

Years of education of wife	According to the interview made in 1969		Number of living children by 1972
	Number of children planned at marriage	Percentage of planners	
0	1·67	37·5	1·50
1–5	1·96	45·5	1·36
6–7	1·77	61·8	1·41
8	1·92	70·7	1·36
9–12	1·99	82·8	1·28
13 and over	2·12	84·7	1·24

It might be hypothesized that the negative relation between achieved fertility and education is simply the consequence of the lower percentage of family planners at the lower levels of education. In that case, with the general acceptance of family planning in Hungary, this relation would disappear. It might similarly be hypothesized, however, that the different percentage of those couples who had distinct family plans at marriage, or at least said that they had plans, is connected to a somewhat different sub-culture, with different values and norms concerning children in the couples with lower levels of education. In that case, the differences by education level might continue in future, the lower education categories having larger families.

In Poland (Smolinski 1974) the fertility survey of 1972 demonstrated a clear negative relation between fertility and education. Likewise, some surveys performed in the Soviet Union indicate that a similar, i.e. traditional, negative relationship prevails in that country. For example, in the Armenian SSR the average number of children in the family at the census of 1959 was (Urlanis 1974):

Education of mother	Average number of children in family
Primary	2·46
Secondary (general secondary and uncompleted secondary)	2·29
High level, specialized secondary	1·88

In 1967 in a district of Baku the number of children ever born was:

Education of mother	Average number of children ever born
Lower than primary	2·59
Primary	2·43
Uncompleted secondary	2·29
Secondary (general and specialized)	1·98
High level	1·39

These differences by education in the Soviet Union and in Poland reflect more or less the differentials by socioeconomic strata. That is, in these countries the professional classes have the lowest fertility.

Similarly, the U-shaped relation of fertility to education was found in societies where fertility differences by socioeconomic strata were also U-shaped. It might be stated that the category of wives with secondary education more or less coincides with the socioeconomic stratum of the simple non-manuals, which in these countries shows the lowest fertility levels. Alternatively, it might be suggested that the wives having secondary education belong (in addition to the simple non-manual group) to that part of the professional stratum which has a comparatively lower family income (couples with professional husband and simple non-manual wife), so that the lower fertility of these women might reflect the positive correlation of relative income (i.e. relative to the couples consisting of two professionals) to fertility.

The main conclusion from all these empirical results seems to be that the special direct impact of education on fertility does not seem to be demonstrated by them. Fertility differentials by education seem to be of a similar nature to those by socioeconomic status. However, it is still possible that, by using more sophisticated methods of investigation, a special direct (probably depressing) effect of the wife's education on the fertility of the couple could be demonstrated. The influence of education on fertility suggests the need for a similar type of explanation to that for the influence of socioeconomic status – i.e. taking into consideration the mediating effect of the values and norms of particular educational categories, which are essentially social strata.

5.5 Social mobility

If fertility is influenced by the socioeconomic status of the parents, an obvious further assumption is that any change in status – either inter-generationally, i.e. from parent to child, or intragenerationally, i.e. during the career of the respondent – will have an impact on the number of children. In fact, a well-known thesis on the impact of social mobility on fertility – or rather, of the impact of fertility on social mobility – was formulated in 1890 by Arsène Dumont. The thesis of '*Capillarité sociale*' states that 'just as a column of liquid has to be thin in order to rise under the force of capillarity, so a family must be small in order to rise in the social scale' (quoted according to Blau and Duncan 1967, p. 367).

R. A. Fisher, a geneticist, suggested an even more general hypothesis – that upward mobility of families with a small number of children and downward mobility of families with a large number of children are the predominant causes of the negative association of fertility with socio-economic status (Fisher 1929). It is worthwhile quoting his explanation:

> That the economic situation in all grades of modern societies is such as favours the social promotion of the less fertile is clear, from a number of familiar considerations. In the wealthiest class, the inherited property is for the most part divided among the natural heirs, and the wealth of the child is inversely proportioned to the number of the family to which he belongs. In the middle class the effect of the direct inheritance of wealth is also important: but the anxiety of the parent of a large family is increased by the expense of a first-class education, besides that of pro-fessional training, and by the need for capital in entering the professions to the best advantage. At the lower economic level social status depends less upon actually inherited capital than upon expenditure on housing, education, amusements, and dress: while the savings of the poor are depleted or exhausted, and their prospects of economic progress often crippled, by the necessity of sufficient food and clothing for their chil-dren. (p. 252)

Sorokin, in his classic work on social mobility, considered that social differences in fertility, as well as the fact that those who are most gifted (and therefore mobile from the lower classes into the élites) must have a similar low fertility in order to be able to achieve the upward movement, might lead to a gradual deterioration in the quality of the population, because fertility of the less gifted is higher (Sorokin 1959, first published 1927).

Thus all these authors hypothesized a special impact on fertility by social mobility causing it to be lower in mobile (or only upwardly mobile) couples than in non-mobile ones. Alternatively, it might be hypothesized that only the additive effects of mobility are existent – that is, the number of children of mobile couples is intermediate between that of couples in their group of origin and couples in their group of destination. In this latter case, it is also worthwhile studying the effect of mobility, since the fertility of mobile couples might be nearer to that of the group of origin or to that of the group of destination, which might be rather different, if fertility differences by social status are significant.

These more or less hypothetical interpretations of the influence of social mobility on fertility were tested in several demographic surveys – initially in surveys of relatively small scope and performed on rather special social groups.

The Indianapolis survey can be classified into this group of surveys. It was supposed that social mobility has an influence both on the efficiency of fertility planning and on the size of family, because socially mobile couples are exposed to various difficulties in achieving mobility and adjusting to new occupational and social environments. The couples thus tend to be more careful in fulfilling family plans, and also they have fewer children, in order to diminish the burdens associated with child rearing and education (Kantner and Kiser, in Whelpton and Kiser 1954).

The influence of both intergenerational (parent–child) and intragenerational or career mobility was examined. Examining the data of intergenerational mobility, the numbers of children in the main diagonal of the

Table 5.29 Children ever born, per 100 couples, by intergenerational mobility: Indianapolis survey.

Occupation of father	Occupation of son (respondent)						
	Professional	Proprietary	Clerical	Skilled	Semi-skilled	Unskilled	Farmer
Professional	162	175	145	*	*	*	*
Proprietary	145	207	184	202	176	*	*
Clerical	*	*	144	*	180	*	*
Skilled	237	196	160	253	218	*	*
Semi-skilled	*	*	145	221	256	*	*
Unskilled	*	*	221	212	*	310	*
Farmer	150	147	182	206	217	*	312

* Rate not shown because based on fewer than twenty cases.
Source: Kantner and Kiser, in Whelpton and Kiser (1954), p. 976.

mobility table (table 5.29), i.e. of the non-mobile couples, are generally higher than those of the mobile ones who are in the same column (i.e. who have attained the same group of destination), or in the same row (i.e. who are from the same social group of origin). The most notable exception is that of the clerical stratum, where the size of family of the non-mobile couples is the smallest. This fact draws our attention to the rather peculiar position of clerical occupations in modern societies, which is also reflected in their demographic behaviour – i.e. in their very low fertility in some economically developed societies at present.

The lower fertility of mobile couples is even more clearly demonstrated when socioeconomic status is measured by a socioeconomic index which takes into account several characteristics of social status (table 5.30), both upwardly and downwardly mobile couples having fewer children than the non-mobile couples at the status level attained by them. This seems to demonstrate the existence of a special social mobility effect on fertility in the case of intergenerational mobility.

Table 5.30 Number of births per 100 couples, by social mobility of husband and wife, as well as their present social position characterized by a socioeconomic index: Indianapolis survey.

Present social position characterized by socioeconomic index	*Social mobility of husband and wife*		
	Non-mobile	*Upward mobility*	*Downward mobility*
I (high)	205	187	—
II	187	158	170
III	225	212	175
IV	246	214	209
V (low)	340	304	344

Source: Kantner and Kiser, in Whelpton and Kiser (1954), p. 979.

Concerning the effect of intragenerational mobility after marriage, different hypotheses were formulated for upwardly and downwardly mobile couples. The upwardly mobile couples were supposed to have smaller families (and smaller planned families) than the non-mobile couples, at both levels of origin and destination, and to have a larger proportion of efficient fertility planners than the non-mobile couples at the level of origin, and a proportion at least as high as the non-mobile couples at their level of destination. The downwardly mobile couples were supposed to have intermediate family sizes between those of the levels of origin and destination, but smaller planned families than the non-mobile couples at both levels of origin and destination, and also to have a smaller proportion of efficient fertility planners than the non-mobiles at both levels of origin and destination. The reason for the hypotheses for downwardly mobile couples is that less efficient fertility planning and larger families (especially at young ages) necessitate much money, time and energy to be devoted to the family, and therefore there is less energy to be devoted to occupational advancement, which leads eventually to downward mobility. On the other hand, downward mobility causes problems and stresses that result in lower fertility, if fertility is planned (Riemer and Kiser, in Whelpton and Kiser (1954)).

Distinguishing two social strata – the non-manuals and the manuals – the following figures emerged.

Mobility	Per cent efficient planners	Average number of living children
Upward from manual to non-manual	47·1	1·44
Downward from non-manual to manual	36·8	1·38
Immobile non-manual	50·9	1·34
Immobile manual	34·1	1·46

Thus the percentages both of efficient fertility planners and of the size of family of mobile couples are intermediate between those of their levels of origin and destination. Formulated in another way, the mobile couples partly maintain the fertility planning and behaviour of their stratum of origin, and partly adapt themselves to those of their stratum of destination. No special effects of mobility, as supposed in the hypotheses concerning mobile couples, could be traced. That, however, does not exclude the possible existence of this type of special mobility effects on fertility, since the sample was relatively small and in consequence the social groups distinguished were rather crudely defined.

These results encouraged the planners of the Princeton survey to concentrate their attention on social mobility. It was hypothesized that a family-centred orientation associated with higher fertility is incompatible with upward social mobility, because:

The ideal type of the couple either in the actual process of vertical mobility or effectively geared toward its anticipation probably has the following characteristics: a maintained rationality of behaviour; intensive competitive effort; careerism with its accompanying manipulation of personalities; psychological insecurity of status with attendant anxieties; and an increasing exhaustion of nervous and physical energies;

in short, a pervasive success-orientation and all that is implied with it. (Westoff 1956, p. 404)

These characteristics are all inimical to having a larger family.

The results, however, failed to support this hypothesis (see pp. 199–200). Fertility did not show any consistent relation to social mobility, and the relation was different for particular denominational groups. The authors even stated that a hypothesis might be developed that upward mobility among Catholics, particularly among more religious Catholics, signifies an opportunity to have more children, while among the Protestants upward mobility neither requires restriction of fertility nor has any positive effect on fertility (Westoff, Potter and Sagi 1963). Another of Westoff's interpretations points to the gradual disappearance in the United States of fertility differences by social strata that might result in social mobility – i.e. that changed social status would have no influence. The problem is, however, whether social fertility differences are actually disappearing, and whether there is any special mobility impact on fertility that is independent of the fertility of the levels of origin and destination (i.e. of the additive effects).

In a survey of a more specialized sample – that of the social élite of Philadelphia – Baltzell (1953) found signs of this last kind of impact, as the newcomers into the élite (i.e. the upwardly mobile couples) had a lower fertility than both their group of origin and the traditional élite – i.e. the group of destination. It might be surmised that the efforts necessary for the upward mobility into the élite induced these newcomers to limit the size of their families, while the traditional élite, who were not obliged to make similar efforts, were less induced to have small families.

In Europe the first studies on the influence of social mobility on fertility were similarly based on rather specialized samples. For example, Lehner (1954), in an investigation limited to Rome, found that people originating from small families were more likely to be upwardly mobile than those coming from larger families. Girard (1951) investigated students of some French universities and secondary schools and found that in these schools the number of siblings of the pupils showed a positive correlation to social status of origin, i.e. those originating from higher status groups had more siblings. This was contrary to the whole population where a negative relation prevailed in the period when these students were born. Girard interpreted this result by supposing that young men coming from low status groups could enter the schools providing higher education only if the number of their siblings was relatively small, thus enabling their parents to concentrate their financial resources on one or two children.

In a survey of social mobility in France, also using a rather special sample, the status achieved by children was characterized by a score (the

higher the score, the higher the status achieved), and this status achievement or mobility performance score was investigated by social origin and
by the number of children in the family (Brésard 1950):

| Social origin | Average status achievement score by number of children in family | | | |
	1	2	3	4 and over
Industrialist and professional	5·7	5·0	5·5	6·1
High-level executive	4·6	5·1	4·3	4·4
Merchant	4·4	4·2	4·2	3·9
Self-employed farmer	4·4	4·2	4·2	3·9
Medium-level clerical	3·6	3·5	3·4	3·2
Worker	2·9	2·7	2·7	2·5
Agricultural worker	2·5	2·5	2·2	2·1

Thus, with the exception of the two strata at the highest level in the social
hierarchy, there was a clear negative relationship between achieved social
status and fertility. In the two top level groups of origin, probably the
existing higher number of children did not constitute an obstacle, because
the high income level assured adequate care and education of several
children without causing too much strain on the family.

The number of siblings in the parental family and the number of children
of the respondents soon became a standard item in surveys of social
mobility. The first large-scale national social mobility survey investigating
the relations of fertility and mobility was a British survey, the fertility data
of which were analysed by Berent (1951–2 1953). He investigated the
impact of intergenerational social mobility on fertility by distinguishing
four social strata (table 5.31). The four strata are ordered according to
their position in the social hierarchy. Also the average fertility follows a
clear pattern in the generation of both fathers and sons. The average
number of children of mobile men in almost all cases was intermediate
between the fertility of the non-mobile men in the group of origin and the
non-mobile men in the group of destination. This result might be interpreted simply by stating that mobile people are influenced by the attitudes
and opinions of their group of origin on the one hand, and by those of the
group of destination on the other. This is often called the additive effect of
social mobility on fertility. Hope (1972) re-analysed Berent's data and
considered that, in addition to the additive or class effect, a special mobility
effect can be demonstrated which causes a flick in the curve of fertility 'in
its two tails' – i.e. in the case of extremely high upward or downward
mobility, the upwardly and the downwardly mobile couples have slightly

Table 5.31 Average number of children per family, by social mobility: England and Wales, 1949.

Social origin of husband	Present social stratum of husband				
	Professional, executive	Other non-manual	Routine non-manual and skilled	Semi-skilled and unskilled	Total
Professional, executive	1·74	1·79	1·96	2·00	1·81
Other non-manual	2·05	2·14	2·51	2·97	2·38
Routine non-manual and skilled manual	1·87	2·01	2·67	3·69	2·81
Semi-skilled and unskilled manual	2·40	3·20	3·22	3·68	3·44
Total	1·88	2·17	2·73	3·56	

Source: Berent (1951–2).

fewer children than expected on the basis of the additive 'half way' hypothesis, according to which the fertility of mobile couples should be 'half way' between the fertility level of the group of origin and that of the group of destination.

A social mobility survey, similar in sample and comprehensiveness to the English survey of 1959, was performed in the United States in 1962. While the earlier surveys (Indianapolis and Princeton) investigating the relations of fertility and mobility used rather special samples, and perhaps therefore failed to provide consistent and convincing proofs of these relations, this 'Occupational Changes in a Generation Survey' (Blau and Duncan 1967) was based on a representative national sample. The hypotheses to be tested were taken from previous work on the relation between fertility and social mobility. A strong form of the mobility hypothesis was taken from Fisher: differential fertility is completely explained by social mobility. The weak form of the mobility hypothesis used by Blau and Duncan was that formulated by Westoff: that social mobility simply has an influence on fertility. The latter hypothesis might be dichotomized as follows: (*a*) the influence of mobility is only of the additive type, and (*b*) there is a special mobility effect which causes fertility of mobile couples to deviate from the status of origin and destination.

In their analysis of the relation between fertility and mobility, Blau and Duncan distinguished five social strata: higher level white collars (professionals, technicals and kindred, managers, officials and proprietors, except farm proprietors), lower level white collars (sales workers, clerical and kindred workers), higher level manuals (craftsmen, foremen, etc.),

Table 5.32 Average number of children born per wife, by husband's father's occupation and husband's 1962 occupation, for wives 42–61 years old, living with husbands: American Occupational Changes in a Generation Survey, 1962.

| Husband's father's occupation | Husband's occupation in 1962 | | | | | |
| | White collar | | Manual | | | |
	Higher	Lower	Higher	Lower	Farm	Total
Higher white collar	1·96	1·68	2·01	2·24	2·53	1·98
Lower white collar	2·01	1·56	2·44	2·18	2·44	1·99
Higher manual	2·31	2·08	2·64	2·52	1·88	2·39
Lower manual	2·13	1·88	2·41	2·52	2·91	2·26
Farm	2·27	2·07	2·78	2·86	3·26	2·84
Total*	2·12	1·92	2·57	2·62	3·18	2·45

* Those couples whose husband's father's occupation or husband's 1962 occupation was not stated are omitted from the table, but included in the totals.
Source: Blau and Duncan (1967), p. 382.

Table 5.33 Average number of children born per wife, by husband's first job and 1962 occupation, for wives 42–61 years old, living with husbands: American Occupational Changes in a Generation Survey, 1962.

| First job | Occupation in 1962 | | | | | |
| | White collar | | Manual | | | |
	Higher	Lower	Higher	Lower	Farm	Total
Higher white collar	1·96	1·44	2·63	1·75	2·25	1·95
Lower white collar	2·03	1·70	2·20	1·98	1·6[	1·94
Higher manual	2·04	1·78	2·53	2·64	1·78	2·30
Lower manual	2·16	2·03	2·51	2·62	3·34	2·46
Farm	3·03	2·69	2·83	2·98	3·32	3·11
Total*	2·12	1·91	2·56	2·61	3·18	2·45

* Those couples whose first or 1962 occupation was not stated are omitted from the table, but included in the totals.
Source: Blau and Duncan (1967), p. 373.

lower level manuals (operatives, service workers, labourers, except farm labourers), and farm workers (farmers, farm managers, farm labourers).

Fertility by intergenerational mobility (table 5.32) and intragenerational mobility (table 5.33) showed the following tendencies:

(1) Fertility in different social strata differs independently of social mobility – i.e. there are fertility differences between non-mobile couples in the particular strata. Thus the strong form of the mobility hypothesis is not justified.

(2) The average fertility of mobile couples seems to verify first of all the existence of additive effects of social mobility, their fertility being in most cases between those of the strata of origin and destination. In the case of intergenerational mobility this relation is somewhat disturbed by the fact that the pattern of fertility differences changed from the generation of fathers to that of the sons. In the generation of fathers the relation is more or less a negative one, while in the generation of sons it is U-shaped. This might be the cause of the fact that the couples entering the stratum of lower white collars show the lowest fertility in the case of whatever stratum of origin, and also the fact that those originating from the lower white collar stratum and entering the higher white collar stratum showed a higher fertility than those who originated and remained in the lower white collar stratum. On the other hand, those who originated from the manual and farm strata and were mobile into the higher or lower white collar strata clearly demonstrate additive effects of mobility on fertility, their fertility being lower than that of the stratum of origin, but higher than that of the stratum of destination. Couples originating from the farm stratum and entering the manual strata show similar effects. The average fertilities of downwardly mobile couples are sometimes rather surprising, but this might be caused by the relatively few cases in these categories. Fertility by intragenerational mobility shows more or less similar tendencies, although somewhat less clearly. Thus Blau and Duncan concluded that 'the major consequence of mobility is simply that mobile couples have a completed family size intermediate between the averages pertaining to their respective origin and destination statuses' (p. 388). They also refer to an earlier work of Blau (1956) in which he suggested that the behaviour of mobile persons in all respects is intermediate between that of the non-mobile persons in the origin and destination strata, as mobile persons are not well integrated into either of these strata and are therefore influenced by the opinions, values and attitudes of both.

(3) By applying a finer analysis method – namely, a regression equation in which the variables explaining the actual fertility of couples were the strata of origin and destination, together with a special mobility effect variable – Blau and Duncan found that there might be a special mobility effect in the case of long-distance downward and upward mobility. Both types of long-distance mobility seem to depress fertility by -0.2 to -0.4 children on the average (by long-distance mobility a downward step by four to nine grades or an upward step by six to nine grades in a scale of seventeen grades is meant). However, less than one tenth of the population is affected, since such long-distance mobility is fairly rare.

Summarizing their results, Blau and Duncan hinted that the hypothesis of a special effect of mobility on fertility might have been characteristic of the actual state of affairs at the turn of the century in the United States, i.e.

in conditions when *per capita* income level was much lower. This interpretation seems to match fairly well the results of the Indianapolis survey, where a special mobility effect seems to have been found.

Considering this hypothetical interpretation, it is interesting to analyse the results of similar surveys carried out in socialist countries. Arutyunyan (1975) published some data from the Armenian SSR in the Soviet Union, showing the desired number of children of couples and the actual number of children of couples where family building was completed:

Head of family	Social origin	Desired fertility	Completed fertility
Worker	Peasant	3·4	3·6
	Worker	3·1	3·1
	Non-manual	2·8	2·9
Non-manual	Peasant	3·7	3·4
(medium level)	Worker	2·9	3·1
	Non-manual	2·8	2·6
Professional	Peasant	2·8	2·7
	Worker	2·7	2·7
	Non-manual	2·4	2·3

The results from this sample (not a national sample) show that, while both social origin and achieved social position influence fertility, the proportions of the influence of origin and present social position do not seem to be identical for all types of mobility. For example, it seems that achieved professional status exerts a fairly strong influence on the fertility of people originating from peasant and worker families.

In the years from 1962 to 1964 a large-scale social mobility survey was performed in Hungary, based on a national sample (Klinger and Szabady 1965, Andorka 1970c). Special emphasis was put on the effects of mobility on fertility, in view of the great social mobility that occurred in Hungary after the Second World War, and also in view of the decline in fertility which occurred in the second half of the 1950s and the first half of the 1960s.

As fertility differences, not only by social strata, but also by type of residence, were fairly significant (Budapest, a metropolis of 2 million people; the other towns, with a population ranging from less than 10 000 up to 160 000; and the villages, where nearly 6 million people, i.e. the majority of population, lived at that time), it was considered advisable to detail the data by residence. The main direction of social mobility was from the peasant stratum into the manual strata, and – to a somewhat lesser extent – from the peasant and manual strata into the professional and other non-manual strata.

The fertility rates by social origin (father's position) and destination (son's position), as well as by residence of the son (table 5.34), seem to indicate that, contrary to the English and American results, the fertility of mobile couples entering a given social stratum from a lower stratum with higher fertility is in general not much influenced by this higher fertility

Table 5.34 Average number of children ever born, of men by age and intergenerational social mobility, and by residence: Hungary, 1962–1964.

Social stratum of son	Age group of son	Social stratum of father	Residence of son		
			Budapest	Other towns	Villages
Professional	20–29	Non-manual	0·2	0·4	1·0
		Manual and peasant	0·5	0·7	1·0
	30–39	Non-manual	1·0	1·4	1·5
		Manual and peasant	0·9	1·4	1·6
	40–49	Non-manual	1·4	1·6	1·6
		Manual and peasant	1·9	1·9	2·1
	50–59	Non-manual	1·5	2·3	2·4
		Manual and peasant	1·7	2·3	1·9
	60+	Non-manual	2·4	1·7	1·2
		Manual and peasant	1·5	1·5	2·1
Other non-manual	20–29	Non-manual	0·4	1·3	0·7
		Manual and peasant	0·5	0·7	0·9
	30–39	Non-manual	1·4	1·9	1·5
		Manual and peasant	1·1	1·5	1·7
	40–49	Non-manual	1·7	2·2	2·7
		Manual and peasant	1·7	1·7	2·0
	50–59	Non-manual	1·3	1·5	2·6
		Manual and peasant	1·1	1·8	2·4
	60+	Non-manual	0·9	2·3	2·5
		Manual	1·4	2·2	2·5
Manual	20–29	Manual	0·5	0·9	1·2
		Peasant	0·4	0·9	1·2
	30–39	Manual	1·3	1·8	2·2
		Peasant	1·7	1·8	2·0
	40–49	Manual	1·7	2·1	2·6
		Peasant	1·6	1·9	2·6
	50–59	Manual	2·0	2·0	2·5
		Peasant	2·5	2·4	3·0
	60+	Manual	2·1	2·9	3·4
		Peasant	2·6	2·8	3·3
Peasant	20–29	Peasant	—	0·8	1·3
	30–39	Peasant	—	1·7	2·2
	40–49	Peasant	—	2·1	2·5
	50–59	Peasant	—	3·1	2·9
	60+	Peasant	—	3·2	3·4

Source: Andorka (1970c), pp. 132–3, 331–6.

'tradition', but adapts itself fairly rapidly to the fertility prevalent in the new stratum of destination. Thus intellectuals originating from manual and peasant strata did not show higher fertility rates than non-mobile professionals (by distinguishing five age groups of men and three types of residence, the fertility of non-mobile professionals is higher in seven cases, equal in three cases and lower in five cases than the fertility of professionals originating from the peasant ᴧnd manual strata). Similarly, in the stratum of other non-manuals no fertility difference by social mobility can be discerned. These results might be interpreted in the following way: social mobility into the non-manual strata imposed fairly great strains on the resources of mobile families, who were therefore forced to restrict their fertility more or less to the level of fertility in the professional and non-manual strata, which level in itself was very low. Thus it seems to be proven that in conditions of a medium-level *per capita* income social mobility has a depressing effect on fertility in the sense that the influence of the higher fertility of the stratum of origin is almost nil – i.e. it does not contribute to the additive effects of mobility. This interpretation is, however, slightly different from that of Blau and Duncan, because here it is not integration into the new social milieu (this interpretation being excluded because of the fact that the new entrants were more numerous than those non-mobiles already in the professional, or non-manual stratum), but simply the economic stress associated with social mobility (adaptation to the requirements of a new social milieu, the necessity for accommodation, the education of children at a higher level, etc.) in conditions of rapid industrialization and urbanization starting from a very low level of economic development (which characterized Hungary at the end of the Second World War) that causes the lower fertility of mobile couples.

In the manual strata as well there is no clear fertility difference between non-mobile workers on the one hand and those originating from the peasant stratum on the other. The exception is the manual stratum in Budapest, where the non-mobiles have a fairly low fertility and the immigrants originating from the peasantry a higher one. It is known from other sociological sources that the proportion of the Budapest working class originating from peasants maintained several other aspects of peasant life style, values and norms, so it is not surprising that their fertility is also somewhat higher. On the other hand, in the villages the fertility levels of non-mobile workers (who are relatively few), workers originating from the peasant stratum and peasants do not differ very significantly. This might be explained by the fact that all the manual and peasant groups in the villages have a fairly similar life style, similar opinions, values and norms, because practically all of them originated from the peasantry. On the other hand, the economic and social situation of peasants became very similar to that of manual workers in other branches after the socialization of agriculture, so there is no strong reason why their fertility should be different from the fertility of manual workers residing in the villages.

The people who were mobile in the opposite direction, i.e. from the non-manual strata to the manual and peasant strata, as well as from the manual stratum to the peasant stratum, showed different fertility rates depending on their place of residence. In Budapest the fertility of manuals originating from non-manual parents was lower than the fertility of both non-manuals and manuals. In other words, a clear special effect of social mobility (in the sense given by Blau and Duncan to this term) is found here. It might be supposed that such a downward mobility in Budapest would have been a rather frustrating experience, causing a decline in fertility. On the other hand, in the other towns and in the villages no such effect is displayed, the fertility of manuals originating from non-manual parents being intermediate in the sense of the additive effects.

The results of the Hungarian social mobility survey thus seem to indicate that the effect of social mobility on fertility cannot be analysed in general, without taking into account the type of mobility and the economic and social conditions in which the mobility processes occur. And obviously the impact of mobility from one stratum to another depends on the pattern of fertility differences of these strata, which might themselves be changing from the generation of fathers to that of their children, and which seem to be currently in transition in the developed countries. This might be the explanation for the different, often contradictory relations that exist between fertility and social mobility in different countries, and even within the same country in different periods (e.g. in the United States).

Obviously the general context in which social mobility takes place also influences its relation to fertility. Namboodiri (1972b), for example, hypothesized that in an 'individualistic entrepreneurial' society, where the individual career contains many uncertain elements and upward mobility requires great efforts during the whole career, the upwardly mobile couples might be inclined to restrict their number of children, but in a more bureaucratic society where the career plan of the individual is much less uncertain and much more determined by his education, upward mobility might have no such effect.

5.6 Urban and rural residence

While the nature of fertility differentials by income is problematical, and those by socioeconomic status and by education seem to be changing, the difference in fertility between urban and rural populations has remained more or less stable for several decades in advanced societies. The census fertility data of the United States and Hungary, dealt with in Chapter 4.2, illustrated the stability of these urban–rural differentials. They do not seem to have changed, even in very recent years, which have been characterized by fairly significant and sometimes unexpected changes in other fertility differentials. Thus it seems to be a more or less universally valid relation in advanced societies that urban populations have smaller numbers of children than rural populations.

It might be questioned, however, whether these urban–rural differences are not simply reflecting the socioeconomic differences of fertility, as the groups that are higher in the socioeconomic hierarchy and have a lower fertility are mostly concentrated in the towns, while the agricultural population, being at the lower end of the social hierarchy and having generally a higher number of children, is residing predominantly in rural areas. In order to verify the existence of urban–rural differences existing independently from socioeconomic differences, we will consider in this chapter only such data that demonstrate fertility by both place of residence and socioeconomic status. One of the first analyses of this type were made with data of the Mälar counties in central Sweden around Lake Mälaren (Edin and Hutchinson 1935). On the basis of data from the census of 1930 communities were divided into four groups according to the level of urbanization. The degree of urbanization was measured by the percentage of three rural occupations and by the degree of concentration of settlements. Age-specific fertility rates were calculated and summarized in a rate standardized with respect to age distribution. Fertility differences were found by occupational groups, the fertility of agricultural workers being the highest, that of others in peasant occupations (primarily self-employed farmers) in the middle and that of urban dwellers the lowest. On the other hand, there were fertility differences by degree of urbanization of the communities, all occupational groups except agricultural workers having higher fertility rates in the less urbanized communities (table 5.35).

Table 5.35   Number of children ever born per 100 married women, standardized with respect to age distribution, by social strata and type of residence: Sweden, Mälar counties, 1930–1931.

Residence, type of community	Social stratum			
	Agricultural worker	Other agricultural	Non-agricultural occupations	Total
75% or more in 3 rural occupations (*a*)	147	132	126	137
50–75% in 3 rural occupations	150	131	105	125
Less than 50% in 3 rural occupations (*b*)	149	117	92	103
Concentrated communities (*c*)	150	103	80	84
Total	148	128	94	113

(*a*) Agriculture, fishing, wood cutting and lumber industry.
(*b*) Not included in the fourth group of communities (concentrated communities).
(*c*) More than 66 per cent of population living in villages of 200 or more inhabitants and less than 50 per cent in three rural occupations.
Source: Edin and Hutchinson (1935), p. 42.

A similar pattern of fertility differences is displayed by data from the Hungarian census of 1930 (Thirring 1969). On the one hand, there were fairly pronounced fertility differences between non-manuals, various groups of workers, self-employed artisans and merchants, self-employed farmers, day labourers in agriculture, and permanently employed labourers in agriculture. On the other hand, there were differences in fertility by type of settlement. These latter differences were caused partly by the concentration of the highest fertility strata in the villages and the lowest fertility strata in Budapest and the ten larger towns, but partly also by the fact that within each stratum more or less consistent fertility differences were found by type of settlement – e.g. industrial workers and miners had lowest fertility in Budapest, intermediate in the other towns and highest in villages. In consequence, the fertility rates of the particular strata overlapped, with, for example, non-manuals living in villages showing a higher fertility than workers in Budapest (table 5.36).

Data from Hungary in the 1960s derived from the social mobility survey (Andorka 1970c) show a similar tendency (table 5.37). Even the differences by residence seem to be more significant than those by social stratum in the case of manual workers and peasants (i.e. manuals working in agriculture), primarily because manual workers employed in industry, construction, transport, etc. (almost half of these workers reside in villages), showed a fertility level similar to that of the peasants living in the

Table 5.36 Number of children ever born per 100 married women, by social strata and residence: Hungary, 1930.

	Residence				
Social stratum	Budapest	10 greater towns	45 other towns	Villages	Total
Self-employed peasant	271	401	394	372	375
Agricultural labourer, permanently employed	356	411	408	422	421
Agricultural day labourer	283	368	382	368	369
Self-employed artisan and merchant	194	264	287	326	289
Worker in industry and mining	202	261	256	298	263
Other worker (transport, commerce, etc.)	188	274	288	323	275
Non-manual	139	186	192	211	176
Pensioner	243	343	363	392	348
Total	187	299	312	357	327

Source: Thirring (1969), p. 318.

villages. As mentioned in Chapter 5.3, the yearly age-specific fertility rates of manual workers seemed in that period to be even higher than those of the peasants, and this was caused primarily by the relatively high fertility of manual workers residing in the villages, whose yearly rates were highest in Hungary at that time, while the fertility of workers in Budapest was rather low. It seems to be clearly proved by these data that the urban or rural character of the residence has an effect on fertility which is independent of the social composition of the population of these settlements, in the sense that all social strata show higher fertility in villages than in towns. This might be conceptualized as the influence of the ecological context on fertility. The ecological context, in turn, is certainly influenced by the social character of the community. This urban–rural ecological context seems to be similar to the ecological context of larger regions, which also influences fertility, as described in Chapter 4.2.

Although the existence of urban–rural fertility differences seems to be proved, it is not at all clear what factors cause this difference. One of the explanations refers to the diffusion of attitudes from urban to rural areas. New attitudes, among others birth control, family planning and the preference for smaller families, arise in towns where the social conditions are more favourable for innovations, and it takes a while for such attitudes to penetrate to the villages. Keyfitz (1952–3) in Canada even found that, in addition to urban–rural differences, there is a positive correlation of fertility to the distance of the given settlement from a city, and this correlation

Table 5.37 Average number of children ever born of men by age, social strata and residence: Hungary, 1962–4.

Age group	Social stratum	Residence		
		Budapest	Other towns	Villages
20–29	Professional	0·5	0·7	1·0
	Other non-manual	0·5	0·7	0·9
	Manual	0·7	0·9	1·2
	Peasant	—	0·9	1·4
30–39	Professional	1·0	1·4	1·6
	Other non-manual	1·3	1·5	1·7
	Manual	1·5	1·8	2·0
	Peasant	—	1·8	2·2
40–49	Professional	1·7	1·8	2·0
	Other non-manual	1·5	1·8	2·2
	Manual	1·5	2·1	2·6
	Peasant	—	2·2	2·5
50–59	Professional	1·6	2·3	2·0
	Other non-manual	1·0	1·7	2·4
	Manual	1·9	2·2	2·9
	Peasant	—	3·1	2·9
60+	Professional	1·9	1·5	2·6
	Other non-manual	1·4	2·0	3·5
	Manual	2·3	2·7	3·3
	Peasant	—	3·3	3·4

Source: Andorka (1970c), p. 130.

remains valid if education and income are controlled in the analysis. Thus, according to this diffusion hypothesis, the fertility differences by types of settlement and by area are caused only by a time lag in the spread of attitudes favouring lower fertility in the period of demographic transition.

Carlsson (1966), on the other hand, strongly criticized this hypothesis, stating that, if the cause of these fertility differences were simply the diffusion of birth control, a widening of the gap between the fertility of towns and villages would necessarily be observed. He analysed fertility rates in seventy-three Swedish districts and found that from 1860 to 1946 their fertility developed along broadly similar lines, and that the total variance in fertility declined from 1910 on, firstly as a result of the decline in within-region variance, and later as a result of the decline in between-region variance. Thus, Carlsson states, birth control was already known before demographic transition in both urban and rural areas, and the decline was caused by a reaction to a new economic and social situation. This reaction occurred in both towns and villages, and the cause of the urban–rural fertility difference was therefore the difference existing before demographic transition – ultimately, the difference in living conditions between towns and villages.

A study of the history of Hungarian fertility differences by type of settlement may help to elucidate the problem of the diffusion versus different living conditions interpretations of urban–rural differences. The birth rates in Budapest, the other towns (all much smaller than Budapest) and in the villages have fluctuated since 1949 more or less in parallel (table 5.38). As the age structure of these settlements is rather different, the 'other towns' having a much higher percentage of young adults than the villages, the total fertility rates give a more exact picture of the fertility differences. These rates, however, are not available before 1960. The total fertility rates also show parallel fluctuations. Clearly, if the development were influenced by some long-term industrialization or similar trend and by the slow diffusion of certain attitudes, the fertility of villages should follow the trend of fertility of the towns with a considerable lag, and a similar lag would exist between Budapest and the other towns. There is in fact a lag, but it is only of one or two years. For example, the downturn of

Table 5.38   Birth rate and total fertility rate in Budapest, other towns and villages:* Hungary, selected years.

Year	Budapest	Other towns	Villages
Birth rate			
1949	15·4	21·0	21·1
1950	15·7	20·8	22·5
1951	16·1	20·2	21·5
1952	16·4	19·5	20·5
1953	21·2	22·8	21·3
1954	19·8	24·3	23·6
1955	14·2	22·4	23·3
1956	11·5	19·6	21·8
1957	10·0	15·6	19·5
1958	10·0	15·3	18·1
1959	9·2	14·2	17·4
1960	8·7	13·9	16·8
Total fertility rate			
1960	1193·5	1818·0	2342·5
1962	1080·5	1616·0	2121·0
1965	1181·5	1644·0	2152·5
1968	1429·0	1916·5	2417·5
1971	1364·5	1796·5	2268·5
1974	1797·0	2178·0	2627·0

* During the period considered in the table the administrative status of some communities changed from village to town.
Source: Demographic Yearbooks.

fertility occurred in 1954 in Budapest, in 1955 in the other towns, and in 1956 in the villages. The lowest level of fertility was attained in Budapest in 1962, and in the villages in 1964. In Chapter 5.11 a hypothetical interpretation of the changes in Hungarian fertility in terms of population policy measures will be described. According to this hypothesis, the downward change around 1954 and the upward change around 1965 were caused by changes in the socio-psychological climate in the country, these changes being motivated by the introduction of population policy measures. The development of the birth rates in Budapest, in the other towns and in the villages seems to indicate that the change in the socio-psychological climate was actually initiated in Budapest, but that it spread very rapidly to all parts of the country. It should be added, however, that Hungary is a relatively small country and communications between towns and villages are fairly rapid, partly because of the mass media, and partly because of widespread commuting between villages and towns.

   The different and sometimes ambiguous definitions of urban and rural areas sometimes cause severe difficulties for the interpretation of urban–rural differentials. For example, in Hungary statistical classification is based on the administrative status of the settlement, some being classed as towns even though administrative position does not strictly follow size of

Table 5.39 Births by 1960 and total number of births expected, for wives, by size of place of residence and by religion: Growth of American Families Survey.

	Average number of births		*Protestant*	*Catholic*
	All religions			
Size of place of residence	*By 1960*	*Most likely expected*	*Most likely expected*	*Most likely expected*
Total	2·3	3·1	2·9	3·7
In standard metropolitan statistical areas:				
12 large cities	2·1	3·0	2·8	3·5
Other cities of 150 000+	2·2	3·0	2·8	3·5
Cities of 50 000–149 000	2·3	3·3	2·9	4·0
Rings of 12 large cities	2·2	3·1	2·8	3·6
Rings of other cities of 50 000+	2·4	3·1	2·9	3·8
Not in standard metropolitan statistical areas:				
Cities of 2500–49 000	2·2	3·0	2·9	3·9
Rural non-farm	2·4	3·1	3·0	3·8
Rural farm	2·7	3·6	3·4	5·2

Source: Whelpton, Campbell and Patterson (1966), p. 118.

population. Thus there are 'villages' with more than 20 000 population and some 'towns' with less than 10 000. Therefore it seems advisable to analyse fertility by population number of settlements.

In the Growth of American Families survey in 1960 fertility differences in towns of different population number were fairly consistent. Differences in the fertility of couples living in cities of different size were not very significant (table 5.39). The differences between cities and rural·farm areas were, however, very marked. It should also be noted that these differences were similar in the case of Protestant and Catholic couples, although almost all other fertility differences by social category investigated were different for these two denominational groups.

In Hungary fertility differences by population number of settlements in 1960 did not follow a completely regular pattern:

Population	Number of children ever born per 100 married women
499	260
500–999	266
1000–1499	269
1500–1999	266
2000–2999	266
3000–4999	266
5000–9999	255
10 000–19 999	250
20 000+	212
Budapest	155
Total	232

Source: *Demografiai jellemzők a települések nagy-ságcsoportja szerint* (1968), p. 29.

It is clear that fertility is not at its highest level in the smallest settlements, and up to a population number of 10 000, no negative relation seems to exist between fertility and population of settlement. One possible interpretation might be that the smaller villages were in general stagnating economically and their population diminished in consequence of a negative migration balance, and that this stagnation or decline might not have encouraged the population living there to have larger families.

Similarly, the fertility level of towns in Hungary in 1960 was not consistently correlated either to their population number or to their agricultural or industrial character (table 5.40). Some relatively large towns had relatively high fertility (e.g. Miskolc), while others of comparative size had very

Table 5.40 Total fertility rate and other social characteristics of selected Hungarian towns in 1960.

Name of town	Region*	Population ('000s)	Percentage employed in agri- culture	Total fertility rate
Balassagyarmat	Central	10·8	9·5	1752
Eger	Central	29·4	14·7	1513
Gyöngyös	Central	22·0	19·6	1531
Győr	Central	57·5	3·5	1518
Gyula	Southern	23·6	26·4	1471
Hajdunánás	Northeastern	18·2	59·8	2802
Hódmezővásárhely	Southern	49·2	39·1	2281
Kalocsa	Southern	11·5	17·3	1784
Kaposvár	Southern	33·5	6·4	1640
Kazincbarcika	Northeastern	5·1	7·6	2567
Kecskemét	Southern	57·3	25·4	1914
Kiskunhalas	Southern	24·3	42·4	2221
Kisújszállás	Northeastern	13·9	45·8	1988
Komló	Southern	7·0	6·1	2468
Kőszeg	Western	8·8	10·1	2123
Makó	Southern	32·0	50·9	1631
Miskolc	Northeastern	109·1	4·0	1811
Ózd	Northeastern	24·8	2·7	2425
Pápa	Western	21·8	7·1	1715
Sopron	Western	15·1	7·9	1935
Szekszárd	Southern	16·3	28·6	1476
Szeged	Southern	86·6	6·5	1401
Tatabánya	Central	40·2	2·9	1844
Túrkeve	Northeastern	13·3	57·8	2665
Várpalota	Western	11·1	4·3	1965
Veszprém	Western	18·2	4·5	1927

* See the regions distinguished in the multiple regression analysis described on pp. 182–3.

low fertility (e.g. Szeged). Some of the smallest towns actually had rather high fertility (e.g. Kazincbarcika and Komló), while others with comparable population showed very low fertility rates (e.g. Balassagyarmat, Gyula, Kalocsa, Szekszárd). Also it was not the predominantly industrialized or agricultural character of towns that determined fertility, as some agricultural towns showed rather high fertility (e.g. Hajdunánás, Túrkeve), while others with a similarly agricultural character had a low fertility (e.g. Makó) (in consequence of the peculiar features in the historical development of Hungarian settlements, some towns grew up as concentrations of peasants). The fertility of industrial towns was also fairly differentiated. The most probable explanation is that the towns where economic development was slow, particularly towns that had been relatively developed but where economic development was slow after the Second World War, tended to show low fertility rates, while the rapidly developing industrial towns, particularly the new towns with a predominantly immigrant population (e.g. Kazincbarcika, Komló), showed generally high fertility rates. Also a regional factor seems to have had some influence, with the towns situated in the northeastern high fertility region (e.g. Kazincbarcika, Hajdunánás, Miskolc, Túrkeve) tending to have relatively high fertility, and the towns in the southern low fertility region (e.g. Szekszárd, Gyula, Makó, Szeged) having low fertility rates.

It might be hypothesized that it is not so much size of settlement, as type of residence, type of neighbourhood and distance from the central city that influence the level of fertility. The Princeton survey (Westoff, Potter and Sagi 1963) investigated the influence of these factors. The type of dwelling seemed to have the clearest influence on the percentage of the couples with two children having a third pregnancy during the period between the first and second interview:

Type of dwelling	Couples having a third pregnancy
Single detached	57%
Attached row	52%
Apartment	41%

The single detached dwellings, mostly with gardens, are clearly the ones where the couples with the highest fertility (among those interviewed) lived, and the apartment houses were the least conducive to larger families.

Similarly, it was found that a smaller percentage (50 per cent) of couples living in central cities had third pregnancies than couples living outside central cities (56 per cent). Also the distance from the central city was positively (although fairly weakly) correlated with fertility.

Obviously two types of causal relations are imaginable here: on the one hand, couples living in single detached houses, outside the central cities and at a greater distance from the central city, may be more prone to have a third child, because these surroundings are more suitable for raising children; but, on the other hand, couples having or planning a third child might tend to migrate to these surroundings, in order to assure more favourable conditions for the upbringing of their children.

However, in spite of all these reservations, urban couples tend to have consistently lower family sizes than rural couples. Although the character of the urban area, the development of the towns, and other factors, might slightly modify this relationship, it seems certain that urbanization had and has a depressing influence on the level of fertility.

These fertility differences by residence were interpreted by Easterlin by different costs of child-rearing and by different preferences of the populations living in these types of residence. He enumerated four types of settlements: frontier areas, settled rural areas, new urban areas, and old urban areas. The effective monetary costs and the needed efforts and time are greater in the last two than in the first two types of settlements; and also consumption alternatives are much more expensive in urban areas than in rural and frontier areas, so that preferences differ with the different availability of alternative goods (Easterlin 1971). Namboodiri (1972b) explained the fertility differences between rural and urban areas, between settlements of different size, between suburban areas and central cities, and between occupants of single-family houses and of apartment houses, by the different life styles of these population groups – i.e. by different child quality standards, child-rearing norms, commitments to non-child-centred activities, etc. As neighbourhood groups can generally be seen as major reference groups, couples living in these different areas influence each other, so that population groups living in given neighbourhood types tend to have similar numbers of children.

5.7 Migration

In the same way as a change in social status (i.e. social mobility) might influence fertility, partly through a special mobility effect and partly in an additive way, migration (i.e. change of residence) might also have two kinds of impact on fertility:

1 A special migration effect, caused by the difficulties and hardships connected with the change of residence and the adaptation to a new geographical and social environment, which might influence migrating couples to have fewer children than non-migrating couples.
2 An additive effect of migration, where migrant couples partly retain the fertility of their original environment and partly adapt themselves to the fertility usual at their destination; in consequence, they have an intermediate fertility between that of the place of origin and that of the destination.

The special migration effect was tested by the Princeton survey (Westoff, Potter and Sagi 1963) and disproved by it, as those couples who migrated during the period between the first and second interview had more (62 per cent) third pregnancies than those who did not move (49 per cent).

As mentioned in Chapter 4.4, the Detroit area studies demonstrated a very clear additive effect of migration on the ideal number of children of the urban couples interviewed: those couples with some rural background considered a higher number of children to be ideal. On the basis of these studies, Goldberg (1959) even hypothesized that urban fertility differences by social strata were only caused by the fact that farm immigrants had higher fertilities and were concentrated in the lower social strata. Goldberg also reanalysed the data of the Indianapolis survey by dividing the 1444 relatively fecund couples into three groups: (1) where both the husband's and the wife's father were urbanites (UU), (2) where one of the fathers had a farm occupation and the other was urbanite (FU), and (3) where both fathers had farm occupations (FF). An urbanite was defined as someone who had a non-farm occupation, independently of the place of his residence (so that a person living in a rural area but with an urban occupation was classified as an urbanite). Taking all couples together, a very weak negative correlation was found in the UU group between fertility and the indicators of socioeconomic status; a somewhat stronger correlation was found in the group FU, and a much stronger correlation in the group FF. When only the 'number and spacing planners' (i.e. the most efficient fertility planners) were taken into consideration, the correlations were positive in group UU, undecided in group FU, and a weak negative in group FF. Goldberg concluded that farm background is thus a very strong factor of fertility and that it also conditions the influence of other factors. The cause of this was, in his opinion, that immigrants from farm areas maintained the fertility values formed in the rural environment after having settled in the towns, however much these fertility values were dysfunctional in the new urban environment.

The Indianapolis and Detroit data analysed by Goldberg each related only to one city, but Blau and Duncan tested the same hypotheses on the basis of a national sample in the framework of a social mobility survey (Duncan 1964, Blau and Duncan 1967). Their results are well summarized in the following data on the average number of children ever born per married women aged 42–61, by socioeconomic status groups, measured by a status index:

	Status index	
	Women with non-farm background	Women with farm background
0–9 (low status)	2·61	3·12
10–19	2·37	2·64
20–39	2·28	2·75
40–59	2·34	2·17
60 and over (high status)	1·94	2·06

Thus couples with farm background (educated in farm areas) had a higher fertility at each status level than couples with no farm background, but the difference diminished from the lower to the higher status groups. On the other hand, there was a negative correlation of fertility to socioeconomic status in both the non-farm background and farm background groups – i.e. the thesis of Goldberg, that differences in fertility by status are only caused by the different intake of farm immigrants with higher fertility, was not verified. Blau and Duncan interpreted their results in the following way:

Movement to non-farm residences from farm backgrounds is, of course, a form of social and occupational mobility. Such a move is accompanied by a reduction of fertility, as compared with that of persons remaining on farms. The amount of reduction is, however, directly related to the degree of upward mobility in the non-farm sector. If the migrants from farms remain in low status occupations or fail to obtain average or greater amounts of education, their fertility remains high relative to other non-farm residents. If they undergo upward mobility their fertility is sharply reduced, though not below the levels of persons with non-farm origins enjoying comparable occupational achievement or educational attainment (p. 390).

Thus a special migration effect on fertility was not demonstrated. Certainly the special depressing effect of migration might be rather weak in social contexts where migration does not entail great efforts on the part of the migrating persons, i.e. when finding a convenient dwelling does not cause difficulties and where working and living conditions are fairly similar in all regions and settlements, so that adaptation to new residential and working neighbourhoods is easy.

Also, this special migration effect might be masked by the additive effects which in the majority of migrants (being rural people coming to towns) have an opposite sign – that is, while the special migration effect might probably depress fertility, the additive effect in the case of migrants with rural background causes their fertility to be higher than that of the native urbanites.

5.8 Employment of women and emancipation of women

As in the case of urban–rural fertility differences, the difference in fertility of employed women and dependent (i.e. non-employed, and not desiring employment) women seems to be very well proved and almost universal in developed countries. Census fertility data, multiple regression analyses and fertility surveys equally displayed unambiguous differences by employment of women. Soviet demographers (Davtyan 1965, Urlanis 1963) laid particularly strong emphasis on the growth of employment of women, and on the emancipation of women associated with it, in explaining the decline of fertility in the Soviet Union. It is worthwhile to analyse here some aspects of this relation, and mention some qualifications of it, in order to understand better the essence of the relation.

The first question related to the correlation of fertility to employment is whether it is not caused by other underlying factors, primarily by the fact that a higher percentage of women is employed in the higher status families and fertility might tend to be lower in these higher status groups. However, the data of the Hungarian censuses described in Chapter 4.2, as well as many other data, seem to prove that there are fertility differences between employed and dependent women at the same status level, although these differences do not always show that employed women have fewer children. For example, the Swedish data given in table 5.41 clearly demonstrates that not only all economically active women taken together have a lower fertility than inactive women, but also within given income groups (of husband's income) active women have lower fertility rates than inactive ones. On the other hand in a survey in Poland (Piotrowski 1963) it was found that not only was there a fertility difference by employment of women at each income level, but also that the negative association between income and fertility was caused solely by the fact that at the higher income levels a higher percentage of women were employed who had a lower fertility in direct consequence of their gainful activity, even though, excluding the dependent women (i.e. considering only the employed ones), the correlation of fertility to income was positive.

The direction of the causal chain, however, is not unambiguous – i.e. while it might be supposed that the desires and plans concerning the number of children, or the attitudes concerning birth control, are

Table 5.41 Average number of children ever born of women married before being 25 years old, marriage cohort 1954-8, by activity of women and income of husband: Sweden, 1967.

Income of husband (kronor)	Active women	Inactive women	Total
Up to 10 000	2·190	2·693	2·514
10 000–15 000	1·753	2·620	2·287
15 000–20 000	1·758	2·384	2·161
20 000–40 000	1·871	2·263	2·159
40 000 +	2·436	2·500	2·482
Total	1·834	2·396	2·213

Source: Tabah (1971), p. 89.

influenced by the employment of women, it might equally be surmised that the number of children influences the decision of the wife concerning seeking a job. Data from the Family Intentions survey of England and Wales in 1967 showed that a much larger percentage of women without children were working at the time of the interview than of women with children. It was supposed that a large part of these women were sterile. Thus sterility is a cause inducing women to engage in some employment, which becomes a factor contributing to the lower fertility of active women. However, also among fertile women, the working ones had a lower fertility. Thus engagement in work outside the home was proved to be a factor reducing fertility (table 5.42).

Table 5.42 Average number of children ever born of married women, by duration of marriage and activity of women: England and Wales, 1967.

Age at marriage	Marriage duration (years)	All married women		Married women having had at least one confinement	
		Total (active and inactive)	Active women	Total (active and inactive)	Active women
Up to 19 years	10–14	2·57	1·93	2·72	2·17
	15–19	2·67	2·13	2·81	2·31
	20–24	2·93	2·42	3·06	2·56
20–24 years	10–14	2·06	1·51	2·29	1·91
	15–19	2·17	1·78	2·38	2·03
	20–24	2·16	1·88	2·38	2·11

Source: Tabah (1971), p. 66.

This survey in England and Wales showed that only 1 per cent of the sample of married women never engaged in any work, but that an important part interrupted the working career for shorter or longer periods during marriage. Thus it is clear that in order to be able to analyse the impact of the wife's employment in more detail, it is necessary to know the whole work history since marriage, and not merely the status of employment at the time of the census or of the survey.

A survey carried out in 1966 in West Germany investigated the work history of married women aged 40–44 (Tabah 1971). The respondents were classified into five groups according to their history, and the number of children living in the household was analysed:

| | Number of children living in the household per 100 women | |
Work history of wife	All women aged 40–44	Marriage cohort of 1950–4
Wives who have never worked	217	236
Wives not working, but having worked with interruptions	200	204
Wives not working, but having worked continuously	208	224
Wives working, but having had interruptions in working career	183	203
Wives working and having worked continuously	217	235
Total	203	218

The results, however, do not confirm the theoretical expectations, as although the women working at the time of the interview had slightly less children than the inactive ones, those who had continuous working careers did not have fewer but tended to have more children than those who interrupted their working career. Thus the working career has no simple influence on fertility, but rather the type of employment (hours of work, character of work, etc.) ought to be taken into consideration.

In the Detroit area studies women were similarly interviewed on their work history and classified according to the years worked since marriage. Married women having had first, second and fourth parity were interviewed, so it was possible to analyse the effects of employment during different stages of family building. In addition to the actual fertility between the subsequent interviews of the longitudinal survey, the preferred and expected number of children was also asked at the first interview.

Number of live births in the period between the interviews was clearly differentiated by the work history of women, and the difference was more pronounced at the higher parities, particularly after the fourth parity. These differences, however, were much smaller in the average preferred number of children at the first interview, and particularly after the first parity. Also the expected number of children was not systematically different after the first parity. Thus the authors (Freedman and Coombs 1966a) concluded that while at the beginning of marriage there were no great differences in preferred and expected fertility between working and dependent wives, the later work history influenced both these preferences and expected fertilities and also the actual fertility (table 5.43).

Table 5.43 Average preferred and expected number of children and number of live births per 1000 women from first to third interview, by work history of women since marriage: Detroit area study.

Wife's work history since marriage	Women who had		
	1st parity	2nd parity	4th parity
Preferred number of children			
Has not worked	3·6	3·5	4·3
Worked under 1 year	3·9	3·8	4·4
Worked 1–4 years	3·4	3·5	4·1
Worked 5 or more years	3·4	2·9	4·2
Expected number of children at first interview			
Has not worked	3·38	3·44	4·95
Worked under 1 year	3·62	3·66	4·93
Worked 1–4 years	3·14	3·36	4·63
Worked 5 or more years	3·81	3·21	4·53
Number of live births per 1000 women			
Has not worked	852	646	430
Worked under 1 year	913	602	511
Worked 1–4 years	656	435	346
Worked 5 or more years	526	333	148

Source: Freedman and Coombs (1966a).

On the basis of the results of the 1960 census in the United States, Sweet (1970) recently investigated the interrelations of employment of women and of fertility by multiple regression analysis and found that causal links go in both directions: on the one hand, the decision to seek employment is influenced by the number of children, women with larger number of children being less able or less liable to engage themselves to employment;

on the other hand, the fact of being employed has a negative effect on fertility.

Thus the classic analysis of Myrdal and Klein (1956) on the situation of women and its relation to fertility seems to be valid in all developed societies: the reproductive role and the gainful employment outside the home of women are conflicting. As long as women used to work in the household, and by that means directly increased the income of the family, the contradiction was much less acute, as the work in the household or the household farm could be organized in such a way that it did not seriously interfere with the care of small children. In modern industrial societies the family unit has lost most of its productive functions; women have to seek employment outside the home in order to contribute to the family income, and work outside the home is difficult to reconcile with the care of small children. The women are urged to seek gainful employment partly because of the needs of the family, but also by the fact that by having a separate personal income her status versus that of the husband is strengthened.

This interpretation seems to be verified by two exceptional cases where fertility seems not to be influenced negatively by the employment of women. One of these is southern Italy where no negative correlation of fertility to the percentage of employed women was found (Federici 1967). These women were to a large extent employed in agriculture, in small family farms, where the conditions of work are not so inimical to fertility. The other example is Hungary after the introduction of the so-called child care allowance in 1967 (Cseh-Szombathy and Miltényi 1969, Cseh-Szombathy, Heinz and Miltényi 1970, Miltényi 1971). By the terms of this population policy measure employed women were given the option of taking leave until the third birthday of the newly born child, and of obtaining during this leave a salary (as a social benefit) equivalent to approximately one third of the average wage of earners (the sum was fixed and equal for every employed woman, so that its relative value as compared to the actual wage of the woman when employed was different for the particular income and occupational groups). Women who were not employed (or who were not members of cooperatives) were not entitled to this social benefit. This measure, therefore, heavily favoured employed women, while women who were not employed received no similar incentive. The possibility of remaining at home and not losing their salary completely, as well as the fact that their jobs were maintained for them, so that they could return when they wished (even before the third birthday of the child), resulted in an increase in the fertility of employed women, while the decline in fertility of dependent women continued following the previous trend. In direct consequence, the fertility difference was inversed, the fertility of employed women becoming higher than that of dependent

Year	Total fertility rate	
	Employed women	Dependent women
1960	1355	2365
1966	1485	2225
1967	1710	2000
1968	1910	1755

This proves that if the conditions of employment of women in a modern industrial society are organized in a way that diminishes the contradictions of the reproductive and working role (i.e. does not make it very hard for working women to care for small children), the negative influence of the employment of women on fertility might be reduced or even nullified.

All these empirical results prove that the impact of employment of women on their fertility depends on the circumstances of their employment. Full-time gainful employment outside the home seems to be negatively correlated to fertility in most circumstances. When however, the birth of a child and a longer break in economic activity does not entail grave income losses and worsening of career chances, employed women might be as prone to have children (even a larger number of children) as dependent women. On the other hand, in circumstances where employment and mother roles are not incompatible (e.g. where mothers work at home or in the family farm or shop, or where they have possibilities for part-time employment), the employment of women might not depress fertility (Stycos and Weller 1967).

5.9 Religious denomination and ethnicity

Religion is a frequently mentioned factor in American investigations into fertility differences. As described in Chapter 4.4, the Princeton survey found that denomination was the strongest and most consistent factor influencing fertility. Also both the Growth of American Families surveys and the National Fertility Studies stated the persistence of these differences, although the second National Fertility Study indicated that they are declining in America.

By religous fertility differences, the authors generally mean the difference between Roman Catholics and Protestants, the fertility of the former being allegedly consistently higher. In some studies it was also asserted that the fertility of Jewish populations tends to be lower than that of Protestants.

It has been supposed that these differences are connected to the fact that the Roman Catholic church is officially opposed to the use of methods of birth control (except the rhythm method and complete abstinence) and is supposed to encourage large families, while the Protestant churches allegedly do not see anything immoral in the use of contraception and consider that responsible parents should have as many children as they can rear adequately – so that an excessive number of children might even be considered immoral, if the parents are unable to provide for them properly (Lenski 1961). The Jewish religion does not profess any special teachings either on contraception or the number of children (Goldscheider 1965).

In addition, differences in fertility by degree of religious interest have sometimes also been studied, and it has been found that couples with higher religious interest have higher fertility, particularly among Roman Catholics. An obvious interpretation of this might be that the higher degree of commitment to the values of a denomination implies a correspondingly greater adherence to any special teachings concerning the number of children.

The influence of religious denomination and interest, however, is not so unambiguous and well explained as might sometimes appear from published material. The following questions need careful discussion:

1 Is the Catholic–Protestant fertility differential universally observable in all advanced societies, or does it appear only in some special circumstances?

2 Do all the Protestant denominations have a lower fertility than Catholics?

3 How does degree of religious interest influence fertility?

4 Are denominational differences of fertility permanent, or are they declining in the same way as some other fertility differentials?

5 Are religous fertility differences simply caused by the fact that the composition of denominational groups varies by socioeconomic status, residence, income, etc., and are the fundamental causes of fertility differentials connected with these differentials? Or, alternatively, do denomination and religious interest have a special impact on fertility, independently of these differentials?

6 Are religious fertility differentials simply the reflections of ethnic differentials?

7 If the differentials by denomination and religious interest are real differences, not caused by other more fundamental factors, then through what mechanism do they influence fertility? The following alternative explanations seem to be possible: (a) more children could be born intentionally because of the teaching of the Catholic church which attaches (perhaps) a higher value to a larger family than the Protestant teaching, which in turn (perhaps) emphasizes more the quality than the quantity of children; (b) more children could be borne unintentionally by Catholic couples, because of the well-known proscription by the Catholic church of the more reliable methods of birth control; (c) the larger families of Catholics might be due to the indirect influence of Catholic ideological encouragement for certain types of behaviour associated with higher natality – e.g. settlement in rural areas, and less motivation for social mobility or migration to towns, or for employment of wives (Day 1968).

Let us consider these questions in turn. Day (1968) investigated the universal existence of Catholic–Protestant differences, by calculating the approximate total fertility rates for different developed countries, for the total population in the case of predominantly Catholic or predominantly Protestant countries, and separately for these two denominations where the population of the country was denominationally mixed. These rates in the late 1950s in some predominantly Protestant countries were:

Denmark	2555
Norway	2825
Sweden	2275
Finland	2630

and in the countries considered by Day to be predominantly Catholic, the rates were:

Ireland	3430
France	2685
Belgium	2470
Luxembourg	2125
Italy (1951)	2365
Austria	2520
Czechoslovakia	2690
Hungary	2175

Thus it cannot be stated that Catholic countries had higher fertility rates than Protestants at that time. On the other hand, in all developed countries where Catholics constituted a significant minority, the fertility rates of the Catholic population were much higher than those of other denominations:

	Total population	Non-Catholic population	Catholic population
Australia	3415	3270	3990
New Zealand	3960	3850	4930
United States	3530	3300	4290
Canada	3890	3245	4705
United Kingdom	2455	2410	2915
Netherlands	3095	2660	3725
Switzerland	2340	2090	2715

West Germany, whose data were not included in this table, constitutes an exceptional case, since there the Catholic–Protestant differential, which was formerly fairly significant, has shown a strong tendency to decline in recent generations (Day 1968, Burgdörfer 1932, Peters 1958, Freedman, Baumert and Bolte 1959). This was interpreted by Day as being due to a Catholic–Protestant difference in the period when the Catholic population was in a minority (until the end of the Second World War), but since then in the German Federal Republic the two denominations have been fairly equal in number and Catholics have been politically somewhat dominant, and the difference has tended to disappear. This was important for Day, as he hypothesizes that the fertility of Catholics exceeds that of Protestants only in those countries where they constitute a significant minority which faces some discrimination but might hope to increase its weight and political influence through increasing its population number more rapidly than rival denominational groups. On the other hand, in predominantly Catholic countries, where Catholics are not discriminated against and there is no need to fight for a dominant position, the teaching of the Catholic church on large families is not so devoutly followed by the masses of Catholics. Thus, Day states, it seems that

> Although Catholic pro-natalism serves to increase natality, it does so only under two conditions – when:
> 1   There exists a high level of economic development; that is, a climate in which one could reasonably expect both the predisposition and the opportunity for effective natality control to be most widespread.
> 2   The persons at whom the pro-natalist teaching is directed define themselves as members of a group constituting a numerically and politically important, but not dominant, *minority* of the population. (p. 45).

Thus it is denomination plus ethnocentrism in a given population group (or maybe primarily ethnocentrism in a group which is expressed among other factors in adherence to the Catholic church) that causes the high fertility of Catholics as compared to Protestants in the countries with mixed denominational composition.

The theory of Day might be used to explain certain peculiarities in the fertility levels of Catholic populations in several countries.

For example, the fact that the fertility of the Hungarian Roman Catholic population equalled that of the Protestant population in the 1930s, even though the Protestants were traditionally more well-to-do and more educated, may fit into the framework of this theory, since the Roman Catholics were for centuries in a politically predominant position in Hungary.

On the other hand, according to Day, the high fertility in Ireland might also be interpreted in terms of this theory, because the Catholic population there have traditionally felt threatened by oppression from Protestants, not inside the country, but from England. Similarly, English Catholics (partly of Irish origin) maintain a relatively high fertility level in face of the predominantly Protestant population (Chou and Brown 1968).

Long before Day, Van Heek (1954 1956–7) interpreted the high fertility of Dutch Catholics in terms of a similar theory. He compared the fertility of some Catholic and Protestant frontier areas in the Netherlands with the fertility of neighbouring Protestant and Catholic territories in Germany and Belgium. These latter German and Belgian territories were selected because their occupational composition and degree of urbanization were similar to the areas investigated in the Netherlands. Van Heek found that the territories inhabited by Catholics in the Netherlands had higher fertility than the comparable territories in Belgium. Thus, he concluded, there must be some special factor influencing the fertility of Dutch Catholics which is related to the position of Catholics in the Netherlands but not in Belgium. He hypothesized that this stems from the fact that Dutch Catholics were a minority with a history of discrimination at the hands of the Protestant majority, but they were an important minority with a real hope of becoming a majority, partly through higher fertility. They were also concentrated in some areas of the country, so that while they influenced each other strongly, they were relatively less influenced by other groups. Therefore they were deeply attached to the Catholic church and followed its teachings strictly, including its teaching concerning the high value given to large families. Paradoxically, the religiosity of Dutch Catholics was also encouraged by the example of the religiosity of Dutch Calvinists, who equally strictly followed the teachings of their religion, although this did not place such a heavy emphasis on the value of large families. Thus the interpretation given by Van Heek was not one based on religion as such, but on the special cultural environment of Catholicism in the Netherlands.

On the basis of this theory, it might be suggested that the recent decline in the Catholic–Protestant fertility differential in the Netherlands is the consequence of the fact that the Catholics have more or less equalled the population number of Protestants, and that the political influence of Catholics (as seen from the percentage of votes given for the denominational political parties) seems to be even stronger than that of Protestants in the Netherlands.

The best example of the combination of Catholic religion and ethnocentricity is Canada, where in 1961 45·7 per cent of the population belonged to the Catholic church, nearly two-thirds of the Catholics being of French origin. The population of French origin, which constituted 30·4 per cent of the total population in 1961, descended from French settlers who were dominated for centuries by England and by English settlers who immigrated after them. The population of French origin was concentrated mainly in the province of Quebec and was strongly attached to the Catholic church, which to a large extent symbolized national identity. The other important Catholic group in Canada is of Irish origin, also traditionally attached to the Catholic church. These Catholics were mostly in underprivileged positions compared with English Protestants in Canada.

Thus the higher fertility of Catholics than Protestants in Canada fits into the theory of Van Heek and Day (table 5.44). The differences, however, have been declining in recent years (Burch 1966), which might also be interpreted as a consequence of the relative improvement in the social and political position of Catholics (and of the French-speaking population).

As for our second question, it is well known that the various Protestant denominations do not share the same norms, attitudes and values, some of them being more traditionalist (fundamentalist), some others more liberal – the traditionalist groups in general emphasizing more the value of larger families and being less liable to accept birth control, while the more liberal ones accept birth control and smaller family ideals fairly early. The

Table 5.44 Number of children ever born per 1000 women ever married, by age group and denomination: Canada, 1961.

Age of women	Number of children ever born			
	Canada	Catholic	Protestant	Jewish
65+	4038	5731	3171	3442
60–64	3650	4966	2839	2368
55–59	3385	4499	2630	2060
50–54	3154	4143	2495	1873
45–49	3110	3950	2566	1950
40–44	3231	3983	2744	2106
35–39	3102	3590	2757	2263
30–34	2775	3019	2588	2229
25–29	2178	2278	2120	1729
20–24	1327	1347	1346	809

Source: Long (1970), p. 138.

United States seems to be the most appropriate country for studying the impact of the different Protestant denominations on fertility, since in no other country are there as many different Protestant denominations living side by side.

The Indianapolis survey, which was restricted to Protestant couples in that city, has already provided the opportunity of comparing the practice of family planning and fertility. Four denominational groups, which were relatively large within the sample, were selected here for comparison: the fairly liberal Presbyterians, the more fundamentalist Baptists and Methodists, and the Christians, a denomination having its centre in Indianapolis. The percentage of efficient planners was highest in the liberal Presbyterian group and lowest in the two fundamentalist denominations (table 5.45). The number of children ever born of all couples belonging to the particular denominational group showed a similar tendency – i.e. the Presbyterians had the lowest and the Methodists the highest number of children, with the Christians and Baptists in intermediate positions. However, in the particular fertility planning status groups the differences in fertility showed dissimilar patterns. In the group of number and spacing planners the order of denominations was reversed: Presbyterians had the highest and Baptists the lowest fertility. On the other hand, in the category of excess fertility Presbyterians had the lowest and Methodists the highest fertility. Thus it seems to be confirmed that the attitude of the given denomination towards birth control and rational planning of life in general does have an influence on the practice of fertility planning by its adherents, but that the influence on fertility is much more complicated than was initially supposed by demographers.

Table 5.45 The relation of fertility planning status and number of children ever born to the denomination of wife for four religious denominations in the Indianapolis survey.

Denomination	Total	Number and spacing planned	Number planned	Quasi- planned	Excess fertility
Per cent distribution by fertility planning status					
Presbyterian	100	38·4	16·4	30·1	15·1
Baptist	100	22·3	18·1	22·9	36·7
Christian	100	24·8	19·4	33·5	22·3
Methodist	100	21·3	9·5	40·9	28·3
Births per 100 *couples*					
Presbyterian	171	134	242	182	245
Baptist	201	97	203	174	280
Christian	201	105	236	194	289
Methodist	214	124	219	199	301

Source: Freedman and Whelpton, in Whelpton and Kiser (1950), pp. 429, 453.

The 1960 Growth of American Families survey also showed fairly marked differences in both the number of children already born and the most likely expected number of children of the liberal and the fundamentalist Protestant denominations – the fertility of the former being near to that of the Jews, and the fertility of the latter similar to that of the Catholics (the Congregational, Episcopal, Presbyterian and Quaker churches were considered liberal, the Baptist, Christian, Lutheran and Methodist churches were considered intermediate, and the Mormon, Nazarene and Pentecostal churches, and Jehovah's Witnesses, were classified as fundamental) (table 5.46).

Similarly, the National Fertility Study of 1965 showed marked differences in fertility, both in the number of children ever born and the expected number of children, by Protestant denomination (table 5.47). The fundamentalist Protestant sects showed current fertilities similar to the Catholics, although their expected final fertility was lower. On the other hand, Episcopalians, Congregationalists, Presbyterians, etc., showed fertility levels similar to those of the Jews.

Thus Protestant fundamentalism seems to be a fairly strong factor favouring high fertility. In addition to the adherence to particular fundamentalist churches, fundamentalism can be measured in more detail, according to De Jong (1965), by studying the answers given to questions concerning attitudes towards gambling, drinking alcohol and card playing, ultimate reliance upon biblical authority, degree of importance attached to

Table 5.46   Births by 1960 and total number of births
expected for wives, by religion of wife: Growth of
American Families survey.

Religion and denomination of wife	Average number of births	
	By 1960	Most likely expected
All Protestants	2·2	2·9
Liberal	2·1	2·8
Intermediate	2·2	2·9
Fundamentalist	2·5	3·3
Catholics	2·5	3·7
Jews	2·1	2·5
Other	2·2	3·0
Total	2·3	3·1

Source: Whelpton, Campbell and Patterson (1966), pp. 71, 74.

Table 5.47   Births by 1965 and total number of births
expected for wives, by religion of wife: National Fertility
Study, USA.

Religion and denomination of wife	Average number of births	
	By 1965	Most likely expected
All Protestants	2·3	3·0
Fundamentalist sects	2·8	3·4
Baptist	2·3	2·9
Lutheran	2·5	3·2
Episcopalian	2·1	2·9
Methodist	2·2	2·9
Presbyterian	2·2	2·9
Congregationalist	2·2	2·9
Evangelical	2·2	2·8
Other Protestants	2·4	3·2
Catholics	2·8	3·9
Jews	2·1	2·9

Source: Ryder and Westoff (1971), p. 71.

the ministry, and views on the approach of the end of the world. He found
that the fundamentalism scale based on these items was very strongly
correlated with high fertility in the region of the Southern Appalachians in
the United States.

Similar differences were demonstrated in the Netherlands, where most Protestants belong to the Dutch Reformed church, a fairly liberal Protestantism, while the Calvinist church, sometimes named the Orthodox Reformed church, is fairly fundamentalist. The number of children ever born, by married women, at the census of 1960 was:

Roman Catholics	3·4
Dutch Reformed	2·6
Calvinist	3·2
Other religions	2·5
No religion	2·1
Total	2·8

Thus, as in the United States, the more traditionally oriented Protestants had a fertility level very similar to that of the Roman Catholics. In fact, while in recent years the fertility of the Roman Catholic population seems to have declined strongly, that of the Calvinists declined much less, so that the fertility of the Calvinists seems to be the highest in the Netherlands at present.

If the denomination to which couples belong influences their number of children, it seems logical to hypothesize that the degree of religious interest, i.e. the degree of commitment to the norms and values professed by these denominations, also influences fertility.

The authors of the Indianapolis survey in the United States hypothesized that the degree of interest and participation in religious activities is an indicator of the acceptance of traditional values. It was supposed that the more religious people act with reference to their socially defined role within a larger unit rather than in terms of a deliberate calculation of alternatives. Non-religious people, on the other hand, tend to consider all questions within a narrow conception of self-interest, and since tradition has no value for them, they do not accept traditional high fertility values and tend to plan their fertility on the basis of rational calculations of the costs and benefits of having children; they thus tend to have smaller families.

This hypothesis formulated by the authors was not completely confirmed by the results (table 5.48). For example, religious interest of the wife since marriage, one of the many indicators of religious interest and participation, seems to be fairly positively correlated to the percentage of fertility planners. However, the relation is not clear, probably because the group showing very little interest in religion seems to have been very heterogeneous, containing both very effective planners and couples who were not successful in planning their number of children.

Table 5.48 The relation of fertility planning status and number of children ever born to the religious interest of the wife since marriage in the Indianapolis survey.

Interest in religion of wife since marriage	Total	Number and spacing planned	Number planned	Quasi- planned	Excess fertility
Per cent distribution by fertility planning status					
Very little	100	38·1	5·8	23·7	32·4
Little	100	33·8	16·9	25·7	23·6
Some	100	25·0	12·9	34·0	28·1
Much	100	24·2	15·3	35·2	25·3
Very much	100	29·5	18·7	29·1	22·7
Total	100	27·9	14·2	31·4	26·5
Births per 100 couples					
Very little or little	188	84	170	192	325
Some	204	103	231	202	286
Much	208	115	237	199	294
Very much	211	135	254	201	286
Total	203	106	228	199	296

Source: Freedman and Whelpton, in Whelpton and Kiser (1950), pp. 424, 446.

Similarly, the number of children ever born did not unanimously confirm the original hypothesis, as in the whole sample the size of family showed only a slight positive association with religious interest. The relation was, however, positive and very strong in the number and spacing planned group – i.e. among the most efficient family planners – and in the number planned group, but in the group of couples having excess fertility the relation was negative, couples with little religious interest having the largest families. It seems that other additional factors (e.g. socioeconomic status) interfered with the influence of the degree of religious interest.

The Princeton survey distinguished Protestants and Catholics actively participating in the church and others whose religious interest seemed low. From among the women having already had two parities the Catholics had more third pregnancies than the Protestants, and the active Catholics significantly more than the non-active Catholics, while among the Protestants an opposite relation seemed to prevail: non-active Protestants had more third pregnancies. Also the mean desired number of children of active Catholics was higher than that of the other Catholics, while there was no difference between active and other Protestants. Jewish couples showed the lowest actual and desired fertility. The percentage of couples

Table 5.49 Selected fertility differences by religion in the Princeton survey.

Fertility measure	Denomination and activity							
	Protestant total	Catholic total	Jewish	Active Protestant	Other Protestant	Active Catholic	Other Catholic	All Couples
Mean number of children desired at first interview	3·0	3·6	2·8	3·0	2·9	4·2	3·4	3·2
Mean number of children desired at second interview	3·0	3·6	2·7	3·0	3·0	4·2	3·3	3·2
Per cent planning all pregnancies	34	34	61	43	27	27	37	38
Per cent planning no pregnancies	19	24	8	14	24	28	23	20
Per cent having a third pregnancy	51	62	31	43	59	72	59	54

Source: Westoff, Potter and Sagi (1963), p. 89.

planning all pregnancies was lowest among Catholics (table 5.49). The authors concluded that these differences prove the influence of the degree of commitment to the teachings of the churches, since the Catholic church advocates larger families and is against the practice of birth control, except the rhythm method.

Similarly, the 1960 Growth of American Families survey showed fertility differences by religious activity of women in the case of Catholics (table 5.50). However, the differences in most likely expected fertility were much higher than the differences in achieved fertility at the time of the survey. It does not seem completely unjustified to conjecture that the practising Catholic couples were mentioning higher numbers of expected children under the influence of Catholic ideals, but that these higher expected numbers of children were not necessarily realized later.

Table 5.50 Births by 1960 and total number of births expected by wife, for Catholic wives, by frequency with which they received the sacrament: Growth of American Families survey.

Frequency with which sacrament was received	Average number of births	
	By 1960	*Most likely expected*
All Catholic wives	2·5	3·7
Never	2·4	3·2
Once a year or less	2·4	3·3
A few times a year	2·6	3·7
Once a month	2·5	3·7
Two or three times a month	2·6	4·1
Once a week or more	2·6	4·4

Source: Whelpton, Campbell and Patterson (1966), p. 83.

The trends for no fertility differences between Protestants of different religous interest and for actively religious Catholics to have a higher fertility than actively religious Protestants, however, are not valid in all other advanced countries. For example, in the Netherlands the fertility survey performed at the end of 1968 on three marriage cohorts showed that both the effective and the expected number of children was higher among Protestants characterized by a high degree of religiosity, than among Catholics of similar religiosity. However, since the number of couples characterized by low religiosity was higher among Protestants, the overall number of children ever born and expected of Catholics and Protestants was more or less similar (table 5.51). The degree of religous interest of Protestants in the Netherlands, however, is overlapped by the

Table 5.51 Average number of children ever born and expected number of children of the marriage cohorts 1958, 1963 and 1968, by denomination and religiosity: fertility survey of the Netherlands.

Denomination	Religiosity	1958		1963		1968	
		Effective	*Expected*	*Effective*	*Expected*	*Effective*	*Expected*
Protestant	High	2·6	3·3	1·9	3·6	0·3	3·4
	Medium	2·2	2·6	1·8	2·9	0·3	2·9
	Low	2·3	2·7	1·7	2·6	0·4	2·7
Catholic	High	2·6	3·0	1·8	3·0	0·3	3·2
	Medium	2·4	2·7	1·7	2·8	0·3	2·7
	Low	—	—	—	—	0·3	2·6

Source: Tabah (1971), p. 49.

two Protestant denominations, the more liberal Dutch Reformed church and the more traditionalist Calvinist church.

Thus, although it seems that under special circumstances the degree of religious interest has an influence on the fertility of the couples, this influence can be observed only in certain contexts, these contexts being most probably associated with the norms and values concerning fertility professed by the given denomination. This fact also suggests that the influence of religion on fertility should be seen in the wider context of the

Table 5.52 Births by the time of interview and total number of births expected, for wives, by religion and by age, in the 1955 and 1960 Growth of American Families surveys.

Religion and age of wife	Average number of births			
	By interview		*Most likely expected*	
	1955	*1960*	*1955*	*1960*
Total	2·1	2·3	3·0	3·1
All Protestants	2·1	2·2	2·9	2·9
18–24	1·1	1·3	2·9	2·8
25–29	2·0	2·3	3·0	3·1
30–34	2·4	2·6	2·9	3·0
35–39	2·6	2·7	2·8	2·8
All Catholics	2·1	2·5	3·4	3·7
18–24	1·2	1·3	3·8	3·6
25–29	1·9	2·5	3·4	4·1
30–34	2·4	3·0	3·3	3·8
35–39	2·6	3·0	3·1	3·4

Source: Whelpton, Campbell and Patterson (1966), p. 78.

influence of the cultural environment of population groups – denomination and religiosity being only one facet of this culture.

Denominational fertility differences were interpreted differently by American demographers. The authors analysing the second Princeton survey (Westoff, Potter and Sagi 1963) considered that denominational differences were the most stable fertility differentials in the United States (see pp. 198–9). On the basis of the two Growth of American Families surveys, it was in fact stated (Whelpton, Campbe.l and Patterson 1966) that fertility differences by denomination increased, since from 1955 to 1960 the average number of children ever born of Catholic women in different age groups increased more than that of the Protestant women of the same age, and while the most likely expected number of children of Protestants only slightly changed, that of the Catholics increased strongly (table 5.52). The greatest rise in the case of Catholics occurred in the age group of 25–29 years, and also the difference in expected fertilities of Catholics and Protestants was highest in this age group.

Still in 1965 the first National Fertility Study found Catholic–Protestant differences in the expected number of children almost unchanged:

Age of wife	Protestant	Catholic
18–24	2·9	3·5
25–29	3·1	4·0
30–34	3·1	4·1
35–39	3·0	4·0

(Ryder and Westoff 1971, p. 84)

If this difference of nearly one child per married couple had been realized, a significant difference in the natural growth of the Catholic and Protestant populations in the United States would have resulted. However, the next National Fertility Study in 1970 indicated a sharp decline in these differences, and Westoff (1975) predicted the disappearance of the Catholic–Protestant fertility differential within the coming decade. Thus within twelve years the judgment of this distinguished American demographer, who participated in the analysis of the Princeton survey, as well as that of the two National Fertility Studies, underwent really dramatic changes: he first considered the denominational differences to be very stable and very large, and later stated that they were quickly diminishing and would soon disappear.

The reduction in Catholic–Protestant fertility differences is even more pronounced in Canada (Long 1970). However, the basic difference between the fertility of Catholics in the United States and in Canada is that while in the United States the fertility of the Catholics increased strongly in the baby boom period, that of the Catholics in Canada did not increase, although the downward trend that had begun much earlier was halted during the period of the baby boom. Since the fertility of Protestants in Canada increased in the baby boom period, the decline of denominational fertility differences was in process during the baby boom period – i.e. it began much earlier than in the United States, where it started only after the baby boom in the second half of the 1960s.

A similar development seems to have been happening in the Netherlands since the first half of the 1960s. The fertility of Catholics, as measured by the average birth order, declined from the level characteristic of the more traditionally oriented Calvinist church to that of the more liberally oriented Dutch Reformed church, so that the fertility of Protestants might be currently higher than that of Catholics (table 5.53).

Table 5.53   Average number of children ever born of women having a birth between 1960 and 1968, by religion: Netherlands.

	Denomination				
Year	Roman Catholic	Reformed Church	Calvinist	Without denomination	Total
1960	3·0	2·6	3·0	2·3	2·8
1961	3·0	2·6	2·9	2·2	2·7
1962	3·0	2·5	2·9	2·2	2·7
1963	2·8	2·5	2·9	2·2	2·6
1964	2·8	2·5	2·8	2·2	2·6
1965	2·6	2·4	2·8	2·1	2·5
1966	2·4	2·3	2·7	2·0	2·3
1967	2·3	2·3	2·6	2·0	2·3
1968	2·2	2·2	2·6	1·9	2·2

Source: Tabah (1971), p. 47.

This also seems to be confirmed by the results of the multiple regression analyses of factors of fertility in the Netherlands, described in Chapter 4.3, where the influence of the percentage of Catholics on fertility was much smaller in 1967 than previously.

It would be premature to give a definite explanation for the change in denominational fertility differences in these three countries, which has been caused primarily by the larger decline in Catholic fertility than in Protestant fertility. But this decline clearly contradicts any hypothesis about the unambiguous and direct relationships between the teachings of a religious denomination and the number of children of the adherents of that religion.

As for our fifth question, several demographers have denied the existence of denominational differences that are independent of other socioeconomic fertility differences. For example, Petersen (1969, p. 538)
considered that:

The effect of religion *per se* on the reproductive behaviour of most
persons in the West is now probably close to nil. What may seem to be a
religious influence often reflects the fact that the members of any
denomination are typically concentrated in a very few places in the social
structure as defined by occupation, education, income, or any other of
the usual indices.

It is well known that the members of Protestant denominations are
concentrated in certain social strata, the Congregational, Episcopal and
Presbyterian denominations having more adherents in the upper strata,
while the Methodist and Baptist denominations have many members from
the lower strata.

There is also a clear difference between the three great denominational groups, Protestants having a socioeconomic composition similar
to the national average, Catholics being overrepresented in the lower
(mostly lower urban) strata, and Jews being overrepresented in the upper
strata.

Thus it might be supposed that denominational fertility differences
simply reflect socioeconomic differences. The surveys performed in the
United States, however, seem to contradict this supposition. When socioeconomic status was measured in the Princeton survey by a composite
index, Protestants in almost all status categories showed lower percentages
of third pregnancies than Catholics and higher ones than Jewish couples.
The difference between Protestants and Jews disappeared when only
completely successful planners were taken into consideration (table 5.54).
From the point of view of the independent influence of denomination, it is
even more significant that the relationship between fertility and socioeconomic status differed between each particular denomination: the fertility of Catholic couples was positively correlated with status, while in the
case of Protestants and Jews the relation is not clear. Similarly, the fertility
of Catholics showed a different relation to all the other socioeconomic
characteristics investigated by the Princeton surveys than did the fertility of
Protestants, as described in Chapter 4.4. Thus it seemed that denomination
is such a strong influencing factor that it modifies the impact of other
socioeconomic factors on fertility.

Freedman, Whelpton and Smit (1961) reanalysed the data of the first
Growth of American Families survey in order to discover whether
denominational fertility differences are caused by combinations of different
social and economic factors. They selected from the sample sixty-six

Table 5.54 Per cent reporting at least one additional pregnancy since the second birth, by religion, socioeconomic status and fertility-planning success: Princeton survey.

Index of socioeconomic status	Total sample		Protestant	
	All couples	Completely successful planners	All couples	Completely successful planners
0–10 (low)	66	33		
11–13	57	15	67	27
14–16	48	27	49	13
17–19	58	36	52	29
20–22	47	32	41	21
23–26	52	35	42	27
27–30	50	37	48	35
31–36 (high)	58	48		

Index of socioeconomic status	Catholic		Jewish	
	All couples	Completely successful planners	All couples	Completely successful planners
0–16 (low)				
11–13	59	28		
14–16	51	36		
17–19	64	45	22	0
20–22	63	55	33	23
23–26	75	58	29	29
27–30	81	78	35	37
31–36 (high)				

Source: Westoff, Potter and Sagi (1963), p. 118.

Catholic, Protestant and Jewish couples who had the following characteristics in common: husband's occupation and income, wife's education, duration of marriage, metropolitan character of present residence, and farm background. Only couples where husband and wife had the same denomination were selected (the number sixty-six was dictated by the fact that there were only sixty-six Jewish couples in the total sample).

Several indicators of fertility and family planning behaviour were compared (table 5.55). In general it might be stated that the Protestant–Jewish fertility differences seem to disappear, while the Protestant–Catholic differences seem to have risen compared with the differences found in the total sample. This might be caused by the fact that most of the Jewish couples had relatively high status levels, so the matched Catholic

Table 5.55 Fertility behaviour of all Protestant, Catholic and Jewish couples in the national sample of the United States, as well as of sixty-six matched Protestant, Catholic and Jewish couples.

Characteristics of fertility behaviour	Total national sample			Matched groups		
	Protes-tants	Catho-lics	Jews	Protes-tants	Catho-lics	Jews
Mean number of births to date	2·1	2·1	1·7	1·4	2·0	1·7
Mean expected number of births	2·9	3·4	2·4	2·4	3·4	2·4
Mean number of children wanted when interviewed	3·0	3·5	2·6	2·8	3·7	2·6
Mean number of children wanted if could start life over	3·4	3·8	3·2	3·2	4·2	3·2
Mean number of children considered ideal for Americans	3·4	3·6	3·1	3·2	3·2	3·1
Percentage expressing unqualified approval of family limitation methods	73	32	89	92	18	89
Percentage of couples having ever used an appliance or chemical method of contraception	67	26	83	78	15	83

Source: Freedman, Whelpton and Smit (1961), p. 610.

couples were at a higher status level than the average Catholic couples, and these higher status Catholics tended to have higher fertilities. On the other hand, the matched Protestant couples were also somewhat above the average, but the higher status Protestants tended to have lower fertilities than the average. The authors concluded from these results that denomination exerts an influence on fertility that is independent from socioeconomic status, income, education and residence.

On the basis of the Detroit Area studies Lenski came to a similar conclusion, but formulated a deeper and more detailed interpretation of the influence of the religious factor (Lenski 1961). By dividing the sample into four groups, he found that the mean number of children ever borne by women of all ages was 3·0 in the group of Negro Protestants, 2·7 in that of white Catholics, 2·2 in that of Jews and 1·9 in that of white Protestants. Incidentally, these mean numbers coincided fairly well with the results of a fertility survey made by the Census Bureau in 1957, except that in this latter survey the fertility of Jews was slightly lower (2·0) and that of Protestants higher (2·4). This might be explained, according to Lenski, by the fact that in the Detroit Area studies only northern urban white Protestants were included, while the southern rural white Protestants, who were obviously not represented in the Detroit sample, had higher than average fertilities.

Lenski also stated that these denominational fertility differences were not caused by the socioeconomic composition of the different denominational groups.

As he found similar differences by denomination in many other social behaviours (e.g. in economic, familial and political behaviour), he stated that socioreligious group membership is a variable similar to socioeconomic class in explaining different aspects of behaviour, among them fertility.

The term 'socioreligious group' is used deliberately instead of 'religious group', because it is not merely religion, but the whole special subculture, of which religion is only a part, that influences fertility, as well as economic, social and family behaviour. Thus white Catholics are influenced by Catholic teachings which oppose the use of the more efficient means of contraception as immoral and stress the view that large families are a value. On the other hand, white Protestants are influenced by the standpoint of Protestant churches that modern and efficient contraceptive methods are not immoral, and even that the failure to limit family size can be immoral if the parents cannot provide adequate care and education for their children because of lack of resources. However, the influence of religious teachings is not exclusive, since Negro Protestants, for example, stand in every respect (including fertility) closer to white Catholics than to white Protestants. Thus it seems that in different settings Protestantism produces different behaviours, among which are different fertility levels.

Data from the Netherlands provide an opportunity for investigating the influence of denomination on fertility while keeping social status constant, because detailed data have been published on the average number of children ever born by duration of marriage, social stratum and denomination (table 5.56). It can be concluded from the data that denominational differences in fertility are caused not only by the different social position of the particular denominations (although this too is a factor of denominational differentiation of fertility), but also by denominational differences in fertility within each social stratum. Fertility of Roman Catholics was the highest in all strata, followed by the fertility of Orthodox Calvinists, and the fertility of the 'no denomination' group was the lowest. It is remarkable that the same differences are found in the younger group, those being married for 10–14 years, where U-shaped curves can be observed in the case of each denominational group. The recent decline in the fertility of Catholics in the Netherlands, however, has probably changed these differences.

The studies described above, then, seem to prove the existence of a religious factor of fertility, which is independent of other socioeconomic factors.

Table 5.56 Average number of children born of married women in existing first marriage, by duration of marriage, social stratum and denomination: Netherlands, 1960.

Social stratum	Duration of marriage (years)	Religious denomination of wife				
		All	Roman Catholic	Dutch Reformed	Calvinist	None
Professional	10–14	2·91	3·61	2·61	3·23	2·20
	21–25	3·04	4·17	2·67	3·70	2·25
Senior manager	10–14	2·83	3·57	2·51	3·27	2·54
	21–25	3·12	4·26	2·75	3·82	2·34
Other non-manual employee, annual income 5500 and over	10–14	2·62	3·20	2·28	3·06	2·00
	21–25	2·99	4·00	2·56	3·75	2·15
Other non-manual employee, annual income under 5500	10–14	2·65	3·14	2·33	2·98	2·02
	21–25	3·16	4·04	2·74	3·61	2·27
Self-employed with employees	10–14	2·90	3·46	2·42	3·33	2·08
	21–25	3·68	4·64	3·02	4·31	2·36
Self-employed without employees	10–14	2·63	3·07	2·30	3·00	2·02
	21–25	3·00	3·79	2·51	3·45	2·49
Worker with annual income 5500 and over	10–14	2·69	3·11	2·40	3·12	2·10
	21–25	3·28	4·18	2·87	3·92	2·38
Worker with annual income 3750–5500	10–14	2·86	3·30	2·56	3·20	2·27
	21–25	3·64	4·53	3·22	4·16	2·65
Worker with annual income under 3750	10–14	2·87	3·17	2·54	3·08	2·38
	21–25	3·79	4·51	3·34	4·04	2·94
Farmer, self-employed	10–14	3·60	4·56	2·64	3·61	2·37
	21–25	4·50	6·21	3·28	4·52	2·46
Farm worker	10–14	3·27	4·06	2·80	3·57	2·70
	21–25	4·25	5·51	3·61	4·70	3·77

Source: Glass (1968), p. 125.

Hungary, on the other hand, is a country where fertility differences by denomination seem to be interpretable in terms of the different socio-economic compositions of the different denominations. Here, however, the denominations lived in a completely different context than in the countries examined above. Roman Catholics were in a strong majority: in 1949 (the last census when denomination was asked) 68 per cent of the population was Roman Catholic, 22 per cent Calvinist, 5 per cent Lutheran, 3 per cent Greek Catholic, and 2 per cent belonged to other denominations (Jewish, etc.). The Catholics traditionally had a predominant share of political power.

In order to understand the development of denominational fertility differences in Hungary, it is necessary to investigate in some detail the social background of the particular denominations in Hungary, following the explanations given in Part 3 in connection with the signs of early birth control and low fertility in the region of Ormánság, in southern Transdanubia.

In the sixteenth century the majority of the Hungarian population became Protestant. At the same time, the territory of the country became divided into three parts; the central part was under Turkish occupation, the western and northern part belonged to the Habsburg empire, while the eastern part of the Great Plain and Transylvania were independent. In the seventeenth century the Habsburgs tried to impose the Counter Reformation on their territories, while the Turkish empire did not bother much about religion, and in Transylvania a denominational peace was instituted, the most energetic princes of Transylvania being Calvinists. These political differences influenced the social background of denominations very much. While in the territories belonging to the Habsburg empire during the Counter Reformation period, relatively few Protestants remained, most of them being wealthy burghers (many of them of German origin) who adhered to Lutheran Protestantism, in the territories occupied by the Turks the native population (which was predominantly serfs and smallholders) remained Calvinist. After the expulsion of the Turks the Counter Reformation drive of the Habsburgs was already weakening, so a significant portion of these smallholder serfs (who after the abolition of serfdom in 1948 became independent peasants) managed to remain Calvinists, while immigrants from parts of the country formerly unoccupied by the Turks were generally Catholics and at the same time mostly landless agricultural workers. So in the western and central part of the country the denominational difference was strongly connected with social differences, the Protestants being generally wealthier and in consequence more independent (this independence being the basis of their ability to remain Protestant). On the other hand, in the northeastern parts of the Great Plain which formerly belonged to independent Transylvania (which after the expulsion of the Turks again became part of Hungary, i.e. also of the Habsburg empire), the great masses of the population (i.e. not only the wealthier peasants and burghers) were Protestants, mostly Calvinists. This region in general was poorer and developed more slowly after the Turkish wars.

It is obvious that birth control and decline in fertility began in those population groups whose members owned some property and had attained a relatively high standard of living; they therefore had something to lose by having many children. These were the burghers and smallholder peasants in the more developed regions. Part of them happened to be Protestants, but in those regions almost all Protestants belonged to these social groups. This fact was the cause of the Catholic–Protestant differences in the more developed regions and of the theory that birth control and decline in fertility was a phenomenon associated only with Protestantism.

The exclusive association between birth control and Protestantism was contradicted, however, by the analyses of census and vital statistical data in Hungary from 1880 to 1910 (Demény 1968, Tekse 1969). Three population groups having especially low marital fertility were distinguished in that period in Hungary: the Calvinist Hungarian population in southern Transdanubia (the same that was found by historical demographic studies to have a low fertility already by 1800), the Roman Catholic German population (settlers who immigrated after the liberation of the territory from Turkish rule) in the Banat region (southern part of the Great Plain), and the Greek Orthodox Romanian population in the counties Krassó-Szörény and Hunyad in Transylvania. Demény explained these findings by 'the paramount importance of economic aspirations – specifically the desire to acquire, to hold on to, and to accumulate land under the increasingly adverse combination of growing population pressures, stable or expanding *latifundia*, and limited availability of alternative employment opportunities' (p. 521), and points also to the fact that early decline in fertility tends to be associated with lower infant mortality and higher literacy.

After the First World War a Catholic clergyman, Pezenhoffer, wrote a book on religious fertility differences in prewar Hungary, based on the same census and vital statistical data, and found that in each county of Hungary taken separately the Catholic villages had higher birth rates than the Protestant villages. He concluded that Protestantism in Hungary was strongly associated with birth control, and even with the one child system, while Catholicism was the surest, and even the only antidote to the decline in population growth. Therefore, he stated, 'the logical conclusion from our data is that Protestantism has no justification for existence in Hungary and it is a national interest and requirement that the Hungarian Protestants should be converted to Catholicism' (Pezenhoffer 1922, p. 6). In the context of the sharp struggles between the Catholic and Protestant denominations, this statement raised heated discussions in the interwar period. As the arguments of the discussants throw some light on the causative mechanisms of denominational fertility differences, it is worthwhile following them here.

Before the First World War in Hungary the fertility of the Roman Catholic population was in fact somewhat higher than that of the Protestant denominational groups, and higher also than the fertility of any other denomination (Kenéz 1906, p. 140):

Denomination	Number of births in 1900–01	
	Per 1000 population	Per 1000 women aged 15–49
Roman Catholic	40·2	162·3
Greek Catholic	40·6	170·7
Greek Orthodox	36·9	151·8
Lutheran	35·3	143·8
Calvinist	35·4	145·5
Unitarian	34·1	146·0
Jew	33·6	130·9
Other and unknown	30·7	103·5
Total	38·4	156·2

The denominational differences were even clearer in particular regions of the country, as Pezenhoffer (1922) correctly stated. He failed, however, to make a comparison between Catholic and Protestant populations, or between predominantly Catholic and Protestant villages on the national level. The denominational differences were less pronounced at the national level, as the bulk of the Protestant population lived in the eastern part of the country, mostly in the eastern Great Plain region, which was not only poorer at the beginning of the eighteenth century, but also developed more slowly, as it was further away from the agricultural markets in central and western Europe. Also the decline in fertility began later in the eastern part of Hungary, so that gradually a fertility differential developed between the western and eastern regions of Hungary.

In the interwar period the Catholic–Calvinist fertility difference gradually disappeared. (It should be mentioned that the following data refer to the population of Hungary after the First World War, i.e. to a much smaller population, than the above data from 1900–10). The crude birth rates were (Schneller 1936, p. 10):

	Roman Catholic	Calvinist	Lutheran	Jew
1921–1925	30·5	29·3	27·2	15·4
1926–1930	26·9	26·2	23·1	12·9
1931	24·6	24·0	20·4	11·7
1932	24·1	24·0	20·3	11·3
1933	22·5	22·6	19·3	10·9
1934	22·3	22·7	19·1	10·8

The disappearance of the Catholic–Calvinist fertility difference at the national level was associated with further changes on the regional map of fertility: the fertility of the predominantly Protestant eastern counties of the Great Plain declined less than the fertility of the central and western counties inhabited predominantly by Roman Catholics. Because of the east–west fertility difference within the Protestant population, the poorer Protestants in eastern Hungary slowly became more and more numerous relative to the Protestants living in Transdanubia. In addition, immigration into the newly developing towns in the second half of the nineteenth century affected more the Catholic population of landless peasants, while the smallholder Protestants tended to remain in the villages at their farms, so the decline in fertility connected with urbanization was less important in the Protestant population groups. In consequence of all these factors, Calvinists became relatively less developed, less urbanized and poorer, but retained a relatively higher fertility than the Catholics.

Changes in regional fertility differences and also in denominational differences caused the multiple regression analysis based on the data of the census of 1930 and the fertility data of the same year for the counties and towns of Hungary to show a positive correlation between the percentage of Protestant population and fertility (see p. 187), although it is quite obvious that this positive correlation was caused by an ecological fallacy – i.e. it is not at all certain that in this year the fertility of the Protestant population was really not higher than that of the Roman Catholic population. Nevertheless, it seems to be clear that since the First World War the fertility of the Calvinist population in Hungary has not been significantly lower than that of the Catholic population.

The exceptional character of Catholic–Protestant fertility differences in Hungary might be explained by the rather exceptional character of the composition of Hungarian Protestants, particularly the Calvinists: unlike those in western Europe and North America, in Hungary the Calvinists are less urbanized, more agricultural and rather more traditional in outlook. (Lutherans, on the other hand, were the second most educated and urbanized group after the Jews.) Thus it might be stated that the socio-economic and cultural characteristics of denominational groups have a strong influence on their fertility differences.

In the same way as the composition of denominational groups by socio-economic characteristics might cause their fertility differences, it might be supposed that the different ethnic background of denominational groups might be associated with their fertility levels. As is well known, particularly in the United States and Canada, denominational groups are to a large extent linked to different ethnic groups – i.e. population groups who have immigrated from different European countries. In this case it is not easy to distinguish the influence of denomination and ethnicity. In the same way as denominational groups profess different norms and values concerning birth control and the number of children in family, so also in the culture of different European national populations differing norms and values are maintained, and these can survive through several generations in America.

In order to investigate this question, it is necessary to have fertility data detailed by religion and by national background. In the Princeton survey this type of two-way tabulation was elaborated (table 5.57). The percentages having a third pregnancy out of those who had already two children

Table 5.57   Per cent reporting at least one additional pregnancy since the second birth, by religion and national background of the wife: Princeton survey.

Religion	National background						
	Irish	Italian	Slavic	German	British	Scandi-navian	Spanish and Latin American
Active Protestant	50	*	*	50	36	30	*
Other Protestant	41	*	33	66	64	*	*
Active Catholic	78	60	62	73	*	*	*
Other Catholic	68	53	55	49	70	*	65
Jewish	*	*	31	37	*	*	*

* Less than 10 cases.
Source: Westoff, Potter and Sagi (1963), p. 103.

were differentiated both by denomination and extent of religious activity and by national background. Among the active Catholics, the women of Irish origin showed the highest fertility rate, the Italians and those of Slavic (Polish, Czech, Croatian, Slovenian, etc.) origin lower fertilities. A similar tendency can be observed among non-active Catholics. These fertility differences reflect to a certain extent the fertility levels of the corresponding national populations in Europe: the very high marital fertility in Ireland and the lower levels of marital fertility in most Slavic Catholic populations (except Poland), as well as the moderate fertility level in Italy in recent decades. The low level of fertility of Jewish women originating from German and Slavic cultural backgrounds might also be interpreted as a parallel phenomenon of the low fertility of these Jewish population groups in the corresponding European countries, where they were mostly more urbanized and better educated and had a higher living standard than the average. The small number of couples in the sample and the fact that many cells of the table are empty, as well as the peculiar nature of the sample (only couples having had a second birth), do not allow definite conclusions to be drawn from these results. Nevertheless, it seems that fertility levels are differentiated by denomination and ethnicity both jointly and also independently from each other.

A special survey of Polish immigrants and their descendants in the small American town Hamtrack, which was based on the assumption of the famous survey of 'Polish peasants' in the United States and Poland (Thomas and Znaniecki 1927), that immigrant groups retain for a long time their traditional family values and attitudes, proved that this theoretical assumption should not be generalized, as these Polish immigrants rapidly adapted their fertility to that of their surroundings (Mayer and Marx 1957). This was interpreted as due to the fact that these Polish immigrants saw a reference group of native Americans whose standards of living was much higher and whose fertility was lower. That reference group was formed by the workers of the automobile industry in Detroit, where the majority of the male population of Hamtrack had jobs.

In Canada, where child/woman ratios from the census of 1961 can be analysed, the populations with the same denomination but different ethnic background show different fertility levels (Krotki and Lapierre 1968):

Denomination and ethnicity of women	Number of children aged 0–4 per 1000 women aged 15–44
Catholic	
Total	666
British background	753
French background	640
Italian background	654
Polish background	578
Hungarian background	598
Protestant and other non-Catholic	
Total	553
British background	535
French background	616
Italian background	682
Polish background	526

Thus the fact that the majority of Canadian Catholics are of French and Irish (British) origin contributes strongly to their higher fertility, as compared with the Protestants who are mostly of English origin, whose fertility is lower than that of the Catholic populations.

The mechanism through which the alleged influence of denomination on fertility is exerted has hitherto not been much investigated, except for the survey of Westoff and Potvin (1967) on the values and attitudes concerning fertility of women attending college, described in Chapter 4.4 (see pp. 201–3). On the basis of their findings, they formulated a theoretical explanation of the mechanism through which fertility of college women is influenced in America by the denomination, or, more precisely the cultural environment to which they belong. The desired number of children is an ideal, probably unconsciously formulated during late childhood and early adolescence – i.e. in the years of elementary and early secondary schooling. The number of children in the family in which the given persons have grown up is especially important. In addition to the number of siblings, the number of children in the families of friends and neighbours, and generally in the families of reference groups, all influence the desired fertility. Family size is a norm to which the individual is socialized, in the same way as to other norms of behaviour, values and styles of life.

Denomination, ethnic and social stratum backgrounds are all elements of this cultural environment, through which ideas and desires concerning fertility are formed. The influences of some religious and ethnic sub-cultures is relatively strong, while that of others is weaker. For example, the Irish Catholic middle class subculture and the Mormon subculture, having very clear cut values on family size, have very strong influence on the desired size of family. Members of subcultures that do not contain strict norms on family size more or less accept the two to four children family ideal and react within these limits fairly flexibly to the changes of economic conditions.

The strength of norms on family size is influenced by the extent of the continuity and consistency of the reference groups of a person in adolescence and adulthood. Norms learned by socialization in childhood and adolescence prevail most strongly in those families living later (in college and after having finished education) in a social environment with similar norms and values. Naturally, the subculture from which the spouse originated also influences the desired number of children of the individual. It should be emphasized, however, that the reference groups (schools, friends, spouses, neighbourhoods) are generally selected by the individual, and by his parents, in such a way that they correspond as much as possible to the subculture in which they were socialized. Catholic families with strong religious interest, therefore, tend to choose Catholic primary and secondary schools and colleges for their children, tend to have Catholic friends, etc. The influence of all these reference groups strengthens the primary influence of the family on the norms concerning the number of children.

The norms and values concerning fertility in a given subculture are thus similar to the norms concerning moral behaviour or life style. While, however, moral norms change relatively slowly and life styles change quickly, like fashions, fertility norms and values are in a somewhat intermediate position, changing more slowly than fashions, but being less stable than ethnic norms. Thus basic economic and social conditions are slowly influencing (and with fairly long lags) the norms on fertility.

Studies on the influence of denomination on fertility have in many cases pointed out the influence of ethnicity parallel with that of denomination, and also the similarity of the influence of these two factors, both being elements of a cultural environment containing some norms and values concerning fertility. Therefore it seems reasonable to study in this chapter the influence of ethnicity, which has been thoroughly investigated in a few countries where the racial, ethnic and national background characteristics of the population are heterogeneous.

Differences of fertility in the United States by national background – (distinguishing foreign-born and second-generation immigrant families) were demonstrated by census data described in Chapter 4.2 (see pp. 158–62). Similar differences by ethnicity, but strongly overlapped by denominational differences, were found in Canada. Here the marital fertility of the population of French ethnic origin was higher than that of Irish ethnic origin, and the fertility of the Irish population group was higher than that of the population of British background (excluding Irish population) (table 5.58). However, the differences, similar to the denominational differences in Canada, are declining, as the French population does not seem to have experienced the baby boom, while the population of British background clearly had a baby boom. Most interestingly, the Irish population of mainly Catholic religion also experienced a baby boom, similar to the British one. In this case, the evolution of the fertility of the Catholic Irish population seems to have followed the pattern characteristic of ethnic differences (non-French groups experiencing a baby boom) and not that characteristic

Table 5.58   Number of children ever born per 1000 women ever married, by age and ethnicity of women: Canada, 1961.

| | Ethnicity of women | | |
Age of women	French	British (excluding Ireland)	Irish
65+	6242	3130	3391
60–64	5483	2817	3034
55–59	4979	2626	2732
50–54	4524	2519	2704
45–49	4278	2624	2823
40–44	4296	2826	3043
35–39	3892	2847	3052
30–34	3190	2675	2805
25–29	2371	2159	2256
20–24	1371	1347	1438

Source: Long (1970), p. 143.

of religion (Catholics not experiencing baby boom). It should be added that the analysis of total fertility might provide a different picture than that of marital fertility, because of the later marriage and higher percentage of celibates in the Catholic population, particularly in Quebec where the French Catholic population is concentrated (Krotki and Lapierre 1968).

The United States, and also Canada to a certain extent, are multiracial societies, and demographers have therefore investigated the influence of race on fertility. As, in the opinion of the author of this book, racial differences are essentially similar to ethnic differences (i.e. they are rooted in the culture of the different racial and ethnic groups), these racial differences are also treated in this chapter.

The fertility of the black population, the largest racial minority in the United States, has been much higher than that of the white population for at least a century, although the black–white differential was not identical in all parts of the United States. The fertility of the black population was higher in the South, although perhaps lower than that of the white population in the North (Okun 1958). The black population also experienced a baby boom after the Second World War, similar to that of the white population. As a result of these parallel booms, black–white fertility differentials did not diminish.

Several authors, however (e.g. Petersen 1969), considered that the higher fertility of the black population is simply the consequence of their socioeconomic characteristics, so that if the characteristics of the black and white populations were equalized, the fertility differences would disappear. Most of the blacks belong the poorest, least educated groups of the population, having the lowest status in the social hierarchy. These social groups (both black and white couples) are characterized by high fertility, but because of the fact that a much larger number of blacks belong to them than whites, the fertility of the black population is consequently higher than that of the white population. The results of the first National Fertility Study (Ryder and Westoff 1971) in fact showed that, although the most likely expected number of children of black couples was higher in all except the three highest income groups (see table 5.17, p. 246) and in all but the highest (4 years college and more) education category (see table 5.26, p. 261), the desired number of children was lower in the case of black women in all except the lowest income and education groups. Thus, although blacks are more numerous in the lower income and education categories, desiring somewhat more children in the case of both races, the average number of desired children is almost equal for both races (that of blacks slightly lower). Therefore Westoff (1975) considered that the excess fertility of black women over white is caused by a higher number of unwanted births, and he predicted a convergence of black and white marital fertility.

As, however, several other surveys have similarly indicated a lower ideal family size of blacks than of whites, Goldscheider formulated a new hypothesis on black fertility, the so-called minority group status hypothesis, according to which not only would black fertility be identical to that of the white population if their socioeconomic characteristics were identical, but in addition factors independent of social and economic characteristics tend to depress the fertility behaviour and attitudes of selected segments of the black population below white fertility levels (Goldscheider and Uhlenberg 1969, Goldscheider 1971). According to this hypothesis, 'membership in, and identification with, a minority group that does not have a normative system encouraging large families, and does not prohibit or discourage efficient contraception methods, depresses fertility below majority levels' (Goldscheider 1971, p. 294). This depressing impact of minority status is interpreted by Goldscheider as a consequence of the insecurities produced by the desire of a minority to acculturate itself to the majority and its permanent structural separation, in consequence of which advancing upwards in society entails more hardships for the minority group than for the majority; thus minorities may tend to compensate for some of their disadvantages by limiting the number of their children. This implies that the depressing minority status effect appears only if the minority (1) wants to acculturate and (2) wants to achieve a higher social status, and (3) does not consider that this can be achieved without acculturation, by strengthening the position of the minority in the given society. These conditions characterize, according to Goldscheider, the situation of blacks, Jews and Japanese in the United States, but do not characterize the situation of Catholics, who on the one hand define themselves as members of an important minority, and on the other hand have a normative system that stimulates them to have large families and not to use efficient methods of birth control. Thus Goldscheider developed from the above fertility differentials a theory of the fertility differentials of minorities.

The minority group status hypothesis has been reanalysed on the basis of American data by several authors. By using data of the number of ever born children of ever married women aged 35–44 detailed by region, education, occupation of husband, and income in 1960, Sly (1970) found that all these factors influence the black–white fertility differentials, and that these differentials are not of the same sign in the four regions. In the South of the United States blacks tended to have a higher number of children, even after having controlled the above socioeconomic variables, while in the North and the North Central regions blacks tended to have (at identical education, occupation and income levels) lower fertilities. The West was in this respect in an intermediate position, as the fertility differences (after having controlled the other variables) were not consistent in sign. Sly concluded from these results that the depressing impact of minority group status does not apply in all circumstances, but only in those areas (regions) where the minority has been institutionally assimilated, i.e. where it does not constitute a separate unit in the social structure.

By using the data from the 1960 census, Roberts and Lee (1974) investigated the fertility differences of black women, women with Spanish surnames and other whites in five southwestern states of America and found higher than average fertilities for both black and Spanish surnamed women. They stated by analyses of variance that these fertility differentials can be explained only to a very limited extent by socioeconomic status and residence (urban or rural) of the investigated couples, so that minority group status seems to have a positive effect on fertility in these regions. Thus the validity of the hypothesis on the depressing impact of minority group status on fertility does not seem to be clarified definitively. The introduction of the distinct notions of structural factors of fertility (occupation, income, education, residence) on the one hand and of cultural factors (norms, values, beliefs, life styles) on the other hand is a significant enrichment to the explanation of denominational, ethnic and other similar fertility differences.

Ethnic fertility differences have been very thoroughly investigated by Soviet demographers, as the Soviet Union, being a country of many nationalities and ethnic groups, provides an excellent field in which to study the influence of the ethnic factor on fertility (Siffman 1971, Belova 1971, Bondarskaya 1970 1971, Bondarskaya and Kozlov 1971, Zeinalov 1968, Arutyunyan 1968, Pirtshalava 1968, Kozlov 1968).

Very significant fertility differentials by the different regions, soviet socialist republics and autonomous republics were demonstrated by both census, vital statistical (pp. 170–1) and fertility survey data (pp. 222–3). As mentioned, the opinions of Soviet demographers differ on the basic cause of these differences, whether it is primarily the different levels of economic and socil development, as well as education, in these territories, or their different ethnic compositions. Mazur (1973) raised the possibility that denominational factors might also have an influence, the fertility of populations with Muslim and Buddhist background having the highest, the populations of Eastern Orthodox background the intermediate and the Baltic groups with Protestant and Catholic background the lowest fertility levels. However, this explanation does not seem to hold in this simple form, as in recent years the fertility level of the three Baltic republics and the other western parts of the Soviet Union seems to have equalized, while the Armenian SSR, with a similar denominational background, maintains a somewhat higher fertility level.

The basic problem is whether the fertility differences observed between the territories are similarly observable between national groups in the

Soviet Union and in the same territories. Bondarskaya (1971) calculated child–woman ratios (number of children aged 0–9 per 1000 women aged 20–49) for ethnic groups at the time of two Soviet censuses:

SSR	1926	1959
Russian SFSR	1223	863
Ukrainian	1354	714
Belorussian	1486	836
Uzbek	1134	1878
Kazakh	1260	1896
Georgian	1483	905
Lithuanian	915	823
Moldavian	1379	1190
Latvian	—	612
Kirgiz	1133	1886
Tadzhik	1257	1782
Armenian	1575	1240
Turkmen	1384	1810
Estonian	—	638

Although the child–woman ratios in 1926 might be strongly influenced by infant and child mortality, it is a conspicuous fact that the fertility of the Slavic ethnic groups strongly declined after 1926, while the fertility of the Asian ethnic groups seems to have risen.

Urlanis (1974) published birth rates of areas inhabited by different ethnic groups in the European part of the Soviet Union in 1927:

Kalmyk Autonomous SSR	31·3
Bashkir ASSR	39·7
Ukrainian SSR	41·3
Karelian ASSR	42·6
Belorussian SSR	43·3
Chuvash ASSR	44·3
Russian SFSR	45·4
Komi ASSR	47·2
Mordvin	48·3
Tatar ASSR	53·1
Mary	53·5
Udmurt ASSR	56·2
Azerbaijan SSR	58·0
Armenian SSR	59·3

Similar birth rates for the whole Soviet Union in the 1960s, as Urlanis stressed, were much more varied than in 1927:

SSR	Average birth rate 1959–1969
Estonian	12·3
Latvian	12·3
Ukrainian	15·8
Russian SFSR	19·0
Belorussian	19·2
Lithuanian	20·6
Armenian	20·8
Georgian	24·0
Moldavian	24·8
Kazakh	41·2
Azerbaijan	43·7
Kirgiz	44·0
Turkmen	45·6
Uzbek	45·2
Tadzhik	45·2

Urlanis also brings examples of fertility differences between populations of different ethnic backgrounds living in the same region of the Soviet Union. For example, in the Chuvash Autonomous Soviet Republic the age-specific fertility rates of Russian and Chuvash women in 1958–9 were:

Age of women	Russian	Chuvash
15–19	24·2	8·4
20–24	162·6	137·4
25–29	159·7	230·8
30–34	91·8	188·6
35–39	51·3	136·8
40–44	16·9	53·6
45–49	2·4	7·0

The lower age-specific fertility of Chuvash women in the two youngest age groups might be explained by their later marriage, but their overall fertility is much higher than that of Russians.

In the Asian republics of the Soviet Union the fertility level of the native population is generally much higher than the average fertility of the population (containing a large number of immigrants from the European parts of the Soviet Union). For example, in Kazakhstan some age-specific fertility rates in 1968 were:

Age of women	Total population	Kazakh population
20–24	188·6	337·6
25–29	182·3	332·8
30–34	133·7	320·1

Urlanis also provides data to prove that, even if the level of education of women is kept constant, differences in fertility by ethnic background are maintained. For example, in Baku in 1967 the average number of children ever borne by women was:

Education of women	Azerbaijani women	Russian women
University level and unfinished university level	1·46	1·32
Secondary (general and specialized)	2·51	1·47
Unfinished secondary	3·20	1·64
Primary	3·39	1·69
Without full primary	3·02	1·99

Thus, according to Urlanis, a very strong ethnic factor is influencing the fertility of women in the Soviet Union.

These studies in the Soviet Union seem to demonstrate the existence of an ethnic factor, similar to but much stronger than the denominational and ethnic factor found in the United States, Canada and some west European countries. It seems reasonable to conclude, following the thesis of Lenski on the influence of the religious factor (1961), that the culture of a population group (i.e. denominational, ethnic or any other group having a distinct subculture within a nation) has a clear influence on fertility. The special characteristics of this culture influence the development of personality in the decisive years of socialization in childhood, and therefore their influence remains more or less prevalent in adult life, even if the actual economic and social conditions of the given family change and induce other fertility goals. However, it is clear that these cultural norms and values are changing, sometimes quickly, as in the case of Catholics in the United States since the second half of the 1960s.

The basic question remains of how these norms and values concerning fertility are formed and under what kind of influences do they change. It might be supposed that the culture of a population group, being a response by this group to the challenges coming from its economic, social and political environment, is developed and changed under the influence of economic, social and political conditions. However, this is only slightly more than a truism, as it is clear that no one factor of fertility has a direct influence on the decisions of the couples, but that all of them (i.e. income, socioeconomic status, education, etc.) exert their influence through conditioning norms, values and attitudes concerning fertility. Therefore any study of the social factors of fertility ought to include investigation of the formation and change of these social norms, values and attitudes – i.e. the social psychological processes of a given culture.

5.10 Psychological factors

Some years ago Stycos stated that 'until the past few years scientific research on motivational aspects of demographic problems has been virtually non-existent. In a science dealing with three of the most basic human events and processes – births, death, and migration – psychological, social and cultural factors have been all but ignored as objects of scientific inquiry' (Stycos 1963).

Recently, however, population psychology, an interdisciplinary research area linking the traditional topics of demography with the approaches of personal and social psychology (Fawcett 1973 1974), has been developed. Unfortunately, its results are still hypothetical and contradictory, so that we must wait for some years before we know more about the psychological factors influencing fertility.

These factors might be conceptualized to act on three different levels:

1   On the level of personal psychological characteristics.
2   On the level of interactions in small groups, primarily the family.
3   On the macro social psychological level, forming the beliefs, opinions, values and norms of societies, social groups, communities.

On the level of personal psychology, psychoanalysts and authors in related fields have dealt with the desire to have a child (Benedek 1959, Erikson 1964, Kestenberg 1956a 1956b 1968). Freud himself considered that the desire for a child is derived from the castration complex and is formed in the pre-oedipal phase of development.

Pohlman (1969) described some other psychoanalytical explanations for the desire to have a child, among which were:

1   Having a child fulfils the need of men to show virility.
2   A woman can compete with her mother by having a baby.
3   Husbands may want their wives to suffer with pregnancy, childbirth and child care to atone their own guilt.
4   The child is considered an extension of the ego and may satisfy the desire for immortality.

All these factors allegedly act on the subconscious level. In addition to the almost insurmountable difficulties of measuring them in surveys, it is also questionable how these factors might explain the variations and differences in fertility at the societal level. From the point of view of researches directed to explain these variations and differences, an additional problem of these hypotheses is that they try to explain the desire for a child or children in general, but not the desire to have few or many – one, two, three, four, etc. – children, which would be most interesting for demographic research on fertility, because the level of fertility in a society is very little influenced by the number of those who do not want to have children, but is mostly determined by the proportion of those who want one, two, etc., children.

Two theories that try to explain the size of family by measurable psychological factors on the personal level, whose changes at the societal level might explain fertility changes in advanced societies, utilize the concepts of alienation and modernization, both considered to be characteristics of advanced societies. Hoffman and Wyatt (1960) hypothesized that the increasing alienation and loneliness of men and women in modern mass societies enhance the value of the family and of children, since they might alleviate these feelings by providing companionship and a sense of life. The growth of the role of the nuclear family in providing psychological support to the individual in modern societies where the other primary groups are losing importance was stressed by family sociologists in other contexts (e.g. Schelski 1960). Hoffman and Wyatt pointed to two other developments in modern society that favour larger families. Changes in the status of women can mean that the household no longer provides a meaningful role for them, while employment outside the household might be considered by some of them. In these conditions, having a child (or an additional child when the first, second, etc., child is starting school and needing less maternal care) provides an escape from both the dull housewife role and the problematical working wife role. At the same time, another development in these societies – a growing emphasis on the importance of the parental role – reinforces the desirability of this escape role. Thus, according to this theory, some developments of advanced societies favour a rise in fertility.

The modernization theory, on the other hand, posits that the development of advanced societies in the direction of increased modernization, both at the societal level and at the personal level – i.e. the fact that individuals show more and more modern character traits – leads to a decline in fertility (Fawcett and Bornstein, in Fawcett 1973). Modernization is supposed to be a syndrome of personality traits, among which can be listed the following: readiness for new experience and openness to innovation and change; opinions of others not automatically accepted or rejected on the basis of their status or power; time orientation towards the present and future, rather than the past; acceptance of fixed hours, punctuality; orientation towards planning; a belief that man can dominate his environment to achieve his goals; faith in science and technology. It might be that the spread of these traits in developing societies is parallel with the decline in fertility during demographic transition, but it is questionable whether this modernity syndrome is related to the number of children of individuals in an advanced society.

The achievement motive investigated by McClelland (1961) might be conceptualized as one facet of the modernity syndrome. It was supposed by him to be related to a lower number of children. However, his results failed to confirm this hypothesis.

An opposite syndrome of different psychological traits is the so-called 'culture of poverty'. This concept was elaborated by Oscar Lewis to describe the life style of poor Mexican families (Lewis 1959 1961), but has been applied to poor people in the United States and other advanced countries. This life style includes attitudes of fatalism, apathy, lack of long-range goal orientation, distrust of the official institutions of society, and lack of stability both in employment and in family relations. It is supposed that this life style is also connected with carelessness about family planning and birth control, and consequently, with a high number of children (Chilman, in Fawcett 1973).

The empirical researches performed in advanced societies, particularly in the United States, were not very successful in finding correlations between fertility variables and personality traits.

In the Indianapolis survey size of family tended to be negatively correlated to a feeling of personal inadequacy and fear of pregnancy and positively correlated to an ego-centred interest in children, a desire to insure against childlessness, a general liking for children, and the belief that the only child is handicapped. The correlations, however, were very weak. It was considered by the authors that the 'failure to secure good measures of the psychological characteristics may account for their apparent lack of relation to fertility' (Kiser and Whelpton 1953, pp. 108–19).

The tendency to plan, measured by questions of the type 'Do you plan things in advance or wait until the time comes?' and 'How often have you run out of money between pay checks?', was found to be negatively related to the number of children. Traditionalism, measured by questions of the type 'Should mothers do paid work?', was positively correlated to the size of family. However, as both lack of planning and traditional views are more characteristic for lower strata in America, which also have higher fertility, the relations found might be merely reflections of the influence of social status.

The Princeton survey, planned with even more ambitious research aims concerning psychological factors, did not show any important correlation between fertility and the psychological traits taken into consideration: generalized manifest anxiety, excessive and unsatisfied dependency needs, tolerance of ambiguity, cooperativeness, ability to delay gratification of impulses, need achievement.

The surveys providing most information on the factors of personal psychology influencing the size of family are those of Rainwater (1960 1965). He deplored the fact that family planning research was defined primarily as a field of demographical research, and considered that family sociologists and social psychologists could provide far more interesting insights into the causes of high and low fertility. He used a rather new research technique in this field, the depth interview. His interviews were very long and detailed and contained many unformalized conversational elements. They were concentrated on the practice of contraception, the ability to engage in contraceptive practice, and the desire for children, especially a larger number of children.

In his first survey he conducted ninety-six interviews in two cities of the United States (Rainwater 1960). In the second survey he conducted 409 interviews in three cities (Rainwater 1965). The first survey was concentrated on the working class, and the second also included middle class couples. The results unfortunately cannot be considered as representing the opinions and motivations of couples in the United States.

Rainwater first states that fertility is to a large extent determined by social norms, the most basic norm being that 'one should not have more children than one can support, but one should have as many as one can afford' (Rainwater 1965, pp. 281–2). A couple having fewer children than it can afford is considered selfish, ill or neurotically weak, while one having more than it can afford is considered as having poor judgement and lacking discipline. Thus the alternative is essentially 'selfishness versus responsibility'. According to Rainwater, however, economic considerations play a fairly minor role in determining how many children a couple can afford. He points out instead the psychological motivations influencing the couples.

Following the hypothesis of Hoffman and Wyatt (see p. 334), he states that 'larger families are functional for resolving the housewife's conflict over whether or not, and how to be active in the world outside the home, either through a job or through other kinds of activities' (Rainwater 1965, p. 285). That is, for working class wives who do not desire to engage in an occupation outside the home, the existence of small children provides a justification for remaining dependent. The more so, because in conditions where housekeeping activities become more mechanized and prepackaged, the housewife's role is both becoming more dull and providing less justification for remaining in the household. Rainwater also found that women who were very concerned with their responsibilities as homemakers, tended to have smaller families, and found an absorbing role for themselves in housekeeping activities.

Mothers desiring several children also tended to emphasize the moral virtue inherent in motherhood. Thus, by wanting a large number of children, they were 'reaching out to embrace an identity in which they are loving and creative persons and to deny or overcome tendencies to seek purely self-centred gratifications' (p. 195). Men who wanted large families tended to consider those who wanted small families as 'selfish', and 'simply catering to their own convenience and as selfishly concerned to have more goods and time' (p. 178). Thus a larger family helps to provide these couples with a positively valued self-identity.

Children are also considered to be a major source of affection and variety. As expressed by his respondents, within a larger family 'something new is always happening', and 'there's never a dull moment here'.

As for the hypothesis of Hoffman and Wyatt concerning the role of children, especially a larger family, as a compensation for the alienation and loneliness in modern society outside the home, Rainwater did not find it completely verified. He hypothesized that the relation might be curvilinear, deeply alienated persons not wanting to become responsible for large families, and deeply integrated persons not being very interested in having many children, so that higher fertility would characterize those couples who 'feel threatened by a tendency toward aloneness and alienation, but who are still hopeful about possibilities of avoiding the pain of that state' and 'may seek to do so by creating a meaningful primary group with a larger number of children' (p. 288). This explanation seems very attractive, but it would be very difficult to try to verify it because of the well-known problems encountered in trying to define and measure alienation.

Groat and Neal (1967) conceptualized alienation in terms of four dimensions: meaninglessness of life, powerlessness in controlling political and economic events, normlessness, and social isolation. Although it was hypothesized that all four measures would be positively related to fertility, it was found (on the basis of a small sample of the population of Toledo, USA) that only meaninglessness and normlessness showed the expected relation. This result seems to indicate the need for further clarification of the concept of alienation, before its relation to fertility can be determined.

In spite of these interesting insights, however, one might agree with the conclusion of Clausen and Clausen (in Fawcett 1973) that the studies of personality in relation to fertility have hitherto failed to demonstrate significant differences between the personalities of parents with one or two children and those of parents with three and more children.

Recently, Hoffman and Hoffman (in Fawcett 1973) elaborated a scheme for the values the children might provide for their parents. In addition to the economic utility of children (as income earners, household helpers, economic helpers in old age, etc.), the following eight psychological benefits of children were distinguished:

1   The birth of a child assures the adult status and adult social identity of the parents. This status and identity may need reconfirmation by subsequent births.
2   Children may give feelings of expansion of self for the parents, of immortality, of a tie to a larger society or community. The strength of this feeling is well documented by the fact that 75 per cent of the respondents of the Indianapolis survey answered affirmatively when asked 'Is one of your greatest satisfactions in being a parent knowing that after you are gone some part of you will live on in your children?'
3   Children help to develop the feeling in the parents that they are moral, altruistic, following the commands of their religion, doing good for their social group; women having children are tended to be viewed as 'good women', more faithful to their husbands.
4   The birth of children strengthens the nuclear family, the one important primary group in advanced societies that has permanence and therefore serves as a bulwark against impersonalization and loneliness. Children especially are apt to fulfil the needs for affection of parents, particularly perhaps of women.
5   Children are a source of constant stimulation, novelty and fun for parents.
6   Rearing of children provides an outlet for creativity, achievement and accomplishment. Needs for such activities are probably emerging more and more strongly in advanced societies, as basic subsistence needs are satisfied for most families within society.
7   The birth of a child enhances the power of the parent in the kinship group, enhances the position of the mother vis-à-vis the husband, and even vis-à-vis her own parents. At the same time, the children afford both parents opportunities for another form of power – namely, to guide, teach, control and influence them.
8   Children may enhance the prestige of parents in the larger primary groups to which they belong.

Obviously, it would be most interesting to obtain information on the relative strengths of each of these motivations and values in advanced societies and also within particular social strata and other population groups in advanced societies. The East–West Population Institute in Hawaii recently engaged in such a survey in several countries, the only advanced country among them being the United States, more precisely Hawaii (Fawcett and Arnold 1973, Arnold *et al.* 1975).

The major code categories were fairly similar to but not identical with the values defined by Hoffman and Hoffman. The advantages of children were coded as:

1   Happiness, love and companionship provided by the existence of children.
2   Personal development of the parents.
3   Child-rearing satisfactions.
4   Economic benefits and security.
5   Benefits for the nuclear family unit.
6   Benefits for the larger kin group.
7   Social and religious values.
8   Intrinsic value of having children.

Disadvantages were also investigated and coded according to the following categories:

1   Financial costs.
2   Emotional costs.
3   Restrictions on alternative activities (career, recreation, etc.).
4   Problems caused in marriage.
5   Costs for the kin group.
6   Societal costs, overpopulation.

The results (Arnold *et al.* 1975) point to the dominant position of the emotional-psychological values of children, particularly in the urban middle classes of Hawaii and the other investigated Asian countries. It would be most interesting to know the relative weights of these advantages and disadvantages in advanced societies.

On the level of interactions within the family, between spouses, the influence of marital adjustment was investigated thoroughly. In the Indianapolis survey marital adjustment showed a strong and interesting relation both to family planning and to the size of family (Reed, in Whelpton and Kiser 1950, pp. 259–301). The hypothesis that the more satisfactory the marital adjustment, the higher the proportion practising contraception efficiently, and the larger the planned families of the efficient planners, was confirmed. However, taking all couples together, larger family size was associated with less marital adjustment. That, however, might have been the effect of social status, since those of higher social status had smaller families and at the same time tended to have fewer problems with marital adjustment, or were at least less liable to talk about them to the interviewer.

The Princeton survey (Westoff *et al.* 1961, Westoff, Potter and Sagi 1963) and several other studies (e.g. Farber and Blackman 1956) later investigated the same relationship, but the results were inconclusive. As Pohlman (1969, p. 98) stated when reviewing these studies.

It seems clear that there is no single correlation between children and marriage happiness. A happier marriage may lead some people to be more willing to have children; a marriage threatening break-up may lead others to want and have children. Children may promote marital happiness in some cases; and children, especially unwanted children, may hurt marital happiness in others.

Clearly, the cause-and-effect may go in both directions: children causing marital happiness or unhappiness – or, alternatively, a happy marriage may lead to either many or few children.

Another feature of marital interaction investigated was the pattern of dominance – namely, the size of family of husband-dominated and wife-dominated, as well as of egalitarian-democratic couples. The results of different studies, however, are contradictory. In the Princeton survey only a very weak negative correlation was found between the extent of the husband's dominance and the number of children desired, egalitarian and wife-dominated families favouring a slightly larger family on the average (Westoff et al, 1961), but at the second interview the percentage of third pregnancies did not show any association with the dominance pattern. Similarly, an analysis of 731 Detroit households by Blood and Wolfe (1960) indicated no such associations.

Role segregation, a phenomenon strongly associated with dominance versus egalitarian family pattern, was found to be positively associated to fertility by Rainwater (1965). His findings suggest that in couples where the male and female roles are strictly segregated and women feel that they cannot participate extensively in the lives of their husbands (a feature much more frequently found in lower strata than in the middle strata) there is a tendency to want more children, as they can provide a role for the wife and might also compensate for the lack of interest and affection from the husband. Rainwater's data suggest that for the husband the relationship is of the same direction, but not statistically significant.

Reanalysing the Indianapolis survey data, Goldberg (1960) formulated a much more complicated theory of the influence of role segregation and fertility. He found that different motivations are influencing husbands and wives, as with higher income and status husbands tend to desire more children, considering that they can afford it, while wives desire fewer children at higher status (and education) levels, because their interest in activities outside the home has increased. In lower class families, especially in farm families, roles are strongly segregated; the care for children being the wife's role, her desires concerning fertility prevail, so there is a strong negative relation of fertility to her education. In higher status urban families, however, roles are not so segregated, the desires of the husband begin to prevail, and so the relation of fertility to the status of the couple tends to be positive. This is certainly a possible explanation for the U-shaped curve of the relation of fertility to status, education and income.

Thus, as is the case with the influence of personality characteristics, the impact of the psychological traits of the wife-husband relationship is not well known at present.

However, we know even less of socio-psychological processes, in which the beliefs, opinions, values and norms of societies are formed and changed. Two case studies reveal how these changed in given circumstances: in Victorian England and in Vienna after the First World War.

The spread of family planning and the decline of fertility in Victorian England was investigated by Banks and Banks (Banks 1954, Banks and Banks 1954–5 1964).

As described in Chapter 4.1, fertility levels remained fairly high in England until the 1870s. The earliest signs of a decline in fertility occurred in the occupational groups of military and naval officers, clergymen, lawyers, doctors, authors, journalists and architects, and somewhat later fertility began to decline in the groups of civil service officials, clerks, dentists, schoolmasters, teachers, professors and lecturers, accountants and people employed in scientific pursuits. Thus it was essentially a middle class phenomenon.

Banks and Banks explain this change of attitude in the following way. Between 1850 and 1870 the situation of the English middle class was relatively prosperous. Although newly married couples expected to begin their married life at their parents' level, as an article in *The Times* stated, and although the normative standards of life in the middle class were widening so that the costs necessary to maintain a living standard considered adequate in this class rose rapidly because of the ostentatious display with which middle class families tried to imitate the gentry, the economic prosperity of the times was so great and the rise of income level in the middle class was so rapid that on the average the members of this class, as well as those who strove to enter it, were able to achieve these goals. This economic prosperity resulted in excessive optimism; it was considered that Victorian progress and prosperity were limitless, and that conditions would continue to expand. Although some unsuccessful people were deeply frustrated, the majority were successful in attaining an ever increasing standard of living, and were able to buy more expensive foods and wines, to hire servants, keep carriages, entertain friends, travel, etc. In these circumstances a larger number of children did not cause too much strain on the family.

However, in the 1870s the situation changed. In 1873 a great depression occurred, which was followed by the lean years of the 1870s and 1880s. The income of the middle class did not diminish in real terms, as the decrease in nominal income was compensated for by the fall in prices, but opportunities narrowed and the rapid growth of income was stopped. At the same time, the aspirations of middle class families did not cease to grow, so the actual feeling of these families was one of a worsening of their economic situation. Their sense of security had also been very badly shaken and their previous optimism faded. In these circumstances, the burden of a larger family was felt more intensely than in the previously prosperous years. Outlays deemed necessary for the children's future could hardly be curtailed, so it was necessary to limit the number of children. It was not considered wrong to prevent them from coming if their future living standard seemed to be less bright than that of their parents, and more siblings was certainly equivalent to a lower standard of living for them.

Economic conditions were thus such as might induce parents to control their fertility severely. According to Banks and Banks, the acceptance of the idea of birth control and family planning was prompted by the trial of Charles Bradlaugh and Annie Besant in 1877, which received huge publicity. They were put on trial because they republished a pamphlet of Charles Knowlton, written several decades earlier, which dealt with birth control. As the pamphlet was sold in the bookshops freely for about forty years, it is rather surprising that the authorities decided to bring a trial for its republication. The reason for the decision might have been the illustrations in the pamphlet. Bradlaugh and Besant actually took the opportunity to propagate their ideas at the trial, and the press reporting on the trial unwillingly gave extensive publicity to their ideas. In consequence, thousands of families who had been unaffected by earlier propaganda became aware of the possibility and even the acceptability of birth control, as they were made familiar with the Bradlaugh and Besant arguments for birth control. Middle class families, burdened by the depression, were provided with a reason for adopting birth control and limiting the number of their children, and they were even convinced that by doing so they would serve the public interest and behave in an up-to-date way. This feeling was strengthened when Bradlaugh and Besant were acquitted by the appeal court. After the trial the Malthusian League was formed and a monthly journal, *The Malthusian*, was published. Thus the publicity connected with the trial acted as an accelerator for the twin processes of the spread of birth control and the decline of fertility, which had already begun and for which the public was already prepared by the economic depression. These processes were further strengthened by the feminist movement in the 1890s, when members of it began to cry against the 'madness of large families'. Birth control, however, as Banks and Banks stated, was primarily not a women's revolt, but a parents' revolt. Thus the influence of the Bradlaugh–Besant trial was more decisive and certainly came earlier. Fertility would have declined without it, but the trial accelerated the process.

The other case study deals with the very low fertility of the city of Vienna in the period between the two World Wars and the first postwar decade

(Jolles 1957). The fertility level of the population of Vienna dropped to a remarkably low level, as the crude birth rates show:

1880s	34·0–39·7
1890s	32·1–34·3
1900s	23·4–31·7
1910s	9·7–22·1
1920s	8·7–15·2
1930–1938	5·4–7·4

In the same period the birth rate in Budapest, a neighbouring capital of similar size, was much higher (12·8–16·4 in the 1930s). In the War years the birth rate rose to a higher level, then dropped again in the first half of the 1950s to a level of 6·7–8·0. It should be added that, in the 1960s, the birth rate was higher, around 11–13 per 1000. The population of Vienna slowly declined from 2·3 million in 1910 to 2·1 million in 1934 and 1·8 million in 1951.

Jolles analysed the press of Vienna from 1912 to 1950, as well as other documents, and conducted 2500 interviews with families as well as ten detailed case studies. The main conclusions of his investigations are that this low level of fertility cannot be completely explained by economic factors, housing shortage, urbanization, emancipation of women, or religion, so therefore the explanation should be sought in the social psychological atmosphere which developed under the impact of all these and other factors.

He also stated that the reasons for couples having only two or three children instead of more are very different from the reasons for couples having only one child or no children. The latter type of families were very numerous in Vienna and Jolles tried to find out first of all the causes inducing families to have no children or only one child.

Economic factors certainly had a role. Before the First World War Vienna was the centre of a large empire, and as such served the function of administering a large area in central Europe. After the War, however, this function was lost and in consequence the large administration apparatus became partly unemployed. It is characteristic that in 1926 (i.e. in a year when the business cycle in other parts of Europe was in the phase of prosperity) the unemployment rate was 12 per cent in Vienna. In consequence, real social security diminished, although social insurance systems were fairly well developed. The population was afraid of the future, and it was felt that at best a minimum level of acceptable social existence could be attained, and thus every unforeseen event might upset the delicate balance between needs and resources.

Instead of long-term perspectives, an orientation towards actuality and actual consumption developed. Investments bringing long-term benefits were generally neglected and instead consumption and the purchase of consumer durables filled the focus of interest. This tendency was enhanced by the fact that Vienna was historically a centre of consumption rather than a centre of production. The consumption-oriented way of life might be interpreted, according to Jolles, as a manifestation of escape from hard economic realities, which on the one hand do not provide a perspective and on the other hand require everyday initiative and responsibility.

To bear and educate children means a certain confidence in the continuity of life and in the security of future conditions. Therefore such a climate of economic uncertainty and consumption orientation tends to depress fertility.

The types of social mobility prevalent in Vienna were all associated with low fertility. Jolles distinguishes the following types:

1   Upward social mobility:
   1.1   Unsuccessful, associated with low fertility – e.g. artisans unable to expand their business or to become higher level non-manuals.
   1.2   Successful, perhaps associated with a moderately high fertility level.
   1.3   Unexpected, in consequence of outside forces – e.g. the general improvement of the situation, workers having no special influence on fertility.
2   Change of status at similar level:
   2.1   Successful, maybe associated with relatively high fertility.
   2.2   Unsuccessful, associated with low fertility.
3   Immobility:
   3.1   Rigid clinging to the level attained, leading to very low fertility, particularly in bad and uncertain periods.
   3.2   No change, with no ambitions – e.g. workers remaining in the same class, associated with high fertility.
4   Downward mobility:
   4.1   For impersonal reasons – e.g. unemployment, loss of job because of political changes, leading to very low fertility.
   4.2   For personal reasons – e.g. unsuccessful business management of artisans, leading to very low fertility.

This typology, although Jolles did not completely prove its validity by data in Vienna, is especially interesting because it takes into consideration not only the fact of mobility, but also its psychological correlates – the motivations and interpretations given by the particular persons experiencing the mobility.

Jolles proves that all immigrant population groups in Vienna, which were fairly numerous and came from different parts of the former Austro-

Hungarian empire, adapted themselves to the low fertility of Vienna, although their areas of origin were characterized by much higher fertility. Here, too, Jolles gives a socio-psychological explanation by stating that most of these immigrants were by ethnic background Germans, and actually fled from the countries which became independent after the First World War. They experienced a certain 'atmosphere of cultural and social defeat' (p. 279). Non-German immigrants rapidly accepted the fertility behaviour of the Germans in Vienna. That they did not want to maintain their nationality was manifested by the fact of their emigration from their native countries which had become independent.

The lack of a feeling of patriotism towards the countries of origin of the immigrants, however, was not replaced by a similar feeling towards Austria. As Jolles pointed out, in the Habsburg empire there was a Bohemian, Croatian, Rumanian, Slovakian and Hungarian patriotism, but nobody, especially in Vienna, felt patriotic toward Austria. Those who were attached to the Habsburg empire were not Austrian patriots, but partisans of a supranational community. Also the sharp opposition between Catholics and socialists impeded the development of a feeling of Austrian patriotism. Jolles considers that the feeling of attachment and belonging to institutions representing the continuity of human social groups (as e.g. nation, church, the extended family, and kinship) tends to favour a higher fertility, while the lack of that kind of attachment results in low fertility.

The Catholic church had no consistent influence in the direction of a higher fertility. It is characteristic that the Lutheran families interviewed by Jolles had a higher fertility than the Catholic ones, the families without religion having the lowest, and readers of socialist newspapers had a somewhat higher fertility than readers of Catholic newspapers. This last difference might be caused, Jolles stated, by underlying social differences in fertility, non-manuals having lower fertility than workers.

While the Catholic party in principle disapproved of birth control as something materialistic, but did not do anything in practice to induce a higher fertility, the Socialist Party was strongly in favour of birth control and small families in the period before the Second World War. It formulated the slogan of 'No children for the rich!', and also strongly supported the emancipation of women and considered that large families impeded the realization of this goal. After the Second World War the standpoint of the Socialist Party was modified to a certain extent, and it began to emphasize that maternity should be recognized as a social performance, which deserved to be assisted.

The Nazi Party and the government of Nazi Germany which occupied Austria in 1938 urged the population to have a higher number of children. However, the racist and antisemitic overtones of the Nazi propaganda for higher fertility harmed the increase of fertility in the longer term, since it discredited every moderately populationist idea.

Thus Jolles seems to have proved, by the case of Vienna, that social psychological factors that develop in consequence of economic, social and political developments have a strong influence on fertility.

Thus both case studies of the social psychological factors of fertility seem to demonstrate that these social psychological factors are developed on the basis of economic and social conditions. There might be, however, a lag between the change in economic conditions and the appropriate change in values, norms and attitudes concerning fertility; and the means influencing public opinion might have an important impact by modifying the lag between economic and socio-psychological phenomena.

5.11 Population policy

Population policy in the wide sense of the concept includes measures intended to influence fertility, mortality, marriage and divorce, as well as migration. Here, however, we deal only with measures whose aim is to influence fertility. In principle, this intended influence might be positive or negative – i.e. aiming either at an increase in fertility, or at a decline. Recently in some developed countries demographers and politicians have expressed fears because of the moderately high rate of population growth, and have considered that it might be necessary to introduce measures to encourage a diminution in fertility. Up to now, however, such measures have not been implemented. Therefore, when we speak of population policy we mean measures introduced in order to increase fertility. Such measures have been initiated by countries in which fertility dropped below the level necessary for long-term simple reproduction, the net reproduction coefficient being considered a crude, but to some extent usable indicator of the level of reproduction. That is, when the net reproduction coefficient falls below 1·0, it has generally been considered in developed societies that something should be done to induce an increase in fertility.

Population policy measures introduced in different periods by developed countries have not been at all similar. The following typology of population policies might be useful in the analysis of the effects of population policy:

1 By the principal goal of the measures we might distinguish:
   (a) Policy measures whose principal aim was to increase the level of fertility.
   (b) Policy measures whose principal aim was to alleviate the inequalities of *per capita* income of families caused by the smaller or larger number of children.
2 By the *means* used by population policy we might distinguish:
   (a) Measures using coercion, primarily the prohibition and prosecution of induced abortions, and sometimes also a prohibition on the sale of contraceptives.
   (b) Measures using no coercion, but incentives, primarily different social benefits given to families with children. These measures might also be differentiated by their monetary or 'in kind' character, the monetary benefits being given in cash to families who may

use them as they like, while the benefits 'in kind' are provided directly to the children (e.g. free meals in schools, cheap milk, etc.).

Naturally, in practice most concrete population policies do not belong to these 'pure' types, but utilize a mixture of such measures. The impact of population policy depends very much on the type of it, as the following case analyses of national population policies will probably show. When in the interwar period fertility fell to a very low level in some west European countries, different measures were introduced.

The decline was very rapid and deep in Germany, where the gross reproduction rate in the 1880s was still 2·459, but reached 0·862 in 1931 and 0·800 in 1933 (Glass 1967). After the Nazi party came to power, different measures were introduced with the aim of increasing fertility: induced abortions were criminally prosecuted (criminal laws were not changed, but the already existing laws were implemented more severely) and propaganda for birth control was forbidden; a tax on unmarried men and women was introduced; a marriage loan was given to politically 'right minded' young couples, the repayable sum of the loan being diminished at the birth of each child by 25 per cent; families with four and more children were given a grant if they were found to need it; family allowances were paid by the state to families having five or more children under 16 years of age, later also for families with three or more children, the sum of these allowances being fairly low, as they reached only 12 per cent of the annual income in the case of an average family with seven children.

Thus the benefits in cash given to families with children were not very great. Therefore the population policy of Nazi Germany might be characterized by the prevalence of coercive measures and by the emphasis laid on natalist goals.

The immediate impact of these measures seemed to be great, as the crude birth rate rose from 14·7 in 1933 to 18·0 in 1934 and to 19·7 in 1938. However, it is not possible to distinguish the influence of the population policy from that of the decrease in unemployment. Burgdörfer (1937) considered that the rise in fertility was to an important (although non-measurable) extent due to the 'psychological' effect of population policy, but he pointed out that the actual level of fertility still remained in 1936 11 per cent below that necessary for the 'maintenance of the stock of population'. In the years of the War fertility declined again, due to the absence of men in the army and to the hardships of the war. Thus it might not be an exaggeration to state that this population policy produced only short-lived results.

The population policy of Fascist Italy was laid down on similar lines to the German policy: induced abortions were prosecuted, propaganda for birth control was forbidden; a tax on unmarried men and women was introduced; but the benefits in cash given to the families were even less than in Germany. These measures failed to produce even a temporary increase in fertility.

Also in the 1930s, Sweden introduced a population policy based on quite different, even opposite principles. The situation was not less severe than in Germany, as the gross reproduction rate attained the level of 0·811 in 1935. In the same year in Stockholm it was 0·394. The population situation was analysed and a policy was proposed by Alva and Gunnar Myrdal who later were active members of a Royal Commission on the population problem (Myrdal and Myrdal 1934, G. Myrdal 1940, A. Myrdal 1945).

The Myrdals distinguished two equally unacceptable standpoints: a conservative one which considered as many births as possible to be desirable, and a neo-Malthusian standpoint which considered birth control to be desirable and thought that the number of children should be adapted to the economic conditions of the families regardless of the requirements of population reproduction. The conservatives had in fact nothing else to propose than exhortations to the individual to do his duty and bear children, and some small honorary grants for families with several children. On the other hand, the approach of the neo-Malthusians, which consisted of exhortations to adjust size of family to social malformations, did not readjust the malformations, but led in the direction of extinguishing the human content of society. As Àlva Myrdal (1945) stated, 'It is certainly more rational and more promising for the future, though much more difficult, to remake society so that it fits the children rather than to abolish the children in order to fit society.'

The principles of a democratic population policy should be:

1   Freedom for the individual to decide the number of children, i.e. voluntary parenthood, which implies no coercion, the permission of abortions on therapeutic, eugenic, ethical and also social grounds, and at the same time widespread reliable information for everybody on methods of birth control, in order to avoid an increase in the number of abortions.

2   Couples should be encouraged to have larger families by social benefits given to families with children; in the Swedish population policy these measures were mostly given in kind, although the benefits in cash were also important.

3   Social benefits given to families with children serve also to assure the equality of conditions for children originating from different social strata and from smaller or larger families.

4   Quality of children should not be sacrificed for a larger quantity of children; social benefits serve to improve quality by providing better opportunities for children.

The Swedish population policy introduced in the 1930s and developed further in subsequent decades was essentially based on these principles. It included: family allowances (for all children, i.e. also for the first child), amounting to about one third of the average cost of the care and education of a child; marriage loans; free delivery, and free prenatal and postnatal care for mothers; free medical care for children; free nursery education; free meals in schools; subvention of house building costs, etc. Abortion was permitted first on therapeutic, eugenic and ethical grounds, later also on medico-social grounds. However, the number of induced abortions remained low. Thus the Swedish population policy was strongly equality-oriented and based on incentives, without using coercion. After the introduction of these population policy measures, the level of fertility rose to that necessary for simple reproduction. It is, however, difficult to separate the direct effect of the policy from the indirect effect of the discussions on population problems and of the introduction of the measures, which caused a change in 'informed public opinion' (Glass 1967), as well as from the factors producing a baby boom some years later in other advanced countries.

The decline in fertility was considered to be the most problematical in France. Although the level of fertility was not especially low compared with some other west European countries, the low level was prolonged, so that in some years effectively only immigration prevented the population of France from declining in the interwar period.

As a matter of curiosity, it should be mentioned that France already had a population policy in the seventeenth century, as in 1666 exemption of taxes was granted to families with many children. This exemption was repealed in 1683, and the Marquis of Turbilly wrote in 1762 that this contributed to the spread of birth control in the villages (Lautman 1972).

Before the First World War the low level of fertility was considered disadvantageous, and in 1920 a law was enacted which prohibited not only induced abortion, but also propaganda for birth control. However, this law had almost no effect, as the level of fertility continued to decline.

Therefore, after a rather long scientific and journalistic discussion on the problems of low fertility, a new comprehensive law, the *Code de Famille*, was enacted in 1939. It became effective in 1940 – i.e. almost at the same time that France was defeated by the German armies. This law did not change the prohibition on induced abortions and propaganda for birth control, but it introduced very important benefits for families with children. Family allowances were concentrated on second and subsequent children, and a mother remaining at home (not being employed) also received a certain allowance, which was called 'unique salary' (*salaire unique*). The following data give some illustration of the importance of the allowances. The family allowance paid for the second child amounted in 1944 to 10 per cent of the average income in the department where the couple lived, and this was raised to 20 per cent in 1946. The family allowance for the third child amounted to 30 and later 50 per cent, and for the fourth and subsequent children to 30 per cent of the average income. The unique salary was (in addition to the above family allowances) 20 per cent in the case of one child, 25 and later 40 per cent in the case of two children, and 30, later 50 per cent in the case of three and more children (Watson 1954). This meant that a three child family obtained more than the average wage in the form of family allowances and unique salary. Up till the present day, French family allowances have remained very high when compared with any other developed country. Thus the population policy of France was characterized by a strong emphasis on population goals (putting less emphasis on equality, as the first child did not qualify for a family allowance) and by very high benefits in cash. Although abortion was prohibited, this prohibition has not been taken very seriously and many clandestine illegal abortions are apparently carried out in France. Thus coercion may not be considered a distinctive feature of French policy.

The new *Code de Famille* and the demographic situation of France was very much in the focus of public interest. Many scientific works were widely read by the non-scientific public (Sauvy 1944, Boverat 1946). After the War a Demographic Research Institute, the INED, was organized which was and remains the largest institute in social sciences financed by the state. The scientific journal of demography, *Population*, which was first published in 1945, constantly followed and commented on the demographic situation in France, pointed to the dangers of a too low fertility, stressed the opinion that France was underpopulated and that a higher population would be more optimal from the point of view of economic effects. Alfred Sauvy, the long-time director of the Demographic Institute and editor in chief of *Population*, had an important role in communicating demographers' ideas to the public, as he combined scientific imagination and sophistication with the style of an excellent journalist (Sauvy 1944 1959 1963 1973).

The impact of all this seems to be really remarkable. Fertility increased almost immediately after the enactment of the *Code de Famille*, and by 1942 fertility was already higher than in the previous year. Thus the population policy increased fertility in the worst period for France, when more than half of the country was occupied by German armies, the living standard dropped to a very low level and there were shortages of the most basic goods. After the War the increase in fertility continued and fertility remained at a comparatively high level. This is illustrated by the fact that the total number of children born in the marriages of the year 1925 was 2000 per 1000, while in the marriage cohort of 1941–3 it increased to 2200–2300 per 1000.

French demographers (Henry 1954, Girard and Bastide 1958, Febvay 1959, Sauvy 1961) considered that the population policy measures certainly contributed to the increase in fertility, but could not be considered the unique cause of it. When the Demographic Research Institute prepared a report on the possible effect of the spread of contraception and the eventual effects of legalization of induced abortions, it was considered that family allowances should be increased to compensate for the effect of these changes, and also that great emphasis should be laid on the fact that French society should be interested continuously in a high level of fertility, because a rapid rate of technological development requires large young generations, and because the possibility of paying relatively high pensions is only assured in the case of relatively large young generations (INED 1966).

Although the impact of the population policy in France seems incontestable, it is not completely clear through what kind of mechanism it influenced fertility. The obvious inference would be that it directly influenced the decisions of the French couples by alleviating the costs of having children. This surely had some impact, but some signs suggest that there was also an indirect effect, which influenced fertility through creating a social atmosphere favourable for larger families. For example, the increase in fertility was not completely proportional to the relative benefits given to particular social strata – e.g. although professionals got relatively lower benefits (compared to their income level) than other non-manual employees, their fertility increased more than that of the other non-manuals. As Sauvy stated (1961), social psychological atmosphere plays a very important role in determining fertility. Fertility declines when a general impression becomes widespread that newly born children are not positively accepted and valued by society. A negative valuation is manifested in such phenomena as contempt for and ridicule of large families, or even of children at all, lack of institutions for children (nurseries, public gardens, etc.). The introduction of the *Code de Famille*, as well as the great publicity given to demographic problems, certainly contributed to the suppression of such negative attitudes and to the development of a positive attitude toward children.

The other problem encountered in an explanation of the influence of population policy on fertility is that at the same time when fertility increased after the War there was a general prosperity in all western Europe, unemployment declined, and income levels rose rapidly, so there were many reasons for fertility to rise. And fertility did in fact increase in other developed countries that did not introduce similar population policies, or introduced much more restricted ones – e.g. in the USA and the UK. However, it could be argued that the change in the tendency of fertility was more pronounced in France (partly because the low fertility was very prolonged here and partly because fertility rose to a somewhat higher level in France than in neighbouring countries), and also that the decline beginning in Western countries in the mid 1960s was less pronounced in France than elsewhere.

Bourdieu and Darbel argued that the fundamental cause of the increase in fertility after the War was an increase in feelings of security, determined mainly by the increased rate of economic growth and full employment, as well as by the guarantees and aids provided by the state, by population policy, of which only one element was family allowance, and by social security institutions. The fundamental cause was not the population policy itself, but it might have contributed to the development of a feeling of security, without which (in their opinion) no population policy can be effective (Bourdieu and Darbel 1966).

After the Second World War, and particularly in the 1960s, fertility declined to a very low level in some east European socialist countries, and therefore different measures of population policy were introduced in some of them. Here we shall investigate two fairly different cases – namely, the population policies of Romania and Hungary.

In Romania the birth level was 14·7 per 1000 and the gross reproduction rate was 0·919 in 1966. In October 1966 a new decree was enacted which completely changed the population policy (which since 1957 had allowed free legal abortion) prohibiting induced abortion under any circumstances except in cases where the life of the mother was in danger, congenital malformations were probable, rape could be proved, or the woman was over 45 or had four or more children, and in some exceptional physiological and psychological conditions. At the same time, a tax on unmarried men and women and on couples without children was introduced, some tax alleviations were introduced for families with three or more children, and the maternity confinement grant was increased. The importation of contraceptive pills and intrauterine devices was stopped. Thus this new Romanian population policy was concentrated exclusively on population goals and was characterized by extended use of coercion combined with weak monetary incentives.

At first the impact of the decree, which came into force on 1 November 1966, was tremendous. Nine months later, in the period from July to September 1967, the birth rate rose to 38·5–40·0, but by October it had already begun to decline. This decline continued uninterrupted and in 1972 the birth rate was 18·8 (Pressat 1967, Teitelbaum 1972, David and Wright 1972).

Thus, the impact of these Romanian population policy measures seems to have been short lived. The very low number of desired children documented by some studies (Mehlan 1965, Potts 1967) – e.g. in Bucharest only 1·3 children per couple – prevailed in spite of the legal restrictions on induced abortion and the difficulties in obtaining contraceptives. At the same time, the restriction on abortions had some serious consequences, e.g. the rates of stillbirths and of infant mortality increased (although later the downward tend resumed).

As already described in Chapter 4.1, the temporary postwar increase in the birth rate in Hungary was fairly short, and in 1952 a slight decline in fertility had already been noted. At that time the prohibition on induced abortions, which was based on a law enacted several decades earlier but which had never been strictly followed (as, for example, in France), was strictly enforced, some doctors who had carried out clandestine abortions being condemned to prison sentences with great publicity in the mass media. A very short-lived rise in the birth rate ensued, its peak being in 1954 (23·0). At the same time, some extra benefits in cash for mothers with several children were introduced, although these amounted to a very moderate sum.

After 1954 the birth rate declined sharply. In Budapest the decline had already begun in 1954 – i.e. in the period when the prohibition on abortions was implemented very strictly. In following years the prohibitions were gradually alleviated, and in 1956 induced abortions were made free and legal, performed in public hospitals on demand for women having a pregnancy not more than twelve weeks advanced. During these years the number of births declined in parallel with the increase in the number of induced abortions. However, it would be erroneous to attribute the decline of fertility simply to the legalization of abortions, as at the same time the planned number of children also declined strongly (from 2·25 in 1958 to 1·89 in 1966). It would be more correct to state that the gradually diminishing planned number of children of couples was achieved by means of the more easily available means of induced abortions.

Considering that the level of fertility declined so much that the simple reproduction of population in the long run did not seem to be assured, and population projections indicated a decline in the population number beginning from the mid-1980s, the outlines and long-term plans of a comprehensive population policy were elaborated (Huszár *et al.* 1969, Iván and Mausecz 1971, Huszár 1973). The basic principles were formulated in the following way:

1 Fertility should increase at least to a level assuring the simple reproduction of the population – i.e. to a cohort reproduction rate of 1·0, or slightly above that rate.
2 This increase should be attained by incentives, without using coercive measures, since an increase in births of unwanted children was considered disadvantageous, both for the family and the society as a whole.
3 The main instruments of population policy should be benefits in cash, given to the families with children. In addition to contributing to the

attainment of the population goals, these family allowances and other cash benefits were also considered necessary to lessen income differences between families with different numbers of children. The long-term aim should be, both for the population goals and for reasons of social equality, to 'socialize' the costs of children.

Family allowances were raised considerably (table 5.59). Preference was given to the third child in the family. In the longer perspective it is planned to provide family allowances for the first child as well until it attains the age of 3 or 4, when the second child is supposed to be born. (Mothers with no husband, having one child, receive family allowances for the first child at present.)

Table 5.59   Family allowances in Hungary, monthly sum in forint.

Employment status of family head	Number of children under 16	1959	1965	1966	1968	1972
Workers and employees	2	75	200	300	300	300
	3	360	360	510	510	810
	4	480	480	680	680	1080
	each following child	+120	+120	+170	+170	+260
Members of agricultural cooperatives	2	—	—	140	200	400
	3	210	210	210	360	660
	4	280	280	280	480	880
	each following child	+70	+70	+70	+120	+120
Average *per capita* income (wages, other money income, social benefits in money and in kind)		989*	1236	1285	1460	1940

* In 1960.
Source: Népesedéspolitika Magyarországon (1972), p. 53, and Statistical Yearbook (1972).

The second important measure of population policy is the so-called child care allowance, introduced in 1967 and further developed in 1969 and 1974 (Miltényi 1971). This allowance provides the opportunity for working women to remain at home after the maternity leave of five months (in which period she gets her total wage) until the child reaches its third birthday, during which time she receives an allowance of 600 ft (members of agricultural cooperatives 500 ft) monthly. The allowance was increased in 1974 to 800 ft in the case of the first, to 900 ft in the case of the second and to 1000 ft in the case of third and subsequent children. If a new child is born during the period of three years, the mother gets the allowance for both children. In the meantime, the mother retains the right to return to her job automatically after the third birthday of the child.

These measures, as well as some others of minor importance, seem to have had an immediate impact on fertility. Family allowances were first increased in 1965 and already in 1966 the gross reproduction rate had risen slightly to 0·907 (having been 0·875 in 1965), then after the introduction of the child care allowance enacted in 1966 and becoming effective from 1 January 1967, the rate rose to 0·970 in 1967 and to 0·997 in 1968.

The effectiveness of the introduction of the child care allowance might be evaluated on the basis of the percentage of working women having a birth who claimed it (72 per cent in 1967, 70 per cent in 1971). Women with lower education and with lower income in general claimed it to a larger extent than working women with higher education and income. For example, in 1967 the monthly average wage of women receiving the allowance was 1325 ft, while the average wage of all women employed in the 'state' sector (i.e. enterprises and institutions under state ownership) was 1859 ft.

The development of the fertility of employed and dependent women, however, demonstrates even more strongly the impact of this type of allowance. While the fertility of dependent women who could not claim it, as the precondition of the allowance was employment for at least one year, continued to decline, the fertility of employed women began to rise (table 5.60). The fertility of women working in agriculture was not affected by the introduction of this allowance, as the conditions for claiming it were somewhat more difficult for members of agricultural cooperatives, where a

Table 5.60 Number of children born per 1000 women aged 15–49, by employment status of the women: Hungary.

Year	Employment status		
	Other branches than agriculture		Agriculture
	Employed	Dependent	Employed and dependent
1949	30	102	80
1960	48	78	53
1963	50	64	50
1966	51	62	53
1967	60	57	54
1968	67	50	51
1969	66	49	48

Source: Miltényi (1971), p. 820.

precondition was a certain number of working days in the previous year, which was not always assured because of the seasonal employment in agriculture of some working women.

The rise in fertility, following the introduction of the different measures of population policy was not simply a phenomenon of timing, since the planned number of children, ascertained by fertility and family planning surveys, also increased at the same time, proving that a change in norms and values concerning fertility had occurred in recent years (see p. 216).

A very similar demographic situation developed in the 1960s in Czechoslovakia, where similar population policy measures (a rise in family allowances and the introduction of a child care allowance until the second birthday) produced similar effects: the level of fertility increased to a level considered sufficient for the long-term development of the population (Heitlinger 1976).

From 1 January 1974, new measures of population policy were introduced in Hungary: family allowances, as well as the child care allowance, were increased. At the same time legal abortions were slightly restricted (see p. 138). The aim of the latter measure was to reduce the number of abortions and it was again stressed that it would not be advantageous to increase the number of unwanted births (Huszár 1973). Parallel with the new restrictions on abortions, great efforts were made to spread family planning and contraceptives in the population.

As for the reduction in the number of abortions, the measures were successful. While in 1973 169 650 legal induced abortions were performed, their number in 1974 dropped to 102 022, the age-specific induced abortion rates being:

	Number of induced abortions per 1000 women	
Age of women	1973	1974
15–19	38·3	26·7
20–24	98·3	52·5
25–29	105·6	54·6
30–34	95·1	55·8
35–39	68·5	50·1
40–49	14·0	11·3
Total	63·3	38·2

Almost parallel with the decline of induced abortions, the number of pill users increased, the number of monthly sales of doses of contraceptive pills being 242 000 in the first nine months in 1973 and 425 000 in the first half of 1975. While in 1973, 91 per 1000 women aged 17–49 used pills, in June 1975 the rate increased to 173 per 1000.

In consequence of the substitution of pills and other contraceptives for induced abortions in the birth control practice of Hungarian women, less than 3000 demands for induced abortions were rejected by the committees deciding on permitting legal abortions. Thus, the coercive effect of the restrictive measures proved to be minimal.

Although the restriction on induced abortions was not planned to be a natalist measure – i.e. its professed aim was not to increase fertility – the birth rate increased after its introduction from 15·0 in 1973 to 17·8 in 1974 and 18·4 in 1975. However, only part of this increase might be attributed to the population policy measures. About one third of the increase is due to the entering of the larger birth cohorts born in the first half of the 1950s into the age groups showing the highest fertility (20–24 years). The other two thirds of the increase resulted mostly from first and second births, i.e. from timing changes, as probably most of these first and second births would have occurred one or two years later, so that the average birth order remained below 2·0 (Central Statistical Office 1975). In the second half of 1975 signs of a beginning decline had already been observed, which continued in 1976.

Thus Hungarian population policy measures produced a certain rise in the level of fertility, nearly to that necessary for the long-term reproduction of the population. Obviously, a final judgement on its success cannot be made until years later when the effects of timing of parities will cancel each other out and the cohort fertility rates can be estimated. As with French population policy, the question might be raised whether it was population policy or other factors that caused the increase in fertility. As the increases in fertility occurred after the introduction of the particular measures, and as the increase occurred primarily in those strata (manual workers) where the amounts of family allowances and child care allowance were relatively (compared with wages) the highest, it might be stated that these measures of population policy certainly had an impact on fertility. But it seems very probable that, as in France, in addition to the direct effect on the costs of children, these measures had a socio-psychological impact, helping to change the cultural norms and attitudes concerning fertility, children and families with several children. In consequence of the widespread publicity given to the introduction of these measures, and perhaps even more in consequences of the lively discussion carried on in newspapers, scientific and literary journals, as well as on the radio and television before the introduction of the measures, the Hungarian public was well aware of the demographic situation of Hungarian society and appreciated the value of children for society.

Thus it seems probable that in addition to the direct effect on the economic position and calculations of young couples deciding on the number of their children, the population policy measures have also had an indirect influence on fertility, which might be compared with the influence of religion and ethnic background. Like religion and other cultural factors, measures of population policy contribute to the shaping of cultural norms, values and attitudes accepted by members of society. However, as unpopular measures, such as coercive measures and taxes on unmarried men and women, surely do not contribute to increasing the norms for number of children per family, not every measure of population policy has a long-term positive influence on fertility. The case studies described here seem to demonstrate, on the contrary, that coercive measures have only temporary effects.

PART SIX

Recent attempts to develop a theory of fertility

Since the mid 1960s a new interest in building a theory of fertility has grown rapidly. This seems to be stimulated both by the new developments of fertility in advanced societies – the baby boom and the ensuing decline in fertility – and by the availability of a large mass of research findings, which were partly contradictory and inconsistent and could not be easily fitted into the framework of existing theories. The renewed interest in theory building was partly embodied in the development of the economic theory of fertility and partly in the sometimes sharp reactions to it. The common characteristic of these new theoretical developments – both those following the economic theory of fertility and those refuting it and trying to find alternative theoretical explanations, as well as the attempts to synthesize the two approaches – is the relatively weak empirical verification of them. However, this is understandable in the light of the fact that these theoretical attempts are fairly new and require new kinds of data and partly also new research methods.

6.1 New developments in the economic theory of fertility

Following the line of Becker (1960), and partly as a reaction to its critics, the economic theory of fertility has been further developed in several respects.

Firstly, it was integrated into the new consumer theory (Lancaster 1965). The essence of this new approach is, that

1   It is not goods, *per se*, but their different characteristics that give rise to utility.
2   In general a good will possess more than one characteristic and many characteristics will be shared by more than one good.
3   Goods in combination may possess characteristics different from the characteristics pertaining to the goods consumed separately.

These characteristics are sometimes called basic commodities (to distinguish them from goods). The preferences of consumers are exercised on these characteristics or commodities, the goods and services purchased being only intermediate elements in the process of satisfaction of wants.

Applied to the theory of fertility, this implies that:

1   It is not children but 'child services' that provide utility to the parents.
2   Child services consist of at least two elements: the number of children and the quality of children, an increase in both number and quality being able to raise the utility, but at the same time numbers and qualities being more or less substitutable (Willis 1973).

Secondly, the theory of fertility was integrated into an economic theory of the family (Schultz 1974), or – as it is alternatively called – a theory of household production and consumption (Terleckij 1975). This theory tries to explain most part of the observable market and non-market behaviour of families and households by means of the tools of the traditional theory of the firm. According to this approach, families behave in a rationally calculating way, similar to firms in classical and neoclassical theory – i.e. optimizing the results attainable with the available resources. The resources of the family are: the incomes of the members of the family, the wealth of the family, the time budget of the members of the family. The outputs are the basic commodities consumed by the members of the family, as well as other satisfactions. Human investments into family members constitute one part of the output, being decided in view of the future benefits arising out of these investments. Both resources (e.g. time spent in the household and time spent in earning activities outside the household, or leisure time and wage income) and outputs are considered substitutable (Becker 1965). Thus households are producing units on the one hand and utility maximizers on the other hand.

Applied to the theory of fertility, this means that families use their available time budget, the time of wife and husband, in order to produce monetary incomes (by engaging in earning activities), to produce goods in the household (e.g. home-produced bread versus store-bought bread), and to produce different kinds of family amenities, among others children. The time input into the production of children might be used to increase their number or to enhance their quality. The efficiency of the particular members of the family in producing monetary income, producing goods in the household, and rearing and educating children might be very different. For example, the wife might be more efficient in household activities and in rearing children, while the husband might be more efficient in gaining monetary income. Expressed in other terms, this means that the wage rate per hour of the husband might be higher, while the output in household activities (e.g. cooking) and child rearing of one hour of the wife might be higher than that of the husband. Accordingly, families allocate the available time of their members in a way leading to maximal utility.

Thirdly, the theory of social interactions developed by Becker (1974b) has implications for the theory of fertility. According to this theory, individuals – among others, the heads of households – try to maximize their 'social income', which is the sum of the person's own income and the monetary value to him of the relevant characteristics of others. These characteristics might be of very varied type, like sex, age, race (of colleagues, etc.), worthiness of esteem, personality characteristics. The characteristics of the members of the family obviously enter the utility function of the individual, as he is not indifferent to their well being, their feeling toward him, etc. He, therefore, chooses his spouse and decides on the number and quality of children in such a way that their relevant characteristics should provide him maximum satisfaction (Becker 1973, 1974a). In this way, the family's utility function can be considered to be identical with that of one family member, e.g. the head of the family, or of both parents, who decide on the number and quality of children. This concept of the individual's utility function might better explain how child services enter into this function.

The economic theory of fertility was formulated by several authors in terms of a mathematical model (Willis 1973, De Tray 1973, Becker and Lewis 1973). The formulations are slightly different. Here we follow the presentation of De Tray.

The household utility function can be written in the following way:

$$U = U(C, Z)$$

where U is utility, C is the quantity of child services and Z the quantity of all other basic commodities.

Child services are composed of two parts:

$$C = C(N, Q)$$

i.e. the number of children (N) and the quality of children (Q).

The household production of the number of children, of the quality of children and of all other basic commodities is governed by the following relations:

$$N = N(t_{m,N}, t_{f,N}, X_N; \beta, \gamma)$$

$$Q = Q(t_{m,Q}, t_{f,Q}, X_Q; \beta, \gamma)$$

$$Z = Z(t_{m,Z}, t_{f,Z}, X_Z; \beta, \gamma)$$

where the meaning of the different inputs into the production of number and quality of children, as well as other basic commodities are:

$t_{m,N}, t_{m,Q}, t_{m,Z}$ = The time of the husband (or of other male members) spent on the number, quality of children and on other basic commodities respectively

$t_{f,N}, t_{f,Q}, t_{f,Z}$ = The time of the wife (or of other female members) spent on the same purposes

X_N, X_Q, X_Z = The market goods and services used in the production of number of children, quality of children, and production of other basic commodities

β, γ = Two indices, characterizing the husband's and the wife's efficiency in producing number of children, quality of children and other basic commodities

Households tend to maximize utility by means of these different inputs through the three production processes, described by the above-mentioned relations. The quantity of the available inputs that can be used by households is constrained by the following relations:

Market goods and services used cannot be more than the quantity that can be purchased by the earnings (wages) of the family members plus any initial wealth or wealth transfers:

$$X_N . P_N + X_Q . P_Q + X_Z . P_Z \leq Y_m + Y_f + V$$

where P_N, P_Q, P_Z are the prices of the market goods and services purchased for the production of number and quality of children, as well as for the production of other basic commodities, Y_m and Y_f are the total (lifetime) earnings or wages of the husband and the wife or other family members, V is the wealth and non-wage-related income of the family.

The time spent on the production of number and quality of children, as well as on the production of other basic commodities, cannot be more than the total time available of the husband and the wife, or other family members:

$$T_m = L_m + t_{m,N} + t_{m,Q} + t_{m,Z}$$

$$T_f = L_f + t_{f,N} + t_{f,Q} + t_{f,Z}$$

where T_m and T_f are the total amounts of lifetime available for the husband and wife or other family members, L_m and L_f are the time of husband and wife spent in earning activities in the market.

Obviously, the total lifetime earnings of husband and wife (or other family members) are equal to the time spent in earning activities multiplied by the male (W_m) and female (W_f) lifetime wage rates per unit of time:

$$Y_m = L_m \cdot W_m$$

$$Y_f = L_f \cdot W_f$$

Time spent on non-market activities (child rearing and household production of basic commodities) can be freely exchanged for time spent in earning activities, gaining income by means of which market goods and services can be purchased. Therefore the 'full lifetime wealth' of the family can be formulated in the following way:

$$I = T_m \cdot W_m + T_f \cdot W_f + V$$

$$= \pi_Z \cdot Z + \pi_N \cdot N + \pi_Q \cdot Q$$

where I is the full wealth of the family, and π_Z, π_N, π_Q, are the shadow prices to the household of number of children, quality of children and of other basic commodities.

The most important exogenous factors of the model influencing the number and quality of children are the prices of different kinds of goods and services at the market (P_N, P_Q, P_Z), the male and female wage rates (W_m and W_f), and the efficiencies of males and females in household production (β and γ). From the mathematical model, however, it is not possible to deduce the impact of these factors on number and quality of children, as these impacts depend on the elasticities of substitution of N, Q and Z, as well as their income elasticities, which are not *a priori* known. Therefore, this model should rather be considered as a theoretical framework and not as a theory of fertility (Ashenfelter 1973).

Several authors tried to calculate parameters of this and similar other models by means of estimations based on different samples (Willis 1973,

De Tray 1973, Gardner 1973, Michael 1973). The most important result of these computations was that the wage rate or potential income of the husband was positively related to fertility, while the wage rate of the wife was rather strongly negatively related to it. This implicitly means that the higher the education of the wife, the lower, *ceteris paribus*, will be the number of children of the family, since a woman having a higher education may achieve a higher lifetime wage income. The explanation given is that child services require much more time input from wives than from husbands, as women's efficiency in rearing children and enhancing their quality is supposed to be much higher than that of men. On the other hand, as female education increases the relative efficiency of wives in enhancing child quality, it is supposed that families where the wives are highly educated concentrate on improving the quality of their children.

There are several possibilities for the extension of this model. The fact that fertility control is both uncertain and involves costs (money costs as well as forgone time, sexual pleasure, conflicts with religious beliefs, etc.) was incorporated into the model (Michael and Willis 1975). The stochastic nature of conception was taken into consideration (Heckman and Willis 1975). It was suggested that each subsequent parity of a family is influenced by a somewhat different set of factors, among others by the experiences with the preceding children, so that the economic theory of fertility should use a sequential model (Namboodiri 1972a). Similarly, the relative dominance of husbands and wives might be a factor influencing decisions (Namboodiri 1972b).

The problem with empirical investigations attempting to verify the economic theory of fertility is that it is rather difficult to operationalize the variables of the model. Number of children is a clear concept, but difficult to measure, as only families with completed fertility ought to be taken into consideration. Quality of children is operationalized in some studies by the expected school investment per child (De Tray 1973). It is fairly difficult to obtain data on potential lifetime wage incomes, particularly of women. Prices of goods and services are sometimes considered to be identical for families belonging to different social strata and for residential groups in cross-sectional samples, although it is a questionable assumption. The efficiencies of husband's and wife's work in household production are sometimes measured by years of schooling (De Tray 1973), but this is a very crude measure. Thus the opinion of Gardner (1973, p. S103), that 'the theory on the economics of family size has outrun the data available to test it', seems to be justified.

In addition to the fact that the economic theory of fertility ought to be considered more as a theoretical framework for investigating the empirical data, and not as a theory of fertility, and to the fact that the data basis on which this framework can be used is rather deficient, this approach raises one further and (in the opinion of the author of this book, more important) reservation – namely, that the basic assumption of the approach is that individuals and couples engage in activities and make decisions independently of the society in which they live. In other words, that they decide on the number (and quality) of their children by taking into consideration only their own costs and benefits, as if society would have no influence on these decisions.

The development of economics itself in recent years seems to point in the direction of a growing recognition of the fact that, even in their purely economic activities, in their decisions on what to produce and how many to produce, individuals and economic organizations do not completely follow the precepts of profit (or economic utility) maximization, but take into consideration the opinions and expectations of the society or particular groups of the society in which they live. As Alfred Sauvy (1963, p. 3), an economist who became one of the most original demographers, expressed it several years ago, men cannot be locked into the 'role of *Homo economicus*', particularly when we investigate such a central phenomenon of the life and survival of society as reproduction.

As Ryder (1973b, p. S66) formulated in a comment to one of the papers treating the economic theory of fertility (Willis 1973), 'just as no act is devoid of economic content, so no act is devoid of normative content', these norms being the institutionalized solutions of society to the pervasive problems of society. These solutions are different in particular societies and social groups, and also change over time, so we cannot neglect them in a theory that is trying to explain changes and differences in the level of fertility.

6.2 Outlines of a sociological theory of fertility

As Duesenberry put it in an often quoted sentence of a comment on Becker's first formulation of the economic theory of fertility (Becker 1960), 'economics is all about how people make choices; sociology is all about how they don't have any choices to make' (Duesenberry 1960). While economic theory presumes that individuals think and behave in a rational, calculating way, comparing the necessary costs and the expected outsomes of their actions, uninfluenced by any exogenous considerations, sociological theory tends to emphasize the fact that individuals are governed in their actions and even in their beliefs and opinions by values and norms embedded in the culture of the surrounding society.

It does not seem to be an understatement that a sociological theory of fertility does not exist as yet. However, the elements and outlines of such a theory have been elaborated. As a precursor of this approach, we might mention the general theory of population of Sauvy (1959), who – although an economist – emphasized the importance of the 'collective will' (an expression used by Landry) and of collective attitudes. However, he also stressed that this collective attitude conerning the number of children is not necessarily prompted by the real public good or by the society's sense of preservation. As illustrative examples he cites the collective scorn for children in France during the period until the Second World War, and the spread of the feeling that more children are welcome for society during the period of the revival in fertility in France. The collective attitude concerning fertility, as he demonstrates it by the example of the 'Malthusian spirit' (a generalized aversion to expansion and change), is not independent of other aspects of economic and social attitudes of the society.

The basic idea of the sociological theory of fertility is that

> when many members of a society face a recurrent common problem with important social consequences they tend to develop a normative solution for it. This solution, a set of rules for behaviour in a particular situation, becomes part of the culture, and the society indoctrinates its members to conform more or less closely to the norms by implicit or explicit rewards and punishments. (Freedman 1963)

Thus in each society and population group there are norms prescribing what the pattern of family growth should be. These norms and patterns might first arise as a result of the responses of individual couples to new economic and social circumstances, e.g. to urbanization, but they gradually develop a compelling power and are reinforced with social sanctions. It is supposed that even unwanted fertility does not cause important deviation from these norms and patterns, as the number of children born as a result of ineffective planning is more or less balanced by the number of those not born because of fecundity impairments, though wanted by couples (Freedman, Baumert and Bolte 1959).

An extreme example of this approach is the critical article of Blake (1968) on the economic theory of fertility of Becker (1960), as well as her recent evaluations of the decline in fertility in the United States (Blake 1967a 1974), in which she consistently explains the development of fertility by the ideal values on family size of American couples (see pp. 36–8).

Hawthorn (1970), attempting to formulate the framework for a sociological theory of fertility, is strongly critical of the kind of approach that is satisfied with the explanation of fertility by norms and values. He acknowledges that fertility cannot be explained without taking into consideration the mental states of the actors, i.e. the intentions of the couples, and the norms, values and goals existing in these mental states. In his interpretation, norms are prescriptions present in society and recognized, though not necessarily accepted, by at least some members of society. Values, on the other hand, are expressions of the desirability of certain things and phenomena. Goals are of the same logical order as values, but less general, more related to the individuals and couples, expressing something they would like to attain. Taking into consideration norms, values and goals is necessary for a sociological theory of fertility, although they should not be considered – as sociologists tend to do – as causes of fertility levels. An explanation by the norms should be followed by the explanation of the development of these norms and values.

A sociological theory of fertility including an explanation of the norms, values and goals concerning fertility has not been elaborated as yet.

6.3 An attempt to combine the economic and sociological theories of fertility

Following the theory elaborated by Becker and the other pioneers of the economic theory of fertility, and the critique of it by Blake, but preceding the more recent elaborations and refinements of the economic theory, Easterlin (1969, 1975) developed a theoretical framework in which he tried to combine the points of view of the economic and sociological theories.

He assumes that fertility is the result of deliberate choices taken by the couple, similar to other decisions on consumption, production and engaging in earning activities. Thus the number of children of the couple is also determined by their income, the prices (costs) of children and other goods and their tastes. He considered that children are included in the preference map of the satisfaction-yielding goods of the family, and in consequence households decide on the basis of their available income, as well as on the costs of children and the relative costs of other goods, how many children they want to have. Thus the preference for the number of children should not be viewed independently from the household's desires for other goods. Therefore, research on family size preference, (the desired or ideal number of children) should not be confined to the fertility dimension alone, but should take into consideration desires for other goods competing with children for the household's resources. Preferences or tastes for the number of children are – similar to preferences for other goods – not of an 'either-or' nature, but of a 'more or less' nature, and there are marginal rates of substitution which express how many of the individual goods the couples are willing to 'trade off' for an additional child.

Easterlin, however, used somewhat different concepts of income and costs from those of Becker's original theory. It is not the income observed at any point in time that influences the decisions on fertility of the household. Rather, these decisions are governed by the long-term income prospects of the household, the 'permanent income', in terms of Milton Friedman, or (as termed by Easterlin) the 'potential income'. This is the potential income flow through time, including all income which might be attained by the family by utilization of its total earning capacity. Obviously, for example, the potential income of a family where the wife is a remedial reading tutor and earns in eight hours as much as the wife in another family earns by working forty hours is not identical with the potential income of this second family, although their observable income might be identical. The first family, considering its higher potential income, might be inclined to have more children than the second family. As cross-sectional analyses of fertility and income generally are based on the observed income of families, the positive relation of fertility to income is not displayed.

The concept of costs of children is also refined by Easterlin. He does not agree with Duesenberry (1960), who considered that these costs are higher for rich families. Thus he confirms Becker's thesis that these costs are more or less identical and the higher expenditures per child in rich families reflect both the preference for better quality children and the higher income available for spending on children. Extending Becker's cost concept, he considers that costs should include the opportunity costs of the time needed for the care of children. Obviously a mother with four children must spend much time on the children, and therefore has less time left either for earning activities, or for recreation. This cost might be measured by the income she could achieve by being employed during the time she spends on child care.

The earning possibilities of the wife have a double effect on fertility. The rise in potential income she might achieve by being employed tends to increase fertility, but on the other hand, by being employed the opportunity costs of child care are increased, which tends to diminish fertility. The two effects might be called income effect (a greater number of children can be achieved with higher income) and substitution effect (at higher income levels alternatives to child care come into the foreground). The negative substitution effect might outweigh the favourable income effect. This also might be an explanation for the negative relation of fertility to income found by some investigations.

Easterlin introduced a further element into the theory – namely, the costs of contraception. These are partly monetary costs, but the psychological costs (the annoyances caused by the practice of birth control) might be even more important. When a couple decides on the use of birth control and chooses between the different methods, and through that decision and choice obviously decides also partly the possibility (or probability) of a further birth or its avoidance, it takes into consideration the costs of birth control and compares them with the costs of an additional child. Thus Easterlin does not consider that unwanted pregnancies are simply the consequences of lack of information, as supposed by Becker, but hypothesizes that people are more or less universally aware of methods of fertility control. However, since these methods, particularly the traditional folk methods, are somewhat unpleasant, couples might consider that it is more worthwhile to take the risk of another pregnancy than to accept the annoyances connected with fertility control. Fertility control methods (e.g. induced abortion) also have a price, which is taken into consideration when deciding on fertility. Modern methods of birth control, obviously, cause much less annoyance than traditional methods, and this explains the wider use of contraception in recent decades in developed societies. Thus the course is not the higher level of knowledge, information or rationality in these societies as compared to their underdeveloped periods.

The most important innovation of Easterlin in the economic theory of fertility, however, is that he considered tastes to be different for individual families, social strata, denominational or ethnic groups, etc., as well as changing over time. The neglect of the question of the formation of tastes by other exponents of the economic theory of fertility was not accidental, since for most economists 'explanation of behaviour in terms of tastes is anathema' (Easterlin 1969, p. 133). Economists used to consider that tastes are determined by exogenous factors and are fixed. Easterlin considers them to be varied and changing, moulded by socialization, by education, and in general by the influence of social environment during the whole span of life. Through the tastes it is possible to introduce into the economic theory of fertility the influence of such factors as religion, ethnic background, place of residence, social status, and education, since all these might influence the development of preferences.

When analysing the baby boom and the recent decline in fertility in the United States, Easterlin points out a mechanism that might determine changes in tastes. He considers that tastes are shaped by the relative status position of couples. They compare their social status and economic position (income, security of employment, etc.) at the time of the family building process with that of their parents at the time of their adolescence. Young couples raised in homes where the parents had high income, and where goods and services were therefore abundant, tend to have high aspirations concerning their own consumption of goods and services, i.e. preference curves biased towards having more goods and less children at identical income levels. Therefore a cohort of young couples originating from a cohort of relatively prosperous parents might have higher expectations than a cohort originating from relatively less well-to-do families. In consequence, their indifference curves, expressing their tastes, would differ (see fig. 6.1).

Leibenstein (1976) refined the conceptual framework of Easterlin by adding that, in addition to the influence of the parental family, peer groups might also influence the tastes or (in Leibenstein's expressions) the aspirations of young couples. Part of the young couple's income is committed to the fulfilment of aspirations concerning their living standard and only the 'free', i.e. uncommitted, portion of the income is taken into consideration

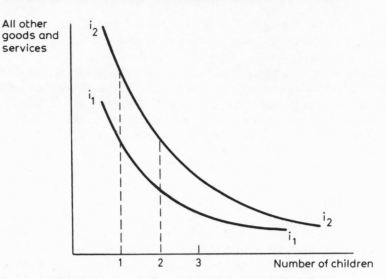

Figure 6.1 Indifference curves of couples with different aspirations for material goods and services.

$i_1 - i_1$ Indifference curve of a couple with higher aspirations for material goods and services.

$i_2 - i_2$ Indifference curve of a couple with lower aspirations for material goods and services.

by the couples when deciding on the number of their children. It might happen that committed income is rising more rapidly than total income, and in that case the number of children declines.

Oppenheimer (1976) similarly considered that consumption aspirations are formed not only during adolescence in the parental family, but also in adult life, by comparing the income of the young couple to that of couples who are some years older, as young couples desire to achieve their standard of living and consumption. Another problem arises from the evaluation of the influence of the wife's income on the number of children. On the one hand, this additional income increases the total family income but on the other hand some of the women (and the proportion may be changing) engage in a gainful occupation because of the economic hardships of the family, so that the employment of the wife (providing additional income) might really be the sign of the relatively lower living standard of the family, and at the same time might directly depress the number of children, as employed women have lower fertility.

By considering tastes to be varied and changing, Easterlin considered that he introduced the basic characteristic of the sociological approach into his theory. In his opinion, social norms are the conceptual equivalents of tastes, and are embodied in preference curves. However, Hawthorn (1970) rightly stated that tastes are not the equivalents in economic theory of what sociologists used to understand by norms, but are more similar to the concepts of values.

Notwithstanding this conceptual problem, the idea of investigating the forces influencing formation and change of tastes seems to be fruitful. As yet, however, few really important steps have been taken in this direction, except perhaps the earlier case study of Banks and Banks on the change of fertility behaviour and contraceptive practice in the middle classes of Victorian England (see pp. 341–2).

PART SEVEN

Some tentative conclusions

In view of the bewildering mass of data on the development of fertility under the influence of different social determinants, and on fertility differentials by social categories, described in this book and in other demographic works, it seems audacious to try to formulate a theory of the determinants of fertility in advanced countries, which would explain its changes and differentials in all the advanced societies and in all periods of their historical development. Nevertheless, it seems worthwhile to summarize at the end of this book some main conclusions which can be drawn from different researches, and to formulate tentative opinions on some controversial subjects.

Contrary to the opinion of many demographers, the author of this book is convinced by many research findings that knowledge of birth control and access to different means of birth control have only a minor and short-term influence on fertility. It seems to be proved that folk methods of contraception and of induced abortion were widely known in almost all societies and in almost all historical periods. The lack of use of these birth control methods, and even the imperfect knowledge of them by individual couples, are, in the opinion of the author, proof of a lack of strong motivation to limit the size of family. Obviously there are differences in the costs and in the nuisances of using different birth control methods, the up-to date methods being clearly less annoying, less risky and more easily accessible than the traditional methods used in earlier centuries; therefore, it is quite possible that couples for whom only the traditional methods were accessible in preceding centuries and decades (and in some societies also today), were somewhat more inclined to accept an additional child than to take upon themselves the difficulties and annoyances connected with such methods, while at present a couple similarly disposed to have an additional birth would rather avoid it for the price of the use of less troublesome up-to-date methods. The basic fact, however, seems to be whether the couple wants an additional child or is willing to accept it, though it could avoid it with both traditional and up-to-date methods. This decision is clearly the outcome of the influences of social determinants other than the availability of birth control methods.

One of the most consistent findings of the researches carried out in different societies and in different historical conditions seems to be that income of families, *ceteris paribus*, is positively associated with the number of children. This means that among families of similar socioeconomic status and education, similar residence, similar life history (social origin, occupational career), living in an identical culture, therefore having similar aspirations and life goals, those having higher income are more liable to have more children, and that the same family is more willing to have a larger number of children if its income level is rising than if its income level is stagnating or declining. In this sense the basic tenet of the economic theory of fertility seems to be valid.

This statement, however, is almost useless in explaining long-term historical changes in fertility, or fertility differentials by social strata in a given society and in a given period, as the '*ceteris paribus*' does not hold in most of these cases. Income is more or less closely associated with almost all the above social characteristics – i.e. changes and differences in income are rather closely correlated to socioeconomic status, education, residence, life history and even culture, as well as aspirations and goals. Therefore, it seems impossible to isolate the influence of income changes from that of these other factors correlated to it when investigating long-term processes of change and differences in fertility.

Nevertheless, the verified positive correlation between income and fertility seems to have two very important implications. First, it helps to explain short-term changes of fertility in the face of economic fluctuations, associated with a rapidly or slowly rising (or stagnating, eventually declining) family income level, nearly full employment or widespread unemployment, economic security and optimistic expectations, or economic insecurity and pessimistic expectations concerning the future economic position. Fertility tends to rise in periods of economic prosperity and tends to decline in periods of depression. In both cases part of the change is caused by timing decisions (advancing and postponing of the time of parities), but part also is caused by changes of decisions concerning desired ultimate family size. It might be conjectured that these fluctuations in fertility will grow in importance in the future demographic development of advanced societies. This fact certainly deters us from making any hasty conclusions concerning the trend of fertility, based on its short-term fluctuations related to economic cycles.

The second important implication is for population policies aiming at improving the relative income position of families having children by means of family allowances and other benefits. The positive correlation between income and fertility, on the condition that all other factors remain unchanged, means that this type of population policy measure has a positive influence on fertility, as it improves the living standard of families with children in the given circumstances. Although the influence of the introduction of and the rise in family allowances and similar benefits is often questioned, these measures seem to have had in almost all concrete historical cases a positive impact on fertility. Obviously the extent of this positive impact depends on the relative importance of the benefits when compared with the income level of families. A small rise of income through the benefits has obviously only a limited effect. Also it is clear that when the relative importance of these benefits declines, in consequence of the general rise in income level of the population, their impact also declines. Therefore, if it is intended that they should continuously exert a positive influence on fertility, it is necessary to raise the amount paid to families, at least in parallel with the rise in income levels.

The other factor showing a fairly consistent correlation to fertility in all advanced societies (but not in all developing countries) is the urban or rural character of the place of residence. Couples living in the highly urbanized areas of advanced societies tend to have fewer children than couples living in rural areas. However, it is neither the administrative status of the settlement (i.e. a town or a village status in the administrative system of the country), nor the simple number of population of the settlement, that determines the level of fertility, but the urban or rural character of the natural or man-made environment. In this sense, by urban areas we mean densely built up and populated areas, mostly with many storeyed apartment blocks, with little space left for public parks, private gardens and other places where children can spend time outside the home, and where the traffic is dense, so that children cannot safely walk on streets. On the other hand, areas of rural character are those where the population lives predominantly in one-family houses with gardens or in relatively small apartment houses, where there is plentiful space for children outside the home, where life is quieter and thus more appropriate for young children. Couples living in the former type of areas tend to have fewer children than those living in the latter type. This differential seems to be connected to the fact that the monetary costs and even more the efforts necessary for raising and educating children are much greater in the urban areas than in the rural ones. This seems to be in accordance with the basic viewpoints of the economic theory of fertility.

However, it does not follow from these tentative conclusions concerning the direct influence of the type of residence that urbanization necessarily has a depressing effect on fertility, only that the type of urbanization that most advanced societies have experienced in recent centuries is associated with a lower number of children per family. It is quite conceivable that with some new form of urbanization, some new types of urban areas that might develop in the future, where the living space is larger and more appropriate for children, the depressing effects of urban surroundings will not be operating.

The third factor that seems to have a direct effect on the number of children seems to be the employment status of women. A women who is employed full time outside the home according to a fixed time schedule tends to have fewer children than a woman who is spending a large part of her time at home, either as a dependant, or as working at home in the farm or shop of the household, or having some other means of earning at home.

However, it is clearly not the current employment status of the woman that determines her future (or past) fertility, but the lifelong plans and experiences of employment. A woman who intends to be employed as continuously as possible, and wants to avoid, or cannot afford interruptions of her occupational career when her children are small and require constant care, will be less liable to have a larger family than another who intends to remain at home. This is simply connected with the fact that the role of mother and the role of a woman employed in the circumstances usual in present advanced societies (i.e. employed full time outside the home) are more or less in conflict with each other. Expressed in terms of the economic theory of fertility, the opportunity costs of rearing children (i.e. the time spent in rearing the children, instead of in income earning activities) are taken into consideration by couples when they decide their fertility.

But it should be stressed that not all forms of income earning activity of women depress their fertility. For example, the opportunity of doing a job at home, or the possibility of part-time work, might have no negative effect on fertility. Similarly, the development of nursery facilities might tend to weaken the negative correlation between fertility and employment of the mother.

Also it is clear that current employment status at the beginning of marriage might not be correlated to the future ultimate fertility of the woman, or might eventually be positively correlated to it, if the fact of being employed provides some advantages for the mother (as e.g. in Hungary at present where she obtains the child care allowance only in the case of having been previously employed).

Similarly, the employment of women after the period when her children are young (under 6 or under 10 years of age) is not necessarily related to the number of children, or might even be positively related, if the family needs the extra income earned by the mother.

Thus, income, residence and employment of women seem to have a direct effect on fertility – not only by influencing social norms, values and attitudes, but also by directly influencing the decisions of individual couples when they decide their number of children within the limits set by the norms and values accepted in the given society. On the other hand, all the other determinants of fertility treated in this book – i.e. socioeconomic status (and its change, i.e. social mobility), education, religious denomination and the intensity of religiousness, ethnicity and similar cultural characteristics – seem to have only an indirect impact on fertility, through shaping and changing the norms, values and attitudes held by societies and social groups concerning the number of children. It should be added that income, residence and employment of women – having a hypothesized direct impact on fertility – might also have an indirect effect through the norms, values and attitudes. In addition, measures of population policy seem to exert a significant part of their influence through shaping the norms, values and attitudes of society.

It is undeniable that societies (nations), social strata, ethnic and religious groups, regional population groups and communities (e.g. villages or groups of villages) develop within their culture certain norms, values and attitudes concerning the basic problems of life. The growth of population and the number of children per family are clearly among the most basic phenomena of the life of societies and individual families, so it is quite understandable that social norms, values and attitudes are formulated concerning these matters. Some social scientists tend to consider that advanced societies are becoming more and more permissive, which means that the strictness of norms is weakening and that a plurality of values is growing. The author of this book, however, is convinced that an opposite tendency is evolving in parallel – namely, that individuals and families living in advanced societies are more and more acting (consciously or even unconsciously) under the influence of the cultural norms and values of the society in which they live. These social norms and values exert their influence through the opinions of family members, neighbours, friends, colleagues – in other words, expressed in a more sophisticated way, of the reference groups of individuals and families.

It has been shown in this book that norms concerning the number of children per family used to be very strict and involved in cases of deviance very strong social sanctions (contempt from other members of the microsociety, etc.), as in the early birth control using areas of Hungary. In the opinion of the author of this book, and of other demographers (e.g. Bourgeois-Pichat 1976), the norms, values and attitudes in advanced societies concerning fertility are also very strong, and are perhaps becoming even stricter, although their influence is exerted in a fairly subtle way.

This hypothesis obviously underlines the importance of the socio-psychological processes through which the norms, values and attitudes of national societies and social groups are developed and changed.

Thus a true sociological investigation of the determinants of fertility should try to find out, in addition to describing the influences of the direct factors (income, residence, employment of women), how these norms, values and attitudes concerning fertility of societies and social groups are influenced by different kinds of social conditions (Hawthorn 1970). Expressed in a less abstract way, we should ask: What kind of factors contribute to the emergence and persistence of the 'Malthusian spirit' (an expression used by Sauvy in his works on fertility), i.e. an attitude that fears the consequences of growth and is inimical to all kinds of changes which might ensue from, among other things, demographic growth? Or, alternatively: What kind of circumstances favour the development of a spirit that considers growth, among other things of population and of individual families, a desirable phenomenon.

Essentially we know very little about these socio-psychological processes, but several case studies (e.g. of the early birth control using population groups in Hungary, of the population of Vienna in the interwar years, and of the Roman Catholic population of the Netherlands) seem to indicate the importance of the underlying economic and social conditions of the given populations in shaping the socio-psychological processes through which norms, values and attitudes are developed. Expectations of economic prosperity and social advancement, and optimistic evaluations of the prospective social position of the population group, seem to contribute to the development of larger family ideals and positive opinions on population growth. On the other hand, expectations of economic stagnation and depression, or of decline in the social position of a population group, seem to have an influence in the direction of the development of the above-mentioned Malthusian spirit and – in the framework of that spirit – to the emergence of small family ideals.

It seems that the long-term impact of population policy measures is also to a large extent mediated through the influence exerted by these measures on the norms, values and attitudes of society – i.e. through the development of a situation favourable for families having children, or a relatively large number (three to four) of children. It follows from this hypothesis that only popular measures might have a lasting positive effect, while unpopular measures (coercive measures used to be unpopular) might have no effect at all in the long run, or lead to the opposite effect (reducing the number of children). In the opinion of the author of this book, this fact seems to be proved by historical case studies on the impact of population policies.

As for the theories of fertility treated in this book, it seems that the theory of demographic transition – which might be considered a rather crude description of the demographic development of advanced societies in past centuries and decades (more or less from the first phase of industrialization and urbanization to the level of development attained by the most developed countries in the 1930s) – does not seem to be at all usable in explaining the changes and differentials of fertility in most of the advanced societies today. As Arthur Campbell (1974) most concisely stated, they are 'beyond the demographic transition' – i.e. they have entered a new phase of demographic development in which the birth rates are influenced by other factors than in the period of the secular decline in fertility.

As hinted several times in these concluding remarks, the new economic theory of fertility seems to provide a useful framework for pinpointing the influence of some (mostly short-term) determinants of fertility that have exerted a direct effect on the decisions of couples concerning their fertility. Although these determinants of fertility are not without importance, particularly in the short run and for formulating a population policy, the most important long-term changes of fertility are influenced by determinants that are embodied – in terms of the economic theory – in the shape and change of preferences or indifference curves. These preferences, i.e. the indifference maps, are mostly left out of consideration by exponents of the economic theory of fertility. The exception is Easterlin, who intends to integrate sociological viewpoints into the economic theory through tastes – i.e. through indifference maps. Some authors, not belonging to this school of economic theory (Terhune and Kaufman 1973, Coombs 1974), have carried out investigations which might help the understanding of indifference maps concerning the number of children.

Without better knowledge of these preferences, the economic theory of fertility seems to miss the most important factors determining long-term changes of fertility in advanced countries. It is not obvious that indifference maps expressing the preferences of couples for children and material goods and services are of similar shape to maps expressing preferences only for goods and services. It might be quite conceivable, for example, that in some societies the indifference map is similar to that represented in fig. 7.1 – i.e. on the one hand there is no substitution between children and material goods and services, and on the other hand a very strict two-children family norm is prevailing. The introduction of changing costs of child-rearing and different qualities of children (which might be explained also by the norms prevailing in the given society or social group) makes the explanation even more complicated. Nay, it might be questioned whether the economic theory and the indifference maps are really the useful framework to investigate the changes of norms, values and attitudes.

Thus the main conclusion developed by the author during the work on this book seems to be that a sociological theory of fertility would be necessary, which – as postulated by Hawthorn (1970) – would explain the influence of social conditions on fertility through the development of norms, values and attitudes concerning fertility. In order to elucidate these influences, however, new research methods seem to be necessary, which – in combination with the fairly traditional methods treated in this book – could follow the processes of actual fertility, as well as of the norms, values

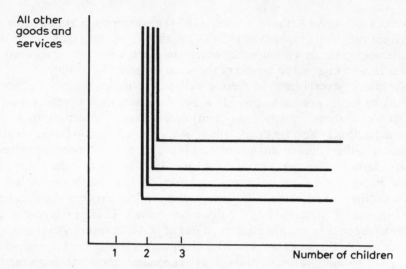

Figure 7.1 A hypothetical special indifference map.

and attitudes, and the factors that determine them. The development of these new lines and methods of research will become increasingly necessary, because, in the opinion of the author, as expressed in the preface to this book, the level of fertility might cause grave problems in advanced countries in coming decades.

BIBLIOGRAPHY

Abramowitz, M. (1961) The nature and significance of Kuznets cycles. *Economic Development and Cultural Change*, **9**, 225–48.

Acsádi, G., and Klinger, A. (1959) A termékenység, a családtervezés és szül-etésszabályozás néhány kérdése (Some problems of fertility, family planning and birth control). *Demográfia*, **2** (2–3), 176–216.

Acsádi, G., Klinger, A., and Szabady, E. (1969) Survey techniques in fertility and family planning research: experience in Hungary. *KSH Népességtudományi Kutató Intézet Közleményei*, no 26. 152 p.

Acsádi, G., Klinger, A., and Szabady, E. (1970) Családtervezés Magyarországon: az 1966. évi termékenységi és családtervezési vizsgálat (TCS) fontosabb adatai (Family planning in Hungary: main results of the 1966 fertility and family planning study). *KSH Népességtudományi Kutató Intézet Közleményei*, no 27. 204 p.

Adelman, I. (1963) An econometric analysis of population growth. *American Economic Review*, **53** (3), 314–39.

Adelman, I., and Morris, C. T. (1966) A quantitative study of social and political determinants of fertility. *Economic Development and Cultural Change*, **14** (2), 129–57.

Adelman, I., and Morris, C. T. (1967) *Society, Politics and Economic Development: A Quantitative Approach*. Baltimore: Johns Hopkins Press. 307 p.

Adonts, M. A., and Davtyan, M. (eds) (1968) *Materiali vsesoyuznoy nauchnoi konferentsii po problemam narodonasseleniya Zakavkazya (Materials of the All-Union Scientific Conference on the Population Problems of Transcaucasus)*. Yerevan.

Agren, K., Gaunt, D., Eriksson, I., Rogers, J., Norberg, A., and Akerman, S. (1973) *Aristocrats, Farmers, Proletarians: Essays in Swedish Demographic History*. Uppsala: Scandinavian University Books. 119 p.

Akerman, J. (1937) Bevölkerungswellen und Wechsellagen. *Schmollers Jahrbuch für Gesetzgebung, Verwaltung und Volkswirtschaft im Deutschen Reiche*, no 1, 91–8.

Andorka, R. (1967) A magyar népesség termékenységének alakulását befolyásoló gazdasági és társadalmi tényezők (Economic and social factors influencing the changes of fertility in Hungary). *Demográfia*, **10** (1), 87–102.

Andorka, R. (1968) *Economic and Social Factors Influencing Regional Fertility Differences in Hungary*. Paper presented at the International Symposium on the Problems of the Human Reproduction, Varna. 13 p.

Andorka, R. (1969a) A születésszám gazdasági és társadalmi tènyezői Magyarországon (Economic and social factors of the birth rate in Hungary). *Valóság*, **12** (3), 26–39.

Andorka, R. (1969b) A regionális termékenység különbségeket befolyásoló gazdasági és társadalmi tényezők (Economic and social factors influencing regional fertility differences). *Demográfia*, **12** (1–2), 114–24.

Andorka, R. (1969c) A déldunántuli egykekutatások története (History of the studies of birth control in Southern Transdanubia). *Statisztikai Szemle*, **47** (12), 1245–57.

Andorka, R. (1969d) Demographic factors in the planning of location of economic activity. *Regional Science Association Papers*, **22**, 149–55.

Andorka, R. (1970a) Születésszabályozás az Ormánságban a 18. század vége óta (Birth control in the region Ormánság since the end of the 18th century). *Demográfia*, **13** (1–2), 73–85.

Andorka, R. (1970b) *Multiple Regression and Covariance Analysis of the Factors Influencing Fertility in Hungary*. Paper presented at the World Conference of the Econometric Society, Cambridge. 10 p.

Andorka, R. (1970c) A társadalmi átrétegződés és demográfiai hatásai in Hungary (Social mobility and its demographic effects in Hungary). *KSH Népességtudományi Kutató Intézet Közleményei*, no 30. 394 p.

Andorka, R. (1971a) La prévention des naissances en Hongrie dans la région 'Ormánság' depuis la fin du XVIIIe siecle. *Population*, **25** (1), 63–78.

Andorka, R. (1971b) Regression analysis of the factors influencing regional fertility differences in Hungary. *International Population Conference, London, 1971*, vol. 1, 488–94.

Andorka, R. (1972) Un exemple de faible fécondité dans une région de la Hongrie, l'Ormansag a la fin du XVIIIe siecle et au début du XIXe: controle des naissances ou faux-semblants? *Annales de Démographie Historique*, 25–53.

Andorka, R. (1973) *Adatok az Ormánság népességtörténetéhez: Vajszló és Besence családrekonstituciós vizsgálatának eredményei* (*Data on the Demographic History of the Region Ormánság: the Results of the Family Reconstitution Study of Vajszló and Besence*). Unpublished. 100 p.

Andorka, R. (1974) *A család és háztartás nagysága és összetétele 1800 körül két déldunántuli faluban, Alsónyéken és Kölkeden* (*Size and composition of Family and Household around 1800 in two Transdanubian Villages, Alsónyék and Kölked*). Unpublished. 40 p.

Andorka, R. (1975) Az ormánsági születéskorlátozás története (History of birth control in the Ormánság). *Valóság*, **18** (6), 45–61.

Andorka, R. (1976) *Fertility, Nuptiality and Household Structure of Peasant Communities of Hungary in the XVIII–XIXth Centuries*. Paper presented at the Colloquium on Agrarian Structure and Regional Development in the XIXth century, Gödöllő. 11 p.

Anicic, Z. (1971) Certain indicators of recent fertility trends of Yugoslav population. *International Population Conference, London, 1971*, vol. 1, 495–509.

Ariès, P. (1953) Sur les origines de la contraception en France. *Population*, **8** (3), 464–72.

Ariès, P. (1954) Deux contributions à l'histoire des pratiques contraceptives, II: Chaucer et Madame de Sévigné. *Population*, **9** (4), 692–8.

Arnold, F., Bulatao, R. A., Buripakdi, C., Chung, B. J., Fawcett, J. T., Iritani, T., Lee, S. J. and Wu, T.-S. (1975) *The Value of Children: A Cross-National Study*, vol. 1. Honolulu: East–West Population Institute. 251 p.

Arutyunyan, L. A. (1968) Nekotoriye osobennosti planirovaniya semi v Armyanskoj SSR (Some aspects of family planning in Armenia). In Adonts and Davtyan (1968), 37–40.

Arutyunyan, L. A. (1975) *Socialisticheski zakon narodonaselenia*. Moscow: Nauka. 95 p.

Ashenfelter, O. (1973) Comment. *Journal of Political Economy*, **81** (2, pt 2), S96–S98.

Axelrod, M., Freedman, R., Goldberg, D., and Slesinger, D. (1963) Fertility expectations of the US population: a time series. *Population Index*, **29**, 23–51.

Back, K. W. (1967) New frontiers in demography and social psychology. *Demography*, **4**, 90–7.

Baltzell, E. D. (1953) Social mobility and fertility within an élite group. *Milbank Memorial Fund Quarterly*, **31** (4), 411–20.

Banks, J. A. (1954) *Prosperity and Parenthood*. London: Routledge & Kegan Paul. 240 p.

Banks, J. A. (1968) Historical sociology and the study of population. *Daedalus*, Spring, 397–414.

Banks, J. A., and Banks, O. (1954–5) The Bradlaugh-Besant trial and the English newspapers. *Population Studies*, **8** (1), 22–34.

Banks, J. A., and Banks, O. (1964) *Feminism and Family Planning in Victorian England*. New York: Schocken Books. 142 p.

Barsy, Gy., and Sárkány, J. (1963) A művi vetélések hatása a születési mozgalomra és a csecsemőhalandóságra (Impact of induced abortions on the birth rate and infant mortality). *Demográfia*, 6 (4), 427–67.

Basavarajappa, K. G. (1971) The influence of fluctuations in economic conditions on fertility and marriage rates, Australia 1920–1 to 1937–8 and 1946–7 to 1966–7. *Population Studies*, **25** (1), 39–53.

Bastide, H., and Girard, A. (1966) Les tendances démographiques en France et les attitudes de la population. *Population*, **21** (1), 9–50.

Bastide, H., and Girard, A. (1975) Attitudes et opinions des français à l'égard de la fécondité et de la famille. *Population*, **30** (4–5), 693–750.

Bean, F. D. (1975) Review symposium. Economics of the family: marriage, children, and human capital. *Demography*, **12** (3), 557–61.

Beauchamp, P., Charbonneau, H., and Lavoie, Y. (1973) Reconstitution automatique de familles par le programme 'Hochelaga'. *Population*, **28** (1), 39–58.

Becker, G. S. (1960) An economic analysis of fertility. In National Bureau of Economic Research (1960), 209–31.

Becker, G. S. (1965) A theory of the allocation of time. *Economic Journal*, **75** (299), 493–517.

Becker, G. S. (1973) A theory of marriage, pt I. *Journal of Political Economy*, **81** (4), 813–46.

Becker, G. S. (1974a) A theory of marriage, pt II. *Journal of Political Economy*, **82** (2, pt 2), 11–26.

Becker, G. S. (1974b) A theory of social interactions. *Journal of Political Economy*, **82** (6), 1063–93.

Becker, G. S., and Lewis, H. G. (1973) On the interaction between the quantity and quality of children. *Journal of Political Economy*, **81** (2, pt 2), S279–88.

Behrman, S. J., Corsa, L., Jr, and Freedman, R. (eds) (1969) *Fertility and Family Planning: A World View*. Ann Arbor: University of Michigan Press. 503 p.

Belova, V. (1971) Obsledivanie mienenii o nailuchsem i ozhidaemom chisle detai v sem'e (A survey of the opinions about optimal and expected family size). *Vestnik Statistiki*, no 6, 23–34.

Belova, V. A., and Darski, L. E. (1968) Mnenia zhenshin o formirovanii semi (Opinions of women on the formation of family). *Vestnik Statistiki*, no 6, 27–36.

Benedek, T. (1959) Parenthood as a developmental phase. *Journal of the American Psychoanalytic Association*, **7**, 389–417.

Benjamin, B. (1959) Recent fertility trends in England and Wales. In Internationaler Bevölkerungskongress, Wien (1959), 249–56.

Berelson, B. (1964) On family planning communications. *Demography*, **1**, 94–105.

Berend, T. I., and Ránki, Gy. (1955) *Magyarország gyáripara 1900–14 (Manufacturing Industry of Hungary 1900–14)*. Budapest: Szikra. 396 p.

Berend, T. I., and Ránki, Gy. (1969) *Közép-Kelet-Európa gazdasági fejlődése a 19–20. században (Economic Development of Eastern Central Europe in the 19th to 20th Centuries)*. Budapest: Közgazdasági és Jogi Könyvkiadó. 416 p.

Berend, T. I., and Ránki, Gy. (1972) *A magyar gazdaság száz éve (Hundred Years of Hungarian Economy)*. Budapest: Közgazdasági és Jogi Könyvkiadó. 329 p.

Berend, T. I., and Szuhay, M. (1973) *A tőkés gazdaság története Magyarországon 1848–1944. (History of Capitalist Economy in Hungary 1848–1944)*. Budapest: Közgazdasági és Jogi Könyvkiadó. 365 p.

Berent, J. (1951–2) Fertility and social mobility. *Population Studies*, **5** (3), 244–60.

Berent, J. (1953) The relationship between family sizes of two successive generations. *Milbank Memorial Fund Quarterly*, **31** (1), 39–50.

Berent, J. (1970) Causes of fertility decline in Eastern Europe and Soviet Union. *Population Studies*, **24** (1), 35–58, (2), 247–92.

Bernhardt, E. M. (1972) Fertility and economic status. Some recent findings on differentials in Sweden. *Population Studies*, **26** (2), 175–84.

Beshers, J. M. (1967) *Population Processes in Social Systems*. New York: Collier-Macmillan. 207 p.

Bhattacharyya, A. K. (1975) Income inequality and fertility: a comparative view. *Population Studies*, **29** (1), 5–20.

Biraben, J.-N. (1975a) La conjoncture démographique: la France. *Population*, **30** (3), 569–84.

Biraben, J.-N. (1975b) La conjoncture démographique: l'Europe. *Population*, **30** (4–5), 849–53.

Biraben, J.-N. (1976) La conjoncture démographique: l'Europe. *Population*, **31** (4–5), 917–24.

Biraben, J.-N., Fleury, M., and Henry, L. (1960) Inventaire par sondage des registres paroissiaux. *Population*, **15** (1), 25–58.

Blacker, C. P. (1947) Stages in population growth. *Eugenics Review*, **39**, 81–101.

Blacker, J. G. (1957) Social ambitions of the bourgeoisie in 18th century France and their relation to family limitation. *Population Studies*, **11** (1), 46–63.

Blake, J. (1965) Demographic science and the redirection of population policy. In Sheps and Ridley (1965), 41–69.

Blake, J. (1966) Ideal family size among white Americans: a quarter of a century's evidence. *Demography*, **3**, 154–73.

Blake, J. (1966–7) The Americanization of Catholic reproductive ideals. *Population Studies*, **20** (1), 27–43.

Blake, J. (1967a) Reproductive ideals and educational attainment among white Americans 1943–66. *Population Studies*, **21** (2), 159–74.

Blake, J. (1967b) Income and reproductive motivation. *Population Studies*, **21** (3), 185–206.

Blake, J. (1967c) Family size in the 1960s: a baffling fad? *Eugenics Quarterly*, **14** (1), 60–74.

Blake, J. (1968) Are babies consumer durables? *Population Studies*, **22** (1), 5–25.

Blake, J. (1974) Can we believe recent data on birth expectations in the United States? *Demography*, **11** (1), 25–44.

Blau, P. M. (1956) Social mobility and interpersonal relations. *American Sociological Review*, **21**, 290–5.

Blau, P. M., and Duncan, O. D. (1967) *The American Occupational Structure*. New York: Wiley, 520 p.

Blaug, M. (1963) The myth of the Old Poor Law and the making of the New. *Journal of Economic History*, 24 (1), 229–45.

Blayo, Ch. (1968) Fécondité des mariages de 1946 à 1964 en France. *Population*, **23** (4), 649–738.

Blayo, Ch. (1972) La baisse de la fécondité française. *Population*, **27** (3), 471–90.

Blayo, Ch. (1975) Natalité, fécondité. *Population*, **29**, 51–80.

Blayo, Ch., and Festy, P. (1975) La fécondité à l'Est et à l'Ouest de l'Europe. *Population*, **30** (4–5), 855–88.

Blayo, Y. (1971) *Couplage des données d'état civil et des listes nominatives de recensement*. Paper presented at the Colloque International de Démographie Historique, Firenze. 4 p.

Blayo, Y., and Henry, L. (1967) Données démographiques sur la Bretagne et l'Anjou de 1740 à 1829. *Annales de Démographie Historique*, 91–171.

Blood, R. O., and Wolfe, D. M. (1960) *Husbands and Wives: The Dynamics of Married Living*. New York: Free Press.

Bodmer, W. F., and Jacquard, A. (1968) La variance de la dimension des familles, selon divers facteurs de la fécondité. *Population*, **23** (5), 869–79.

Bodrova, V. (1972) La politique démographique dans les républiques populaires de l'Europe. *Population*, **27** (6), 1001–18.

Bogue, D. J. (ed.) (1967) *Mass Communication and Motivation for Birth Control: Proceedings of the Summer Workshops at the University of Chicago*. Chicago: Community and Family Study Center, University of Chicago.

Bogue, D. J. (1969) *Principles of Demography*. New York: Wiley. 917 p.

Bogue, D. J. (1971) *Demographic Techniques of Fertility Analysis*. Chicago: Community and Family Study Center, University of Chicago. 116 p.

Bogue, D. J., and Harris, D. L. (1954) *Comparative Population and Urban Research Via Multiple Regression and Covariance Analysis*. Oxford, Ohio: Scripps Foundation, Miami University, and Chicago: Population Research and Training Center, University of Chicago, Studies in Population Distribution no 8. 75 p.

Bogue, D. J., and Heiskanen, V. S. (1963) *How to Improve Written Communication for Birth Control*. Chicago: Community and Family Study Center, University of Chicago. 90 p.

Bondarskaya, G. A. (1970) Rol etnicheskovo faktora v formirovanii territorialnykh razlichii rozhdayemosti (The role of the ethnic factor in the formation of territorial differentials of fertility). In Volkov *et al.* (1970), 160–75.

Bondarskaya, G. A. (1971) Vliyanie etnicheskovo faktora na uroveni rozhdaye-mosti (The influence of the ethnic factor on the level of fertility). In Volkov (1971), 52–62.

Bondarskaya, G. A., and Kozlov, V. I. (1971) Natsionalni sostav nasseleniya kak faktor differentsyatsii rozhdayemosti (Nationality composition of population as a factor of differential fertility). In Volkov (1971), 63–76.

Bourdieu, P., and Darbel, A. (1966) La fin d'un malthusianisme? In Darras (1966), 135–54.

Bourdieu, P., Darbel, A., and Febvay, M. (1964) *Essai d'explication des tendances de la natalité française.* Colloque d'Arras. 120 p.

Bourgeois-Pichat, J. (1965a) Les facteurs de la fécondité non dirigée. *Population,* **20** (3), 383–424.

Bourgeois-Pichat, J., and Taleb, S. A. (1970) Un taux d'accroissement nul pour les since the eighteenth century. In Glass and Eversley (1965), 474–506.

Bourgeois-Pichat, J. (1976) Baisse de la fécondité et descendance finale. *Population,* **31** (6), 1045–97.

Bourgeois-Pichat, J. (no date) *Manuel: Le concept de population stable,* vols 1–4. 595 p.

Bourgeois-Pichat, J., and Taleb, S.-A. (1970) Un taux d'accroissement nul pour les pays en voie de développement en l'an 2000: rêve ou réalité? *Population,* **25** (5), 957–74.

Boverat, F. (1946) *Le vieillissement de la population.* Paris: Les Éditions Sociales Françaises. 164 p.

Braun, R. (1960) *Industrialisierung und Volksleben: Die Veränderungen der Lebensformen in einem ländlichen Industriegebiet vor 1800 (Zürcher Oberland).* Zürich: Eugen Rentsch Verlag. 287 p.

Brésard, M. (1950) Mobilité sociale et dimension de famille. *Population,* **5** (3), 533–66.

Breznik, D. (1967) A jugoszláv népesség termékenysége (Fertility of Yugoslavian population). *Demográfia,* **10** (3–4), 328–42.

Breznik, D. (1969) Rozwój zjawisk demograficznych w Jugoslawii (Development of demographic phenomena in Yugoslavia). *Studia Demograficzne,* **18**, 25–38.

Breznik, D., Mojic, A., Rasevic, M., and Rancic, M. (1972) *Fertilitet stanovnistva u Jugoslaviji.* Beograd: Institut Drustvenih Nauka. 429 p.

Breznik, D., *et al.* (1974) *Évolution de la population de la Yougoslavie pendant la période de l'après-guerre.* Beograd: Institut des Sciences Sociales. 84 p.

Brooks, H. F., and Henry, F. J. (1958) An empirical study of the relationship of Catholic practice and occupational mobility to fertility. *Milbank Memorial Fund Quarterly,* **36**, 222–81.

Buday, D. (1909) Az egyke (The one child system). *Huszadik Század,* **10** (2), 260–8, 408–15.

Buissink, J. D. (1971) Regional differences in marital fertility in the Netherlands in the second half of the nineteenth century. *Population Studies,* **25** (3), 353–74.

Bumpass, L. (1969) Age at marriage as a variable in socio-economic differentials in fertility. *Demography,* **6** (1), 45–54.

Bumpass, L. (1975) Comment on J. Blake's 'Can we believe recent data on birth expectations in the United States?' *Demography,* **12** (1), 155–6.

Bumpass, L., and Westoff, C. F. (1969) The prediction of completed fertility. *Demography,* **6** (4), 445–54.

Bumpass, L., and Westoff, C. F. (1971) *The Later Years of Childbearing.* Princeton: Princeton University Press. 183 p.

Burch, T. K. (1966) The fertility of North American Catholics: a comparative overview. *Demography,* **3** (1), 174–87.

Burch, T. K., and Gendell, M. (1971) Extended family structure and fertility: some conceptual and methodological issues. In Polgar (1971), 87–104.

Burgdörfer, F. (1929) *Der Geburtenrückgang und seine Bekämpfung.* Berlin: Schoetz. 192 p.

Burgdörfer, F. (1932) *Volk ohne Jugend.* Berlin: Vawinckel. 448 p.

Burgdörfer, F. (1937) *Völker am Abgrund.* München: Lehmann. 76 p.

Caldwell, J. C. (1976) Toward a restatement of demographic transition theory. *Population and Development Review,* **2** (3–4), 321–66.

Calot, G., Hémery, S., and Piro, C. (1969) L'évolution récente de la fécondité et de la nuptialité en France. *Population,* **24** (2), 263–92.

Campbell, A. A. (1974) Beyond the demographic transition. *Demography,* **11** (4), 549–61.

Cantillon, R. (1931) *Essai sur la Nature du Commerce.* London: Kelley. 436 p.

Carlsson, G. (1966) The decline of fertility: innovation or adjustment process. *Population Studies,* **20** (2), 149–74.

Carlsson, G. (1970) Nineteenth-century fertility oscillations. *Population Studies,* **24** (3), 413–22.

Casetti, E. (1968) A formalization of the demographic transition theory. *Regional Science Association Papers,* **21**, 159–64.

Centers, R., and Blumberg, G. (1954) Social and psychological factors in human procreation: a survey approach. *Journal of Social Psychology,* **40**, 245–57.

Central Statistical Office (1975) Jelentés a népesedéspolitikai intézkedések eredményeiről. (Report on the results of population policy). *Statisztikai Szemle,* **53** (10), 1021–36.

Chambers, J. D. (1957) The Vale of Trent 1670–1800. *Economic History Review,* Suppl. 3.

Chambers, J. D. (1965) Three essays on the population and economy of the Midlands. In Glass and Eversley (1965), 308–53.

Charbonneau, H. (1970) *Tourouvre-au-Perche aux XVIIe et XVIIIe siècles.* INED Travaux et Documents, no 55. 423 p.

Charbonneau, H. (1975) *Vie et mort de nos ancêtres.* Montréal: Presses de l'Université de Montréal. 267 p.

Chasteland, J. C., and Henry, L. (1956) Disparité régionale de la fécondité des mariages. *Population,* **11** (4), 653–72.

Chaunu, C. (1966) La civilisation de l'Europe Classique. Paris: Arthaud. 705 p.

Chilman, G. (1968) Fertility and poverty in the United States: some implications for family planning programs, evaluation and research. *Journal of Marriage and Family,* **30**, 207–27.

Chojnacka, H. (1976) Nuptiality patterns in an agrarian society. *Population Studies,* **30** (2), 203–26.

Chou, R.-C., and Brown, S. (1968) A comparison of the size of families of Roman Catholics and non-Catholics in Great Britain. *Population Studies,* **22** (1), 51–60.

Christensen, H. T. (1968) Children in the family: relationship of number and spacing to marital success. *Journal of Marriage and the Family,* **30**, 283–98.

Cicourel, A. (1967) Fertility, family planning and the social organization of family life: some methodological issues. *Journal of Social Issues,* **23**, 57–81.

Cipolla, C. M. (1962) *The Economic History of World Population*. Harmondsworth: Penguin. 126 p.

Cipolla, C. M. (1965) Four centuries of Italian demographic development. In Glass and Eversley (1965), 570–87.

Clark, C. (1967) *Population Growth and Land Use*. London: Macmillan. 406 p.

Coale, A. J. (1963) Estimates of various demographic measures through quasi-stable age distribution. In Milbank Memorial Fund (1963).

Coale, A. J. (1965) Factors associated with the development of low fertility: an historic summary. In World Population Conference (1965), vol. 2, 205–9.

Coale, A. J. (1969) The decline of fertility in Europe from the French Revolution to World War II. In Behrman *et al.* (1969), 3–24.

Coale, A. J. (1973) The demographic transition. In International Population Conference, Liège (1973), vol. 1, 53–72.

Coale, A. J., and Demény, P. (1966) *Regional Life Tables and Stable Populations*. Princeton: Princeton University Press. 871 p.

Coale, A. J., and Hoover, E. M. (1958) *Population Growth and Economic Development in Low Income Countries*. Princeton: Princeton University Press. 389 p.

Cochrane, S. H. (1975) Children as by-products, investment goods and consumer goods: a review of some micro-economic models of fertility. *Population Studies*, **29** (3) 373–90.

Collomb, P. (1976) De quelques facteurs structurels de la baisse de la fécondité française. *Population*, **31** (6), 1099–1117.

Commission on Population Growth and the American Future (1972) *Population and the American Future: Report of the Commission on Population Growth and the American Future*. 186 p.

Connell, K. H. (1965) Land and population in Ireland 1780–1845. In Glass and Eversley (1965), 423–33.

Coombs, L. C. (1974). The measurement of family size preferences and subsequent fertility. *Demography*, **11** (4), 587–611.

Coombs, L. C., and Freedman, R. (1970) Pre-marital pregnancy, child-spacing, and later economic achievement. *Population Studies*, **34** (3), 389–412.

Cowgill, D. O. (1949) The theory of population growth cycles. *American Journal of Sociology*, **55**, 163–70.

Cseh-Szombathy, L., and Miltényi, K. (1969) Gyermekgondozási segély (Child care allowance). *KSH Népességtudományi Kutató Intézet Közleményei*, no 25. 98 p.

Cseh-Szombathy, L., Heinz, E., and Miltényi, K. (1970) Gyermekgondozási segély (Child care allowance). *KSH Népességtudományi Kutató Intézet Közleményei*, no 28. 104 p.

Dányi, D. (1960) Az 1777. évi lelkek összeirása (A demographic description from the year 1777). *Történeti Statisztikai Évkönyv*, 167–93. Budapest: Központi Statisztikai Hivatal Könyvtára.

Dányi, D. (1972) La migration et les méthodes nominatives: l'exemple hongrois. *Annales de Démographie Historique*, 69–82.

Dányi, D. (1973) *Győr város történeti demográfiája (Historical Demography of the Town Győr)*. Unpublished. 90 p.

Darras (1966) *Le partage des bénéfices: Expansion et inégalités en France*. Paris: Les Éditions de Minuit. 444 p.

David, H. P. (1970) *Family Planning and Abortion in the Socialist Countries of Central and Eastern Europe*. New York: The Population Council. 306 p.

David, H. P., and Wright, N. H. (1972) La législation sur l'avortement: l'expérience roumaine. *Etudes de Planning Familial*, **2** (10), 369–79.

Dávid, Z. (1957) Az 1715–1720. évi összeirás (Census of 1715–1720). In Kovacsics (1957), 145–99.

Dávid, Z. (1963) A történeti demográfiai források értékelésének kérdései (Problems of evaluation of sources of historical deomography). *Demográfia*, **6** (4), 515–25.

Davis, K. (1945) The world demographic transition. *Annals of the American Academy of Political and Social Sciences*, **273**, 1–11.

Davis, K. (1959) The sociology of demographic behavior. In Merton *et al.* (1959), 309–33.

Davis, K. (1963) The theory of change and response in modern demographic history. *Population Index*, **29** (4), 345–66.

Davis, K., and Blake, J. (1956) Social structure and fertility: an analytical framework. *Economic Development and Cultural Change*, **4**, 211–35.

Davtyan, L. M. (1965) *The Influence of Socio-economic Factors on Natality from the Example of the Armenian SSR*. Paper presented at the World Population Conference, Belgrade. 8 p.

Day, L. H. (1968) Natality and ethnocentrism: some relationships suggested by an analysis of catholic-protestant differentials. *Population Studies*, **22** (1), 27–50.

Deane, P., and Cole, W. A. (1962) *British Economic Growth 1688–1959: Trends and Structure*. Cambridge: Cambridge University Press. 348 p.

De Jong, C. F. (1965) Religious fundamentalism, socio-economic status, and fertility attitudes in the Southern Appalachians. *Demography*, **2**, 540–8.

De Laszlo, H., and Henshaw, P. S. (1954) Plant materials used by primitive groups to affect fertility. *Science*, **119**, 621–36.

Demény, P. (1965) Estimation of vital rates for populations in the process of destabilization. *Demography*, **2**, 516–30.

Demény, P. (1968) Early fertility decline in Austria–Hungary: A lesson in demographic transition. *Daedalus*, Spring, 502–22.

Demográfiai jellemzők a települések nagyságcsoportja szerint, 1900–1960 (Demographic data by size of towns and villages, 1900–1960). (1968) *KSH Népességtudományi Kutató Intézet Közleményei*, no 22. 509 p.

Den Hollander, A. N. J. (1960–1) The Great Hungarian Plain: a European frontier. *Comparative Studies in Society and History*, **3**, 74–88, 155–67.

Deniel, R., and Henry, L. (1965) La population d'un village du Nord de la France, Sainghin-en-Mèlantois. *Population*, **20** (4), 563–602.

Deprèz, P. (1965) The demographic development of Flanders in the eighteenth century. In Glass and Eversley (1965), 608–30.

Derksen, J. B. D. (1966) *On the Use of Cross-Section Analysis in Demography, Illustrated by a Study of Regional Variations of Fertility in the Netherlands*. Paper presented at the European Population Conference, Strasbourg. 11 p.

Derksen, J. B. D. (1970) *Economic and Social Factors Explaining Interregional Variations in Marital Fertility in the Netherlands*. Paper presented at the World Conference of the Econometric Society, Cambridge. 11 p.

De Tray, D. N. (1973) Child quality and the demand for children. *Journal of Political Economy*, **81** (2, pt 2), S70–S95.

Devereux, G. (1955) *A Study of Abortion in Primitive Societies.* New York: Julian Press. 394 p.

Devereux, G. (1967) A typological study of abortion in 350 primitive, ancient and preindustrial societies. In Rose (1967), 97–152.

De Wolff, P., Meerdink, J. (1957) La fécondité des mariages à Amsterdam selon l'appartenance sociale et réligieuse. *Population*, **12** (2), 289–318.

Dinkel, R. M. (1952) Occupation and fertility in the United States. *American Sociological Review*, 17 (2), 178–83.

Douglas, M. (1966) Population control in primitive groups. *British Journal of Sociology*, **17**, 263–73.

Drake, M. (1969) *Population and Society in Norway* 1735–1865. Cambridge: Cambridge University Press. 256 p.

Draper, W. H., Jr (1969) Is zero population growth the answer? Address at testimonial dinner in Washington, D.C., 2 December 1969. Population Crisis Committee.

Duesenberry, J. S. (1960) Comment. In National Bureau of Economic Research (1960), 231–4.

Dumont, A. (1890) Dépopulation et civilisation. Paris: Lecrossier-Babe. 520 p.

Duncan, O. D. (1964) Residential areas and differential fertility. *Eugenics Quarterly*, **11**, 82–9.

Duncan, O. D. (1965) Farm background and differential fertility. *Demography*, **2**, 240–9.

Duncan, O. D., Freedman, R., Coble, J. M., and Slesinger, D. P. (1965) Marital fertility and size of family of orientation. *Demography*, **2**, 508–15.

Dupaquier, J. (1971) Bilan et perspectives des recherches françaises en démographie historique. In International Population Conference (1971), vol. 4, 2331–5.

Dupaquier, J., and Lachiver, M. (1969) Sur les débuts de la contraception en France ou les deux malthusianismes. *Annales E.S.C.*, **24** (6), 1391–406.

Dziennio, K. (1964) Zmiany poziomu plodnosci kobiet w Polsce (Changes of the level of fertility of women in Poland). *Studia Demograficzne*, **7**, 79–92.

Easterlin, R. A. (1961) The American baby boom in historical perspective. *American Economic Review*, **51** (5), 869–911.

Easterlin, R. A. (1966) Economic-demographic interactions and long swings in economic growth. *American Economic Review*, **56** (5), 1063–1104.

Easterlin, R. A. (1968) *Population, Labor Force, and Long Swings in Economic Growth: The American Experience*. New York: National Bureau of Economic Research. 298 p.

Easterlin, R. A. (1969) Toward a socio-economic theory of fertility. In Behrman *et al.* (1969), 127–156.

Easterlin, R. A. (1971) Does human fertility adjust to the environment? *American Economic Review*, **61** (2), 399–407.

Easterlin, R. A. (1975) Analyse de la fécondité dans un cadre économique approprié. *Études de Planning familial*, **6** (3), 87–101.

Easterlin, R. A. (1976) The conflict between aspirations and resources. *Population and Development Review*, **2** (3–4), 417–25.

Eaton, J. W., and Mayer, A. J. (1953) The social biology of very high fertility among the Hutterites: the demography of a unique population. *Human Biology*, **25**, 256–62.

Edin, K. A., and Hutchinson, E. P. (1935) *Studies in Differential Fertility in Sweden.* London: King. 116 p.

Eldridge, H. T. (1954) *Population Policies: A Survey of Recent Developments.* Washington: International Union for the Scientific Study of Population. 153 p.

Elek, P., Gunda, B., Hilscher, Z., Horváth, S., Karsay, Gy., Kerényi, Gy., Koczogh, Á., Kovács, I., Pócsy, F., and Torbágyi, L. (1936) *Elsüllyedt falu a Dunántulon (A Sunken Village in Transdanubia).* Budapest: Sylvester. 159 p.

Engels, F. (1964) Outlines of a critique of political economy. Appendix to Mark, K., *The Economic and Philosophical Manuscripts of 1884.* New York: International Publishers.

Erdei, F. (no date) *A magyar paraszttàrsadalom (Hungarian Peasant Society).* Budapest: Franklin. 170 p.

Erikson, E. H. (1964) Inner and outer space. *Daedalus,* Spring, 582–606.

Eversley, D. E. C. (1959) *Social Theories of Fertility and the Malthusian Debate.* Oxford: Clarendon Press. 313 p.

Eversley, D. E. C. (1961) *Population in England in the Eighteenth Century: An Appraisal of Current Research.* Paper presented at the International Population Conference, New York.

Eversley, D. E. C. (1965a) Population, economy and society. In Glass and Eversley (1965), 23–69.

Eversley, D. E. C. (1965b) A survey of population in an area of Worcestershire from 1660 to 1850 on the basis of parish registers. In Glass and Eversley (1965), 394–419.

Eversley, D. E. C. (1968) Evaluation of family data relating to a religious sect in Ireland in the 17th and 18th century: a preliminary report on methods and results of an investigation into the demography of Quakers. In Kovacsics and Thirring (1968), 42–52.

Farber, B., and Blackman, L. S. (1956) Marital role tensions and number and sex of children. *American Sociological Review,* **21,** 596–601.

Fawcett, J. T. (1970) *Psychologie et population.* New York: Population Council. 142 p.

Fawcett, J. T. (1973) *Psychological Perspectives on Population.* New York: Basic Books. 522 p.

Hoffman, L. W. and Hoffman, M. L., The value of children to parents, 19–76.

Back, K. W., and Hass, P. H., Family structure and fertility control, 77–105.

Fawcett, J. T., and Bornstein, M. B., Modernization, individual modernity, and fertility, 106–31.

Chilman, C. S., Some psychological aspects of fertility, family planning, and population policy in the United States, 163–182.

Clausen, J. A., and Clausen, S. R., The effects of family size on parents and children, 185–208.

Fawcett, J. T. (1974) Psychological research on family size and family planning in the United States. *Professional Psychology,* **5** (3), 334–44.

Fawcett, J. T., and Arnold, F. S. (1973) The value of children: theory and method. *Representative Research in Social Psychology,* **4** (1), 23–35.

Febvay, M. (1959) Niveau et évolution de la fécondité par catégorie socio-professionnelle. *Population,* **14** (4), 729–39.

Federici, N. (1955) Fattori soziali ed omogeneozzazione del comportamento demográfico. *Statistica,* **15,** 537–58.

Federici, N. (1967) A női munka hatása a termékenységre (The influence of female employment on fertility). *Demográfia*, **10** (3–4), 343–9.

Ferenbac, I. (1962) A technikai fejlődés és a szocialista termelési viszonyok hatása a születésekre és halálozásokra a Román Népköztársaságban (The impact of technical development and of socialist relations of production on the birth and death rates in the Romanian People's Republic). *Demográfia*, **5** (4), 463–70.

Ferenbac, I. (1971) Changes in the evolution of birth rates in the Socialist Republic of Romania. In International Population Conference, London, (1971), vol. 1, 688–9.

Festy, P. (1970) Évolution de la fécondité en Europe occidentale depuis la guerre. *Population*, **25** (2), 229–74.

Festy, P. (1974) La situation démographique des deux Allemagnes. *Population*, **29** (4–5), 795–824.

Firth, R. (1936) *We, the Tikopia: A Sociological Study of Kinship in Primitive Polynesia*. London: Allen & Unwin. 605 p.

Firth, R. (1939) *Primitive Polynesian Economy*. London: Routledge & Sons. 387 p.

Fisher, R. A. (1929) *The Genetical Theory of Natural Selection*. New York: Dover Publications. 272 p.

Flandrin, J.-L. (1969) Contraception, mariage et relations amoureuses dans l'Occident Chrétien. *Annales ESC*, **24** (6), 1370–90.

Fleury, M., and Henry, L. (1958) Pour connaitre la population de la France depuis Louis XIV: Plan de travaux par sondage. *Population*, **13** (4), 663–86.

Fleury, M., and Henry, L. (1965) *Nouveau manuel de dépouillement et d'exploitation de l'état civil ancien*. Paris: INED. 182 p.

Flew, A. (1970) Introduction. In Malthus (1970), 7–56.

Ford, T. R., and De Jong, C. F. (eds) (1970) *Social Demography*. Englewood Cliffs: Prentice Hall. 690 p.

Forster, C., and Tucker, G. S. L. (1972) *Economic Opportunity and White American Fertility Ratios 1800–1860*. New Haven: Yale University Press. 121 p.

Foster, G. N. (1965) Peasant society and the image of limited good. *American Anthropologist*, **67**, 293–315.

Freedman, D. S. (1963) The relation of economic status to fertility. *American Economic Review*, **53** (3), 414–26.

Freedman, R. (1961–2) The sociology of human fertility. A trend report and bibliography. *Current Sociology*, **10–11** (2), 35–121.

Freedman, R. (1962) The American studies of family planning and fertility: a review of major trends and issues. In Kiser (1962), 211–27.

Freedman, R. (1963) Norms for family size in underdeveloped areas. *Proceedings of the Royal Society*, **B159**, pt 974, 220–45.

Freedman, R., Baumert, G., and Bolte, M. (1959) Expected family size and family size values in West Germany. *Population Studies*, **13** (2), 136–50.

Freedman, R., and Coombs, L. C. (1966a) Economic considerations in family growth decisions. *Population Studies*, **20** (2), 177–222.

Freedman, R., and Coombs, L. C. (1966b) Childspacing and family economic position. *American Sociological Review*, **31** (5), 631–48.

Freedman, R., Coombs, L. C., and Bumpass, L. (1965) Stability and change in expectations about family size: a longitudinal study. *Demography*, **2** (2), 250–75.

Freedman, R., Goldberg, D., and Sharp, H. (1955) Ideals about family size in Detroit Metropolitan Area, 1954. *Milbank Memorial Fund Quarterly*, **33** (2), 187–97.

Freedman, R., Goldberg, D., and Slesinger, D. (1963) Current fertility expectations of married couples in the United States. *Population Index*, **29**, 366–91.

Freedman, R., and Sharp, H. (1954–5) Correlates of values about ideal family size in the Detroit Metropolitan Area. *Population Studies*, **8** (1), 35–45.

Freedman, R., Whelpton, P. K., and Campbell, A. A. (1959) *Family Planning, Sterility, and Population Growth*. New York: McGraw-Hill. 515 p.

Freedman, R., Whelpton, P. K., and Smit, J. W. (1961) Socio-economic factors in religious differentials in fertility. *American Sociological Review*, **26** (4), 608–14.

Frenkel, I., 1976, Attitudes toward family size in some East European countries. *Populations Studies*, **30**, no 1. 35–57 p.

Freyka, T. (1973) *The Future of Population Growth*. New York: Wiley. 268 p.

Fridlizius, G. (1975) Some new aspects on Swedish population growth. *Economy and History*, **18** (1), 3–33 (2), 126–54.

Friedlander, D. (1969) Demographic responses and population change. *Demography*, **6** (4), 359–81.

Friedlander, D. (1973) Demographic patterns and socioeconomic characteristics of the coal-mining population in England and Wales in the nineteenth century. *Economic Development and Cultural Change*, **21 21** (1), 39–51.

Friedlander, S., and Silver, M. (1967) A quantitative study of the determinants of fertility behavior. *Demography*, **4** (1), 30–70.

Frigyes, E. (1964) A munkás és alkalmazotti jövedelmi rétegződés legfontosabb tényezői (Principal factors of stratification of the workers and employees by income). *Statisztikai Szemle*, **42** (7), 748–66.

Fülep. L. (1929) Interview and articles. *Pesti Napló*. 15, 17 and 26 November, 4 and 15 December.

Galbraith, V. L., Thomas, D. S. (1941) Birth rates and the interwar business cycles. *Journal of the American Statistical Association*, **36**, 465–76.

Ganiage, J. (1963) Trois villages de l'Ile de France. *INED Travaux et Documents*, no 40. 148 p.

Gardner, B. (1973) Economics of the size of North Carolina rural families. *Journal of Political Economy*, **81** (2, pt 2), S99–S122.

Gaunt, D. (1973) Family planning and the pre-industrial society: some Swedish evidence. In Agren *et al.* (1973), 28–59.

Gaunt, D. (1976) Familj, hushall och arbetsintensitet. *Scandia*, **42** (1), 32–59.

Gautier, E., and Henry, L. (1958) La population de Crulai paroisse normande. *INED Travaux et Documents*, no 26. 234 p.

Gerhard, D. (1959) The frontier in comparative view. *Comparative Studies in Society and History*, **1**, 205–29.

Gerschenkron, A. (1966) *Economic Backwardness in Historical Perspective*. Cambridge, Mass.: Harvard University Press. 456 p.

Gille, H. (1948–9) Recent developments in Swedish population policy. *Population Studies*, **2** (1), 3–70, (2), 129–84.

Gille, H. (1949–50) The demographic history of the Northern European countries in the eighteenth century. *Population Studies*, **3** (1), 3–65.

Girard, A. (1951) Mobilité sociale et dimension de la famille. Deuxième partie: enquête dans les lycées et les facultés. *Population*, **6** (1), 103–24.

Girard, A. (1977) Dimension idéale de la famille et tendances de la fécondité: Comparaisons internationales. *Population*, **31** (6), 1119–46.

Girard, A., and Bastide, H. (1958) Une enquête sur l'efficacité de l'action sociale des caisses d'allocations familiales. *Population*, **13** (1), 39–45.

Girard, A., and Bastide, H. (1960) Les problèmes démographiques devant l'opinion. *Population*, **15** (2), 245–88.

Girard, A., and Henry, L. (1956) Les attitudes et la conjoncture démographique: natalité, structure familiale et limites de la vie active. *Population*, **11** (1), 105–41.

Girard, A., Roussel, L., and Bastide, H. (1976) Natalité et politique familiale: Une enquête d'opinion. *Population*, **31** (2), 355–77.

Girard, A., and Zucker, É. (1967) Une enquête auprès du public sur la structure familiale et la prévention des naissances. *Population*, **22** (3), 401–54.

Girard, A., and Zucker, É. (1968) La conjoncture démographique: régulation des naissances, famille et natalité. Une enquète auprès le public. *Population*, **23** (2), 225–64.

Girard, P. (1959) Aperçu de la démographie de Sotteville-les-Rouen vers la fin du XVIIIe siècle. *Population*, **14** (3), 485–508.

Glass, D. V. (1951) A note on the under-registration of births in Britain in the nineteenth century. *Population Studies*, **5** (1), 70–88.

Glass, D. V. (1965a) Population growth and population policy. In Sheps and Ridley (1965), 3–24.

Glass, D. V. (1965b) Population and population movements in England and Wales, 1700 to 1850. In Glass and Eversley (1965), 221–46.

Glass, D. V. (1967) *Population Policies and Movements in Europe*, 2nd ed. London: Cass. 490 p.

Glass, D. V. (1968) Fertility trends in Europe since the Second World War. *Population Studies*, **22** (1), 103–46.

Glass, D. V., and Eversley, D. E. C. (eds) (1965) *Population in History*. London: Edward Arnold. 602 p.

Glass, D. V., and Grebenik, E. (1954a) *The Trend and Pattern of Fertility in Great Britain: A Report on the Family Census of 1946. Part I: Report*. London: HMSO. 306 p.

Glass, D. V., and Grebenik, E. (1954b) *The Trend and Pattern of Fertility in Great Britain: A Report on the Family Census of 1946. Part II: Tables*. London: HMSO. 253 p.

Goldberg, D. (1959) The fertility of two-generation urbanites. *Population Studies*, **12** (3), 214–22.

Goldberg, D. (1960) Another look at the Indianapolis fertility data. *Milbank Memorial Fund Quarterly*, **38**, 23–36.

Goldberg, D. (1965) Fertility and fertility differentials: some observations on recent changes in the United States. In Sheps and Ridley (1965), 119–42.

Goldscheider, C. (1965) Ideological factors on Jewish fertility differentials. *Jewish Journal of Sociology*, **7**, 92–105.

Goldscheider, C. (1971) Population, modernization, and social structure. Boston: Little, Brown. 345 p.

Goldscheider, C., and Uhlenberg, P. R. (1969) Minority group status and fertility. *American Journal of Sociology*, **74** (4), 361–72.

Goldstein, S., and Mayer, K. B. (1965) Residence and status differences in fertility. *Milbank Memorial Fund Quarterly*, **43** (3), 291–310.

Goodwin, A. (ed.) (1967) *The European Nobility in the Eighteenth Century*. London: Black. 204 p.

Goubert, P. (1960) *Beauvais et le Beauvaisis de 1600 a 1730: Contribution à l'histoire sociale de la France du XVIIe siècle*, vols 1–2. Paris: École Pratique des Hautes Études. 653 and 118 p.

Goubert, P. (1965) Recent theories and research in French population between 1500 and 1700. In Glass and Eversley (1965), 457–73.

Goubert, P. (1968) Legitimate fecundity and infant mortality in France during the eighteenth century: a comparison. *Daedalus*, Spring, 593–603.

Gregory, P. R., Campbell, J. M., and Cheng, B. (1972a) A cost-inclusive simultaneous equation model of birth rates. *Econometrica*, **40** (4), 681–7.

Gregory, P. R., Campbell, J. M., and Cheng, B. S. (1972b) A simultaneous equation model of birth rates in the United States. *Review of Economics and Statistics*, **54** (4), 374–80.

Griliches, Z. (1974) Comment. *Journal of Political Economy*, **82** (2, pt 2), S219–S221.

Groat, H. T., and Neal, A. G. (1967) Social psychological correlates of urban fertility. *American Sociological Review*, **32**, 945–59.

Gronau, R. (1973) The effect of children on the housewife's value of time. *Journal of Political Economy*, **81** (2, pt 2), S168–S199.

Habakkuk, H. J. (1963) Population problems and European economic development in the late eighteenth and nineteenth centuries. *American Economic Review*, **53**, 607–18.

Habakkuk, H. J. (1965a) The economic history of modern Britain. In Glass and Eversley (1965), 147–59.

Habakkuk, H. J. (1965b) English population in the eighteenth century. In Glass and Eversley (1965), 269–84.

Habakkuk, H. J. (1967) England. In Goodwin (1967), 1–21.

Hajnal, J. (1965) European marriage patterns in perspective. In Glass and Eversley (1965), 101–43.

Hansen, A. H. (1939) Economic progress and declining population. *American Economic Review*, **18** (1), 1–15.

Hauser, P. M. (1967) Family planning and population programs: a book review article. *Demography*, 4.

Hawthorn, G. (1970) *The Sociology of Fertility*. London: Collier-Macmillan. 161 p.

Heberle, R. (1942) Social factors in birth control. *American Sociological Review*, **6** (6), 794–805.

Heckman, J. J., Willis, R. J. (1975) Estimation of a stochastic model of reproduction: an econometric approach. In Terleckij (1975), 99–138.

Heckscher, E. F. (1949–50) Swedish population trends before the industrial revolution. *Economic History Review*, ser. 2, **2**, 266–77.

Heer, D. M. (1966) Economic development and fertility. *Demography*, **3** (2), 423–44.

Heer, D. M. (1968) Economic development and the fertility transition. *Daedalus*, Spring, 447–62.

Heer, D. M. (1973) Évolution récente de la politique démographique en Union Soviétique. *Études de Planning Familial*, **3** (11), 485–99.

Heitlinger, A. (1976) Pro-natalist population policy in Czechoslovakia. *Population Studies*, 30 (1), 123–35.

Henripin, J. (1954) La population canadienne au début du XVIIIe siècle. *INED Travaux et Documents*, no 22. 118 p.

Henry, L. (1953) *Fécondité des mariages*. Paris: Presses Universitaires de France. 180 p.

Henry, L. (1954) Mise au point sur la natalité française. *Population*, **9** (2), 197–226.•

Henry, L. (1956) Anciennes familles genevoises. *INED Travaux et Documents*, no 26. 234 p.

Henry, L. (1961a) Some data in natural fertility. *Eugenics Quarterly*, **8**, 81–91.

Henry, L. (1961b) La fécondité naturelle: Observation, théorie, résultats. *Population*, **16** (4), 625–36.

Henry, L. (1961c) La population d'Irlande en 1703. *Population*, **16** (1), 122–33.

Henry, L. (1965) The population of France in the eighteenth century. In Glass and Eversley (1965), 434–56.

Henry, L. (1968) Historical demography. *Daedalus*, Spring, 385–96.

Henry, L. (1971) *Variations des noms de famille et changements de prénom: Les problèmes qui en résultent pour le couplage automatique des données*. Paper presented at the Colloque International de Démographie Historique, Firenze, 5 p.

Henry, L. (1972) Fécondité des mariages dans le quart sud-ouest de la France de 1720 à 1829. *Annales ESC*, **27** (3), 612–40.

Henry, L., and Houdaille, J. (1973) Fécondité des mariages dans le quart nord-ouest de la France de 1670 à 1829. *Population*, **28** (4–5), 873–924.

Henry, L. and Lévy, C. (1960) Ducs et pairs sous l'ancien régime. *Population*, **15** (5), 807–30.

Hidvégi, J. (no date) Hulló magyarság (Decaying Hungarian population). Budapest: Athaeneum. 213 p.

Higgins, E. (1963) Some fertility attitudes among white women in Johannesburg. *Population Studies*, 16 (1), 70–8.

Hill, R., Stycos, J. M., and Back, K. (1959) *The Family and Population Control*. Chapel Hill: University of North Carolina Press. 481 p.

Himes, N. E. (1963) *Medical History of Contraception*. New York: Gamut Press. 521 p.

Hoffman, L. W., and Wyatt, F. (1960) Social change and motivations for having larger families: some theoretical considerations. *Merril-Palmer Quarterly*, **6**, 235–44.

Hofstee, E. W. (1954) *Regional verscheidenheid in der ontwikkeling van het antal geborten in Nederland in de twede helft van de 19e eeuw*. Amsterdam: Koninklijke Akademie van Wetenschappen. 59–106.

Hofstee, E. W. (1966) Over het modern-dynamisch cultuurpatroon. Weerens, de gebortecijfers in Nederland: Commentaar op commentaar. *Sociologische Gids*, **13**, 139–54, 173–5, 187–9.

Hofstee, E. W. (1968) Population increase in the Netherlands. *Acta Historiae Nederlandica*, **3**, 43–125.

Hölbling, M. (1845) *Baranya vármegyének orvosi helyirata* (*Medical Description of the County of Baranya*). Pécs. 151 p.

Hollingsworth, T. H. (1957–8) A demographic study of the British ducal families. *Population Studies*, **11** (1), 4–26.

Hollingsworth, T. H. (1964–5) The demography of the British peerage. *Population Studies*, **18** (2), suppl. 108 p.

Hollingsworth, T. H. (1965) The demographic background of the peerage, 1603–1938. *Eugenics Review*, **57** (2), 55–65.

Hollingsworth, T. H. (1968) The importance of the quality of the data in historical demography. *Daedalus*, Spring, 415–32.

Hollingsworth, T. H. (1969) *Historical Demography*. London: The Sources of History Ltd., in association with Hodder & Stoughton. 448 p.

Hollingsworth, T. H. (1971) *Migration and Temporary Absences in Nominative Demographic Research*. Paper presented at the Colloque International de Démographie Historique, Firenze. 11 p.

Hope, K. (ed.) (1972) *The Analysis of Social Mobility: Methods and Approaches*. Oxford: Clarendon Press. 254 p.

Hopkin, W. A. B., and Hajnal, J. (1947–8) Analysis of births in England and Wales, 1939, by father's occupation. *Population Studies*, **1** (2), 187–203, (3), 275–300.

Hopkins, K. (1965–6) Contraception in the Roman Empire. *Comparative Studies in Society and History*, **8**, 124–51.

Houdaille, J. (1961) Un village du Morvan: Saint-Agnan. *Population*, **16** (2), 301–12.

Houdaille, J. (1967) La population de Boulay (Moselle) avant 1850. *Population*, **22** (6), 1055–84.

Houdaille, J. (1970) La population de Remmesweiler en Sarre aux XVIIIe et XIXe siècles. *Population*, **25** (6), 1183–95.

Houdaille, J. (1971) La population de sept villages des environs de Boulay (Moselle) aux XVIIIe et XIXe siècles. *Population*, **26** (6), 1061–72.

Hughes, R. B. (1959) Human fertility differentials: the influence of industrial urban development on birth rates. *Population Review*, **3** (2), 58–69.

Huszár, I. (1973) Népesedéspolitikánk időszerű kérdéseiről (Actual problems of our population policy). *Társadalmi Szemle*, **28** (8–9), 3–15.

Huszár, I., Hoch, R., Kovács, J., and Timár, J. (1969) Hipotézisek a foglalkoztatás és az életszinvonal alakulására Magyarországon 1985-ig (Hypotheses on the trends of employment and level of living in Hungary until 1985). *Gazdaság*, **3** (3), 17–41.

Hyrenius, H. (1958–9) Fertility and reproduction in a Swedish population group without family limitation. *Population Studies*, **12** (2), 121–30.

Illyés, Gy. (no date) *Magyarok (Hungarians)*. Budapest: Nyugat Könyvkiadó. 468 p.

INED (1966) Rapport de l'Institut National d'Études Démographiques à Monsieur le Ministre des Affaires Sociales sur la régulation des naissances en France. *Population*, **21** (4), 645–90.

Innes, J. (1938) *Class Fertility Trends in England and Wales 1876–1934*. Princeton: Princeton University Press. 152 p.

International Population Conference, London (1971). Liège: International Union for the Scientific Study of Population. Vols 1–4. 3050 p.

International Population Conference, Liège (1973). Liège: International Union for the Scientific Study of Population. Vols 1–3. 494, 416 and 469 p.

Internationaler Bevölkerungskongress, Wien (1959). Vienna: Union Internationale pour l'Étude Scientifique de la Population. 735 p.

Isard, W. (1942) Transport development and building cycles. *Quarterly Journal of Economics*, **57** (4), 90–110.

Iván, P., and Mausecz, Zs. (1971) Népesség és foglalkoztatáspolitika: Prognózis 1985-re (Population and employment policy: A prognosis for 1985). *Gazdaság*, **5** (3), 7–24.

Jagielski, A. (1970) Niektóre problemy wspólczesnego rozwoju ludnosci ZSRR. *Studia Demograficzne*, **21**, 35–67.

Jankó, J. (1902) *A balaton-melléki lakosság néprajza (Ethnography of the Population Living Around Lake Balaton)*. Budapest: Kilián. 429 p.

Johnson, G. Z. (1960) Differential fertility in European countries. In National Bureau of Economic Research (1960), 36–72.

Jolles, H. M. (1957) *Wien: eine Stadt ohne Nachwuchs.* Assen: Van Gorcum. 395 p.

Jurecek, Z. (1966) Differencni plodnost podle vysledku scitani lidu Z.R. 1961 (Differential fertility according to the results of the 1961 census). *Demografie*, **8** (2), 97–106 (3), 207–15.

Jutikkala, E. (1965) Finland's population movement in the eighteenth century. In Glass and Eversley (1965), 549–69.

Kápolnai, I. (1962) Adalékok a XIX. század népmozgalmához: Mezőkövesd, Mezőkeresztes, Szentistván, Tard 1820–1869 (Some data on vital statistics in the nineteenth century: the villages Mezőkövesd, Mezőkeresztes, Szentistván, Tard, 1820–1869). In *Történeti Statisztikai Évkönyv 1961–1962*, 90–130. Budapest: Központi Statisztikai Hivatal Könyvtár.

Kapótsy, B. (1972) The demographic effects of legal abortion in Eastern Europe. *European Demographic Information Bulletin*, **3** (4), 193–207.

Karachanow, M. (1966) Dynamika zaludnienia i rozwój gospodarczy USSR (Population dynamics and economic development of the Soviet Union). *Studia Demograficzne*, **9**, 67–80.

Kassabov, V. S. (1974) La natalité en Bulgarie: Résultats, perspectives, politique. *Population*, **29** (2), 275–90.

Katkova, I. P. (1971) *Rozdaemost v molodich semiach.* Moscow: Isdatelstvo Medicina. 112 p.

Katus, L. (1970) Economic growth in Hungary during the age of dualism 1867–1918. *Studia Historica Academiae Scientiarum Hungaricae*, **62**, 35–127.

Kenéz, B. (1906) *Magyarország népességi statisztikája (Population Statistics of Hungary)*. Budapest: Stampfel. 314 p.

Kenéz, B. (1934) Népesedési politikai kérdések (Problems of population politics). *Magyar Statisztikai Szemle*, **12** (6), 441–56.

Kestenberg, J. (1956a) On the development of maternal feelings in early childhood. *Psychoanalytic Study of the Child*, **11**, 257–91.

Kestenberg, J. (1956b) Vicissitudes of female sexuality. *Journal of the American Psychoanalytic Association*, **4**, 453–76.

Kestenberg, J. S. (1968) Outside and inside, male and female. *Journal of the American Psychoanalytic Association*, **16**, 457–520.

Keyfitz, N. (1952–3) Differential fertility in Ontario: an application of factorial design to a demographic problem. *Population Studies*, **6** (2), 123–34.

Keynes, J. M. (1937) Some consequences of a declining population. *Eugenics Quarterly*, **29** (1), 13–17.

Kirk, D. (1960) The influence of business cycles on marriage and birth rates. In National Bureau of Economic Research (1960), 241–57.

Kirk, D., and Nortman, D. L. (1958) Business and babies: the influence of the business cycle on birth rates. *Proceedings of the American Statistical Association, Social Statistics Section*, 151–60.

Kiser, C. V. (1960) Differential fertility in the United States. In National Bureau of Economic Research (1960), 77–116.

Kiser, C. V. (ed.) (1962) *Research in Family Planning*. Princeton: Princeton University Press. 664 p.

Kiser, C. V. (1967) The Growth of American Families studies: an assessment of significance. *Demography*, **4**, 388–96.

Kiser, C. V., Grabill, W. H., and Campbell, A. A. (1968) Trends and variations in fertility in the United States. Cambridge, Mass.: Harvard University Press. 338 p.

Kiser, C. V., Mishler, E. G., Westoff, C. F., and Potter, R. G. (1956–7) Development of plans for a social psychological study of the future fertility of two-child families. *Population Studies*, **10** (1), 43–51.

Kiser, C. V., and Whelpton, P. K. (1953) Résumé of the Indianapolis study of social and psychological factors affecting fertility. *Population Studies*, **7** (2), 95–110.

Kiss, G. (1937) *Ormánság (The Region of Ormánság in Hungary)*. Budapest: Sylvester. 427 p.

Kitagawa, E. M. (1953) Differential fertility in Chicago, 1920–1940. *American Journal of Sociology*, **58** (5), 481–92.

Klinger, A. (1964) A differenciális termékenység ujabb alakulása (Recent development of differential fertility). *Demográfia*, **7** (3–4), 394–408.

Klinger, A. (1969) Magyarország népesedési helyzete az 1960-as években (Demographic situation of Hungary in the 1960s). *Statisztikai Szemle*, **47** (11), 1067–96 (12), 1171–88.

Klinger, A. (1970) Magyarország népesedési helyzete az 1960-as években (Demographic situation of Hungary in the 1960s). *Statisztikai Szemle*, **48** (3), 227–52, (11), 1111–37, (12), 1215–40.

Klinger, A. (1971) Magyarország népesedési helyzete az 1960-as években (Demographic situation of Hungary in the 1960s). *Statisztikai Szemle*, **49** (1), 1215–40.

Klinger, A. (1975) Az ujabb magyar családtervezési vizsgálatok főbb eredményei (Main results of the recent surveys in family planning in Hungary). *Statisztikai Szemle*, **53** (2), 127–37, (3), 233–48.

Klinger, A., Bárány, L., Kamarás, F., and Varga, L. (1974) *Az 1966. évben házasságot kötöttek családtervezési, termékenységi és születésszabályozási magatartása 1966–1972 között (Family Planning, Fertility and Birth Control of Couples Married in 1966 in the Years 1966–1972)*. Budapest: KSH. 231 p.

Klinger, A., and Szabady, E. (1965) A társadalmi átrétegződés és demográfiai hatásai, vol. 1: Budapesten és a városokban. (Social mobility and its demographic effects, vol. 1: In Budapest and in the other towns.) *KSH Népességtudományi Kutató Intézet Közleményei*, no 7. 325 p.

Klinger, A. et al. (1972–5) *A népmozgalom főbb adatai községenként 1828–1900. (The Main Vital Statistical Data by Villages 1828–1900)*, vols 1–5. Budapest: Central Statistical Office. 173, 173, 160, 164 and 175 p.

Knodel, J. (1970) Two and a half centuries of demographic history in a Bavarian village. *Population Studies*, **24** (3), 353–76.

Knodel, J. E. (1974) *The Decline of Fertility in Germany 1871–1939*. Princeton: Princeton University Press. 306 p.

Kodolányi, J. (1941) *Baranyai utazás (Journey in Baranya)*. Budapest: Bólyai Akadémia. 110 p.

Kooy, G.-A. (1959) *De oude samenwoning op het nieuwe platteland*. Assen.

Kovács, A. (1913) Az egyke és a katolikusok. *Magyar Kultura*, no 22, 423–31.

Kovács, A. (1923) Az egyke és a népszaporodás (The one-child system and the rate of growth of population). *Magyar Statisztikai Szemle*, **1** (3–4), 65–79).

Kovács, A. (1925) Magyarország népmozgalma vallásfelekezetek és nemzetiség szerint az 1921–1924 években (Vital statistics of Hungary by denomination and nationality). *Magyar Statisztikai Szemle*, **3** (11–12), 439–43.

Kovács, I. (1940) *A parasztéletforma csődje (Breakdown of the Peasant Way of Life)*. Budapest: Bólyai Akadémia. 214 p.

Kovács, I. (no date) *A néma forradalom (The Silent Revolution)*. Budapest: Cserépfalvi. 264 p.

Kovacsics, J. (ed.) (1957) *A történeti statisztika forrásai (Sources of Historical Statistics)*. Budapest: Közgazdasági és Jogi Könyvkiadő. 460 p.

Kovacsics, J. (ed.) (1963) *Magyarország történeti demográfiája. (Historical Demography of Hungary)*. Budapest: Közgazdasági és Jogi Könyvkiadó. 442 p.

Kovacsics, J., and Thirring, L. (eds) (1968) Colloque de démographie historique, Budapest, 23–26 Septembre 1965. *KSH Népességtudományi Kutató Intézet Közleményei*, no 21. 150 p.

Kováts, Z., and Cs. Tóth, P. (1962) Csurgói jobbágy-családok demográfiai viszonyai 1720–1950 (Demography of serf families in Csurgó 1720–1950). In *Történeti Statisztikai Évkönyv 1961–1962*, 22–47. Budapest: Központi Statisztikai Hivatal Könyvtára.

Kozlov, V. I. (1968) O vliyänii religioznovo faktora na plodovitnost (On the influence of religious factors on fertility). In Volkov (1968), 184–206.

Krause, J. T. (1958) Changes in English fertility and mortality, 1781–1850. *Economic History Review*, **11** (1), 52–70.

Krause, J. T. (1959) Some neglected factors in the English industrial revolution. *Journal of Economic History*, **19**, 531–4.

Krause, J. T. (1965) The changing adequacy of English registration 1690–1837. In Glass and Eversley (1965), 379–93.

Krotki, K., and Lapierre, É. (1968) La fécondité au Canada, selon la réligion, l'origine ethnique et l'état matrimonial. *Population*, **23** (5), 815–34.

Kruegel, D. L. (1975) Further comment on J. Blake's 'Can we believe recent data on birth expectations in the United States?' *Demography*, 12 (1), 157–61.

Kucera, N. (1967) Reprodukcje obyvatelstva v letech 1961–1966 (Reproduction of population in 1961–1966). *Demografie*, **9**, 193–205.

Kuznets, S. (1930) *Secular Movements in Production and Prices*. New York: Houghton Mifflin. 536 p.

Kuznets, S. (1956) Quantitative aspects of economic growth of nations: levels and variability of rates of growth. *Economic Development and Cultural Change*, **5**, 1–94.

Kuznets, S. (1958) Long swings in the growth of population and in related economic variables. *Proceedings of the American Philosophical Society*, 25–52.

Kvasha, A. J. (1971) Etapi demograficheskogo razvitia SSSR. In Volkov (1971), 77–88.

Lachiver, M. (1967) *La population de Meulan du XVIIe au XIXe siècle*. Paris: SEVPEN. 339 p.

Lancaster, K. J. (1965) A new approach to consumer theory. *Journal of Political Economy*, **74** (2) 132–57.

Landry, A. (1934) *La révolution démographique*. Paris: Sirey. 227 p.

Landry, A. (1945) *Traité de démographie*. Paris: Payot. 651 p.

Laslett, P. (1965) *The World We Have Lost.* London: Methuen. 280 p.

Laslett, P. (ed.) (1972) *Household and Family in Past Time.* Cambridge: Cambridge University Press. 623 p.

Laslett, P. (1975) *The Family and Industrialization: A 'Strong Theory'.* Paper presented at the Bad Homburg Symposium. 24 p.

Laslett, P., and Oosterveen, K. (1973) Long-term trends in bastardy in England: a study of the illegitimacy figures in the parish registers and in the reports of the Registrar General, 1561–1960. *Population Studies,* **27** (2), 255–86.

Lautman, F. (1972) Naissances illégitimes et abandons d'enfants en Anjou au XVIIIe siècle. *Annales ESC* **27** (4–5), 1183–96.

Le Bras, H. (1971) Géographie de la fécondité française depuis 1921. *Population,* **26** (6), 1093–24.

Lee, R. (1973) Probleme der Bevölkerungsgeschichte in England 1750–1850. *Vierteljahrschrift für Sozial- und Wirtschaftsgeschichte,* **60** (3), 290–310.

Lee, R. (1974) Estimating series of vital rates and age structures from baptisms and burials: a new technique, with applications to pre-industrial England. *Population Studies,* **28** (3), 495–512.

Lehner, A. (1954) Social mobility in relation to size of family. In World Population Conference (1954), vol. 6, 911–32.

Leibenstein, H. (1957) *Economic Backwardness and Economic Growth.* New York: Wiley.

Leibenstein, H. (1974) An interpretation of the economic theory of fertility: promising path or blind alley? *Journal of Economic Literature,* **12** (2), 457–79.

Leibenstein, H. (1975) The economic theory of fertility decline. *Quarterly Journal of Economics,* **89** (1), 1–31.

Leibenstein, H. (1976) The problem of characterizing aspirations. *Population and Development Review,* **2** (3–4), 427–31.

Lenski, G. (1961) *The Religious Factor: A Sociological Study of Religion's Impact on Politics, Economics and Family Life.* New York: Doubleday. 381 p.

Le Roy Ladurie, E. (1966) Révolution française et contraception. *Annales de Démographie Historique,* 417–36.

Lewis, O. (1959) *Five Families: A Mexican Case Study in the Culture of Poverty.* New York: Basic Books. 351 p.

Lewis, O. (1961) *The Children of Sanchez: Autobiography of a Mexican Family.* New York: Random House. 499 p.

Lewis-Faning, E. (1949) *Report on an Enquiry into Family Limitation and its Influence on Human Fertility During the Past Fifty Years.* London: HMSO. 204 p.

Livi-Bacci, M. (1960) Sui fattori economici e sociali della ripresa della natalità nei paesi anglosassoni. *Rivista Italiana de Economica, Dem..g..fia e Statistica,* **14,** 5–119.

Livi-Bacci, M. (1961) Sulle cause della ripresa della natalità verificatasi in taluni paesi industrializzati. *Studi Politici,* **8,** 53–67.

Livi-Bacci, M. (1968a) Fertility and nuptiality changes in Spain from the late 18th to the early 20th century. *Population Studies,* **22** (1), 83–102, (2), 211–34.

Livi-Bacci, M. (1968b) Fertility and population growth in Spain in the eighteenth and nineenth centuries. *Daedalus,* Spring, 523–35 p.

Livi-Bacci, M. (1971a) *Some Problems in Nominal Record Linkage in Tuscany, XVII–XVIII Century.* Paper presented at the Colloque International de Démographie Historique, Firenze. 9 p.

Livi-Bacci, M. (1971b) *A Century of Portuguese Fertility*. Princeton: Princeton University Press. 149 p.

Long, L. H. (1970) Fertility patterns among religious groups in Canada. *Demography*, **7** (2), 135–49.

Lösch, A. (1956) Population cycles as a cause of business cycles. In Spengler and Duncan (1956), 292–301.

Loschky, D. J., and Krier, D. F. (1969) Income and family size in three eighteenth century Lancashire parishes: a reconstitution study. *Journal of Economic History*, **29** (3), 429–48.

McClelland, D. C. (1961) *The Achieving Society*. Princeton: Van Nostrand. 512 p.

McKenna, E. E. (1974) Marriage and fertility in postfamine Ireland: a multivariate analysis. *American Journal of Sociology*, **80** (3), 688–705.

Mackenroth, G. (1953) *Bevölkerungslehre*. Berlin: Springer. 531 p.

Mackensen, R. (1967) Theoretical considerations regarding differential transition. In Sidney Conference (1967), 37–46.

McKeown, T. (1965) Medicine and world population. In Sheps and Ridley (1965), 25–40.

McKeown, T., Brown, R. G., and Record, R. G. (1972) An interpretation of the modern rise of population in Europe. *Population Studies*, **26** (3), 345–82.

Macura, M. (1966) Razmisljanja povodom osnova demografske teorije. *Stanovnistvo*, **4** (1), 5–25.

Malinowski, B. (1929) *The Sexual Life of Savages in North-Western Melanesia*. London: Routledge. 603 p.

Malthus, T. R. (1966) *First Essay on Population: A Reprint in Facsimile of 'An Essay on the Principle of Population as it Affects the Future Improvement of Society'*. London: Macmillan. 396 p.

Malthus, T. R. (1970) *An Essay on the Principle of Population, and A Summary View of the Principle of Population*. Harmondsworth: Penguin. 297 p.

Malthus, T. R. (no date) *An Essay on the Principle of Population, Or A View of its Past and Present Effects on Human Happiness*, reprinted from the last edition revised by the author. London: Ward Lock. 614 p.

Marchal, F., and Rabut, O. (1972) Évolution récente de la fécondité en Europe Occidentale. *Population*, **27** (4–5), 838–47.

Marczewski, J. (1965) Le produit physique de l'économie française de 1789 à 1913 (comparaison avec la Grande-Bretagne). *Cahiers de l'ISEA*, no 103. 212 p.

Marshall, A. (1898) *Principles of Economics*, vol. 1. London: Macmillan. 820 p.

Marshall, T. H. (1965) The population problem during the industrial revolution: a note on the present state of the controversy. In Glass and Eversley (1965), 247–68.

Matras, J. (1965) The social strategy of family formation: some variations in time and space. *Demography*, **2**, 349–62.

Matras, J. (1965–6) Social strategies of family formation: data for British female cohorts born 1831–1906. *Population Studies*, **19** (2), 167–81.

Matthiessen, P. C. (1970) *Some Aspects of the Demographic Transition in Denmark*. Copenhagen: Kobenhavns Universitets Fond. 226 p.

Mayer, A. J., and Klapprodt, C. (1955) Fertility differentials in Detroit, 1920–1950. *Population Studies*, **9** (2), 148–58.

Mayer, A. J., and Marx, S. (1957) Social change, religion, and birth rates. *American Journal of Sociology*, **62** (4), 383–90.

Mazur, P. (1967) Fertility among ethnic groups in USSR. *Demography*, **4** (1), 172–95.

Mazur, P. (1968) Birth control and regional differentials in the Soviet Union. *Population Studies*, **22** (3), 319–33.

Mazur, P. (1973) Relation of marriage and education to fertility in the USSR. *Population Studies*, **27** (1), 105–15.

Mazur, D. P. (1975a) Social and demographic determinants of abortion in Poland. *Population Studies*, **29** (1), 21–36.

Mazur, D. P. (1975b) The influence of human fertility on the economic conditions of the rural population in Poland. *Population Studies*, **29** (3), 423–38.

Mead, M. (1950) *Male and Female: A Study of Sexes in a Changing World.* London: Gollancz. 477 p.

Meadows, D. H., Meadows, D. L., Randers, J., Behrens, W. W. (1972) *The Limits to Growth.* New York: Universe Books. 205 p.

Measurement in Economics: Studies in Mathematical Economics and Econometrics in Memory of Yehuda Grunfeld (1963). Stanford: Stanford University Press. 319 p.

Mehlan, K. H. (1965) Legal abortions in Romania. *Journal of Sex Research*, **1**, 31–8.

Merton, R., Broom, L., and Cottrell, L. S. (eds) (1959) *Sociology Today.* New York: Basic Books. 623 p.

Meuvret, J. (1965) Demographic crisis in France from the sixteenth to the eighteenth century. In Glass and Eversley (1965), 507–22.

Michael, R. T. (1973) Education and the derived demand for children. *Journal of Political Economy*, **81** (2, pt 2), S128–S164.

Michael, R. T., and Willis, R. J. (1975) Contraception and fertility: household production under uncertainty. In Terleckij, N. E. (1975), 27–93.

Milbank Memorial Fund (1955) *Current Research in Human Fertility.* New York: Milbank Memorial Fund. 164 p.

Milbank Memorial Fund (1963) *Emerging Techniques in Population Research.* New York: Milbank Memorial Fund. 306 p.

Miller, A. (1962) *Kultur und menschliche Fruchtbarkeit.* Stuttgart: Enke. 152 p.

Miltényi, K. (1964) A müvi vetélések hatásainak kérdéséhez (On the effects of induced abortions). *Demográfia*, **7** (1), 73–87.

Miltényi, K. (1971) A gyermekgondozási segély népesedési és gazdasági hatásai (Demographic and economic effects of the child care allowance). *Statisztikai Szemle*, **49** (8–9), 816–26.

Miltényi, K. (1973) *Population Policy Impacts on Differential Fertility and Social Mobility.* Paper presented at the International Population Conference, Liege. 13 p.

Mincer, J. (1963) Market prices, opportunity costs, and income effects. In *Measurement in Economics* (1963), 67–82.

Mishler, E. G., and Westoff, C. F. (1955) A proposal for research on social psychological factors affecting fertility: concepts and hypotheses. In Milbank Memorial Fund (1955), 121–50.

Moberg, S. (1950–1) Marital status and family size among matriculated persons in Sweden. *Population Studies*, **5** (1), 115–27.

Moess, A. (1972) Velem népessége 1711–1895 (Population of the village Velem 1711–1895). *Vasi Szemle*, **26** (2), 277–86, (3), 420–32.

Moess, A. (1973a) Velem község történeti demográfiája (Historical demography of the village Velem). Unpublished. 10 p.

Moess, A. (1973b) *Baranya megyei katolikus községek történeti demográfiája (Historical Demography of Catholic Villages in the County of Baranya)*. Unpublished. 8 p.

Moors, H. G. (1974) *Child Spacing and Family Size in the Netherlands*. Leiden: Stenfert Kroese. 195 p.

Morsa, J. (1959) Travail des femmes et natalité. *Revue de l'Institut de Sociologie*, **2**, 233–63.

Morsa, J. (1967) Une enquête nationale sur la fécondité: Présentation. *Population et Famille*, **13**, 1–12.

Morsa, J. (1970) Une enquête nationale sur la fécondité, II: Stérilité – pratiques contraceptives. *Population et Famille*, **70**, 37–91.

Moulin, L. (1972) *L'aventure européenne*. Bruges: De Tempel. 243 p.

Murdock, G. P. (1934) *Our Primitive Contemporaries*. New York: Macmillan. 614 p.

Myrdal, A. (1945) *Nation and Family: The Swedish Experiment in Democratic Family and Population Policy*. London: Kegan Paul. 441 p.

Myrdal, A., and Klein, V. (1956) *Women's Two Roles: Home and Work*. London: Routledge & Kegan Paul. 208 p.

Myrdal, A., and Myrdal, G. (1934) *Kris i befolkingsfragan*. Stockholm: Albert Bonniers Förlag. 403 p.

Myrdal, G. (1940) *Population: A Problem for Democracy*. Cambridge, Mass.: Harvard University Press. 237 p.

Naldal, J., and Saez, A. (1971) *La fécondité à St Joan de Palamos, Catalogne, de 1700 à 1859*. Paper presented at the Colloque International de Démographie Historique, Firenze. 9 p.

Nag, M. (1962) Factors affecting human fertility in non-industrial societies: a cross-cultural study. *Yale University Publications in Anthropology*, no 66. 227 p.

Namboodiri, N. K. (1972a) Some observations on the economic framework for fertility analysis. *Population Studies*, **26** (2), 185–206.

Namboodiri, N. K. (1972b) The integrative potential of a fertility model: an analytical test. *Population Studies*, **26** (3), 465–85.

Namboodiri, N. K. (1975) Review symposium: Economics of the family: marriage, children, and human capital. *Demography*, **12** (3), 561–9.

National Bureau of Economic Research (1960) *Demographic and Economic Change in Developed Countries*. Princeton: Princeton University Press. 536 p.

Népesedéspolitika Magyarországon (Population policy in Hungary) (1972) *KSH Népességtudományi Kutató Intézet Közleményei*, no 35. 105 p.

Nerlove, M. (1974) Household and economy: toward a new theory of population and economic growth. *Journal of Political Economy*, **82** (2, pt 2), S200–S218.

Nizard, A., and Pressat, R. (1965) La situation démographique. *Population*, **20** (6), 1115–46.

Noin, D. (1973) *Géographie démographique de la France*. Paris: Presses Universitaires de France. 158 p.

Notestein, F. W. (1945) Population: the long view. In Schultz (1945), 36–57.

Notestein, F. W. (1953) Economic problems of population change. In *Proceedings of the Eighth International Conference of Agricultural Economists*, 13–31. London: Oxford University Press.

Notestein, F. W., Taeuber, I. B., Kirk, D., Coale, A. J., and Kiser, L. (1944) *The Future Population of Europe and the Soviet Union*: Population Projections, 1940–1970. Geneva: League of Nations. 315 p.

Ogburn, W. F., and Thomas, D. S. (1922) The influence of the business cycle on certain social conditions. *Journal of the American Statistical Association*, **18**, 324–40.

Okun, B. (1958) *Trends in Birth Rates in the United States Since 1870*. Baltimore: Johns Hopkins Press. 203 p.

Oppenheimer, V. K. (1976) The Easterlin hypothesis: another aspect of the echo to consider. *Population and Development Review*, **2** (3–4), 433–57.

Palli, H. (1973) *Ajaloolise demograafia probleeme Eestis* (*Historical Demographic Problems of Estonia*). Tallin: Eesti NSV Teaduste Akadeemia Ajaloo Institut. 130 p.

Pataki, J. (1937) A Sárköz népességtörténete és az egyke kifejlődése (Population history of the region Sárköz and the development of the one-child system). *Történetirás*, **1** (1), 85–96, (2), 193–205.

Patlagean, E. (1969) Sur la limitation de la fécondité dans la haute époque byzantine. *Annales ESC*, **24** (6), 1353–69.

Pavlik, Z. (1971) Nombre désiré et nombre idéal d'enfants chez les femmes rurales en Bohème. *Population*, **26** (5), 915–33.

Perevedentzev, V. (1975a) Semia, vchera, sivodnia, zavtra (The family yesterday, today and tomorrow). *Nash Sovremennik*, no 6, 118–31.

Perevedentzev, V. (1975b) Naselenie: prognoz i deistvitelnost (Population: prognosis and reality). *Nas Sovremennik*, no 11, 122–33.

Perjés, G. (1973) *Az 1728. évi adóösszeirás* (*The Tax Census of 1728*). Unpub. MS. 12 p.

Perlman, M. (1975) Review symposium: Economics of the family: marriage, children, and human capital. *Demography*, **12** (3), 549–56.

Perrenoud, A. (1974) Malthusianisme at protestantisme: 'Un modèle démographique weberien'. *Annales ESC*, **29** (4), 975–88.

Peters, H. (1958) Die Geburtenhäufigkeit nach der Religions-zugehörigkeit. *Wirtschaft und Statistik*, **10** (1), 24–5.

Petersen, W. (1954–5) John Maynard Keynes's theories of population and the concept of 'optimum'. *Population Studies*, **8** (3), 228–46.

Petersen, W. (1960) The demographic transition in the Netherlands. *American Sociological Review*, **25** (3), 334–47.

Petersen, W. (1969) *Population*. New York: Macmillan. 735 p.

Pezenhoffer, A. (1922) A demográfiai viszonyok befolyása a nép szaporodására (*Influence of Demographic Conditions on the Natural Growth Rate of Population*). Budapest: Author's edition. 276 p.

Phillips, A., Votey, H. L., Jr, and Maxwell, D. E. (1969) A synthesis of econometric and demographic models of fertility: an econometric test. *Review of Economics and Statistics*, **51** (3), 298–308.

Pierce, R. M., and Rowntree, G. (1961) Birth control in Britain, Part II: Contraceptive methods used by couples married in the last thirty years. *Population Studies*, **15** (2), 121–60.

Piotrowski, J. (1963) *Praca zawodowa kobiety a rodzina* (*Employment of Women and Family*). Warszawa: Ksiazka i Wiedza. 365 p.

Pirtshalava, G. V. (1968) Dinamika i niekotoriye osobennosti rozhdayemosti v

Gruzii (The dynamics and some characteristics of fertility in Georgia). In Adonts and Davtyan (1968), 43–5.

Pohlman, E. (1967) A psychologist's introduction to the birth planning literature. *Journal of Social Issues*, **23**, 13–28.

Pohlman, E. (1969) *The Psychology of Birth Planning*. Cambridge, Mass.: Schenkman. 496 p.

Polgar, S. (ed.) (1971) *Culture and Population: A Collection of Current Studies.* Cambridge, Mass., and London: Carolina Population Center, University of North Carolina, Chapel Hill, and Schenkman. 195 p.

Population and Australia. A Demographic Analysis and Projection. Canberra: Australian Government Publishing Service. 761 p.

Potter, J. (1965) The growth of population in America, 1700–1860. In Glass and Eversley (1965), 631–79 p.

Potts, M. (1967) Legal abortions in eastern Europe. *Eugenics Review*, **59** (4), 232–50.

Poussou, J. P. (1973) Les sources et méthodes classiques de la démographie historique. In International Population Conference, Liège, (1973), vol. 3, 23–43.

Pressat, R. (1961) *L'analyse démographique*. Paris: Presses Universitaires de France. 168 p.

Pressat, R. (1967) Suppression de l'avortement légal en Roumanie: Premiers effets. *Population*, **22** (1), 116–17.

Pressat, R. (1969a) Interprétation des variations à court terme du taux de natalité. *Population*, **24** (1), 47–56.

Pressat, R. (1969b) Les naissances en France de 1946 à 1980. *Population*, **24** (3), 417–26.

Pressat, R. (1971) *Démographie sociale*. Paris: Presses Universitaires de France. 168 p.

Pressat, R. (1972a) La conjoncture démographique: L'Europe. I: Données statistiques. *Population*, **27** (4–5), 805–8.

Pressat, R. (1972b) La population de l'URSS: données récentes. *Population*, **27** (4–5), 809–37.

Pressat, R. (1974a) *A Workbook in Demography*. London: Methuen. 292 p.

Pressat, R. (1974b) Évolution générale de la population française. *Population*, **29** (spécial), 11–29.

Pressat, R, (no date) *Principles d'analyse*. Paris: Éditiones de l'INED. 153 p.

Prioux-Marchal, F. (1974) Le mariage en Suede. *Population*, **29** (4–5), 825–60.

Proceedings of the Eighth International Conference of Agricultural Economists (1953). London: Oxford University Press. 608 p.

Rabin, A. I. (1965) Motivation for parenthood. *Journal of Projective Techniques and Personality Assessment*, **29** 405–11.

Rabin, A. I., and Greene, R. J. (1968) Assessing motivation for parenthood. *Journal of Psychology*, **69**, 39–46.

Rainwater, L. (1960) *And the Poor Get Children*, Chicago: Quadrangle. 202 p.

Rainwater, L. (1965) *Family Design*. Chicago: Aldine. 349 p.

Rasevic, M. (1965) Neki socio-economiki faktori kao determinante fertiliteta jugoslenskog stanovnistva (Some socioeconomic factors as determinants of the fertility of the Yugoslavian population). *Stanovnistvo*, **3** (1), 23–8.

Rasevic, M. (1971) Determinante fertiliteta stanovnistva v Jugoslaviji (Determinants of fertility in Yugoslavia). Belgrade: Institut Drustvenih Nauka Centar za Demografska Inskarivania. 201 p.

Razzel, P. E. (1972) The evaluation of baptism as a form of birth registration through cross-matching census and parish register data: a study in methodology. *Population Studies*, **26** (1), 121–46.

Razzel, P. E. (1974) An interpretation of the modern rise of population in Europe: a critique. *Population Studies*, **28** (1), 5–17.

Reddaway, W. B. (1939) *The Economics of Declining Population*. New York, London: Macmillan. 270 p.

Ridley, J. C. (1959) Number of children expected in relation to non-familial activities of the wife. *Milbank Memorial Fund Quarterly*, **37** (3), 277–96.

Riquet, R. P. (1949) Christianisme et population. *Population*, **4** (4), 615–36.

Ritchey, P. N. (1975) The effect of minority group status on fertility: a re-examination of concepts. *Population Studies*, **29** (2), 249–58.

Roberts, R. E., and Lee, E. S. (1974) Minority group status and fertility reviewed. *American Journal of Sociology*, **80** (2), 503–23.

Robinson, W. C., and Horlacher, D. E. (1971) Population growth and economic welfare. *Reports on Population/Family Planning*, **6**, 1–39.

Roeske-Slomka, I. (1973) Wspólzaleznosc naturalnego rozwoju demograficznego i wzrostu gospodarczego regionów (The interrelationship between natural demographic development and economic growth of regions). *Studia Demograficzne*, **31**, 85–100.

Roeske-Slomka, I. (1974) Wspólzaleznosc dochodów i dzietnosci rodzin (The correlation of income and number of children of families). *Studia Demograficzne*, **37**, 45–61.

Roheim, G. (1950) *Psychoanalysis and Anthropology*. New York: International University Press. 496 p.

Rose, H. (ed.) (1967) *Abortion in America*. Boston: Beacon Press.

Roussel, L. (1969) Les mobiles de la limitation des naissances dans les ménages de un ou deux enfants: Enquête d'opinion. *Population*, **24** (2), 309–34.

Roussel, L. (1975) Le mariage dans la société française. *INED Travaux et Documents*, no 73. 407 p.

Rowntree, G., and Pierce, R. M. (1961) Birth control in Britain, part I: attitudes and practices among persons married since the First World War. *Population Studies*, **15** (1), 3–31.

Russel, J. C. (1940) *British Medieval Population*. Albuquerque: University of New Mexico Press. 398 p.

Ruwet, J. (1954) Crises démographiques. Problèmes économiques ou crises morales? *Population*, **9** (3), 451–76.

Ruzsás, L. (1964) *A baranyai parasztság élete és küzdelme a nagybirtokkal 1711–1748 (Life and struggle with the large estates of the peasants in the county of Baranya, 1711–1748)*. Budapest: Akadémiai Kiadó. 254 p.

Ryder, N. B. (1969) The emergence of a modern fertility pattern: United States, 1917–1966. In Behrman *et al.* (1969), 99–123.

Ryder, N. B. (1971) The time series of fertility in the United States. In International Population Conference, London (1971), vol. 1. 587 p.

Ryder, N. B. (1973a) A critique of the National Fertility Study. *Demography*, **10** (4), 495–506.

Ryder, N. B. (1973b) Comment. *Journal of Political Economy*, **81** (2, pt 2), S65–S69.

Ryder, N. B. (1973c) Recent trends and group differences in fertility. In Westoff (1973), 57–68.

Ryder, N. B., and Westoff, C. F. (1969) Fertility planning status: United States, 1965. *Demography*, **6** (4), 435–44.

Ryder, N. B., and Westoff, C. F. (1971) *Reproduction in the United States*. Princeton: Princeton University Press. 419 p.

Sallume, X., and Notestein, W. W. (1932) Trends in size of families completed prior to 1910 in various social classes. *American Journal of Sociology*, **37**, 398–408.

Sándor, V. (1964) *Nagyipari fejlődés Magyarországon 1867–1900* (*Development of Large-Scale Industry in Hungary 1867–1900*). Budapest: Szikra. 771 p.

Sauvy, A. (1944) *Richesse et population*. Paris: Payot. 327 p.

Sauvy, A. (1959) *Théorie générale de la population*, vol. 2: *Biologie sociale*, 2nd ed. Paris: Presses Universitaires de France. 397 p.

Sauvy, A. (1961) Fécondité des populations: Évolution générale des recherches. *Population*, **16** (4), 699–712.

Sauvy, A. (1963) *Théorie générale de la population*, vol. 1: *Économie et croissance*, 3rd ed. Paris: Presses Universitaires de France. 371 p.

Sauvy, A. (1973) *Croissance zéro?* Paris: Calmann-Lévy. 329 p.

Schelsky, H. (1960) *Wandlungen der deutschen Familie in der Gegenwart*. Stuttgart: Enke. 418 p.

Schneller, K. (1936) *A református lakosság szociális és gazdasági viszonyai* (*Social and Economic Conditions of the Calvinist Population*). Kecskemét: Első Kecskeméti Hirlapkiadó. 64 p.

Schofield, R. S. (1971a) *Representativeness and Family Reconstitution*. Paper presented at the Colloque International de Démographie Historique, Firenze. 4 p.

Schofield, R. S. (1971b) *The Standardization of Names and the Automatic Linking of Historical Records*. Paper presented at the Colloque International de Démographie Historique, Firenze. 4 p.

Schram, F. (1970) *Magyarországi boszorkányperek 1529–1768* (Witchcraft Trials in Hungary 1529–1768), vols 1–2. Budapest: Akadémiai Kiadó. 571 and 780 p.

Schultz, T. W. (ed.) (1945) *Food for the World*. Chicago: University of Chicago Press. 353 p.

Schultz, T. W. (1973) The value of children: an economic perspective. *Journal of Political Economy*, **81** (2, pt 2), S2–S13.

Schultz, T. W. (ed.) (1974) *Economics of the Family: Marriage, Children, and Human Capital*. Chicago: University of Chicago Press. 584 p.

Schwartz, K. (1965) Nombre d'enfants suivant le milieu physique et social en Allemagne. *Population*, **20** (1), 77–92.

Scott, W. (1958) Fertility and social mobility among teachers. *Population Studies*, **11** (3), 251–61.

Sheps, M. C., and Ridley, J. C. (eds) (1965) *Public Health and Population Change*. Pittsburgh: University of Pittsburg Press. 557 p.

Shorter, E., Knodel, J., and Van de Walle, E. (1971) The decline of non-marital fertility in Europe 1880–1940. *Population Studies*, **25** (3), 375–93.

Siegel, J. S., and Akers, D. S. (1969) Some aspects of the use of birth expectation data from sample surveys for population projections. *Demography*, **6** (2), 101–15.

Stiffman, R. I. (1967) Age at marriage as a demographic factor in conditions of high fertility. In World Population Conference (1965), vol. 2. 177–8.

Siffman, R. I. (1971) Plodovitnost zenchin v Baku (Fertility of women in Baku). In Volkov (1971), 22–34.

Silver, M. (1965) Births, marriages and business cycles in the United States. *Journal of Political Economy*, **73**, 237–55.

Silver, M. (1965–6) Births, marriages and income fluctuations in the United Kingdom and Japan. *Economic Development and Cultural Change*, **14** (3), 302–15.

Simon, J. L., 1969, The effect of income on fertility. *Population Studies*, **23** (3), 327–41.

Simon, J. L. (1975a) The mixed effects of income upon successive births may explain the convergence phenomenon. *Population Studies*, **29** (1), 109–22.

Simon, J. L. (1975b) Puzzles and further explorations in the interrelationships of successive births with husband's income, spouse's education and race. *Demography*, **12** (2), 259–74.

Sklar, J. L. (1974) The role of marriage behaviour in the demographic transition: the case of Eastern Europe around 1900. *Population Studies*, **28** (2), 231–48.

Slicher van Bath, B. M. (1958) Historical demography and the social and economic development of the Netherlands. *Daedalus*, Spring, 604–21.

Sly, D. F. (1970) Minority-group status and fertility: an extension of Goldscheider and Uhlenberg. *American Journal of Sociology*, **76** (3), 443–59.

Smolinski, Z. (1964) O teritorialnym zrócnicowaniu i zmianach plodnosci kobiet w Polsce (Regional differences and changes of fertility in Poland). *Wiadomosci Statystyczne*, **9** (3), 21–5.

Smolinski, Z. (1965) Kisérlet a népességfejlődés általános gazdasági elméletének megfogalmazására (An attempt to formulate the general economic theory of population development). *Demográfia*, **8** (1), 60–70.

Smolinski, Z. (1969) Wplyw czynników ekonomicznych na proces reprodukcji ludnosci (Influence of economic factors on the process of reproduction of population). *Studia Demograficzne*, no 19, 41–62.

Smolinski, Z. (1971) *Rozrodczosc w latach 1945–2000 (Fertility in the Years 1945–2000)*. Warsaw: GUS. 270 p.

Smolinski, Z. (1973a) *Stan i perspektiwy dzietnosci rodzin (The Present State and Perspective of the Number of Children in Families)*. Warsaw: GUS. 430 p.

Smolinski, Z. (1973b) Efektywny okres rozrodczy (Effective fertile period). *Wiadomosci Statystyczne*, **18** (8), 6–9.

Smolinski, Z. (1974) *Statystyczna analiza dzietnosci kobiet (Statistical Analysis of the Number of Children of Women)*. Warsaw: GUS. 183 p.

Sorokin, P. A. (1959) *Social and Cultural Mobility*. Glencoe, Ill.: Free Press. 645 p.

Spengler, J. J. (1938) *France Faces Depopulation*. Durham: Duke University Press. 313 p.

Spengler, J. J., and Duncan, O. D. (eds) (1956) *Population Theory and Policy*. Glencoe, Ill.: Free Press. 522 p.

Srb, V. (1972) Research in marriage reproduction (1970). *Demosta*, **4**, 442–49.

Srb, V., Kucera, M., and Vysusilova, D. (1964) Une enquête sur la prevention des naissances et le plan familial en Tchécoslovaquie. *Population*, **19** (1), 79–94.

Srb, V., and Vomackova, O. (1971, 1972) Vyzkum reprodukce malzenstvi v CSSR (1970). *Demografie*, (3), 233–39, (4), 327–34, **13** (1), 5–18, (2), 110–16.

Stycos, J. M. (1955) *Family and Fertility in Puerto Rico*. New York: Columbia University Press. 322 p.

Stycos, J. M. (1962) Experiments in social change: the Caribbean fertility studies. In Kiser (1962), 305–33.

Stycos, J. M. (1963) Obstacles to programs of population control: facts and fancies. *Marriage and Family Living*, **25**, 5–13.

Stycos, J. M., and Weller, R. H. (1967) Female working roles and fertility. *Demography*, **4**, 210–17.

Stys, W. (1957) The influence of economic conditions on fertility of peasant women. *Population Studies*, **11** (2), 136–48.

Stys, W. (1959) *Wspólzaleznosc rozwoju rodziny chlopskiej i jej gospodarstwa (Relation of the Peasant Family to its Family Farm)*. Wroclaw: Wroclawskiego Towarzystwa Naukowego. ser. A, no 62. 556 p.

Sutter, J. (1953) Un démographe engagé: Arsène Dumont. *Population*, **8** (1), 79–82.

Sweet, J. A. (1970) Family composition and labor force activity of American wives. *Demography*, **7** (2), 195–209.

Sydney Conference (1967) Contributed papers. Liège: International Union for the Scientific Study of Population. 1099 p.

Szabady, E. (1962) A társadalmi-foglalkozási átrétegeződés és demográfiai hatásai (Socio-occupational mobility and its demographic impacts). *Demográfia*. **5** (4), 494–500.

Szabady, E. (1964a) Születésszámunk nemzetközi és történeti megvilágitásban (The birth rate of Hungary in historical and international comparison). *Demográfia*, **7** (3–4), 373–83.

Szabady, E. (ed.) (1964a) *Studies on Fertility and Social Mobility*. Budapest: Akadémiai Kiadó. 331 p.

Szabady, E. (1967) A családtervezési vizsgálatok egyes kérdései (Some problems of family planning surveys). *Demográfia*, **10** (2), 219–37.

Szabady, E. (ed.) (1968a) *World Views of Population Problems*. Budapest: Akadémiai Kiadó. 447 p.

Szabady, E. (1968b) Családtervezési trendek: a magyar vizsgálat (Family planning trends: the Hungarian survey). *Demográfia*, **11**, (3–4), 333–46.

Szabady, E. (1969a) Magyar termékenységi és családtervezési vizsgálatok (Hungarian fertility and family planning studies). *Demográfia*, **12** (4), 417–36.

Szabady, E. (1969b) Les effets sociaux et démographiques d'une nouvelle mesure de politique démographique. *Population et Famille*, no 18, 1–17.

Szabady, E. (1971a) A társadalmi tényezők szelektiv szerepe a gyermekgondozási segély igénybevételénél (Study of the selective role of social factors in taking advantage of the child care allowance). *Statisztikai Szemle*, **49** (4), 339–47.

Szabady, E. (1971b) Économie et population: la situation de la Hongrie. *Économie et Statistique*, no 22, 21–9.

Szabady, E. (1971c) Some characteristics of fertility in Hungary after World War II. In International Population Conference, London (1969), vol. 1, 621–5.

Szabady, E. (1972a) Termékenységi változások és a társadalmi-gazdasági fejlődés összefüggései a kelet-európai szocialista országokban (The interrelations of fertility changes and socioeconomic development in east European socialist countries). *Gazdaság*, **6** (4), 103–15.

Szabady, E. (1972b) Impact of the new child care allowances. *New Hungarian Quarterly*, **48**, 99–110.

Szabady, E., and Klinger, A. (1966) Az 1965–6. évi termékenységi, családtervezési és születésszabályozási vizsgálat (The 1965–6 Hungarian study on fertility, family planning and birth control). *Demogràfia*, **9** (2), 135–61.

Szabady, E., Tekse, K., and Pressat, R. (1966) La population des pays socialistes européens. *Population*, **21** (5), 941–70.

Taba, I. (1962) Baranya megye család- és lélekszáma 1696-ban (The number of families and of population in the country of Baranya in 1696). *Történeti Statisztikai Évkönyv*, 131–58. Budapest: Központi Statisztikai Hivatal Könyvtára.

Tabah, L. (1971) *Rapport sur les relations entre la fécondité et la condition sociale et économique de la famille en Europe: leurs répercussions sur la politique sociale.* Council of Europe. 149 p.

Teitelbaum, M. C. (1972) Fertility effects of the abolition of legal abortion in Romania. *Population Studies*, **26** (3), 405–17.

Tekse, K. (1969) A termékenység néhány jellemzője Közép-és Déleurópában az első világháboru előtt (Some characteristics of fertility in Central and Southern Europe before the First World War). *Demográfia*, **12** (1–2), 23–48.

Terhune, K. W., and Kaufman, S. (1973) The family size utility function. *Demography*, **10** (4), 599–618.

Terleckij, N. E. (ed.) (1975) *Household Production and Consumption.* New York: National Bureau of Economic Research. 669 p.

Termékenységi adatok (Fertility data) (1966). *KSH Népességtudományi Kutató Intézet Közleményei*, no 14. 349 p.

Terrisse, M. (1961) Un faubourg du Havre: Ingouville. *Population*, **16** (2), 285–300.

Tery, G. B. (1975) Rival explanations in the work-fertility relationship. *Population Studies*, **29** (2), 191–206.

Theiss, E. (1966) Családnövekedési valószinüségek és modellek (Parity progression rates and models). *Demográfia*, **9** (1), 67–87.

Thirring, L. (1941) Tanulmányok as 1930. évi népszámlálás köréből (Studies on the census of 1930 in Hungary). *Magyar Statisztikai Társaság Kiadványai*, no 16. 196 p.

Thirring, L. (1959) Vizsgálódások a termékenység alakulásának foglalkozási, társadalmi-gazdasági jellegzetességeiről (Studies on the occupational and socio-economic characteristics of the development of fertility). *Demográfia*, **2** (1), 54–73.

Thirring, L. (1969) Adatok a termékenység alakulásának város és vidék közötti különbségeiről (Data on the development of fertility differences between urban and rural areas). *Demográfia*, **12** (3), 307–22.

Thomas, W. I., and Znaniecki, F. (1927) *The Polish Peasant in Europe and America*, vols 1–2. New York: Knopf. 2250 p.

Thompson, W. S. (1929) Population. *American Journal of Sociology*, **34**, 959–75.

Thompson, W. S. (1944) *Plenty of People.* Lancaster: Jacques Cattel Press. 246 p.

Tranter, N. (1973) *Population Since the Industrial Revolution.* London: Croom Helm. 206 p.

United Nations, Population Division (1953) *The Determinations and Consequences of Population Trends.* New York: United Nations. 403 p.

United Nations Dept of Social Affairs, Population Branch (1955) *Age and Sex Patterns of Mortality: Model Life Tables for Underdeveloped Countries.* New York: UN Dept of Social Affairs. 38 p.

United Nations Dept of Economic and Social Affairs (1973) *The Determinants and Consequences of Population Trends: New Summary of Findings on Interaction of Demographic, Economic and Social Factors*, vol. 1. New York: United Nations. 661 p.

United Nations Dept of Economic and Social Affairs (1976) *Fertility and Family Planning in Europe Around 1970: A Comparative Survey of Twelve National Surveys*. New York: UN Dept of Econ. & Soc. Affairs Population Studies no 58. 180 p.

Urlanis, B. T. (1963) *Rozhdayemost i prodolzhitelnost zhisni v SSSR (Fertility and Life Expectancy in the USSR)*. Moscow: Gostatisdat. 136 p.

Urlanis, B. T. (1971) The birth rate in the USSR after the Second World War. In International Population Conference, London, vol. 1, 634–47.

Urlanis, B. T. (1974) *Problemy dinamiki naselenia SSSR (Problems of the Dynamics of Population in the USSR)*. Moscow: Nauka. 335 p.

Utterström, G. (1965) Two essays on population in eighteenth-century Scandinavia. In Glass and Eversley (1965), 523–48.

Valentey, D. I. (1967) *Teoria i politika narodonaseleniya (Population Theory and Politics)*. Moscow: Vysshaya Shola. 183 p.

Valentey, D. I. (1970) Les problèmes démographiques de l'Union soviétique. *Population*, 25 (2), 363–72.

Valentey, D. I. (1973) *Narodonaseleniya (Population)*. Moscow: Statistika. 110 p.

Vallot, F., and Roussel, L. (1969) La formation de la famille suivant les groupes socio-professionnelles. *Population*, 24 (5), 897–918.

Valmary, P. (1965) Familles paysannes au XVIIIe siècle en Bas-Quercy. *INED Travaux et Documents*, no 45. 192 p.

Van der Woude, A. M., and Mentink, G. J. (1966) La population de Rotterdam au XVIIe et au XVIIIe siècle. *Population*, 21 (6), 1165–90.

Van de Walle, E. (1968) Marriage and marital fertility. *Daedalus*, Spring, 486–501.

Van de Walle, E. (1969) Problèmes de l'étude du déclin de la fécondité européenne. *Recherches Économiques de Louvain*, 35 (4), 271–87.

Van de Walle, E. (1971) *Analyse non nominative des sources écrites de tout ordre: Méthodologie, relation avec les études nominatives*. Paper presented at the Colloque International de Démographie Historique, Firenze. 32 p.

Van de Walle, E. (1974) *The Female Population of France in the Nineteenth Century: A Reconstruction of 82 Departments*. Princeton: Princeton University Press. 483 p.

Van de Walle, E., and Knodel, J. (1967) Demographic transition and fertility decline: the European case. In Sydney Conference (1967), 47–55.

Van de Walle, E., and Van de Walle, F. (1972) Allaitement, sterilité et contraception: les opinions jusqu'au XIXe siècle. *Population*, 27 (4–5), 685–701.

Van Heek, F. (1954) *Het geboorte-niveau des nederlandse Rooms-Katholiken*. Leyden: H. E. Stenfert Kroese. 201 p.

Van Heek, F. (1956–7) Roman-Catholicism and fertility in the Netherlands. *Population Studies*, 10 (2), 125–38.

Van Nort, L. (1960) On values in population theory. *Milbank Memorial Fund Quarterly*, 38 (4), 387–95.

Vavra, Z. (1962) A városi és falusi népesség születési arányszámának változása (Changes in the birth rate of urban and rural population in Czechoslovakia). *Demográfia*, 5 (4), 529–36.

Vavra, Z. (1964) Changes in the birth rates of urban and rural populations. In Szabady (1964b), 206-13.

Vielrose, E. (1965a) Zróznicowanie czestosci urodzen w Polsce (Differentiation of fertility in Poland). *Przeglad Statystyczny*, **12** (1), 3-10.

Vielrose, E. (1965b) *Elements of the Natural Movement of Population*. Oxford and Warsaw: Pergamon Press and Panstwowe Wydawnictwo Ekonomiczne. 288 p.

Vielrose, E. (1968) Przyczynek do zagadnienia wspólzaleznosci miedzy dochodem narodowym i plodnoscia. *Studia Demograficzne*, no 15, 13-21.

Volkov, A. G. (ed.) (1968) *Izucheniye vosproizvodstva nasseleniya* ((Study of the reproduction of population). Moscow: Nauka. 330 p.

Volkov, A. G. (ed.) (1971) *Faktori rozhdayemosti* (*Factors of Fertility*). Moscow: Statistika. 86 p.

Volkov, A. G., Darski, L. E., and Krasi, A. J. (eds) (1970) *Voprosy Demografii* (*Problems of Demography*). Moscow: Statistika. 278 p.

Voprosi demografii (1968). Moscow: Statistika. 298 p.

Vostrikova, A. M. (1962) A születési mozgalom, a házasság-kötések és a család vizsgálata a Szovjetunióban (The study of fertility, marriage and family in the Soviet Union). *Demográfia*, **5** (4), 537-45.

Vostrikova, A. M. (1964) Examination of fertility, marriages and family in the USSR. In Szabady (1964b), 214-28.

Watson, C. (1954) Population policy in France: family allowances and other benefits. *Population Studies*, **7** (3), 263-286, **8** (1), 46-73.

Weintraub, R. (1962) The birth rate and economic development: an empirical study. *Econometrica*, **15** (4), 182-217.

Wells, R. V. (1971) Family size and fertility control in eighteenth-century America: a study of Quaker families. *Population Studies*, **25** (1), 73-82.

Westoff, C. F. (1956) The changing focus of differential fertility research: the social mobility hypothesis. In Spengler and Duncan (1956), 400-9.

Westoff, C. F. (1959) The social-psychological structure of fertility. In Internationaler Bevölkerungskongress (1959), 355-66.

Westoff, C. F. (ed.) (1973) *Toward the End of Growth*. Englewood Cliffs, N.J.: Prentice Hall. 177 p.

Westoff, C. F. (1975) The yield of the imperfect: the 1970 national fertility study. *Demography*, **12** (4), 573-80.

Westoff, C. F., Mishler, E. G., and Kelly, E. L. (1957) Preferences in size of family and eventual fertility twenty years later. *American Journal of Sociology*, **62** (5), 491-7.

Westoff, C. F., Potter, R. G., Jr, and Sagi, P. C. (1963) *The Third Child: A Study of Prediction in Fertility*. Princeton: Princeton University Press. 293 p.

Westoff, C. F., Potter, R. G., Jr, and Sagi, P. C. (1964) Some selected findings of the Princeton fertility survey. *Demography*, **1** (1), 130-5.

Westoff, C. F., Potter, R. G., Jr, Sagi, P. C., and Mishler, E. G. (1961) *Family Growth in Metropolitan America*. Princeton: Princeton University Press. 433 p.

Westoff, C. F., and Potvin, R. H. (1967) *College Women and Fertility Values*. Princeton: Princeton University Press. 237 p.

Westoff, C. F., and Ryder, N. B. (1970) États-Unis: L'encyclique du Pape: les attitudes et le comportement des catholiques, 1969. *Études du Planning Familial*, **1** (50), 1-15.

Whelpton, P. K. (1954) *Cohort Fertility: Native White Women in the United States.* Princeton: Princeton University Press. 492 p.

Whelpton, P. K., Campbell, A. A., and Patterson, J. E. (1966) *Fertility and Family Planning in the United States.* Princeton: Princeton University Press. 443 p.

Whelpton, P. K., and Kiser, C. V. (eds) (1950) *Social and Psychological Factors Affecting Fertility*, vol. 2. New York: Milbank Memorial Fund.

Whelpton, P. K. and Kiser, C. V., The planning of fertility. 209–57.

Reed, R. B., The interrelationship of marital adjustment, fertility control, and size of family, 259–301.

Whelpton, P. K., and Kiser, C. V., The comparative influence on fertility of contraception and impairments of fecundity, 303–57.

Kiser, C. V., and Whelpton, P. K., Fertility planning and fertility rates by socioeconomic status, 359–415.

Freedman, R., and Whelpton, P. K., Fertility planning and fertility rates by religious interest and denomination, 417–66.

Whelpton, P. K., and Kiser, C. V. (eds) (1952) *Social and Psychological Factors Affecting Fertility*, vol. 3. New York: Milbank Memorial Fund.

Kiser, C. V., and Whelpton, P. K., The interrelation of fertility, fertility planning, and feeling of economic security, 467–548.

Freedman, R., and Whelpton, P. K., The relationship of general planning and fertility rates, 549–74.

Herrera, L. F., and Kiser, C. V., Fertility in relation to fertility planning and health of wife, husband, and children, 575–620.

Clare, J. E., and Kiser, C. V., Preference for children of given sex in relation to fertility, 621–73.

Freedman, R., and Whelpton, P. K., Fertility planning and fertility rates by adherence to traditions, 675–704.

Kantner, J. F., Whelpton, P. K., Fertility rates and fertility planning by character of migration, 705–40.

Westoff, C. F., and Kiser, C. V., The interrelation of fertility, fertility planning, and feeling of personal inadequacy, 741–99.

Whelpton, P. K., and Kiser, C. V. (eds) (1958) *Social and Psychological Factors Affecting Fertility*, vol. 4. New York: Milbank Memorial Fund.

DeGraff Swain, M., and Kiser, C. V., The interrelation of fertility, fertility planning and ego-centered interest in children, 801–34.

Schacter, N., and Kiser, C. V., Fear of pregnancy and childbirth in relation to fertility-planning status and fertility, 835–84.

Westoff, C. F., and Kiser, C. V., An empirical re-examination and intercorrelation of selected hypothesis factors. 953–67.

Kantner, J. F., and Kiser, C. V., The interrelation of fertility, fertility planning, and intergenerational mobility, 969–1003.

Riemer, R., and Kiser, R. C., Economic tension and social mobility in relation to fertility planning and size of planned family, 1005–68.

Kantner, J. F., and Potter, R. G., Jr., The relationship of family size in two successive generations, 1069–86.

Whelpton, P. K., and Kiser, C. V. (eds) (1958) *Social and Psychological Factors Affecting Fertility*, vol. 5. New York: Milbank Memorial Fund.

Borgatta, E. F., and Westoff, C. F., The prediction of total fertility, 1087–123.

Westoff, C. F., and Borgatta, E. F., The prediction of planned fertility, 1125–37.

Riemer, R., and Whelpton, P. K., Attitudes toward restriction of personal freedom in relation to fertility planning and fertility, 1139–87.

Potter, R. G., Jr, and Kantner, J. F., The influence of siblings and friends on fertility, 1189–210.

Pratt, L., and Whelpton, P. K., Interest in and liking for children in relation to fertility planning and size of planned family, 1211–44.

Pratt, L., and Whelpton, P. K., Extra-familial participation of wives in relation to interest in and liking for children, fertility planning, and actual and desired family size. 1245–79.

Solomon, E. S., Clare, J. E., and Westoff, C. F., Fear of childlessness, desire to avoid an only child, and children's desires for siblings, 1281–98.

Kiser, C. V., and Whelpton, P. K., Summary of the chief findings and implications for future studies, 1325–72.

Wilkinson, M. (1967) Evidences of long swings in the growth of the Swedish population and related economic variables 1860–1965. *Journal of Economic History*, **27** (1), 17–38.

Wilkinson, M. (1973) An econometric analysis of fertility in Sweden. *Econometrica*, **41** (4), 633–42.

Willis, R. J. (1973) A new approach to the economic theory of fertility behavior. *Journal of Political Economy*, **81** (2, pt 2), S14–S64.

World Population Conference, Rome (1954) vols 1–6. New York: United Nations. 1040, 1016, 906, 1073, 1115 and 1047 p.

World Population Conference, Belgrade (1965), vols 1–4. New York: United Nations. 349, 509, 435 and 557 p.

Wrigley, E. A. (1961) *Industrial Growth and Population Change*. Cambridge: Cambridge University Press. 193 p.

Wrigley, E. A. (ed.) (1966a) *An Introduction to English Historical Demography*. London: Weidenfeld & Nicolson. 283 p. (Contributors: Armstrong, W. A., Eversley, D. E. C., Laslett, P., Wrigley, E. A.)

Wrigley, E. A. (1966b) Family limitation in pre-industrial England. *Economic History Review*, ser. 2, **19** (1), 82–109.

Wrigley, E. A. (1969) *Population and History*. London: Weidenfeld & Nicolson. 256 p.

Wrigley, E. A. (1975) Baptism coverage in early nineteenth century England: the Colyton area. *Population Studies*, **29** (2), 299–316.

Wrong, D. H. (1960) Class fertility differentials in England and Wales. *Milbank Memorial Fund Quarterly*, **38** (1), 37–47.

Wyatt, F. (1967) Clinical notes on the motives of reproduction. *Journal of Social Issues*, **23**, 29–56.

Yasuba, Y. (1961) *Birth Rates of the White Population in the United States, 1800–1860: An Economic Study*. Baltimore: Johns Hopkins Press. 198 p.

Yaukey, D. (1969) On theorizing about fertility. *American Sociologist*, **4**, 100–4.

Yule, G. U. (1906) On the changes in the marriage and birth rates in England and Wales during the past half century with an inquiry as to their probable causes. *Journal of the Royal Statistical Society*, **66**, 88–132.

Zeinalov, G. N. (1968) Rozhdayemost v Azarbaidjanskoj SSR (Fertility in Azerbaijan). In Adonts and Davtyan (1968), 41–2.

Zyromski, S. (1975) *Rozrodczosc a srodowisko (Natality and Environment)*. Warsaw: PWN. 283 p.

Author index

Abramowitz, M., 122, 385
Acsádi, G., 137, 215–17, 385
Adelman, I., 164, 385
Adonts, M. A., 385
Agren, K., 385
Akerman, J., 119, 385
Akerman, S., 385
Akers, D. S., 209, 413
Andorka, R., 47, 52–3, 68, 69, 71, 86, 90, 178–89, 275–8, 280–2, 385–6
Anicic, Z., 134, 386
Aries, P., 42, 386
Arnold, F., 338–9, 387, 395
Arutyunyan, L. A., 133, 170, 275, 328, 387
Ashenfelter, O., 366, 387
Axelrod, M., 387

Back, K. W., 387, 395, 400
Baltzell, E. D., 270, 387
Banks, J. A., 341–2, 387
Banks, O., 341-2, 387
Bárány, L., 264, 403
Barsy, Gy., 387
Basavarajappa, K. G., 387
Bastide, H., 212–15, 352, 387, 397, 398
Baumert, G., 215, 300, 370, 396
Bean, F. D., 387
Beauchamp, P., 48, 387
Becker, G. S., 30, 37, 231, 363, 364, 369, 370, 371, 372, 387–8
Behrens, W. W., 131, 407
Behrman, S. J., 388
Belova, V., 221, 222, 328, 388
Benedek, T., 333, 388
Benjamin, B., 125, 388
Berelson, B., 388
Berend, T. I., 115, 388
Berent, J., 136, 271–2, 388
Bernhardt, E. M., 240–2, 388

Beshers, J. M., 41, 388
Bhattacharyya, A. K., 388
Biraben, J.-N., 47, 127–8, 129, 388
Blacker, C. P., 18, 388
Blacker, J. G., 91–2, 114, 388
Blackman, L. S., 339, 395
Blake, J., 36–8, 130, 200, 209–10, 370, 371, 388–9, 393
Blau, P. M., 266, 272–5, 277, 278, 290–1, 389
Blaug, M., 101, 389
Blayo, Ch., 120–1, 127–8, 389
Blayo, Y., 47, 48, 77–8, 389
Blood, R. O., 340, 389
Blumberg, G., 391
Bodmer, W. F., 389
Bodrova, V., 389
Bogue, D. J., 18, 389
Bolte, M., 215, 300, 370, 396
Bondarskaya, G. A., 170, 328–9, 389–90
Borgatta, E. E., 419
Bornstein, M. B., 334–5, 395
Bourdieu, P., 232, 254, 353, 390
Bourgeois-Pichat, J., 8, 73, 76, 77, 78, 131, 381, 390
Boverat, F., 351, 390
Braun, R., 112, 390
Brésard, M., 271, 390
Breznik, D., 134, 168–70, 390
Brooks, H. F., 390
Broom, L., 407
Brown, R. G., 41, 100, 102, 406
Brown, S., 301, 391
Buday, D., 94, 390
Buissink, J. D., 177, 390
Bulatao, R. A., 338–9. 387
Bumpass, L., 130, 197, 209, 390–1, 396
Burch, T. K., 302, 391
Burgdörfer, F., 237, 300, 348, 391
Buripakdi, C., 338–9, 387

Caldwell, J. C., 24–5, 391
Calot, G., 391
Campbell, A. A., 9, 125, 151–61, 207, 229, 245, 284, 305, 309, 311, 383, 391, 403, 418
Campbell, J. M., 125, 130, 165, 399
Cantillon, R., 70, 87, 391
Carlsson, G., 42, 80, 104–5, 282–3, 391
Casetti, E., 18, 391
Centers, R., 391
Chambers, J. D., 92, 101, 391
Charbonneau, H., 48, 50, 52, 61–2, 67, 86, 88, 387, 391
Charles, E., 116–17
Chasteland, J., 174, 391
Chaunu, C., 42, 391
Cheng, B., 125, 165, 399
Chilman, C. S., 395
Chilman, G., 335, 391
Chojnacka, H., 90, 391
Chou, R.-C., 301, 391
Christensen, H. T., 391
Chung, B. J., 338–9, 387
Cicourel, A., 391
Cipolla, C. M., 18, 81–2, 392
Clare, J. E., 418, 419
Clark, C., 251, 392
Clausen, J. A., 337, 395
Clausen, S. R., 337, 395
Coale, A. J., 6, 18, 21, 22, 34–44, 73, 116, 131, 392, 409
Coble, J. M., 394
Cochrane, S. H., 392
Cole, W. A., 101, 393
Collomb, P., 392
Commission on Population Growth and the American Future, 130–1, 229, 392
Connel, K. H., 103, 392
Coombs, L., 209, 246–8, 295, 383, 392, 396
Corsa, L., 388
Cottrel, L. S., 407
Cowgill, D. O., 392
Cseh-Szombathy, L., 296, 392

Dányi, D., 43, 96, 392
Darbel, P., 232, 254, 353, 389
Darras, 392

Darski, L. E., 221, 388, 417
David, H. P., 136, 353, 393
Dávid, Z., 45, 85, 93, 393
Davis, K., 18, 25–6, 393
Davtyan, L. M., 292, 385, 393
Day, L. H., 299–301, 302, 393
Deane, P., 101, 393
De Graff, S. M., 418
De Jong, C. F., 304–5, 393, 396
De Laszlo, H., 41, 393
Demény, P. 6, 22, 73, 88, 319, 392, 393
Den Hollander, A. N. J., 93, 393
Deniel, R., 51, 62, 393
Deprez, P., 50, 68, 112, 393
Derksen, J. B. D., 175–7, 393
De Tray, D. N., 364, 367, 393
Devereux, G., 41, 394
De Wolff, P., 394
Dinkel, R. M., 394
Douglas, M., 41, 394
Drake, M., 72, 79, 394
Draper, W. H., 131, 394
Duesenberry, J. S., 369, 372, 394
Dumont, A., 266, 394
Duncan, O. D., 242, 266, 275–5, 277–8, 290–1, 389, 394, 414
Dupaquier, J., 101, 394
Dziennio, K., 394

Easterlin, R. A., 122–5, 126, 130–1, 173, 288, 371–4, 394
Eaton, J. W., 8, 394
Edin, K. A., 237–9, 259–60, 279–80, 395
Eldridge, H. T., 395
Elek, P., 44, 395
Engels, F., 18, 395
Erdei, F., 95, 395
Erikson, E. H., 333, 395
Eriksson, I., 385
Eversley, D. E. C., 13, 42, 92, 112, 395, 398

Farber, B., 339, 395
Fawcett, J. T., 333, 334–5, 337, 338–9, 387, 395
Febvay, M., 129, 213, 232, 254, 352, 390, 395

Federici, N., 174, 296, 395–6
Ferenbac, I., 135, 396
Festy, P., 120–1, 389, 396
Firth, R., 41, 396
Fisher, R. A., 266, 272, 396
Flandrin, J.-L., 42, 396
Fleury, M., 45, 47, 388, 396
Flew, A., 13, 14, 396
Ford, T. R., 396
Forster, C., 173, 396
Foster, G. N., 94, 396
Freedman, D. S., 245–6, 396
Freedman, R., 204–5, 207, 209, 215, 246–8, 295, 300, 304, 307, 313–15, 369, 370, 387, 388, 392, 394, 396–7, 418
Frenkel, I., 397
Freud, S., 333
Freyka, T., 131, 397
Fridlizius, G., 102, 397
Friedlander, D., 114, 397
Friedlander, S., 165, 397
Friedman, M., 371
Frigyes, E., 137, 397
Fülep, Z., 95

Galbraith, V. L., 119, 397
Ganiage, J., 50, 397
Gardner, B., 367, 397
Gaunt, D., 52, 63, 68, 385, 397
Gautier, E., 50, 80, 397
Gendell, M., 391
Gerhard, D., 93, 397
Gerschenkron, A., 115, 397
Gille, H., 397
Girard, A., 212–15, 270, 352, 387, 397–8
Girard, P., 50, 86, 398
Glass, D. V., 74, 75, 110, 118–19, 120, 122, 172, 174, 212, 228, 229, 230, 251, 252, 253, 254, 317, 348, 350, 398
Godwin, W., 13
Goldberg, D., 204–5, 242, 289–90. 340, 387, 396, 397, 398
Goldscheider, C., 298, 327, 398
Goldstein, S., 398
Goodwin, A., 398
Goubert, P., 50, 86, 99, 398–9

Grabill, W. H., 9, 125, 151–61, 403
Graunt, J., 13
Grebenik, E., 121, 212, 398
Greene, R. J., 411
Gregory, P. R., 125, 165, 399
Griliches, Z., 399
Groat, H. T., 337, 399
Gronau, R., 399
Gunda, B., 44, 395

Habakkuk, H. J., 91, 111, 399
Hajnal, J., 22, 23, 66–7, 299, 252–3, 399, 401
Hansen, A. H., 116, 399
Harris, D. L., 389
Hass, P. H., 395
Hauser, P. M., 209, 399
Hawthorn, G., 370, 374–5, 382, 383, 399
Heberle, R., 399
Heckman, J. J., 367, 399
Heckscher, E. F., 102, 399
Heer, D. M., 164–5, 222, 399
Heinz, E., 296, 392
Heiskanen, V. S., 389
Heitlinger, A., 357, 399
Héméry, S., 391
Henripin, J., 52, 399
Henry, F. J., 390
Henry, L., 4, 8, 9, 45, 47, 48, 49, 50, 51, 54, 62, 64–6, 67, 68, 69, 71, 77, 78, 87, 88, 89, 174, 212, 352, 388, 389, 391, 393, 396, 397, 398, 399–400
Henshaw, P. S., 41, 393
Herrera, L. F., 418
Hicks, J., 27
Hidvégi, J., 44, 95, 400
Higgins, E., 400
Hill, R., 400
Hilscher, Z., 44, 395
Himes, N. E., 41, 400
Hoch, R., 354, 401
Hoffman, L. W., 334, 336–8, 395, 400
Hoffman, M. L., 338, 395
Hofstee, E. W., 112, 177, 400
Höbling, M., 44, 54, 400
Hollingsworth, T. H., 46, 47, 64–6, 67, 69, 75, 76, 85, 88, 400–5
Hoover, E. M., 18, 392

Hope, K., 271, 401
Hopkin, W. A. B., 252–3, 401
Hopkins, K., 42, 401
Horlacher, D. E., 411
Horváth, S., 44, 395
Hughes, R. B., 401
Huszár, I., 354, 357, 401
Hutchinson, E. P., 237–9, 259–60, 279–80, 395
Hyrenius, H., 59, 401

Illyés, Gy., 94–5, 401
INED, 352, 401
Innes, J., 401
Iritani, T., 338–9, 387
Isard, W., 122, 401
Iván, P., 354, 401

Jacquard, A., 8, 389
Jagielski, A., 401
Jankó, J., 96, 402
Johnson, G. Z., 254, 402
Jolles, H. M., 343–6, 402
Jurecek, Z., 402
Jutikkala, E., 81, 102, 402

Kamarás, F., 264, 403
Kantner, J. F., 267–8, 418, 419
Kápolnai, I., 96, 402
Kapótsy, B., 402
Karachanow, M., 402
Karsay, Gy., 44, 395
Kassabov, V. S., 135, 402
Katkova, I. P., 133, 221, 402
Katus, L., 115, 402
Kaufman, S., 383, 415
Kelly, E. L., 209, 418
Kenéz, B., 319–20, 402
Kerényi, Gy., 44, 395
Kestenberg, J., 333, 402
Keyfitz, N., 118, 281–2, 402
Keynes, J. M., 116, 402
Kirk, D., 116, 119, 402, 409
Kiser, C. V., 9, 116, 117–18, 125, 151–61, 191–3, 195–7, 242–3, 267–9, 304, 307, 335, 339, 402–3 409, 418–19
Kiss, G., 403
Kitagawa, E. M., 403

Klapprodt, C., 407
Klein, V., 296, 408
Klinger, A., 81–2, 96, 137, 215–19, 256, 263, 264, 275, 296, 385, 403, 415
Knodel, J., 6, 19, 21–2, 51, 68, 72, 189, 227–8, 403, 413, 417
Knowlton, C., 342
Koczogh, A., 44, 395
Kodolányi, J., 95, 403
Kondratieff, N. D., 122
Kooy, G.-A., 403
Kovács, A., 183, 403–4
Kovács, I., 44, 95, 96, 395, 404
Kovács, J., 354, 401
Kovacsics, J., 404
Kováts, Z., 404
Kozlov, V. I., 170, 328, 390, 404
Krasi, A. J., 417
Krause, J. T., 46, 74, 75, 76, 100–1, 404
Krier, D. F., 63, 406
Krotki, K., 323, 326, 404
Kruegel, D. L., 404
Kucera, N., 135, 220, 221, 404, 414
Kuznets, S., 122–3, 404
Kvasha, A. J., 113, 404

Lachiver, M., 394, 405
Lancaster, K. J., 363, 405
Landry, A., 18, 369, 405
Lapierre, E., 323, 326, 404
Laslett, P., 70, 71, 72, 90, 99, 227–8, 405
Lautman, F., 99, 350, 405
Lavoie, Y., 48, 387
Le Bras, H., 174, 405
Lee, E. S., 328, 411
Lee, R., 405
Lee, S. J., 338–9, 387
Lehner, A., 270, 405
Leibenstein, H., 32–4, 373–4, 405
Lenski, G., 298, 315–16, 331, 405
Le Play, F., 101
Le Roy Ladurie, E., 405
Lévy, C., 64, 400
Lewis, H. G., 364, 388, 405
Lewis, O., 335, 405
Lewis-Faning, E., 210–11, 405

Livi-Bacci, M., 48, 78–9, 125, 177–8, 405–6
Long, L. H., 303, 311, 325, 406
Lösch, A., 406
Loschky, D. J., 63, 406

McClelland, D. C., 335, 406
McKenna, E. E., 103, 406
Mackenroth, G., 406
Mackensen, R., 406
McKeown, T., 41, 100, 102, 406
Macura, M., 134, 406
Malinowski, B., 41, 406
Malthus, T. R., 13–17, 406
Marchal, F., 120–1, 406
Marczewski, J., 114, 406
Marshall, A., 27, 406
Marshall, T. H., 74, 406
Marx, S., 323, 407
Matras, J., 90, 406–7
Mathiessen, P. C., 80, 407
Mausecz, Zs., 354, 401
Maxwell, D. E., 177, 410
Mayer, A. J., 8, 323, 394, 407
Mayer, K. B., 398
Mazur, P., 171, 328, 407
Mead, M., vii, 407
Meadows, D. H., 131, 407
Meadows, D. L., 131, 407
Meerdink, J., 394
Mehlan, K. H., 353, 407
Mentink, G. J., 61
Merton, R., 407
Meuvret, J., 99, 407
Michael, R. T., 367, 407
Milbank Memorial Fund, 407
Miller, A., 407
Miltényi, K., 296, 355, 356, 392, 407
Mincer, J., 34–5, 408
Mishler, E. G., 197, 209, 339, 340, 403, 408, 418
Moberg, S., 238–40, 408
Moess, A., 53, 61, 96, 408
Mojic, A., 134, 168, 390
Moors, H. G., 262, 408
Morsa, J., 267, 408
Morris, C. T., 164, 385
Moulin, L., 101, 114, 408
Murdock, G. P., 41, 408

Myrdal, A., 127, 296, 349, 408
Myrdal, G., 127, 349, 408

Nadal, J., 51, 408
Nag, M., 41, 408
Namboodiri, N. K., 278, 288, 367, 408
Neal, A. G., 337, 399
Nerlove, M., 409
Nizard, A., 127–8, 409
Noin, D., 174, 409
Norberg, A., 385
Nortman, D. L., 119, 402
Notestein, F. W., 18, 19–21, 116, 409, 412

Ogburn, E. F., 116, 409
Okun, B., 31–2, 327, 409
Oosterveen, K., 71, 227–8, 405
Oppenheimer, V. K., 374, 409

Palli, H., 52, 409
Pataki, J., 96, 409
Patlagean, E., 42, 409
Patterson, J. E., 207, 246, 284, 305, 309–11, 418
Pavlik, Z., 409
Perevedentzev, V., 409
Perjés, G., 97, 409
Perlman, M., 409
Perrenoud, A., 409
Peters, H., 300, 409
Petersen, W., 112, 117, 313, 326, 409–10
Pezenhoffer, A., 319–20, 410
Phillips, A., 177, 410
Pierce, R. M., 410, 411
Piotrovski, J., 292, 410
Piro, C., 391
Pirtshalava, G. V., 328, 410
Pócsy, F., 44, 395
Pohlman, E., 333, 339–40, 410
Polgar, S., 410
Potter, J., 173, 410
Potter, R. G., 197–201, 244, 270, 287, 289, 307–9, 311, 314, 339, 340, 403, 418
Potts, M., 353, 410
Potvin, R. H., 201–3, 323, 418
Poussou, J. P., 47, 410

Pratt, L., 419
Pressat, R., 4, 5, 43, 127–8, 170, 353, 409, 410, 414
Prioux-Marchal, F., 229, 411

Rabin, A. I., 411
Rabut, O., 120–1, 406
Rainwater, L., 336–7, 340, 411
Rancic, M., 134, 168, 390
Randers, J., 131, 407
Ránki, Gy., 115, 388
Rasevic, M., 134, 168, 390, 411
Razzel, P. E., 46, 74, 75, 411
Record, R. G., 41, 100, 102, 406
Reddaway, W. B., 116, 411
Reed, R. B., 339, 418
Rickman, J., 74
Ridley, J. C., 411, 412
Riemer, R., 243, 269, 419
Riquet, R. P., 42, 411
Ritchey, P. N., 411
Roberts, R. E., 328, 411
Robinson, W. C., 411
Roeske-Slomka, I., 36, 166, 249, 411
Rogers, J., 385
Roheim, G., 95–6, 411
Rose, H., 411
Roussel, L., 213–15, 230–1, 398, 411, 416
Rowntree, G., 410, 411
Russel, J. C., 42, 412
Ruwet, J., 99, 412
Ruzsás, L., 94, 412
Ryder, N. B., 207–8, 210, 246, 252, 261, 305, 311, 326, 368, 412, 418

Saez, A., 51, 408
Sagi, P. C., 197–202, 244, 270, 287, 289, 307–9, 311, 319, 339, 340, 418
Sallume, X., 412
Sándor, V., 412
Sárkány, J., 387
Sauvy, A., 99, 351–2, 368, 369, 382, 412
Schelsky, H., 334, 412
Schneller, K., 320, 412
Schofield, R. S., 46, 48, 412
Schram, F., 43, 412
Schultz, T. W., 363, 412–13

Schumpeter, J., 122
Schwartz, K., 413
Scott, W., 413
Shacter, N., 419
Sharp, H., 204–5, 396, 397
Sheps, M. C., 413
Shorter, E., 72, 227, 413
Siegel, J. S., 209, 413
Siffman, P. I., 328, 413
Silver, M., 125–6, 165, 397, 413
Simon, J. L., 35, 413
Sklar, J. L., 66, 413
Slesinger, D. P., 387, 394, 397
Slicher van Bath, B. M., 413
Sly, D. F., 327, 413
Smit, J. W., 313–15, 397
Smolinski, Z., 36, 122, 133–4, 167, 168, 219–20, 249, 264, 413–14
Solomon, E. S., 419
Sorokin, P. A., 266–7, 414
Spengler, J. J., 116, 414
Srb, V., 135, 220–1, 414
Stycos, J. M., 297, 333, 400, 414
Stys, W., 235–7, 414
Sundbärg, G., 72
Sutter, J., 414
Sweet, J., 295–6, 414
Szabady, E., 137, 217–18, 275, 385, 403, 414–15
Szuhay, M., 115, 388

Taba, I., 415
Tabah, L., 137, 254, 255, 256, 261, 263, 293, 294, 310, 312, 415
Taeuber, I. B., 116, 409
Taleb, S. A., 131, 390
Teitelbaum, M. C., 132, 136, 353, 415
Tekse, K., 22, 183, 319, 415
Terhune, K. W., 383, 415
Terleckij, N. E., 363, 415
Terrisse, M., 50, 62, 86, 415
Tery, G. B., 415
Theiss, E., 415
Thirring, L., 144, 280–1, 404, 415–16
Thomas, D. S., 116, 119, 397
Thomas, W. I., 323, 409, 416
Thompson, W. S., 18, 416
Timár, J., 354, 401
Torbágyi, L., 44, 395

Tóth, P., 404
Tranter, N., 101, 416
Tucker, G. S. L., 173, 396

Uhlenberg, P. R., 327, 398
Urlanis, B. T., 121, 133, 170, 171, 223, 264–5, 292, 329–31, 416
Utterström, G., 80, 102, 416

Valentey, D. I., 416
Vallot, F., 416
Valmary, P., 51, 416
Van der Woude, A. M., 61, 416
Van de Walle, E., 6, 21–2, 42, 72, 74, 77, 78, 90, 111, 113, 227, 413, 416–17
Van de Walle, F., 42, 417
Van Heek, F., 301–2, 417
Van Nort, L., 417
Varga, L., 264, 403
Vavra, Z., 135, 417
Vielrose, E., 166, 417
Volkov, A. G., 417
Vomackova, O., 414
Vostrikova, A. M., 133, 417
Votey, H. L., 177, 410
Vysusilova, D., 135, 220–1, 414

Watson, C., 351, 417
Weintraub, R., 164, 417

Weller, R. H., 297, 414
Wells, R. W., 52, 417
Westoff, C. F., 195–6, 197–203, 207–9, 231, 244, 246, 252, 261, 269–70, 272, 287, 289, 305, 307–8, 311, 314, 323, 326, 339, 340, 390–1, 403, 408, 412, 417–18, 419
Whelpton, P. K., 5, 117–18, 191–3, 207, 242–3, 246, 267–9, 284, 304–5, 307, 309–11, 313–15, 335, 339, 397, 403, 418–19
Wilkinson, M., 126–7, 419
Willis, R. J., 363, 364, 366, 367, 368, 399, 407, 419
Wolfe, D. M., 340, 389
Wright, N. H., 136, 353, 393
Wrigley, E. A., 45, 50, 67, 70, 84–5, 88, 92, 101, 112, 229, 419
Wrong, D. H., 420
Wu, T.-S., 338–9, 387
Wyatt, F., 334, 336–7, 400, 420

Yasuba, Y., 171–2, 420
Yaukey, D., 420
Yule, G. U., 116, 420

Zeinalov, G. N., 328, 420
Znaniecki, F., 323, 416
Zucker, E., 213, 398
Zyromski, S., 111, 420

Subject index

adjustment, spread of birth control as adjustment, 104–5

age at marriage, 15–16, 22–3, 25, 65–6, 66–71, 80, 87–90, 92, 101, 103, 104, 112, 122, 123, 171, 210, 225, 227–31, 248, 330

alienation, 334, 337

aspirations, 244, 248, 250, 319, 343, 373–4, 378

attitudes, 189, 198, 207, 223–4, 225, 281–2, 332, 346, 358, 359, 369, 380–4

Australia, 117, 120, 129, 300

Austria, 22, 85, 116, 117, 228, 300, 342–6, 382

baptist, 303–5, 313

benefits of children, see utilities of children
see value of children

Belgium, 50, 111, 112, 116, 117, 120, 129, 221, 223, 228, 255, 262–3, 300, 301

birth control, 21, 23, 25–6, 30, 41–4, 48–9, 54, 57–9, 61–2, 64, 89–90, 92, 104, 110, 133, 171, 191–3, 208, 216, 225, 231–3, 235, 257, 259, 281, 322, 342, 345, 349, 372–3, 377

Bohemia, 66, 85, 135

Bradlaugh–Besant trial, 342

breast feeding, 42, 101

British aristocracy, 64–6, 90–2

Buddhist, 328

Bulgaria, 22, 117, 129, 131–2, 135

business cycles, see economic fluctuations

Calvinist, 61, 96–8, 175–7, 302, 306, 310, 312, 316–21

Canada, 52, 90, 117, 120–1, 129, 281–2, 300, 302–3, 311–12, 321–3, 325–6, 330

Catalonia, 22, 51, 59, 61, 79, 98

Catholic, see Roman Catholic

celibacy, 15–16, 23, 25, 27, 41, 63, 66–71, 87–90, 92, 101, 104, 228–9

change of income, 200, 243–4, 246–7

child care allowance, 137, 138, 296, 355–7

Christian Church Indianapolis, 303–5

collectivization of agriculture, 135–6, 257

college women in America survey, 201–3, 323–4

Congregational, 304–5, 313

contraception, 21, 23, 25–6, 35, 41, 208–10, 232, 316, 336, 339, 347, 352–5, 358
see also birth control

cost of children, 21, 30–8, 126, 134, 138, 242, 250, 257, 288, 339, 358, 371–3, 379, 383

culture of poverty, 335

Czechoslovakia, 117, 121, 129, 131, 132, 135, 136, 220–1, 228, 300, 357

Denmark, 79–80, 117, 119, 129, 221, 228, 299

denomination, 20–1, 54–61, 165, 171, 175–7, 182, 187, 189, 194, 198–205, 215, 224–5, 243, 246, 270, 284–5, 298–325, 328, 331, 338–9, 343, 359, 373, 381

depression, economic, 116, 118, 120, 122–3, 125–6, 139, 143, 229, 341–2, 378, 382

Detroit Area Studies, 203–4, 209, 246–8, 289–90, 294–5, 315–16

diffusion hypothesis of spread of birth control, of decline of fertility, 281–4
disutility of children, *see* costs of children
divorce, 230
dominance of husband or wife in marriage, 198, 340, 367
dwelling type, 287–8, 379

earning, *see* income
economic activity of women, *see* employment of women
economic crisis, *see* depression
economic development, *see* socio-economic development
economic fluctuations, cycles, 27, 116, 119, 122–4, 139, 234, 378
economic growth rate, 115–16
economic tension, 194, 243
education, 16, 19–23, 36, 110, 117, 125, 133, 134, 136, 141–2, 151–2, 155–6, 163–4, 171, 174–7, 179–89, 192, 195–6, 198, 202, 204–5, 207–8, 215, 220, 223–5, 235, 238–40, 245–6, 248–9, 291, 313–5, 321, 326–8, 332, 340, 367, 373, 378, 381
emancipation of women, 174, 343, 345
emigration, 25, 115, 126, 178
employment of women, 34, 124–5, 133, 141–3, 146–7, 155–7, 163, 165, 171, 174, 176, 178–89, 215, 220, 222, 225, 245, 292–7, 364–7, 371–2, 374, 380–1
England and Wales, 15, 21, 46, 50, 56–7, 59, 63, 67, 69, 71, 74–6, 83, 85, 87, 88, 90–2, 98–101, 110, 112–16, 119–20, 221, 227–8, 230–1, 271–2, 293–4, 301, 341–2
  see also Great Britain, United Kingdom
Episcopal, 304–5, 313
Estonia, 22, 52, 54, 59, 66, 170, 221–3
ethnic background, *see* ethnicity
ethnicity, 158, 160–2, 165, 170–1, 200, 221–5, 299, 321–6, 328–32, 345, 359, 373, 381
ethnocentrism, 301, 302
Evangelical, 305
expected income, 247–8

family, 37, 110, 198, 333–4, 338–9
  extended, 21, 24–5
  nuclear, 21, 24–5
family allowance, 127, 134–5, 137, 139, 257, 350–1, 353, 355–7, 378–9
Family Census of Great Britain, 211–12
Family Intentions survey of England and Wales, 293
farm background, *see* place of birth
feminist movement, 342
fertility control, *see* birth control
Finland, 22, 79, 81, 102, 110, 117, 119, 121, 129, 221, 228, 299
Flanders, 68, 86–7, 112
France, 21–2, 42–3, 50–1, 54–6, 58–61, 67, 69, 70, 76–8, 83, 85–92, 98–9, 101, 110, 113–15, 117, 119–21, 127–9, 174–5, 212–15, 221, 228, 230–1, 254, 261, 270–1, 300, 350–3, 358
French aristocracy, 64, 90–2
frontier situation, 93

Germany, 19, 21–2, 51, 59, 68, 85, 111, 116–17, 122, 126–7, 189, 237, 348–9
  Eastern (DDR), 121, 129, 132, 135, 228
  Western (BRD), 120, 129. 215, 228, 230–1, 294, 300–1
Great Britain, 121, 211–12
Greece, 117, 120
Greek Catholic, 317, 320
Greek Orthodox, *see* Orthodox
Growth of American Families surveys, 19, 205–10, 244–6, 284–5, 298, 304–5, 309–11
Habsburg Empire, 22, 93, 97, 318, 344–5
household, 90, 124
  see also family
housing, 133, 136
  shortage, 343
Hungary, vii, 43–7, 52–4, 56–9, 61, 63–4, 68–9, 81, 85–6, 90, 92–8, 111, 113, 115–17, 121, 129, 131–2, 136–9, 141–50, 162, 178–89, 215–19, 221, 228, 230–1, 256–7, 262–4, 275–81, 283–7, 292, 300–1, 317–21, 354–8, 380–2
Hutterite, 8–9, 48

Iceland, 117, 121
illegitimacy, 66, 71–2, 227–30
illiteracy, 164–5, 168, 178, 319
image of limited good, 94
immigration, *see* migration
income, earning, standard of living,
    level of living, 15–16, 21, 27–38, 104,
    109–10, 117–19, 122, 125–6, 130–1,
    134, 136–7, 145–6, 148, 151, 154–5,
    162–6, 168, 172, 177–8, 181, 189,
    192–6, 204–5, 208, 215, 223, 225,
    234–51, 257, 259, 265, 275, 292–3,
    296, 299, 313–5, 318, 326–7, 328,
    332, 340–1, 352, 367, 371–4, 378–9,
    380–1
Indianapolis survey, 190–7, 200, 209,
    242–3, 260, 267–9, 272, 289–90,
    303–4, 306–7, 335, 338–9, 340
induced abortion, 25–6, 41–4, 135–7,
    181, 216, 221, 232, 347–54, 357–8,
    373, 377
industrialization, 20–2, 74, 100–1,
    110–11, 114–15, 117, 134, 136, 150,
    163–4, 168, 172, 174, 178, 180–9,
    234–5, 259, 277, 283, 382
industrial production, 125
INED, 351–2
infanticide, 41, 42, 44
infant mortality, 21, 23, 85–7, 92–3,
    125–6, 134, 164, 165–6, 168, 176,
    178, 181, 234
inflation, 131, 229, 234
innovation, spread of birth control as
    innovation, 104–5
insecurity, 127, 131, 195, 197, 234–5,
    242–3, 327, 378
Ireland, 21–2, 25, 102–3, 111, 117,
    228, 230, 300–1
Italy, 81–2, 85, 111, 117, 120, 129,
    172–4, 228, 230, 270, 300, 348–9

Japan, 125–6
Jehovah's Witnesses, 304–5
Jew, 198–200, 202, 207, 243–4, 298,
    303–5, 307–8, 313–15, 317, 320,
    322, 327

labour force participation of women, *see*
    employment of women
Latvia, 22, 170, 221–3

level of living, *see* income
literacy, *see* illiteracy
    male-female differential, 171
Lithuania, 22, 66, 170, 222–3
Lutheran, 61, 304–5, 317–18, 320–1,
    345
Luxembourg, 117, 300

marital adjustment, happiness, 194–6,
    198, 339–40
Malthusian League, 342
Methodist, 303–5
migration, 25–6, 61–4, 114, 123–4,
    134, 136, 146, 158–9, 166, 195, 225,
    284, 287, 289–91, 321
    see also emigration
minority group status hypothesis, 327–8
modernization, 35, 134, 164, 166, 171,
    265, 334–5
Mormon, 158, 202, 304–5, 324
mortality, 14, 18–21, 32, 84–7, 93, 98,
    103–4, 109, 111–12, 123–4, 225–6,
    234
    see also infant mortality
Muslim, 328

National Fertility Studies, 191, 205–10,
    244–5, 260–1, 298, 304–5, 311, 326
national income, per capita, 164–5
Nazarene, 304–5
Netherlands, 22, 61, 79, 112, 117,
    119–20, 129, 175–7, 221, 228,
    254–5, 262, 300–2, 306, 309–10,
    312, 316–17, 382
New Zealand, 117, 120, 129, 300
norm, 37, 59, 104, 112, 145, 166,
    186–7, 189, 201, 203, 223–4, 229,
    257–8, 264, 277, 288, 310, 321–2,
    324–5, 328, 331–3, 336, 346, 357–9,
    368–70, 374–5, 380–4
Norway, 22, 72, 79–80, 83, 117,
    119–20, 129, 299
number of siblings in family of origin,
    194–5
occupation, 61–4, 141–8, 153–4, 192,
    194–6, 198, 204–5, 220, 238–40,
    242, 246, 249, 313–14, 327–8, 341
    see also socio-economic status
occupational changes in a generation
    survey, United States, 272–5, 290–1

opportunity cost of children, 35, 37, 372, 380
Orthodox, 319–20, 328

Pentecostal, 304–5
permanent income, 371
place of birth, urban-rural, 158–9, 220, 242, 289–90, 314
    see also migration
Poland, 66, 111, 117, 121, 129, 132–4, 166–8, 219–21, 228, 230, 235–7, 249, 264–5, 292
population density, 164, 172
population policy, 127, 129, 137–9, 212, 214–15, 225, 284, 374–5, 380–4
Portugal, 117, 119–20, 129, 177–8
potential income, 367, 371–3
Presbyterian, 303–5, 313
Princeton survey, 190, 197–200, 209, 243–4, 269–70, 272, 287, 298, 307–8, 311, 313, 322, 335–6, 339–40
prosperity, economic, 122–6, 139, 341, 352, 378, 382
Protestant, 46, 59, 60, 97–8, 182, 187, 194, 198–200, 202, 204–5, 207–8, 215, 243–6, 270, 284–5, 298–325, 328
psychological personality characteristics, 194, 198, 200, 225, 333–7
public opinion, see socio-psychological atmosphere

Quaker, 52, 59, 61, 98, 304–5
quality of children, 30, 299, 349, 363, 365–8, 383

race/black-white fertility differential, 208, 246, 249, 252, 326–8
rate of economic development, 175
rational thinking, 110, 164
recession, economic, see depression
Reformed, Dutch, 61, 306, 310, 312, 317
regional fertility differences, 81–2, 148–50, 157–9, 162, 165–89, 221–3, 318–21, 327–30, 381
relative income hypothesis, 240–2, 245–6
religion, see denomination

religious interest, religiousness, 178, 199, 201, 215, 298, 306, 311, 324, 381
residence, urban-rural and type, 148–9, 151, 155, 158, 168, 171, 175–7, 200, 235, 245–6, 249, 279–88, 314–15, 321, 328, 367, 373, 378–9, 380–1
    see also migration
role segregation, 340
Roman Catholic, 46, 59–61, 96–8, 175–8, 182, 188, 198, 204–5, 207–8, 215, 243–6, 270, 284–8, 298–325, 328, 331, 345
Romania, 117, 121, 129, 131, 132, 135–6, 353–4
Russian, 79, 90, 111, 113, 115, 170, 222–3

Scandinavia, 79
scarcity of land, 27, 94, 98, 154, 172–3
Scotland, 22
security, 118–19, 194–7, 343–4, 353, 373
Slovakia, 135
social benefit, 134–5, 257, 296, 347, 349–52, 354–5, 378–9
social downgrading, 94
social mobility, 20–1, 134, 136–7, 194, 198–200, 225, 266–78, 289, 344, 381
social status, see socio-economic status
social stratum, see socio-economic status
socialization of agriculture, see collectivization of agriculture
socio-economic development, 16–17, 19, 26, 32, 109, 122, 139, 141, 150, 171, 174, 180, 189, 234, 249, 287, 301, 328
socio-economic status, 61–4, 141–8, 153–6, 162, 192–200, 204–5, 208, 211–15, 217–25, 234, 238–41, 245–6, 249, 251–8, 265, 279–82, 289–92, 299, 307, 313–18, 324, 326, 328, 332, 335, 340, 367, 373, 378, 380
socio-psychological atmosphere, climate, 31, 138, 215, 284, 343, 345–6, 352, 381
South Africa, 117, 120

Soviet Union, *see* USSR
Spain, 22, 51, 78–9, 117, 120, 228
standard of living, *see* income
Sweden, 52, 59, 68, 72, 79–81, 83, 85,
  98, 102, 110, 113–21, 126–7, 129,
  228, 230–1, 237–42, 255–6, 259–60,
  282–3, 292–3, 299, 349–50
Switzerland, 51, 59, 61, 68–9, 87–8, 98,
  111–12, 116–17, 119, 121, 300

taste, 373–4
tendency to plan, 194–6
traditionalism, 194–5, 306–7
Transylvania, 22, 318–19

uncertainty, 127, 344
unemployment, 122–3, 125, 127, 131,
  139, 146, 194, 196, 212, 214, 234,
  243, 343–4, 348, 352, 378
unique salary, 350–1
Unitarian, 320
United Kingdom, 116, 117, 121, 125–6,
  129, 210–12, 300, 352
  see also England and Wales
United States, 9, 52, 59, 110, 116–18,
  120–1, 124–6, 129, 150–62, 171–3,

190–210, 228, 231, 242–9, 260–1,
  272–5, 278–9, 284–5, 287, 294–6,
  298, 300, 303–6, 311–16, 321–8,
  330, 335–7, 339–40, 352
unwanted pregnancy, birth, child, 192,
  208, 210, 229, 231–2, 248, 326,
  340, 357, 370, 372
urbanization, 20–3, 110, 114, 117,
  133–4, 163, 172, 176, 178, 189, 235,
  249, 277, 288, 321, 343, 370, 382
USSR, 117, 121, 129, 131–2, 170–1,
  221–3, 264–5, 275, 292, 328–31
utility of children, 32
  see also value of children

value, 104, 201, 203, 207, 221, 223–5,
  244, 257–8, 264–5, 274, 277, 290,
  310, 321–2, 324–5, 332–3, 346, 357,
  369–70, 375, 380–4
value of children, 138, 337–9, 359

wealth, 145

Yugoslavia, 117, 121, 129, 131–3,
  170–1, 221–3, 264–5, 275, 292,
  328–31